South Africa's Tran

South Africa's Transkei

*The Political Economy of an
'Independent' Bantustan*

ROGER J. SOUTHALL

MONTHLY REVIEW PRESS
NEW YORK

Copyright © 1983 by Roger Southall
All rights reserved

Library of Congress Cataloging in Publication Data

Southall, Roger.
    South Africa's Transkei.

    Bibliography: p.
    Includes index.
    1. Transkei—Politics and government. 2. Transkei—Economic conditions. 3. Transkei—Social conditions. I. Title.
DT846.T7S69   968.7   81-84742
ISBN 0-85345-614-3   AACR2
ISBN 0-85345-615-1 (pbk.)

Monthly Review Press
155 West 23rd Street
New York, N.Y. 10011

Manufactured in the United States of America

10 9 8 7 6 5 4 3 2 1

Contents

List of tables vii
List of maps viii
List of abbreviations used in text and notes ix
A note on terminology x
Foreword xi

1 *The problem of bantustan 'independence'* 1
   'Independent' bantustans: non-states or neo-colonies? 4
   The theory of internal colonialism 10

2 *Apartheid and decolonization* 20
   Capitalism, segregation and apartheid 21
   The implementation of apartheid 33
   The evolution of the apartheid neo-colonial design 44

3 *The Transkei as a native reserve* 60
   Annexation and the establishment of colonial rule 60
   Origins of the reserve economy 67
   The development of underdevelopment 73
   Administration and politics 88

4 *The transition to 'independence'* 103
   Bantu Authorities and the Pondo Revolt 104
   From indirect rule to self-government 114
   The electoral process 120
   The TNIP: a party for the patrons 135
   The move to 'independence' 140

5 *Extrusion of the white settlers* 146
   White settlement in the Transkeian Territories 146
   White settlers and the bantustan strategy 149
   Zoning and compensation 157
   'Sold down the Kei River' 160

6	*Class formation in a bantustan*	172
	The Transkeian bourgeoisie: chiefs and politicians	173
	The bureaucrats	176
	The teachers	182
	Traders and businessmen	185
	The emergent petty-bourgeoisie: collaboration, ambivalence and dependence	195
7	*The bantustan economy*	202
	Financial dependence upon South Africa	203
	Transkei as a labour reserve	208
	The agricultural base	219
	Bantustan development strategy	222
8	*The politics of bantustan 'independence'*	247
	The search for recognition	248
	The deracialization of Transkei	251
	Change and continuity in Transkeian politics	255
	Relations with South Africa	264
	The limits of 'independence'	271
	The politics of 'independent' Transkei	274
9	*The bantustan strategy – prospects and possibilities*	281
	Transkei in the context of contemporary policy towards the bantustans	283
	Perspectives and possibilities	295

Postscript	309
Bibliography	313
Index (compiled by Shirley Ross, Research Assistant, University of Ottawa)	329

List of tables

2.1	Predominant ethnic composition, land area and portions, and population of the homelands	35
2.2	The homelands: constitutional stages and political leadership	51
3.1	Estimated African population of the Transkei, 1911–41	74
3.2	Geographical sources of black labour employed by the Chamber of Mines, 1906–43 (%)	78
3.3	Budget for 2 years for family of 5 with adult male at work at mines for 14 months and living in the Transkei for 10 months	81
3.4	Distribution of cattle ownership in 7 districts of the Transkeian Territories in 1942	86
4.1	Immediate post-election party affiliations in the Transkei Legislative Assembly, 1963–76	119
4.2	Voter participation in contested seats in Transkei general elections, 1963–76	141
5.1	Some indicators of increased cash flow in Butterworth and Umtata	167
6.1	Salaries of chiefs and headmen, 1964–78	174
6.2	Occupational distribution of elected members of the Transkei Legislature	175
6.3	Establishment of the Transkeian public service, 1963–79	177
6.4	Professional qualifications of teachers in Transkei, 1978	183
6.5	Financial aid from the Xhosa Development Corporation to African businessmen in the Transkei up to 1975	190
7.1	Sources of revenue of the Transkeian government, 1964/5–1975/6 (R'000s)	204
7.2	Transkei as an exporter of labour to South Africa, 1963–78	209
7.3	The extent of migrant labour from the African homelands in the white areas of South Africa, 1973–5	210
7.4	Locality and sectoral distribution of male labour recruited from Transkei, 1974–8	212
7.5	Sources of African labour employed on the South African gold mines, 1969–80 (monthly averages)	215
7.6	Employment by areas of origin of African workers from South Africa on mines belonging to the Chamber of Mines, April 1977 and April 1978	217

7.7 Average monthly earnings of Africans upon the South African mines compared to subsistence level for an African family of 5 living in Soweto, 1977 and 1978   217

List of maps

1. The African homelands of South Africa   xiii
2. The Transkei in relation to Southern Africa   xiv
3. The Transkei at 'independence'   269

List of abbreviations

ANC	African National Congress
BENBO	Bureau for Economic Research re Bantu Development
BIC	Bantu Investment Corporation
BLS	Botswana, Lesotho and Swaziland
BPC	Black People's Convention
DP	Democratic Party
DPP	Democratic Progressive Party
HAD	*South African House of Assembly Debates*
NDP	New Democratic Party
NP	National Party
NRC	Native Recruiting Corporation
PAC	Pan-Africanist Congress
RDM	*Rand Daily Mail*
SAIRR	South African Institute of Race Relations
SASO	South African Students' Organization
TDC	Transkei Development Corporation
TGC	Transkeian General Council
TLA	Transkeian Legislative Assembly
TNIP	Transkei National Independence Party
TNPP	Transkei National Progressive Party
TPFP	Transkei People's Freedom Party
TTCA	Transkeian Territories Civic Association
TTGC	Transkeian Territories General Council
UP	United Party
UTTGC	United Transkeian Territories General Council
WNLA	Witwatersrand Native Labour Association
XDC	Xhosa Development Corporation

A note on terminology

In the present work, I refer mainly to *the* Transkei or, when appropriate, to the Transkeian Territories. Only for the period after 'independence' in October 1976 do I refer to the territory as Transkei (now the official designation).

As I do not recognize Transkei as a *de jure* state, I often refer to Transkeian 'independence' with the latter word in quotation marks. However, because continual use of such apostrophes is tiresome, I have attempted to restrict their use to points where Transkei's lack of legitimacy as a state requires particular emphasis.

At different times I refer to the Transkei as a reserve, a bantustan and a homeland. The first term is used (1) in the context of the territory serving as an official Native Reserve from the passage of the Natives Land Act of 1913 until the implementation of the Bantu Authorities system in the 1950s (after which former reserves soon became colloquially referred to as bantustans); and (2) in the sense of the territory functioning as a labour reserve for the South African economy – a function which Transkei fulfils to the present day. The words bantustan and homeland I use interchangeably, according to the stylistic needs of the moment. My employment of the term 'homeland' in no way implies my acceptance of the notion that designated tribal areas are in any real sense 'home' for the blacks arbitrarily allotted to them; rather, I accept the label only as a convenience, in recognition that the notion of 'the homelands' now refers to a particular set of official policies and institutional structures designed by whites for black South Africans.

The term 'the Republic' (and any derivatives) refers exclusively to South Africa.

Where I refer simply to Matanzima without any forename, I refer exclusively to Kaiser Matanzima. References to George Matanzima are always specified as such.

Foreword

Transkei is already the most comprehensively studied of all the bantustans, and there will be those who question whether there is a need for yet another book-length study. The pioneering work of Gwendolen Carter, Thomas Karis and Newell Stultz (1967), *South Africa's Transkei: The Politics of Domestic Colonialism*, made a justifiably lasting impact which finds an echo in the title of my own work. However, this first serious work was inevitably outdated by the time that Patrick Laurence, the well-known journalist who works for the *Rand Daily Mail* in Johannesburg, published his *Transkei: South Africa's Politics of Partition* at the time of the homeland's so-called 'independence' in 1976. If the former study was principally concerned to put the theory of separate development to empirical test by surveying the first homeland, the latter was a piece of masterly journalism which put developments into a carefully worked, chronological perspective. The present study has depended heavily on both these earlier works and will, I hope, be regarded as complementary to them in that it seeks to approach the bantustan policy as implimented in Transkei from a perspective that has been much influenced (but not exclusively) by the writings of the 'neo-Marxist' school that is now so busily re-interpreting Southern African political economy. My intention, however, has been not to frighten away the reader who is unfamiliar with the radical literature, and I have accordingly sought to minimize the use of Marxian terminology which might unnecessarily obfuscate rather than elucidate relatively simple points. However, my approach differs sharply from that of Newell Stultz who, in returning to his old haunts, has recently published *Transkei's Half Loaf: Race Separatism in South Africa* (1980), a study which proposes that, although Transkeian 'independence' is hedged around by many severe constraints and inadequacies, it may none the less make a constructive contribution to the resolution of South Africa's 'racial problems'. But Stultz's offering is based upon the thoroughly conservative premise that rule by a 'racial majority' would be unlikely to produce a democratic South Africa and that consequently, the major challenge of the present must be to work towards some political arrangement whereby the future prospects of the white minority will be protected. In contrast, the major purpose of the present study has been to examine, through the particular case of Transkei located within the context of South African political economy, how the bantustan strategy has worked and continues to operate to further the exploitation of the oppressed majority. Although I touch only briefly upon the likely future of South Africa in my conclusion, the implication of my study is that the bantustan policy is devoid of all progressive political potentialities, and that consequently, support must be unambiguously given to the forces of liberation which are struggling to overthrow apartheid rule.

During the course of writing this book, I have incurred a large number of debts. David Kimble, formerly Professor of Government and Administration at what was then the University of Botswana, Lesotho and Swaziland, gave me initial encouragement when, even more ignorant about South Africa than I am now, I arrived in Lesotho in early 1975. Others at what became the National University of Lesotho, notably John Bardill, Chris Goldman and David Hirschmann, read portions of the manuscripts and offered valuable criticisms, while Bob Edgar of Howard University (an old Transkeian hand), attempted to save me from the knives of the historians. Thanks are also due for assistance from Thomas Karis and Ben Turok, together with various publishers' readers who have remained anonymous; and I am particularly indebted to Professor David Butler of Wesleyan University (whose interpretation of South African politics, history and economy diverges considerably from my own) for offering erudite, lengthy and comprehensive commentaries which resulted in major improvements. I would also like to thank Ben Magubane who read the text for Monthly Review Press and whose provocative commentary caused me to rework some of my original formulations. I am indebted to a number of informants in or from Transkei who for obvious reasons are better left unnamed, while I would also like to acknowledge the stimulation that was provided by my students at Roma, Lesotho to whom I had the temerity to teach South African politics. All responsibility for the interpretation of my topic and my treatment of material falls to myself alone. The National University of Lesotho was generous in its financial support and, without it, I would have been unable to conduct my research. I am grateful to Pat Onsworth and Val Hughes for typing the manuscript and to Joanna Mulder for Maps 2 and 3; Susan Lowes of Monthly Review Press has been unfailingly helpful. I owe a special debt of thanks to James Currey of Heinemann for his patience in overseeing successive drafts. But the largest debt of all is owed to my wife, Hilary, without whose constant support I would not have been able to proceed with and complete my work

Roger J. Southall
Ottawa

Map 1 *The African homelands of South Africa*

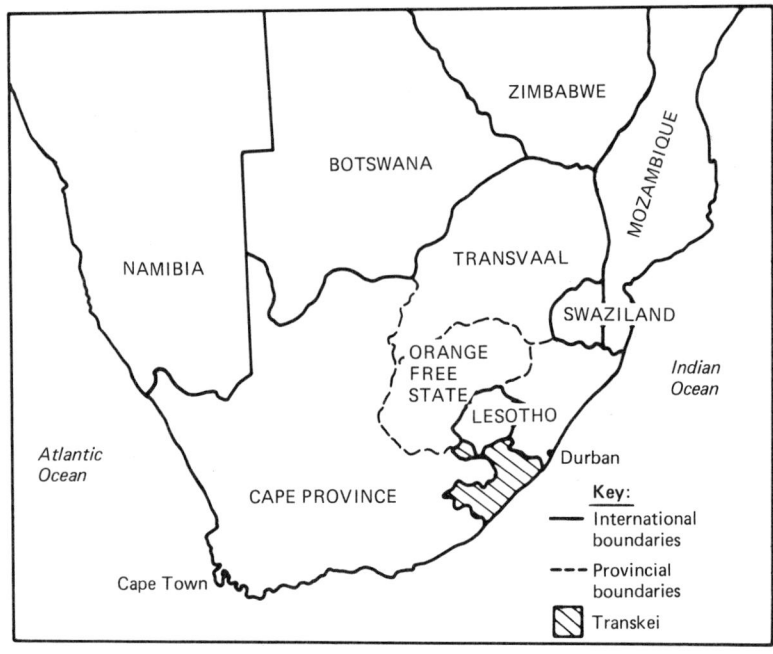

Map 2 *The Transkei in relation to Southern Africa*

Chapter 1
The problem of bantustan 'independence'

> About 30,000 people, including observers from 12 countries, cheered and ululated in spite of a heavy shower as, towards midnight, the South African state President, Dr. Nico Diedrichs, handed over the Status of Transkei Act and a golden pen to sign it to Paramount Chief Matanzima.
> A choir sang *Die Stem* as the South African flag was lowered in Transkei for the last time to be replaced by the ochre, white and green flag of the new state, and the signing of its national anthem: *'Nkosi Sikelel' iAfrica.*
> Torch bearers from each of nine regions of Transkei padded into the stadium to light the flame of independence. As the flames shot up from the bowl high on the stadium wall, a 101-gun salute announced the birth of Africa's 50th independent state.[1]

When the Transkei, one of the two so-called 'homelands' of the Xhosa people, became the first bantustan to obtain juridical 'independence' from South Africa on 26 October 1976, the event was hailed by the National Party government and its supporters as marking the dawn of a new and progressive epoch in the history of Southern Africa. It was viewed, not simply in the light of the transfer of sovereignty to a colonial territory after a lengthy period of preparation, but also as the culmination of all that was positive in the government's policy of 'Separate Development', whereby each racial group is allotted its own political institutions, and the different black ethnic groups supposedly fulfil their aspirations towards full nationhood by steadily assuming control over the machinery of state in their own territorial areas or 'homelands'. In the model of constitutional progress devised by Pretoria, the Transkei had been the first homeland to accede to the stage of 'self-government' in 1963; and now, some thirteen years later, it was also the first to be granted its political independence. 'In so far as the Transkei is concerned,' remarked M. C. Botha, the Minister of Bantu Administration and Development, when introducing the Independence Bill into the House of Assembly:

> we are today arriving at the last step in a long process of evolution and it is the dawn of an exceptionally unique day; the day on which South Africa for the first time takes the necessary legal step to relinquish its guardianship over one of its wards by declaring it to be independent . . . We are witnessing here today the logical outcome of the policy of multinationalism of our Republic of South Africa: the consummation of the inevitable and irreversible passage of our

National Party's constitutional principles and views in regard to the various nations in our midst. We are witnessing here today the confirmation of the earnestness and resoluteness of our National Party concerning its policy, of the sincerity of our endeavours and undertakings concerning the Black nations ... All of us in South Africa are witnessing the fact that each national group in our multinational constellation has a destination of its own which, with the help of our Government, can be arrived at in peace ... Indeed, this is a day of fulfilment for the National Party ...[2]

There was jubilation, too, at the *manner* with which the Transkei acceded to its 'Inkululeko' (or freedom): 'without hatred, without bitterness, without bloodshed, without something which might poison relationships with its neighbours, or which could destroy peace of mind, Transkei reached its political maturity'.[3] It had considerable assets on which it could depend, notably a neighbouring state on whose aid and advice it could rely, while being spared the discord and chaos which had been the lot of so many other states in Africa.[4]

The *substance* of the newly achieved independence was held in no less regard, and the new republic was held up as a model state which other Third World nations would do well to follow. Blessed with 'an auspicious and well-planned' birth, Transkei was a beautiful country with a fertile soil, well endowed with natural resources, and had benefited from a long period of tutelage resulting in the firm establishment of a parliamentary democracy.[5] And in the sense that Transkeian independence was taken to foreshadow the progression along a similar path by all the remaining African homelands, it opened the way to a new political dispensation of 'plural democracy', whereby in time to come South Africa's whites, Indians and coloureds would all have their own separate parliaments within a single state, linked to the independent national units within a regional framework of economic and political co-operation.[6]

But the reception given to the independence of Transkei in other quarters was less ecstatic. Within the remainder of the white body politic itself, there was considerable foreboding of the consequences which would flow from the political fragmentation of the Republic. Both the Opposition United and Progressive-Reform Parties objected to the entire concept of independence, arguing variously that those designated Transkeian citizens had been inadequately consulted, that the newly created state would be economically unviable, that the new constitution inadequately protected minority rights, and that the importation of a further black state into the confines of the South African heartland might pose a military threat to the defence of the Republic. Both were also agreed that granting independence to a rural homeland, which was economically dependent on industries in white areas, would do nothing to resolve the fundamental problem confronting the white minority, namely that of the long-term accommodation of a black, urban, numerous and politically volatile population with so-called responsible rule which would be broadly protective of white interests and security in the future. Yet both these parties concurred that the act of transferring sovereignty to a black government in Umtata, the capital of Transkei, would be irreversible; and accordingly, they pledged themselves to accept Transkeian independence and to offer whatever assistance they could to the fledgling state in the years to come.[7]

Despite government assertions to the contrary, it is clear also that the broad mass of blacks strongly rejected the decision of Kaiser Matanzima (the Transkeian Chief Minister) to opt for a separate political future, as was indicated *inter alia* not only by opposition internal to the Transkei, but by the forthright repudiation of homeland independence by such important bodies as the South African Students' Organization and the Black Peoples' Convention, both of which had played a particularly prominent role in articulating black resistance to apartheid throughout the 1970s.[8] Although there was some support for independence – mainly from the various bantustan élites – it is evidence of the depth of mass feeling against Matanzima that he gained the explicit support of only one other homeland leader, Chief Lucas Mangope of Bophuthatswana (who was himself soon to opt for independence),[9] and otherwise earned only rebuke from his erstwhile colleagues, some of whom reacted to Transkeian independence by linking together with middle-class urban blacks in Soweto to form a Black United Front which was pledged to fight against the partition of South Africa into independent homelands.[10] Meanwhile, other blacks for whom the structures of separate development allowed no adequate institutional means of expression responded violently in the wake of the Soweto upheaval of June 1976 by attacking symbols of bantustan authority in the homelands themselves, the razing to the ground on 9 August of the Bophuthatswana Legislative Assembly being the most spectacular expression of dissent amid a wave of protest that included acts of violence in the Transkei itself.[11]

But perhaps the most telling blow of all to government hopes was the manner in which Transkeian independence was greeted by the international community. Both the Organization of African Unity and the United Nations had long given notice that they would not admit an independent Transkei to their ranks, and the latter body even went so far as to hold a 'Festival of Rejection' during the week in which the homeland received its independence.[12] And taking their cue from the Afro-Asian bloc which they were reluctant to offend, western powers, on whom hopes for recognition had been pinned by the Vorster regime, assumed a tactful diplomatic stance which – although not excluding the possibility of recognition in the future – argued that the Transkei did not currently meet the criteria of nation-statehood. As a result the National Party regime was forced to fall back on assertions both that Transkei would earn international acceptance in time or (rather contradictorily) that the lack of recognition mattered little in any case.[13]

The crux of the argument underpinning this widespread rejection of Transkeian independence was the belief that the entire exercise was essentially fraudulent, specifically designed to entrench white rule in the southern tip of the continent at the expense of the black mass. From this perspective, instead of symbolizing a further stage in the triumphal unfolding of African nationalism, bantustan independence represented an attempt by the South African regime to externalize its race relations into the international arena, and to impose structures of political domination (through the willing co-operation of black 'sell-outs' or 'stooges' headed by Matanzima) upon the unwilling mass of South African blacks. International recognition of bantustan independence would thereby imply acceptance of the white claim that blacks could enjoy meaningful political rights 'in their own areas', and – given the nature of the homelands' economic dependence – an entrenchment of their role as labour reserves servicing the white economy on its own terms.[14]

Yet vital though it is to uncover the fraudulent designs of the Republican government, it is necessary to go beyond a mere exposure of National Party motives and policies if the significance of bantustan independence is to be adequately confronted. In short, it is necessary to locate homeland independence in the overall context of the South African political economy which, in turn, is to decipher the nature of the relationship between the white 'core' of apartheid and its bantustan peripheries. Yet in so doing, it is imperative first to grapple with the very notion of bantustan 'independence', for it is argued here that the very concept of a bantustan as an independent state represents an attempt by the South African government to mystify the peculiar relation that obtains between capital and labour under apartheid by elevating an essentially class relationship (exploitation) to an apparently international transaction between discrete (white and black) nationalities.

'Independent' bantustans: non-states or neo-colonies?

Since Transkei became independent, two other homelands – Bophuthatswana in 1977 and Venda in 1979 – have followed the same path and have claimed the right to assume international sovereign status.[15] The dynamics and nature of this process will be elaborated later in this text as I seek to relate the specific historical circumstances of Transkei as the 'model bantustan' to the more general context of the separate development strategy as a whole. But the very fact that there are now three (and soon four) 'independent' bantustans necessitates that we examine closely the argument (not propagated by the South African government alone) that such entities constitute independent 'states', whether they are internationally recognized as such or not.

When it was launched into independence in 1976, the official South African doctrine proposed that, in terms of such phenomena as land area, population, *per capita* income and so on, Transkei objectively fulfilled the criteria of nation-statehood no less than certain already internationally recognized states such as Lesotho and Swaziland.[16] Although we may note in passing that many of the official statistics produced by Pretoria to put the Transkeian case were intentionally misleading and require careful scrutiny,[17] we should also be quite forthright in acknowledging that there *are* a number of states which are, if anything, poorer and smaller than Transkei. Indeed, Lesotho (the politically independent enclave surrounded by South Africa and which borders on Transkei) is territorially smaller, has a less numerous resident population and possesses even fewer natural resources than its bantustan neighbour, while Newell Stultz (to whose work on Transkei we will return in greater detail in the conclusion) has noted the homeland's claims to statehood (on which he is not prepared to make a personal judgement) as including (notwithstanding the territory's considerable liabilities) a cultural homogeneity that is unusual among contemporary African states, a comparatively long history (since *circa* 1894) as a recognizable politico-administrative entity within the area now known as South Africa, and a government which, compared to most African countries at the time of their independence, had enjoyed considerable self-governing experience.[18] Thus if we could abstract the bantustan from its concrete historical situation (a proposition which Stultz does *not* accept), it would appear that, as South African propaganda eagerly informs us, there would be nothing inherently wrong with our conceiving of Transkei as a distinct polity, even if a far less convincing case could be proposed for our accepting the notion of, say, Bophuthatswana (with six separate pieces of territory, all – bar one – surrounded by 'white' South Africa) as a separate political entity.[19]

Furthermore, leaving aside for the moment the question of such other bantustans as are or would be independent, the notion of Transkei as a separate state has received some considerable support from members of the legal profession who have argued that, from the perspective of constitutional law, there is little doubt that the homeland exists as a discrete entity separate from the South African state itself. Thus John Dugard, the internationally respected Professor of Law at the University of the Witwatersrand, has argued that the denial of international recognition to Transkei as an independent territorial entity is not sufficient to counter its *legal* claim to existence as a state, for 'recognition does not create a new state as it is a *declaratory* and not a *constitutive* act', and accordingly, the critical issue is the fact that the South African legislature has chosen to divest itself of legal responsibility for the administration of part of its territory, this having been passed on to a separate parliament which now forms a legally constituted sovereign authority.[20] However, that there is more to statehood than merely legal components is suggested by Harvey and Dean, Professors of Law at Boston (USA) and Cape Town Universities respectively, who argue that:

> If Transkeian sovereignty and entitlement to recognition as an independent nation were dependent on an assessment of its constitutional–legal order,

there seems to be no doubt that it passes as severe a test of independence as could be extrapolated from the criteria seemingly applied to other new states. Certainly the shaping influence of the former sovereign is readily apparent in the constitutional order; a vast body of pre-independence laws remains in force; appeals still run from the highest court of Transkei to a South African tribunal. All of these features were routinely found, however, in the new polities in Africa spawned by the departing colonial powers. We believe that nothing in the *constitutional order of Transkei* necessitates the description of its Government as a 'puppet', or of its independence as 'fictitious' or 'sham'. We do not assert factually that Transkei is 'independent'; indeed, we are uncertain of the meaning of that term in a complex, highly interdependent community of nations. Our assertion is more modest: if Transkei is a dependent, puppet community and is precluded from pursuing the policies and goals of an independent nation, the reasons for this status with its attendant disabilities *must be sought elsewhere than in the constitutional–legal order as it is formally organised* (my emphasis).[21]

Although Harvey and Dean go on to add grist to the apartheid mill by concluding that, whatever the extra-legal case against Transkeian statehood, denial of independence by the world community of states will serve to reinforce the homeland's dependence upon Pretoria and thus serve as a self-fulfilling prophecy, their analysis clearly points to the fact that statehood is as much, if not more, a political as well as a legal phenomenon.

In summary, therefore, the reason why recognition of Transkei as a state has been withheld by the entire world community (except South Africa) is clearly *neither* because Transkei is a small, dependent and impoverished territory, *nor* because of any inherent inadequacies of its constitution, but *rather* because it is specifically a creation of apartheid, a doctrine and policy founded on racial distinctions which is regarded as abhorrent or impolitic to legitimize at the level of international law.

Those who require a more extended discussion of the claims for and against Transkeian statehood should turn to Stultz's work which has been briefly touched on above. Suffice to say for the moment that, whatever his doubts about the legitimacy of the notion of the homeland as a separate entity, he does in practice treat Transkei as a *de facto* state, regarding this question as being separable from the related issue of recognition. In other words, he advances the proposition that, whether we like it or not, the Transkeian regime exists and that so long as the territory continues to retain its present degree of political and legal independence, we fly in the face of reality if we fail to confront the fact of its being a discrete (albeit ostracized) political entity.

At one level, this is clearly a commonsensical and not unattractive argument, for few would wish to deny the existence of a political–legal unit called Transkei which possesses its own constitution, parliament, bureaucracy and other trappings of independent nationhood. Consequently, moving forward from this position, it could be further proposed from a radical perspective that, given Transkei's continuing heavy dependence upon Pretoria, it forms a *neo-colony* of South Africa, and that the concept of neo-colonialism may be invoked as a useful and critical tool for analysing the political economy of any independent bantustan. Before progressing any further, therefore, it is necessary first to examine briefly what is generally implied by the notion of a neo-colonial state. The concept of neo-colonialism came into prominence in the early 1960s, at a time when the limits of formal political independence were becoming crudely exposed by the failure of the former African colonies to develop economically. Kwame Nkrumah, President of Ghana until he was toppled by military *coup* in 1966, located the cause of this malaise in the continuing domination of the continent through new means by the imperialist powers. Thus he arrived at what has come to be a much quoted, shorthand definition of this phenomenon, which he labelled 'neo-colonialism', subtitling it 'The Last Stage of Imperialism': 'The essence of neo-colonialism is that the state which is subject to it is, in theory, independent and has all the outward trappings of international sovereignty. In reality its economic system and thus its political policy is directed from outside.'[22] Neo-colonialism, he further maintained, was also the worst form of imperialism for it meant, for those who practised it, power without responsibility, and for those who suffered from it, exploitation without redress, for no longer did the imperial power have to justify its colonial activities in the home country.

Nkrumah's framework – which located the phenomenon of neo-colonialism in the context of the post-Second World War crisis in the international capitalist system, the increasing importance of the multi-national corporations, and the rise to hegemony of American capital – offered a promising foundation on which to base an analysis of the continuing economic dependence of now politically independent states upon the metropolitan West. However, his theory none the less suffered from a number of serious deficiencies, these being principally that he failed to examine sufficiently the process now widely referred to as the 'development of underdevelopment'; and secondly, that he failed to pay any attention – except at the most cursory level – to the internal structure of those countries that were subordinated by neo-colonialism. Consequently, the further elucidation of neo-colonialism has been largely subsumed under the more general discussion of underdevelopment and dependence in its historical and contemporary forms.

In painfully brief summary, the outline of this discussion has proceeded from analysis of the characteristics of imperialist expansion (ranging from a crude process of 'primitive accumulation' in the form of plunder or slavery to the formal annexation of an overseas territory by a European power)[23] to examination of the means whereby the 'surplus' of underdeveloped countries is expropriated by advanced capitalist economies on an international scale.[24] This has been conceptualized by Frank[25] in terms of a polarization between metropolitan-centre countries and peripheral satellites, involving the expropriation by a metropolis of economic surplus from its satellites for its own economic development, a process which has necessarily inhibited the possibilities of domestic investment within the satellites themselves. This has therefore created an international division of labour whereby the satellite economies produce materials for transfer and processing in the metropolis, either through an unequal trading relationship, or more directly through the provision of labour for the extraction of raw materials.

From this perspective, therefore, underdevelopment is not an original condition (a lack of development) but is rather a product of exploitation, for it is a further characteristic of imperialism that the contradiction between metropole and satellite is replicated within the regions of the countries which are parties to the relationship. In Frank's words: 'This contradictory metropolitan centre–peripheral satellite relationship, like the process of surplus expropriation–appropriation, runs through the entire capitalist system in chain-like fashion from its uppermost metropolitan world centre, through each of the various national, regional, local and enterprise centres.'[26] Thus, as the capitalist mode of production becomes dominant,[27] new relations of production – which define a specific mode of appropriation of surplus labour and a specific form of social distribution of the means of production – emerge in the peripheral satellite, entailing the creation of a new class structure. In the colonial context this involved either the import of settlers from the metropole or the growth of a class, drawn out from the indigenous community, which had an interest in the maintenance of the broad structures of the economy. Generally (and there were exceptions), these classes were only locally dominant, for their interests were in turn subordinated to those of the metropolitan bourgeoisie (owners of capital in the metropoles) who appropriated surplus from the colonial economy. And because this surplus (or at least the major portion of it) was not invested locally, colonial production had an inherent tendency to be externally oriented, channelling its raw materials and products out and manufactured goods from the metropole in.

In the course of time, the locally prominent classes came to reject the notion of direct rule from overseas. It was not always the case that when a struggle for national independence began, the colonial power was able to devolve political power upon an indigenous class willing to co-operate with imperialism, but in the majority of colonial territories there were emergent groups within the colonial political economy (in trade, the administration and so on) which posed no major threat to the interests of the metropolitan power, so that 'this phenomenon presented an opportunity for imperialism to transfer some amount of political autonomy to this stratum whilst retaining control of the economy through the colonial structure of property relations'.[28] In other words (and the concept should not be regarded as a variant of conspiracy theory), neo-colonialism was often 'a deliberate move to prepared positions', the colonial power 'seeking out social and political forces which, in their own class interests, would not push the national revolution too far nor allow the actions of their people to endanger too greatly the interests of the Western powers'.[29] Such social strata were therefore reckoned to be favourable to the preservation (or rationalization) of colonial economic relationships. 'To the extent that the state in the metropolitan countries was a committee for managing the common affairs of the whole bourgeoisie,' writes Colin Leys paraphrasing Marx, 'the state which emerged in the periphery country was a sort of sub-committee.'[30] In turn, the monopoly control of production and distribution which characteristic of the colonial political economy is maintained under neo-colonialism not only through continuing direct control and ownership in the peripheral countries, but also through such means as the operation of commodity markets and metropolitan advantage in the development of industrial technology. However, neo-colonialism should in no way be regarded as the inevitable and final condition for the majority of mankind, for it is itself a product of a dialectical historical process, and it has become increasingly appreciated that there are different *types* of neo-colonies which vary in their national production relations, class formations and the corresponding connections which locally dominant classes make with the metropolitan bourgeoisies – so that accordingly, these variant neo-colonial formations display different potentialities for economic stagnation, autonomous development or even dependent capitalist growth.[31]

Whatever the inadequacies of the above summary, it should be evident that the concept of neo-colonialism, located in an appropriately broader theoretical framework, strikes a rich vein of ideas which can serve to elucidate the varying conditions of dependence and underdevelopment which are the lot of the majority of the countries of today's world. However, the question remains as to whether the neo-colonial concept is a suitable tool for application to the analysis of bantustan independence. There is no doubt, for example, that the white 'core' of the South African political economy has historically appropriated surplus from the various racially defined peripheries (whether as native reserves or in their contemporary guise as 'black states'); and similarly (as will be elaborated later in this text), it is clear that capital accumulation at the centre has underdeveloped the satellite 'homeland' territories. None the less, promotion of such argument does not necessarily entail acceptance of the neo-colonial thesis in the specific case of the bantustans, for this can apply *if and only if* the relevant bantustans are presented as independent states. In other words, the problem with the neo-colonial thesis if applied to the bantustans is first, that even though it simultaneously provides a critique, it accepts the South African regime's own definition that the independent bantustans are in fact states, and thus (albeit unintentionally) serves to legitimize apartheid ideology and, more importantly, the fragmentation of the Republic into its white core and black peripheral 'states' (with all the oppressive consequences that go with that). If nothing else, therefore, acceptance of the notion of bantustans as neo-colonies presents us with a severe political problem in that it ultimately accepts the South African government's claim to be a decolonizing power.

But secondly, and perhaps more crucially, the neo-colonial thesis may encourage us to isolate developments in the bantustans from the overall context of apartheid. In other words, whether or not the bantustans are granted a formal constitutional sovereignty, they have historically developed (or underdeveloped) as integral parts of the South African political economy, and continue today to perform the essential function of serving as reservoirs whose primary purpose is to serve the labour needs of the white economy, even though the *political form* which the former native reserves now take as ethnic states (whether independent or otherwise) has been modernized in response to the changing requirements of apartheid. The fact that at the economic level the former British Protectorates of Botswana, Lesotho and Swaziland have historically undergone an analogous transformation should not blind us to the fact that, at the political level, theirs has been a substantively different experience which now allows for a qualitatively different (albeit, perhaps, neo-colonial) relationship with South Africa.[32]

However, before we can discard the neo-colonial thesis it is necessary first to confront the problem posed by the theory of *internal colonialism* which has, in a variety of formulations, sought to portray the peculiar essence of South African political economy.

The theory of internal colonialism

Utilization of the neo-colonial framework to analyse the relationship between South Africa as metropole and the Xhosa homeland as periphery would necessarily presuppose that, before it became independent, Transkei was in some way a colony. However, given that since the Act of Union in 1910 South Africa has been internationally recognized as an autonomous state, and that the Transkeian Territories and other African Reserves/Homelands have been regarded as integral parts of it (not least by the National Party until some years *after* it had come to office in 1948), the government in Pretoria cannot be viewed as a colonial power in anything like the same sense as were, for instance, Britain and France, which ruled over territories that were overseas. None the less, largely because South Africa is a historical product of the era of formal imperialism, and because it shares many fundamental similarities with settler colonies such as were Rhodesia and Kenya, the South African social formation has been commonly viewed as having *internalized* a peculiarly colonial content. This has been taken to involve, according to Harold Wolpe, two main elements. First, 'the colonial relationship is conceived of as occurring between different countries, total populations, nations, geographical areas, or between peoples of different races, colours and cultures'; and secondly, the internal colonial relationship 'is characterised, in a general way, as involving domination, oppression and exploitation'.[33]

Given these broad features, the theory of internal colonialism has been used variously. First and foremost perhaps, it has been adopted as the basis upon which to erect the entire ideological superstructure of separate development, which is founded upon the analogy that the 'distinct African peoples', each with their traditional homelands, are akin to the new nations formerly ruled by the other colonial powers, and that as they develop towards full-nationhood they will receive increased responsibility in terms of self-governing authority, culminating in the bequest of independence. Although this model has naturally been seized upon eagerly by conservative and paternalistic writers as proving the alleged goodwill and benevolence of the white man,[34] it has also formed the basis of a number of studies which have sought to contrast the reality of the 'decolonization' process with the official rhetoric of devolution. Thus Carter, Karis and Stultz, in their study of what they termed 'Domestic Colonialism', concluded that 'Transkeian developments have taken territorial separation out of the realm of theory into that of practice and disclosed the hollowness of its pretensions'.[35] In other words, such liberal commentators have undertaken the important (though perhaps not difficult) task of explaining why separate territorial development as presently conceived will not work as a solution to South Africa's 'racial problems'. While admitting that racial/territorial partition *might* be an option so long as whites were genuinely prepared to make sufficient sacrifice to make for a meaningful equality, such writers concede that this is politically unlikely and that too much time has been allowed to pass by in order for this to be really considered a viable way out of the racial dilemma.

A second interpretation of internal colonialism adopts a considerably broader perspective, although again – as Joe Slovo, a leading proponent of this view, argues – the theory is 'based on the historical *analogy* of the classic imperialist–colonialist solution in which the ruling class of the dominant nation "owns" and controls its economic, political and military supremacy against would-be external competitors' (my emphasis). 'But,' continues Slovo, 'analogies are not carbon copies; they are resemblances between situations otherwise different.' South Africa is certainly not free of external imperialist involvement yet control over the economy and the state is exercised by a locally resident ruling class. The social formation is essentially capitalist, pre-capitalist modes of production having been restructured to serve the dominant capitalist mode, and the people as a whole are divided along class lines; but in addition, their function in society – and the manner in which resources are distributed and appropriated – is determined by racial criteria.[36]

The argument that Slovo is putting forward is that advanced by both the African National Congress and the South African Communist Party (both in exile), summarized most precisely by the latter's *The Road to South African Freedom* (1962):

> South Africa is not a colony but an independent state. Yet masses of our people enjoy neither independence nor freedom. The conceding of independence to South Africa by Britain in 1910 ... was designed in the interests of imperialism. Power was transferred not into the hands of the masses of the people of South Africa, but into the hands of the white minority alone. The evils of colonialism, in so far as the non-white majority were concerned, were perpetuated and reinforced. A new type of colonialism was developed, in which the oppressing white nation occupied the same territory as the oppressed people themselves and lived side by side with them.
>
> On one level, that of 'white South Africa', there are all the features of an advanced capitalist state in its final stage of imperialism. There are highly developed industrial monopolies and the merging of industrial and finance capital. The land is farmed along capitalist lines, employing wage labour, and producing cash crops for the local export market. The South African monopoly capitalists, who are closely linked with British, United States and other foreign imperialist interests, export capital abroad especially in Africa. Greedy for expansion, South African imperialism reaches out to incorporate other territories – South West Africa and the Protectorates.
>
> But on another level, that of 'non-white South Africa', there are all the features of a colony. The indigenous population is subjected to extreme national oppression, poverty and exploitation, lack of all democratic rights and political domination by a group which does everything it can to emphasise and perpetuate its alien 'European' character. The African Reserves show the complete lack of industry, communications, transport and power resources which are characteristic of ... territories under colonial rule ... Typical, too, of imperialist rule, is the reliance by the state upon brute force and terror, and upon the most backward tribal elements and institutions which are deliberately and artificially preserved. Non-white South Africa is the colony of white South Africa itself.[37]

This analysis provides the theoretical basis for the conclusion that the character of the struggle in South Africa is first and foremost one of *national liberation* of the African people. Class divisions that are internal to racial groups are viewed as having specifically shaped the form and content of the exploitative process, and to have played a major part in structuring political relations between the races. But, concludes Slovo, 'to identify "white South Africa" with an independent state and "non-white South Africa" with the colony is undoubtedly a useful shorthand, at one level, to depict the reality of the historically specific race factor in both the genesis and the existing nature of class rule.'[38]

The problem with the Slovo/SACP analysis is that it is offered on the basis of analogy and 'useful shorthand' to explain the complex specificity of the South African situation, yet it fails to offer a comprehensive theory of the relationship between class and race. Thus to argue, as does Slovo, that because its objective material interests are served by white minority rule, the white working class is 'a part (albeit subordinate) of the ruling class in its broader meaning',[39] is not only muddled, but contradictory when argued from a Marxian perspective – for by definition, a working class under capitalism *cannot* be a ruling class. What Slovo's analysis would suggest, therefore, is that either his use of the concept of class is over-mechanistic (and that what he terms the 'white working class' is in fact something rather different)[40] or that he is arguing that in capitalist South Africa race relations are the *dominant* source of conflict rather than class division, an argument which has been typically advanced by liberal–pluralist theorists rather than by Marxists.

It is this inconsistency which has been taken to task by Harold Wolpe, who argues that unless race and class exactly coincide (which they do not in the South African case), the concept of exploitation cannot be correctly used to express a relationship between racial groups, because exploitation refers specifically, in the Marxian formulation, to the appropriation of the surplus product of one *class* by another. In the case of internal colonialism, therefore, in order to avoid the abstraction (Slovo's 'shorthand' or 'analogy') involved in treating racial or ethnic groups as undifferentiated or homogeneous, we should consider each group as being made up of distinct classes with contradictory interests, with the social formation as a whole being constituted 'by the complex articulation of class relations within racial or ethnic groups, as well as the relation of classes across these groups, together ... with the ideological and political practices which "fit" these relationships'.[41]

Wolpe goes on to argue that the thesis of internal colonialism as formulated by the SACP fails to specifically relate different types of colonial *domination* (ideological, political, cultural and so on) with variant modes of economic *exploitation*. This he sees as resulting from the failure of the SACP programme to go beyond the rather general proposition that capitalism in South Africa goes hand in hand with the oppression of the majority racial group(s).

However, Wolpe continues, imperialist expansion does not necessarily lead to the *dissolution* of pre-capitalist modes of production, but can alternatively lead to the *preservation* and *domination* of the pre-capitalist forms:

> In certain circumstances capitalism may, within the boundaries of a single state, develop predominantly by means of its relationship to non-capitalist modes of production. When that occurs, the mode of political domination and the content of legitimating ideologies assume racial and ethnic and cultural forms, and for the same reason as in the case of imperialism. In this case, political domination takes on a colonial form, the precise or specific nature of which has to be related to the specific mode of exploitation of the non-capitalist society.[42]

He then goes on to argue that a distinctive feature of the South African social formation is that it has internalized such an imperialist relationship. Thus for Wolpe, the foundation of internal colonialism lies in 'the introduction into the capitalist circuit of production of labour-power physically produced in a non-capitalist economy ... [which] modifies the relationship between wages and the cost of reproducing labour-power in favour of capital'.[43]

His explanation is as follows. In the capitalist mode, the labourer sells his labour-power to the owner of the means of production, and receives in return payment for only part of the value of his product, the capitalist appropriating the balance in terms of unpaid labour or surplus value. Payment to the labourer is made on the basis of a distinction between *necessary* and *surplus* labour, necessary labour being the amount of labour required to allow for the subsistence of his dependants (including such socially necessary items as education). In general, however, the labourer will receive his payment in both direct and indirect forms: directly, in terms of his wage, and indirectly, in terms of the benefits offered by the state – social security payments, health facilities, schooling and so on. But, under certain circumstances, argues Wolpe, the capitalist mode of production is able to avoid bearing the cost of these indirect wages – that is, it is enabled to pay for labour-power below the cost of reproduction – by the availability of a supply of labour-power which is produced and reproduced outside the capitalist mode of production.

As far as South Africa is concerned, Wolpe argues that part of the indirect wages of labour have been met by the maintenance of non-capitalist modes of agricultural production, mainly (but not exclusively) located in the African Reserves (which were politically defined by the Natives Land Act of 1913, which initially restricted African titled occupation to some 7·13 per cent of the total land area). Although this African agriculture has been much restructured under the impact of capitalism, it has retained certain non-capitalist features, notably (given the predominantly communal tenure of land) the sharing of the product of labour among a kin group. But the crucial element is the existence of reciprocal obligation of support and consequently a distribution of the product which includes kin absent temporarily from agricultural production on the land held by the kin group.[44] If the necessary subsistence for a family can be produced in part of the year, then there is a supply of labour-power which can be *politically* coerced into working for the capitalist economy. Alternatively, if the non-capitalist mode can provide for only part of the subsistence of the labourer and his dependants, the labourer is forced on to the market by *economic* need. In either case, however, the capitalist mode is subsidized because it does not have to bear the entire cost of the labourer's subsistence, which raises the rate of the surplus value which the owner of capital is enabled to appropriate. Thus, in the South African case, the capitalist mode has been serviced by the preservation of non-capitalist modes of production in a restructured form, the political expression of this tendency taking a colonial form which has stressed the need to preserve the tribal nature of African societies.

However, it is a further aspect of Wolpe's analysis that the process of internal underdevelopment in the reserves occasioned by the dominance of the capitalist mode of production was such that, by the early 1940s, the latter could no longer effectively subsidize the interests of capital. In concrete terms, Wolpe means by this that so great were the pressures upon African agriculture that the reserves were no longer able to provide for the subsistence needs of their populations, overpopulation and the deliberate preservation of outmoded agricultural practices having led to a crisis of declining productivity, thereby extruding numbers of their inhabitants into the burgeoning urban settlements in white areas. It follows, therefore, that the major function of the reserves was necessarily transformed:

> That is to say, the practice and policy of Separate Development must be seen as the attempt to retain, in a modified form, the structure of the 'traditional' societies, not, as in the past, for the purpose of ensuring an economic supplement to the wages of the migrant labour force, but for the purposes of reproducing and exercising control over a cheap African industrial labour force in or near the 'homelands', not by means of preserving the pre-capitalist means of production but by the political, social, economic and ideological enforcement of low levels of subsistence.[45]

In short, no longer could the economies of the reserves be characterized as retaining predominantly pre-capitalist features, having been absorbed – through their crisis of declining productivity – into the dominant capitalist mode. Consequently, it was necessary for the state to erect a new and more repressive apparatus of political control (apartheid), based initially upon the deliberate cultivation of the authority of the chiefs (under the Bantu Authorities system). And this in turn was combined with the imposition of the entire ideological formulation of separate development and the 'free development' of the various 'African nations' (as expressed on occasions such as the debate on the Promotion of Bantu Self-Government Bill in 1959). Given the new emphasis on racial difference inherent in the ideology of separate development, rather than on the inherent biological–cultural superiority of the white man, the logic led inexorably to the setting of full independence for the various African groups in their own areas as the goal of state policy. In sum, concludes Wolpe, 'The uniqueness or specificity of South Africa, in the period of capitalism, lies precisely in this: that it embodies within a single nation-state a relationship characteristic of the external relationship between imperialist states and their colonies (or neo-colonies).'[46]

Wolpe's argument has been dealt with so extensively here because not only does it represent the most advanced theory of internal colonialism that is available, but it also provides a working explanation for the specific changes that have overcome the reserves/bantustans in the present century. In addition, he links the declining productivity of the reserves to various challenges made to the interests of different white groups; and in particular, he suggests that increasing African proletarianization (itself a reflection of reserve underdevelopment) presented a major threat to the white (predominantly Afrikaner) and enfranchised working class, thus in part being responsible for the ascendancy to power in 1948 of the (Afrikaner) National Party. He thus lays a material basis for the interpretation of a political practice and ideology that is widely recognized as being unique to South Africa. And while he does not include in his analysis the impact of external pressures on domestic policy and the rate of implementation of separate development, these can readily be incorporated into his model of political change. Indeed, the whole force of his argument is that unless there be some economic basis to apartheid, then the entire complex ideology becomes simply, and no more than, an exercise in divide and rule of a subordinate population.

At first sight, the notion of the contemporary Transkei as a neo-colony of South Africa would appear to fit neatly in with Wolpe's formulation, for the 'independence' that has been granted marks above all an acknowledgement that the process of creating a coercive state apparatus, manned by Africans to politically control surplus black population in favour of capital, has been so perfected that – in response to external events – direct political rule can be relaxed and left in the reliable hands of the Matanzima government. Unable to bear the cost of the reproduction of its own labour, it continues to be dependent upon the extrusion of migrant workers on to the South African market. The limited economic and industrial developments which do take place within its borders in no way threaten this supply of labour, yet simultaneously serve to provide a superficial credibility to the notion of Transkei as an independent state.

However, what is not completely clear from Wolpe's presentation is whether he regards the relation of internal colonialism as going beyond analogy to become fact. Elsewhere, for instance, Wolpe has referred to the bantustans as 'sub-states',[47] yet (to my knowledge) he has not sought to confront the problem of whether non-independent bantustans (sub-states) might emerge to independence as states (or neo-colonies). Thus even if the thrust of his analysis proposes that the bantustans, whatever their status, are integrally embedded into the apartheid political economy, the implication of the notion of internal colonialism might appear to be that the relationship it describes can be externalized in the form of a bantustan neo-colonialism. Yet the dangers inherent in such an approach are self-evident, and it would be peculiarly ironic if Wolpe's Marxian analysis were to be distorted into legitimating apartheid ideology.

Yet the fact that internal colonialism is, for Wolpe, the *political expression* of the 'crossing' of different modes of production suggests that he regards it as principally an ideological form and that, correspondingly, bantustan 'independence' is also an ideological rather than a substantive construct. If this be the correct interpretation of Wolpe's analysis, then it endorses the approach of Innes and O'Meara who, in one of the few attempts to elucidate the class dynamics of a bantustan, explain:

> In attempting to come to terms with class formation within the Transkei region we do not pose the question of whether a capitalist mode of production is

dominant within the Transkeian economy. To do so assumes that there exists such a discrete entity as the Transkei economy. It concedes to state ideology the claim that the Transkei region is an autonomous entity (an internal colony to be decolonised) and thus further serves to mystify its position within the South African social formation.[48]

Their position, which is congruent with the perspective adopted here, therefore concludes that 'a capitalist mode of production dominates the South African social formation, of which the Transkei region forms an integral part'. Accordingly, the focus of the present work is to offer, first, a historical survey of the development of classes in contemporary Transkei in the context of South African political economy as a whole; and secondly, to analyse the process whereby the apartheid government has sought to devolve political and administrative functions to a class of indigenous auxiliaries via the creation of a (sub)state apparatus in Transkei. All this is not to say that the South African government did not itself quite consciously emulate and seek to implement a strategy of extremely active neo-colonization (and it will be argued in the text below that this was the model that the white regime pursued), but rather to propose that if we accept the notion of Transkei as *substantively* a neo-colony then we reify the concept of bantustan 'statehood'. Such a concession, whether intentional or not, would clearly be a political act; and accordingly, given that scholarship cannot be value-free, the reverse interpretation (founded upon political and historical but *not* legal grounds) which maintains that a bantustan *cannot* be disembodied from the apartheid state, serves to *confront* rather than to *legitimate* the practice and implementation of apartheid rule and ideology.

Notes

1. *Comment and Opinion*, vol. 3, no. 43, 29 October, 1976.
2. House of Assembly *Hansard*, 7 June 1976, cols 8303, 8320–1.
3. *Die Burger*, 26 October 1976.
4. *Hoofstad*, 26 October 1976.
5. *To the Point*, 29 October 1976.
6. *Comment and Opinion*, 3, 38, 24 September 1976. The idea of introducing a new constitution, with separate Parliaments for the three non-black race groups, was officially launched by Prime Minister Vorster at a National Party Congress in August 1977.
7. See the debate on the Status of the Transkei Bill, 1976, in the Assembly *Hansard* 7–9 June, cols 8297–580. For a summary of the debate, see Horrell *et al.* (1976), pp. 230–3.
8. For opposition within the Transkei, see my article (1977); for the positions of SASO and the BPC see Mbanjwa (1975), pp. 2–3.
9. A survey of opposition to Mangope is offered by Special Report, 'Bophuthatswana: a fraud, Transkei style', *Africa*, no. 73, September 1977.
10. *Rand Daily Mail*, 11 October 1976; and SAIRR, *A Survey, 1976*, p. 28.
11. Anonymous (1976a).

18 THE PROBLEM OF BANTUSTAN 'INDEPENDENCE'

12. Kirby (1976) provides a convenient summary of 'Opposition to the Bantustans from Outside South Africa', Appendix Two, pp. 63–6.
13. *The Citizen*, 15 September 1976; *Comment and Opinion*, 3, 44, November 1976.
14. Much of the literature produced by bodies such as the UN and anti-apartheid bodies is devoted to proving the fraudulence of the bantustan exercise, although paying little attention to the class dynamics involved. See for example Kirby (1976) and Barbara Rogers (1976).
15. See pp. 283–95 below. At the time of final revision of the text, a fourth homeland, Ciskei, is scheduled to become 'independent' on 4 December 1981.
16. For example, BENBO (1976), Chapter III, 'A Comparison between Countries in Africa'.
17. As when, as is often done, earnings of 'Transkeian citizens' who are permanently resident in 'white' South Africa are counted as part of the Gross National Product of Transkei.
18. Stultz (1980), Chapter II, 'Transkei's Share'.
19. For the fragmentation of Bophuthatswana, see Map 1 on page xiii above.
20. Dugard (1976b), p. 2.
21. Harvey and Dean (1978).
22. Nkrumah (1965), p. ix.
23. For a concise and influential overview as applied to Africa, see Amin (1972).
24. The notion of economic surplus is derived from the work of Paul Baran and, as generally utilized by theorists, relates to 'the difference between society's *actual* current output and its *actual* current consumption'. Baran (1957), pp. 22–3.
25. Frank (1971).
26. ibid., p. 34.
27. Capitalist relations of production define a mode of appropriation of surplus labour (that is, the amount of labour over and above that required for the labourer's subsistence and his reproduction as a labourer) which works by means of commodity exchange, whereby owners of capital purchase the labour-power of non-owners by means of wage payment. Capitalist profit thus relies on the value of the labour-power purchased being greater than the value produced by that labour-power, this difference (surplus–labour) itself being capable of being expressed as a commodity, that is, surplus value. Note that one or more modes of production may co-exist within the same economy (thus capitalist with pre-capitalist), although one will always be dominant – Frank seems to ignore this possibility, arguing that the capitalist mode will replicate itself to the exclusion of other modes.
28. Nabudere (1977), p. 216.
29. Woddis (1967), pp. 62, 55.
30. Colin Leys (1975), p. 10.
31. Issa G. Shivji has developed one typology which distinguishes between three forms of neo-colonialism: Neo-colonialism Par-excellence, Bureaucratic Capitalism and State Capitalism, the main differences between the three relating mainly to the size of the public sector (and its relationship to international capital) and the presence or absence of a national bourgeois class. See Shivji (1973), pp. 1–60.
32. I was myself originally persuaded by the constitutional–legal argument which represents Transkei as a *de jure* state and felt accordingly that the neo-colonial framework as applied to Transkei could be helpful in allowing us to

strip away legal forms and thereby to analyse the modernized role of the 'independent' homeland in South African political economy. But the credibility of this approach rests to a considerable extent upon the notion of Transkei (the 'model bantustan') as historically a special case which has subsequently been destroyed by the progression to 'independence' of Bophuthatswana, Venda and Ciskei – entities which, for a whole host of reasons, it is patently absurd (even in 'objective' terms) to regard as potential or actual 'nation-states'.

33. Wolpe (1975).
34. Giniewski (1961); Molnar (1964).
35. Carter, Karis and Stultz (1967), p. 184. For an earlier, related analysis, see Marquard (1957).
36. Slovo (1976), p. 132.
37. South African Communist Party (1962/1970). Also partially reproduced in Wolpe (1975), pp. 231–2, and Slovo (1976), p. 133.
38. Slovo (1976), p. 135.
39. ibid., p. 122.
40. This question has been discussed separately by Wolpe (1976).
41. Wolpe (1975), p. 241.
42. ibid., p. 244.
43. ibid., p. 245.
44. ibid., p. 247.
45. Wolpe (1972), p. 450.
46. Wolpe (1975), p. 248.
47. Wolpe (1978).
48. Innes and O'Meara (1976), p. 70.

Chapter 2
Apartheid and decolonization

Apartheid ideology rests upon an identification by its rulers of South Africa as composed, not of a white minority and a predominantly black majority, but of a mosaic of culturally distinct peoples, each of whose destinies have been woven together by history yet which have continuously sought to assert their own identity. The whites, themselves drawn from a diversity of backgrounds but sharing a common European tradition, are said to have been drawn together by earlier struggles (of black against white, and Boer against Briton) into a homogeneous national group, but those of Bantu stock to have remained differentiated into a number of separate peoples – Xhosa, Zulu, North and South Sotho, Tswana, Swazi, Shangaan, Venda and Ndebele – each of which displays its own distinctive features, just as elsewhere in Africa the black race is made up of a diversity of tribes and nations. Thus it has been the particular contribution of the National Party to recognize (and, we might add, to foster) these differences, and to implement a policy of political separation, basing itself upon a presumed truth that no long-term peace can be attained where one or more nations oppress another.

According to apartheid ideologists, separate development is the only policy yet devised which can accommodate otherwise irreconcilable political differences among the various national groups. The white group, technologically the most advanced and upon whom the other peoples are dependent for economic leadership, has therefore evolved a political model (just as did the colonial powers elsewhere in Africa), whereby each black nation can determine its own future. Each such nation has been allotted its own territorial homeland which, because it is located in a region of ancestral settlement, constitutes a spiritual and emotional home even for those national citizens who physically dwell outside it. But based upon the former Native Reserves as delineated under the 1936 Natives Land and Trust Act, the homelands are unduly fragmented, and the Republican government is accordingly seeking to consolidate them by a process of fair exchange of land between the different groups. Finally, within each homeland, official policy has given expression to the political aspirations of each people by allowing them to evolve their own self-governing institutions, and as each homeland government gains in capability and experience, so it is encouraged to progress along the path of constitutional development until it reaches eventual independence. Ultimately, each Bantu nation will have separated from South Africa, whose body politic will thereafter contain only white, coloured and Asian citizens, each of which peoples will administer its own internal affairs, with all blacks – even though they be permanently working in the Republic – exercising their political rights in their own particular homelands. Thereafter, the various discrete nations of South Africa will co-operate together on a functional basis of 'interdependent independence'.[1]

The above is a summary of separate development theory as currently propounded. A critique of its failure to conform with social and historical reality need not detain us here, as numerous competent observers have undertaken this task elsewhere, focusing upon such aspects as only 13 per cent of the total land area of the Republic being set aside for blacks (who constitute some 70 per cent of the total population); the hopeless fragmentation of the homelands which debars them from ever becoming 'countries' in any meaningful sense of that word; the arbitrary and racist concept of nationality which ignores the extent to which the various African ethnic groups are inextricably and irreversibly interrelated; the effective denial of all political voice to blacks living in urban areas of the Republic; and the fact that all the homelands are thoroughly impoverished, underdeveloped and dependent upon the white economy.[2] Yet, despite all these and many other objections, the South African government continues to justify its policies in terms of its ideology. But apartheid has been a changing creed, theory and practice adjusting in response to pressures upon them from sources both internal and external to South Africa. To place the bantustan strategy in its proper perspective, therefore, it is necessary first to relate apartheid to the development of capitalism in Southern Africa as a whole, and to draw out the connections between the evolution of the bantustan policy and the changing international context.

Capitalism, segregation and apartheid[3]

Apartheid is principally a system whereby capital secures cheap black labour under certain historically defined conditions specific to the development of the South African social formation, its roots lying in the policies of 'segregation' which were adopted by the state subsequent to the inauguration of the Union in 1910. The latter was itself the political expression of an alliance between 'gold and maize', following upon the discovery of diamonds (1867) and gold (1886) and the subsequent Anglo-Boer war (1899–1902), in which the British imperial government sought to curb the independence of the Afrikaner republics of the Orange Free State and the Transvaal in favour of English-dominated mining capital by imposing a united South Africa.[4] From being a peripheral mercantile economy based upon the limited export of agricultural produce (mostly maize) to Europe, South Africa moved rapidly to being the world's foremost supplier of gold, and accordingly it was mining and farming together (and primarily the former) which initially determined the constellation of coercive mechanisms (designated 'segregation') whereby capital secured the labour-power it required through the creation of an extensive system of migrancy. But the stimulus from mining was itself to promote an expansion of secondary industry, which by the mid-1940s had become the predominant sector within the continuously expanding economy. Yet manufacturing, too, had its own specific requirements, and these in turn were to necessitate a massive extension of political controls to maintain the cheapness of African labour at a time when the latter was becoming increasingly proletarianized under pressures stemming from the erosion of the migrant base in the reserves. Thus 'apartheid' was evolved, and following Legassick may be characterized as 'the application of the cheap forced labour system established under segregationism, now applied to secondary industry rather than to mining and farming alone'.[5]

The development of the gold-mining industry in South Africa was, from its earliest days, predicated upon a specific cost structure which determined that profits to capital could be secured only by the absolute minimization of costs and the simultaneous maximization of output.

The unique feature of gold was that, unlike in the case of all other commodities, its price was fixed internationally and remained constant for long periods of time. This had two major consequences. On the one hand, producers were not enabled to pass on cost increases to their consumers; but on the other, as the market would accept all gold that was offered, it meant that the industry was not subject to crises of overproduction in that maximization of output increased, rather than endangered, the level of profits. However, because of certain technical constraints upon output maximization, primary emphasis in the pursuit of profit had therefore to be laid upon the minimization of costs.

The two major components of production costs were the prices of materials and labour respectively. But because the former was determined by external factors beyond the mining companies' control, the profitability of gold mining was necessarily almost wholly dependent upon the minimization of the cost of labour. This was particularly so because of the specific geological characteristics of the Witwatersrand: the average grade of ore was low, and the gold-bearing reef sloped deeply downwards, thus necessitating large-scale mining operations which required large capital outlays. Given also high development and overhead costs attendant upon deep-level mining, and the insufficiency of local capital to exploit the mineral discoveries, the industry from the start became dominated by overseas (mostly English) capital concentrated into several large, monopolistic corporations (or 'Groups').[6]

The requirement of mining capital for cheap labour was matched by that of settler agriculture, which was itself transformed by the development of the gold-mining industry, for directly associated with the latter was a process of rapid industrialization and consequent expansion of the internal market. From being primarily concerned with the production of wool and sugar for export, commercial agriculture became progressively oriented to the satisfaction of local demand, its own expansion thereby drawing it into increasing competition with the mining houses for the limited supply of labour that was available.[7] Yet squeezed by the twin pressures of low-priced wheat imports and low-cost market participation by African producers (who were as responsive to expanding opportunities as the settlers themselves), white farming was no less dependent than the mines upon the acquisition of labour that was cheap. But the effect of their mutual competition was to raise, rather than to depress, the cost of labour – the requisite supply of which was not forthcoming at the low prices which either was able or willing to pay. Thus the response of both alike was to resort, through the state, to the use of 'extra-economic' coercion – the use of political controls to induce a flow of labour at a price below that which would normally obtain under free market conditions.[8]

But the labour that was available was of two kinds – free and unfree, white and non-white – for the emergent working class in South Africa was composed of two racially distinct groups which were involved in quite different relations of production with the owners of capital. In particular, as members of the dominant racial group, white workers were not legally subject to the various forms of extra-economic coercion devised by the capitalist class, and were free in the specific sense that they were able to vote, and to organize collectively through trade union and party political activity, the combined effect of which was to raise the cost of their labour. In bleak contrast, black workers enjoyed no such rights, and were accordingly subject to the full rigour of a racially structured system of class exploitation.

The advantaged status of white workers was critical in that it determined that both the mines and settler agriculture would seek to minimize their costs by coercively inducing politically unfree, black labour. Of course, employers' reliance upon extra-economic coercion to secure labour had a history which well predated Union. Thus in the Cape, measures such as the Caledon Code of 1809 and, later, Masters and Servants Laws (first introduced by the Colony government in 1856), had restricted the contractual rights of black workers, while almost from the earliest days the mines had been dependent upon the importation of semi-slave labour from territories outside South Africa (notably from Portuguese East Africa).[9] But it was only after the consolidation of the alliance between gold and maize in 1910 that coercion was to find its expression in the enactments and policies which defined segregation, these being constituted of three main elements: (1) the limitation of black land ownership to Native Reserves which were designed to function as labour reservoirs; (2) measures to induce and regulate a flow of African labour; and (3) restrictions upon the permanent settlement of Africans in white areas.

1. Territorial segregation of black from white was legally defined by the Natives Land Act of 1913, which not only set aside existing African areas as reserves for exclusive black ownership and occupation, but also prohibited Africans from purchasing land outside the scheduled territories (in order to ensure that what whites had gained by conquest they would not later lose through the market). In sum, 7·13 per cent of the total land area of the Union was demarcated as reserve land (including some individually owned allotments), although provision was made in the Act for further enlargement. It was subsequently decided in 1922 to release a further $7\frac{1}{2}$ million morgen (1 morgen = 2·12 acres) for African purchase, although only $1\frac{1}{2}$ million were in actuality bought by Africans before 1936, in which year the Native Trust and Land Act ordained that the 'final' land settlement between black and white would, at maximum, allow for the reserves to extend to a total of 13·7 per cent of Union territory.[10]

As De Kiewiet has argued,[11] the land wars of the nineteenth century were also labour wars, so that in many areas the effects of appropriation of land were cushioned for blacks by their being absorbed into quasi-feudal arrangements with the new landowners. Rather than sweeping the African inhabitants before them and clearing the land for exclusive white settlement, the conquerors permitted them to retain a restricted access to the means of production, in return for which they were obliged to offer services as labourers, herdsmen and tenants, or in the case of sharecroppers to turn over half of their annual crops to white landowners in exchange for the rights to occupy, graze and cultivate. Although initially easing land utilization problems, especially for larger owners, such arrangements later posed a threat to settler agriculture, for not only did they provide a basis for African peasantization and consequent commercial competition, but they also increased African capacity to resist pressures designed to extrude black labour power upon the market. Thus the immediate *motivation* behind the passage of the Land Act of 1913 was, through the elimination of squatting and occupation rights outside the reserves, to elicit a greater supply of labour for white agriculture, while simultaneously undermining the foundations of African peasant production.[12] But the broader *effect* of the Act was to overburden the reserves, and to limit the ability of Africans to mitigate the results of land pressure by moving beyond the confines of the scheduled areas. The consequent increased flow of cheap labour was thereby to provide a basis for accumulation, not by settler agriculture alone, but by every sector of white capital, and notably the mines.

2. If the principal objective of the 1913 Land Act was to induce a supply of African labour for white capital, its necessary complement was a series of measures more directly coercive of the African workforce. Existing labour legislation was modelled on the Cape Masters and Servants Laws which restricted the rights of non-white workers, regulating the formation, duration and termination of their contracts. The essential feature of

these contracts was that their breach (desertion, disturbance, insubordination and so on) constituted a criminal offence, making the offender liable to imprisonment. In 1911, under the Native Labour Regulation Act, these criminal sanctions were extended to workers in the mines, who were also expressly denied the right to strike.[13] And it was the same Act which made mineworkers also subject to the Pass Laws which, like the Masters and Servants Ordinances, had originated in the nineteenth century and had been consolidated over time. Under these regulations, the movement of labour was directly restricted, black workers being denied the freedom to move their place of residence or to take up alternative employment elsewhere without first obtaining a pass, on which were registered a host of personal details. Taken together with the establishment of monopsonistic recruiting agencies by employers (notably the mines),[14] consequent wage fixing and the extensive incarceration of workers into prison-like compounds, the resulting system can not unfairly be characterized as one of essentially forced labour.

3. Finally, the complement to legislation which restricted African ownership to the reserves and which subjected them to a regimented system of labour were measures to order and control their lives in urban 'locations' where they lived while in white employment. Township Africans were subject to a variety of provincial and municipal statutes prior to the First World War, but in 1923 Parliament ratified the Natives (Urban Areas) Act, which was based on the philosophy of the Stallard Commission of 1921 which deemed that any African was only temporarily resident and 'should only be allowed to enter the urban areas, which are essentially the white man's creation, when he is willing to enter and to minister to the needs of the white man and should depart therefrom when he ceases so to minister'.[15] In essence, therefore, the thrust of this law (and numerous subsequent amendments) was that those Africans who were unemployed, sick or 'idle' could be dispatched to the reserves, there to wait until they were further required to wait upon the white economy.

As a mode of securing cheap labour for capital, segregation was thus responsible for the creation of a system of labour migrancy which extended far beyond the borders of the Union, embracing not only the three High Commission Territories, but also countries as diverse and far apart as Mozambique, Nyasaland, the Rhodesias, Tanganyika, South West Africa and Angola as sources of supply. As such, the development of capitalism in South Africa was, in varying degrees, responsible for the structural underdevelopment of the labour-supplying territories,[16] the extreme case being presented by Basutoland (contemporary Lesotho), whose labour dependence and general impoverishment closely paralleled that of the reserves.[17] Yet this system of labour migrancy was fraught with internal contradictions whose resolution, in the course of time, was to lead to the virtual collapse of the non-capitalist base (notably in the reserves) upon which segregation was founded and thus, taken together with the rise of secondary industry, necessitate the transition to apartheid.

Historically, the system of labour migration represented the crucial mechanism whereby capital was able to obtain the cheap labour that it required. More specifically, because the subsistence requirements of the individual worker were wholly or in part met by the continued existence of non-capitalist modes of production (involving the retention of communal land tenure and the continuing distribution of the social product among kin), capital was enabled to employ labour-power below the cost of its production and reproduction. In concrete terms, by stabilizing the existing distribution of land between black and white, the 1913 Land Act arrested the development of landlessness among the African population in order to provide the foundation for the migrant labour system. By allowing Africans to retain *limited* access to land in the reserves (although *insufficient* to allow for their subsistence), the *necessity* of migrancy for employment was thereby forced upon them; and at the same time, because they were provided with the partial means of subsistence (and their complete separation from the land was simultaneously retarded by legislation restricting their right to move to urban areas), capital was enabled to pay African labourers at a coercively induced cheap wage. In other words, the workforce was paid at a rate below the cost of its physical reproduction as a class, so that, in effect, the productive capacity of the reserves served as an indirect subsidy to white-owned capital.[18]

This relationship, beneficial to capital as it was, could only be maintained so long as the non-capitalist base was capable of bearing a proportion of the real cost of labour (by providing an indirect wage). However, by the early 1940s (and in many cases well before) it had become plainly apparent that the economic base of the migrant labour system was being undermined by the structural underdevelopment of the reserves.[19] Overpopulation, overstocking, soil erosion, a declining productivity of African agriculture, increasing social stratification and landlessness, and the dissolution of communal obligations among kin to distribute the resources that were available, all indicated that the reserves were providing a diminishing proportion of the subsistence requirement of migrant workers: in essence, they were becoming ever less able to subsidize the operations of capital, and the mining industry in particular.

There were two major consequences. In the first place, it followed that growing numbers of migrant workers were becoming free in Marx's sense of their being separated from ownership of or access to the means of production, thereby compelling them to rely for the greater part of their subsistence upon the sale of their labour-power to the capitalist market. The most telling evidence of this was a drift to the towns, despite all the various influx controls and Pass Laws operative under segregation, and the highly visible growth of an African proletariat increasingly cut off from the reserves.[20] And secondly, the declining productive capacity of the reserves 'threatened to reduce the rate of surplus value through pressure on wages and posed, for capital, the problem of preventing a fall in the level of profit'.[21] In other words, if the non-capitalist mode was increasingly less able to provide for the cost of the reproduction of labour-power, this burden was necessarily placed upon the capitalist sector itself.

The resultant crisis presented acute problems for the owners of capital in terms of their continuing need for control over and exploitation of the African labour force. But it was also the case that, with the rise to prominence of manufacturing (which overtook mining in terms of contribution to Gross Domestic Product in the mid-1940s), the labour requirements of the diverse fractions of South African capital were no longer uniform, for secondary industry was less dependent than either the mines or agriculture upon the acquisition of cheap (that is, reserve-subsidized) labour *per se* than upon the rationalization of its existing high-cost structure which was perceived as a barrier to its further expansion. In short, the posited need was, through the extension of mechanization to industry, to replace relatively expensive white labour (upon which the development of manufacturing had hitherto in large measure been based), with a cheaper, semi-skilled black workforce, thereby achieving an overall reduction in cost. But the political implications of such a transition were immense, for they posed a direct threat to the relatively advantaged position of the white working class.

The earliest developments in manufacturing had been mainly in the sphere of light industry (food and beverages, textiles and clothing, footwear and raw materials processing) which were all relatively labour intensive, demanding limited inputs of capital, and were oriented to the production of consumer goods and import substitution. The major exception was the metal products and engineering industry (initially developed around the needs of the mines) which had received a major stimulus with the establishment of the Iron and Steel Corporation (ISCOR) under state auspices in 1928. This latter development foreshadowed a steady expansion of the public sector, and a greater participation by the state in economic planning with a view to expanding the secondary sector and making the economy less dependent upon primary industry (mining and farming). Thus, following the establishment of the Industrial Development Corporation in 1940 (created to funnel public funds towards key areas in the economy), other ventures were later to include SASOL (an enterprise devoted to the production of oil from coal) and FOSKOR (which produces mining phosphates as a base for fertilizers) – a key feature of all such nationalized industries being the extent to which they have, historically, served as channels for upward mobility and instruments for accumulation by Afrikaner personnel. Yet the trend towards state capitalism was accompanied by a vast extension of private industry, which in the postwar period (and stimulated by western investment)[22] has become increasingly capital intensive, major growth taking place in the additional spheres of automobile construction, chemicals, military hardware, capital goods equipment, electronics and computers.[23]

The early development of manufacturing industry had been to a great extent fostered by the adoption by the state of a protective tariff, but in return, employers had had to accept the costs of a higher wage structure sponsored by the government to solve the 'poor white problem'.[24] Historically, the white working class in South Africa had been differentiated into skilled and unskilled elements. Thus although the bulk of work upon the mines could be adequately performed by the unskilled, there were certain technical operations (relating mainly to the extraction of gold from the ore) which demanded a given level of training. However, because of an absence of skilled labourers upon the Rand, mining capital had early resorted to the import of such workers from Britain and Europe. Yet the cost of such labour was high, for not only was it scarce but its economic muscle was from the first enhanced by its organization into trade unions which acted not only to bargain with employers, but to perpetuate scarcity by restricting admission to the ranks of the skilled.[25]

In contrast, the unskilled and larger element among the white working class had been formed by workers subject to a classic process of proletarianization in that they came to be separated from the means of production by a number of discrete economic upheavals (such as the 1899–1902 war), but in particular by the commercialization of agriculture (many landowners ridding themselves of unwanted *bywoners*, or white tenant farmers, who unlike black squatters could not be legally required to offer labour to their proprietors). Nothing to sell but their labour-power, and possessing no special attributes which they could offer to the market, such white proletarians (most of whom were Afrikaners) had flocked to the towns, differentiated from the emergent African working class by their possession of the vote, which in consequence was to become instrumental in promoting their economic advance.

The critical turning point was the election to office in 1924 of the 'Pact government'.[26] Changing conditions initiated during the First World War had led to a series of forceful challenges to capital from both black and white workers. The expansion of all sectors of the economy (and notably manufacturing), combined with the departure of a significant proportion of the white workforce for the battlefields of Europe, had aggravated the perennial shortage of African labour. African workers were not backward in taking advantage of this situation, and put forward a series of claims for higher wages and better working conditions, the expression of their demands taking the form of a series of large-scale strikes (notably involving some 71,000 mineworkers in 1920) and the formation of the Industrial and Commercial Workers Union under Clements Kadalie.

Although such displays of militance were suppressed by force, capital and the state had both been placed on the defensive. Accordingly, the mine employers now sought to accommodate various of the African workers' demands by restructuring their labour policies within limits which did not materially affect the conditions of accumulation. In short, via a process of mechanization they sought to upgrade and to increase wages for semi-skilled black mineworkers and to substitute them for more highly paid skilled white workers, thus securing an overall reduction in costs. But white workers responded sharply to this assault upon their racially entrenched position, their resistance culminating in the Rand Revolt of 1922, an armed uprising against the state which, in distorted echo of the Bolshevik Revolution of 1917, called for 'Workers of the World to fight and unite for a White South Africa'.

The revolt was crushed unhesitatingly and forcefully by the South African Party government of General Smuts, but the unpopularity which the latter gained in so doing led to the white working class pledging its allegiance to an Opposition alliance in the general election of 1924. The resultant Pact government, a coalition of the National and Labour Parties, was no less a servant of capital than its predecessor (even if it was less readily identifiable with the mining magnates). However, its political complexion and electoral interests induced it to adopt a new strategy based upon the neutralization of the white working class and the co-option of a number of its leaders. This involved, first, a drive not only against the African trade union movement, but also a determined assault upon militants among the white workers' leadership. By the end of 1932 the organization of the ICU had been effectively destroyed and black workers beaten into a temporary submission, while the attacks upon white militants had destroyed the unity of the Labour Party (which disintegrated into warring factions in 1928). Secondly, by extending Smuts's policy of promoting secondary industrialization (in part by introducing tariff protection against foreign competition), the Pact government sought (*inter alia*) to increase the employment opportunities available to the white working class; and thirdly, it moved swiftly to introduce a 'Civilized Labour Policy' which was designed to protect poor whites against black competition in the field of unskilled labour and, at a higher level, to prevent skilled whites from being undercut by black artisans.

It was in pursuit of this civilized labour policy that a Wage Board was established in 1925 to make wage determinations in industries where there was no previous provision for collective bargaining and through which the government was to pursue a policy of upgrading wages for unskilled white workers relative to black, while the Mines and Works Amendment Act of the following year secured the interests of skilled workers by the simple expedient of reserving the grant of certificates for participating in skilled trades to whites and coloureds. And with the onset of the Depression, employment opportunities for blacks in both the public and private sectors were deliberately blocked to provide jobs for whites, with tariff concessions to employers being made explicitly dependent upon their adoption of 'satisfactory' labour policies.

The civilized labour policy was directly responsible for placing South African industry at a disadvantage relative to its international competitors. Wages for its skilled workers were high when compared to rates paid to artisans elsewhere, while the availability of an ample supply of cheap, unskilled (black) labour had retarded mechanization, so that productivity lagged behind. Thus once the worst of the Depression was over and the 'poor white' problem had become less politically pressing, both employers and government increasingly advocated the need for a rationalization of the high-wage cost-structure, arguing the necessity to dissolve the craft skills held and protected by the white working class in favour of a long-term substitution by semi-skilled operatives, thereby creating greater scope for the employment of African workers (who were conveniently held to display a peculiar aptitude for monotonous machine processes!): 'The extension of manufacturing industry can be stimulated by a reduction of the high cost structures through increased mechanisation, so as to derive the full benefit of the large resources of comparatively low-paid non-European labour.'[27] Such a development was also deemed to hold out the prospect for increased African purchasing power, thereby providing an expanding market to stimulate yet further industrial growth.

But the increased employment of black labour on a semi-skilled basis necessitated a modification of the existing migratory system. Manufacturing industry was not seeking to undermine the mechanisms whereby mining and agriculture acquired cheap labour from the reserves, but it was concerned to ensure that these should not interfere with its own labour needs, for unless its own African employees could be settled in urban areas on a more permanent basis, skills would be quickly lost by rapid turnover and capital would be unable to receive adequate return on investment expenditures on training facilities and the other social costs attendant upon stabilization of the workforce. This in turn implied that manufacturing capital, with a more flexible cost structure than mining in that it was able to pass on cost increases through higher prices to consumers, accepted the increasing necessity to take up the burden of providing for the full costs of the subsistence of its African workforce.

On the other hand, the dangers of stabilization were clearly recognized as making for the increasing proletarianization of African labour and a consequent development of its political consciousness: 'Racial and Class differences will make a homogeneous Native proletariat which will eventually lose all contact with its former communal rural relations which had previously given their lives a content and meaning,' stated one report. 'The detribalisation of large numbers of Natives congregated in amorphous masses in large industrial centres is a matter which no government can view with equanimity.'[28] That such a threat was not unfounded was indicated by the intensification of industrial and political struggle by the African population. Whereas 171,088 African man-hours had been lost to industry in the period 1930–9, a total of 1,684,915 were lost in the following decade (inclusive of the African mineworkers' strike of 1946, when African workers struck for a ten shilling basic wage and housing for their families – a demand reflective of the erosion of the migrant base).[29] And in a broader sphere, of course, the African National Congress (founded in 1912 but in a state of decline in the 1930s) became revitalized through its Youth League and shifted its strategy to mass boycott and political demonstration.[30]

The stabilization and proletarianization of the African population were, not unnaturally, perceived as a major threat by the white working class in particular (and notably its Afrikaner constituent which was – in general – rather less skilled that its English-speaking counterpart). Hitherto protected by the civilized labour policy, the basis of its privilege was apparently endangered by the exhibited preference of manufacturing capital for the greater employment of black workers. Similarly, mining and agricultural capital were broadly opposed to the process as representing a potential threat to their own interests, mining because of its absolute requirement for cheap labour, and farming (unable to entomb its workers in compounds) because of its inability to prevent its labourers from deserting to the towns without resorting to methods of outright coercion.

These variant interests of the different class elements were to be highlighted in the critical election of 1948, when the two main contestant parties offered divergent programmes to resolve the acute problems posed by the disintegration of the reserves and the employment needs of the different sectors of capital. Yet politically, the landscape was made much more complex by the Opposition National Party promoting itself as the historical manifestation of the Afrikaner *volk*, and seeking to challenge the predominance of English-speaking and British imperial interests.

The ruling United Party had been formed in 1934 by the fusion of the National and South African Parties to confront the crisis of the Great Depression. It had initially coalesced the leading elements of both the Afrikaner and English-speaking oligarchies, while simultaneously serving as the representative of all the major fractions of capital. It had won convincing parliamentary majorities in elections in 1938 and 1943, although in hindsight it is evident that these victories in actuality masked the party's political decline, for it had alienated large numbers of its Afrikaner supporters by its entry into another of 'England's wars' in 1939. This had resulted in the resignation of General Hertzog as Prime Minister (after his failure to win a parliamentary vote to keep the Union out of the war), and his departure from the UP for the Opposition benches, taking with him a considerable body of supporters. This then provided the basis for the formation of the *Herenigde* (reunited) National Party in 1939, which reconciled the main body of the Hertzogites with the

Gesuiwerde (Purified) National Party of D. F. Malan (which had broken away from the former NP when the latter had fused with the SAP in 1934). However, continuing differences between the various factions was to lead to Hertzog's forming a further breakaway Afrikaner Party in January 1941, although this time he succeeded in taking with him only a small handful of followers. Hertzog was soon to withdraw from politics, and in so doing to clear the way for his successor as leader of the Afrikaner Party, N. C. Havenga, to enter an electoral pact with Malan in 1948.

The election programme of the UP in 1948 attempted the difficult task of seeking to accommodate all the diverse pressure to which the party was subjected. In the first place, although the UP itself espoused a broad white South Africanism against the Afrikaner particularism of the Opposition coalition, it was inevitably portrayed by the latter as the vehicle of English-speaking interests. Secondly, it was also seeking to reconcile the conflicting interests of the diverse fractions of capital. Mining and agriculture, both dependent upon a continuing supply of cheap labour, were assured that even if inevitable, the processes of African urbanization and 'detribalization' would be gradual and that they need fear no drastic change. In contrast, manufacturing industry was assured that the stabilization of its African workforce would be facilitated by extension of housing, pension and other welfare benefits to the burgeoning black population, while white workers were informed that their interests would be protected by continuing regulation of the African workforce, modification of the Pass Laws (to become less offensive but more effective) and prohibition of the right of blacks to strike. Finally, to offset the political dangers posed by proletarianization and concentration of the African masses in the urban areas, the UP advocated continuing separate representation through segregated political institutions, in addition to a state-financed rehabilitation programme for the reserves and a policy of regional planning with a view to the decentralization of industry whenever possible.

The ambivalence of the UP appeal was further reflected by a lack of leadership from General Smuts (who had followed Hertzog as Prime Minister in 1939), and the demoralization of the party's organization. In contrast, the National Party's apartheid programme was far more dynamic in that it sought to mobilize political support by unambiguously espousing the cause of Afrikaner reunification (Afrikaans-speakers forming a numerical majority of all South African whites). Principally representing the Afrikaner bourgeoisie (which was still largely located within the agricultural sphere) and playing heavily upon white (notably unskilled Afrikaner) workers' fears of black competition, the NP rejected the UP notion that the demise of African labour migrancy was inevitable, and instead promised to reverse the tide of history by extending the migrant system to secondary industry. African movement into the towns and cities would be strictly controlled by the state according to the needs of industry through a system of labour bureaux located in the reserves, while it was re-emphasized that urban blacks would be regarded as temporary sojourners entitled to remain in white areas only so long as they were in active employment. Political dangers inherent in African proletarianization would be countered by influx control and coercive regulations, and the trend towards concentrations of blacks in urban areas would be reversed by the revitalization of the reserves and a policy of decentralization. Finally, the idea was put forward that Africans would be extended political rights in their tribal 'homelands' (the reserves). Their remaining representation in the central parliament (three white MPs) would be abolished, as would the Natives Representatives Council established in 1936, their political genius to be alternatively realized through a system of self-government on lines similar to those which already existed in the Transkei (through its Bunga or Council), which would uphold the authority of the tribal chiefs.

It was upon this platform that the NP achieved office (though on a minority vote and dependent upon the support of the small Afrikaner Party under Havenga, its slim parliamentary majority reflecting the acute conflicts prevailing between different elements within the white ruling bloc). In particular, its programme had been bitterly opposed by large sectors of manufacturing capital (which feared that their attempts to procure a stabilized, semi-skilled black workforce would be thwarted by the renewed emphasis upon migrancy); and mining capital was alarmed by campaign threats to carry through a policy of nationalization. But the farming interest had found considerable reassurance in the intention to secure its migrant base, and the discriminatory and coercive measures promised against the African labour force had won it the support of large numbers of white workers fearful of black competition. Together, therefore, the electoral combination of the Afrikaner bourgeoisie and the white working class was sufficient to secure a narrow victory for the Nationalists, and to enable them to implement subsequently their policy of apartheid.[31]

The implementation of apartheid

For many western observers, the racial policies of the post-1948 National Party governments have constituted a politically regressive and ideological constraint upon the expansion of the South African economy, for while the officially proclaimed end of apartheid has been to separate the races as far as is practical (on the assumption that racial mixing causes interracial friction), continuing economic development is seen as promoting increasing and inevitable racial integration and interdependence. Yet, as Johnstone has indicated, the *ideology* of apartheid (which justifies the actions of the South African government) needs to be distinguished from apartheid *goals* (which relate to official policies as actually implemented), for the latter are purposefully functional to the promotion and maintenance of white prosperity and white supremacy.[32] In other words, rather than in any way constituting an irrational superstructure imposed upon the economy, apartheid should be viewed as a set of pragmatic policies whereby the government, rather than devoting itself to the literal pursuit of its ideology, caters to the needs of capital and the interests of the dominant racial group.

The implementation of apartheid has affected virtually every sphere of South African society. Social mixing between the races can take place only under extremely limited conditions, and there is an absolute legal bar on sexual contact between white and black. Public amenities are largely segregated, with blacks being offered grossly inferior services and facilities (although in recent years there has been some relaxation of 'petty apartheid' measures with the opening of some public amenities – such as 'international' hotels – to all races). And through the Bantu Education Act of 1953, the state excluded missions and other bodies from the educational sphere, and took over entire responsibility for African schooling, going on to introduce a system designed to be in accordance with the subservient role of blacks in the white economy. But because of its deliberately inferior quality, Bantu education has served as a source of continuous protest by the black community and, importantly, provided the spark which ignited the Soweto explosion in 1976 (after the government had sought to make teaching in Afrikaans compulsory); and similarly, the separate universities which were established for the different ethnic groups after 1958 (following the passage of the Extension of University Education Act), have been in recent years centres of ferment and protest against apartheid, students reacting violently against tribal nationalism and the entire homeland concept.

A major political objective of the post-1948 government has certainly been to advance specifically Afrikaner interests, although this aim has not contradicted the broader cause of maintaining white supremacy, which in turn has remained premised upon the concern to secure a supply of cheap labour power to satisfy the expanding requirements of mining, agriculture and industry. And just as the mechanisms of segregation could be analysed through a threefold characterization, so also is it possible to examine the application of apartheid via (1) the implementation of the bantustan policy in association with the strategy of industrial decentralization; (2) the maintenance of the cheapness of black labour in the context of secondary industrialization; and (3) the continuing restriction on the settlement of blacks in urban areas.

1. At its most basic level, the bantustan programme as implemented since 1948 may be viewed as a policy of 'divide and rule', for in order to counter the unifying effects of urbanization and proletarianization, the African population (which outnumbers whites by five to one) has been redefined into ten (originally eight) ethnic minorities. 'Nationality' has

been given territorial substance by the grouping together of former reserve areas into 'homelands', while a continuing process of 'consolidation' is reducing the latter's fragmentation to more administratively manageable proportions than at first obtained, even though the credibility of the bantustans as potential states is undermined by the supposedly final consolidation plan announced in 1975 which would leave only the Ciskei and the smaller territories of QwaQwa, Kangwane and Ndebele as united entities, with Kwazulu consisting of ten separate fragments, Bophuthatswana of six, Transkei of three and so on (although such territorial divisions in themselves serve as a useful defence against any homeland nationality assuming an unwholesome and unexpected reality potentially embarrassing to white political control – see Table 2.1).[33]

Table 2.1 *Predominant ethnic composition, land area and portions, and population of the homelands*

Homeland	People	Land area (sq. ml)	Land portions	Population de facto 1970 ('000s)	Population de jure 1970 ('000s)
Transkei	Xhosa	14,178	3	1,726	2,997
Ciskei	Xhosa	3,547	19 (1)[a]	525	915
Kwazulu	Zulu	12,141	44 (10)	2,014	4,018
Lebowa	Pedi/N. Ndebele	8,549	13 (6)	1,084	2,097
Venda	Venda	2,333	3 (2)	267	360
Gazankulu	Shangaan/Tsonga	2,576	4 (3)	265	650
Bophuthatswana	Tswana	14,494	8 (6)	865	1,680
QwaQwa	Basotho	144	1	24	1,357
KaNgwane	Swazi	818	2 (1)	116	472
Ndebele	S. Ndebele	?	1	n.a.	(233)[b]

Notes:
[a]Refers to projected number of land portions after implementation of 1975 consolidation proposals.
[b]Total S. Ndebele population 1970. No figure is yet available as to how many of these persons are designated 'citizens' of the Ndebele homeland.
Sources: Malan and Hattingh (1976); Figure 4.4, p. 27; D. A. Kotze (1975), Table 3, II, p.32.

Complementary to the divisive effects of ethnic differentiation has been a revival of chieftaincy and the creation of political institutions in the bantustans designed to employ indigenous auxiliaries in maintaining control over homeland populations. Thus the Bantu Authorities Act of 1951 provided for the establishment of Tribal, Regional and Territorial Authorities, and for the gradual delegation to them of executive and administrative powers. This involved granting to chiefs greater authority than they had previously enjoyed under 'traditional' forms of government, thereby giving them a vested interest in the continuance of separate development; and upon this foundation was subsequently erected a set of political structures allowing for the wider incorporation of an emerging African petty-bourgeoisie into the various homeland governments. The creation of legislative assemblies (initially in the Transkei in 1963 and after 1970 in the other bantustans) has allowed for the broader representation of locally prominent rural interests, and the expansion of bantustan administrations has led to the growth of bureaucratic elements whose material interests and élite status are objectively opposed to those of the impoverished homeland populations. Finally, the Republican administration has been enabled to relieve itself of various burdensome chores (such as the provision of education, the care of the sick, and the payment of pensions) which have now in large part become the responsibility of the homeland governments; and through the devolution of limited (but not unimportant) powers to the bantustan peripheries, regional foci have been created which direct attention away from the political core, deflecting protest and discontent away from the white authorities and on to the black auxiliaries themselves.

The third aspect of bantustan policy has been the state-directed effort to counter the disintegration of the reserves through a programme of agricultural rehabilitation and industrial decentralization. The Tomlinson Commission, reporting in 1955 upon a brief to make recommendations for the socio-economic development of the Bantu Areas, argued for a massive programme of employment creation providing some 50,000 jobs per annum in order to attain an actual reversal of the flow of the (rapidly expanding) African population to the white core. It was proposed that white-owned capital (hitherto barred) should be attracted to the reserves by the provision of financial incentives and guarantees of low-cost labour, while African capitalist investment and enterprise should itself be promoted through the creation of various financial institutions (a development corporation, a bank, an insurance company and a building society) to encourage local capital formation and supply credit to indigenous entrepreneurs; and in the agricultural sphere, a comprehensive revitalization programme was urged involving the revision of communal land tenure and the introduction of freehold title in order to promote a class of capitalistically oriented peasants, non-farmers being transferred to urban settlements where they would be employed by the expansion of industry.[34]

But the government response to Tomlinson has served to illustrate the disjunction between the goals and ideology of apartheid, for although the Commission was established to provide a blueprint for the future of the reserves, its (majority) recommendations were subsequently discarded, diluted or delayed lest their implementation run counter to white interests. Conscious that its electorate would be reluctant to underwrite a suggested outlay of £104·5 million over an initial ten-year period to finance development, the government pared the Commission's estimates down to £36·6 million, while simultaneously refraining from imposing upon itself any long-term financial commitments; and by the Natives Taxation and Development Act (no. 38 of 1958), it increased rates of taxation upon the African population, thereby shifting the burden of development expenditure away from the white taxpayer.[35]

In similar fashion, while the government has explicitly accepted the need to shore up the disintegrating base of reserve agriculture, the impact of its limited reform measures have been largely negated by the continuing contradictions of apartheid. Thus pressures upon agriculture have been much intensified by the 'resettlement' programme (whereby surplus blacks are removed from white areas), so that the density of population actually living upon the land in the bantustans now far outstrips that which exists in comparable areas of other African countries: in contrast to a density of 41 persons per square mile (2·6 square km) in Kenya and 63 in Lesotho, the average figure for the homelands was 119 in 1970.[36] Overpopulation, in turn, has led to increasing landlessness and the reduction of farming lots to an average size well below that capable of providing subsistence for the average family unit under present conditions, while the coercive implementation of soil conservation and land rehabilitation measures have provoked a series of violent protests against the authorities.[37] But perhaps most revealing of all, the government has correctly recognized that extensive reform of the existing land tenure system would undermine the political structure of Bantu Authorities, under which chiefs play a central role in the allocation of land and other material resources. Thus introduction of freehold title would act as a corrosive upon chiefly authority, with the distributive function being transferred to the forces of an impersonal market; the removal from the land of the majority of the present occupants would necessitate the creation of large-scale urban settlements; and, of course, the development of African peasant farming upon a capitalistic basis would pose a potentially competitive threat to white farming interests.[38] Thus bantustan agriculture remains in a state of deepening and perpetual crisis, with the various official schemes to promote stock improvement, establish cooperative marketing and launch irrigation farming failing to arrest the continuing decline in productivity of staple foods.[39]

In the industrial sphere, the Tomlinson recommendations have fared only marginally better. Thus the government initially rejected the proposal to allow white investment to penetrate the reserves lest its low-cost basis should threaten the established interests of white capital and labour outside the homelands, justifying its stand on the grounds that industrial activity within the bantustans should be undertaken exclusively by Africans themselves. To import apparent substance to its decision, in 1959 the government created the Bantu Investment Corporation (although with initial capital of only £500,000), whose objective was to promote and encourage African enterprise through financial, commercial and educational assistance; and subsequently, the Bantu Homelands Development Corporations Act of 1965 provided for the establishment of development corporations for the individual homelands. The Xhosa Development Corporation (XDC) was the first established (in 1966) to operate in both the Ciskei and Transkei, itself separating into two successor bodies when Transkei became independent in 1976. The extent to which the various corporations have actually promoted African enterprise has been limited. Broadly speaking, African economic activity has been encouraged in spheres that present little competitive threat to white industry. Up to 1974, for instance, the BIC had financed 1,300 concerns throughout the homelands, 86 per cent being trading establishments (general dealers, cafés, butchers and bottle stores), 13 per cent service concerns (mainly transport and garages) and only 2 per cent light manufacturing establishments. Similarly, the amounts of capital have been quite small: by 1975 the BIC had loaned only a total amount of R13,076,444 to African businessmen, and the XDC only R$9\frac{1}{2}$ million.[40] None the less, as will be argued below, the corporations have played a decisive role in the creation of a small (but growing) stratum of African businessmen who are to a great extent a product of and dependent upon the structures of separate development within the homelands.

Rather than encouraging white capital to enter the reserves, the government at first favoured the decentralization of industry to areas bordering upon the homelands, stimulus being given by the establishment in 1960 of a Permanent Committee for the Location of Industry and the Development of Border Areas. Capital was thereafter attracted by financial incentives, tax concessions and various other devices, although the most important guarantee was the assurance that wage differentials between regions would be maintained, and that African labour would be considerably cheaper in border than in urban areas because of its supposedly lower productivity and cost of living. Subsequently, border areas which emerged as being the most attractive to industrialists were all relatively near to existing industrial conurbations. Thus Rosslyn, bordering upon Bophuthatswana, offered the advantage of the use of homeland labour while benefiting from the availability of markets, skills and management in the nearby Pretoria–Johannesburg–Vereeniging triangle; and similarly, the other most popular areas were near Durban (bordering on Kwazulu) and near East London (for the Ciskei). Thus from the mid-1960s onwards the government sought to stress development in the more remote border areas – such as Pietersburg and Potgietersrus in the northern Transvaal (bordering of Lebowa), Rustenburg, Brits, Zeerust, and Mafeking near Bophuthatswana, and Queenstown near the Ciskei.[41]

But the overall impact of the decentralization policy has been limited. According to the Permanent Committee itself, additional employment for Africans created in the border areas and homelands between 1960 and 1970 amounted only to 68,500 – well short of the target figure of 50,000 jobs per annum laid down by the Tomlinson Commission; and a major study undertaken by Bell has suggested that industrial growth in South Africa in the 1960s evinced no clear trend either towards or away from the existing centralized pattern of growth, with the extra employment in the decentralized areas probably having occurred even without the offer of incentives and concessions by the government.[42]

It was because of this that in 1968 the government passed the Promotion of the Economic Development of the Homelands Act, by which it reversed its earlier refusal to allow white capital into the reserves. Henceforth, white-owned firms were to be allowed to establish themselves in the homelands under an agency basis, whereby they would be subject to a number of constraints (such as there being no proprietary right to land and investment being limited to a fixed time span), but in return receiving a wide array of concessions, as well as being able to enjoy the benefit of cheap African labour, industrial legislation operative in white areas not being applicable.[43] Industrial growth points were identified within the homelands, basic infrastructure being provided by the BIC and other corporations, these also establishing a number of production ventures (such as small furniture factories or breweries) themselves. Incentives to industry have been generous, and the growth points have accordingly enjoyed a modest degree of success – yet none the less the number of jobs created has fallen far below what is required to absorb the expanding flow of labour, for with an estimated 70,000 new African workers entering the labour market each year, industrial development in the homelands had led to the creation of only 14,235 new jobs by 1976.

Thus industrial decentralization notwithstanding, unemployment is becoming one of the most pervasive features of contemporary homeland life. Indeed, the bantustans are now serving ever more explicitly as reservoirs of surplus population, their function being to regulate black wage levels in the metropolitan centres of industry. Yet an industrial reserve army is not a passive force, and poses a severe threat to the long-term political stability of the auxiliary homeland regimes – and this in turn suggests that there will be a future expansion of the currently fledgling bantustan security forces (army and police) for purposes of internal repression and control.

2. The essence of apartheid, as argued here, relates to the twin goals of the maintenance of white supremacy and the extension of the coercive labour system, established under segregation, to the South African economy as it has increasingly moved away from its mining and agricultural base, coincident with the disintegration of the reserves. These aims have been realized, partly, by the intensive implementation of repressive measures to counter political challenges made by the subordinate racial groups and thereby to ensure the cheapness of black labour; and secondly, by the establishment of a complex and comprehensive regulatory system for the direction and channelling of such labour according to sectoral demand.

As already indicated, the postwar expansion of the secondary and tertiary spheres in the South African economy was, to a large degree, predicated upon the stabilization of the African workforce and the necessity for capital to provide for a greater proportion of the reproduction costs of the black labour force. Yet although manufacturing industry has always enjoyed a more flexible cost structure than both mining and agriculture, the continuing search for profit has ensured that the impetus towards labour-cost minimization has been maintained through a series of highly coercive measures. At one level, this has been achieved through a battery of repressive legislation designed to counter the politically conscientizing effects attendant upon increasing African urbanization, labour stabilization and proletarianization (as evidenced most spectacularly by the mass defiance campaigns in the 1950s and the more spontaneous Soweto events in the mid-1970s). Thus the main enactments – the Suppression of Communism Act of 1950 (updated by the Internal Security Act of 1976), the Criminal Law Amendment Act of 1953, the Riotous Assemblies Act of 1956, the Unlawful Organizations Act of 1962 and the Terrorism Act of 1967 – gave the state sweeping and arbitrary powers to suppress opposition, and to ban, detain and restrict persons virtually at will; and combined with the extensive machinery of a police state (a widespread information network, the habitual use of torture on detainees and so on), have been designed to intimidate the entire African population, and to keep it in a position of perpetual subordination. In consequence, all political movements (such as the ANC, PAC, BPC and SASO), which have sought to give voice to African resistance to apartheid, have been banned as endangering the security of the state, leaving the homeland and other officially appointed leaders (nearly all of whom are rejected by the mass) as the only black spokesmen accepted and recognized by the law.

The suppression of effective opposition to the state has served as a necessary complement to legislation more directly concerned to secure the minimization of the cost of black labour.[44] In particular, apartheid law has restricted the African workforce to a minimal role in collective bargaining, the main instrument being the Bantu Labour (Settlement of Disputes) Act of 1953, which buttressed the existing prohibition on the right of African employees to strike by the introduction of heavier sanctions to deal with such action – so that when (in spite of the law) African workers have gone on strike, they have been subjected to criminal prosecution and legal dismissal. In addition, the same law further provided that registered trade unions were not to include Africans among their members, for African interests were to be alternatively represented by appointed white officials; and while the same Act also made provision for the election by African workers of consultative works' committees, these were (designedly) wholly inadequate substitutes for unions, and in fact some eighteen years after the passage of the Act there were only some twenty-eight such committees in existence.

Further legislation (notably the Industrial Conciliation Act of 1956 and the Wage Act of 1957) was later to deny the right of Africans to participate in collective bargaining agreements with employers, and to establish the principle that official investigations into wages and working conditions could be made on behalf of African workers only by direct order of the Minister of Labour, who would also decide upon any subsequent recommendations that might be made. In addition, income levels for blacks have been contained by the operation of job colour bars, whereby certain employment spheres are reserved for whites, these also being associated with the maintenance of large wage differentials between white and non-white workers – even though such discriminatory measures have in practice been flexibly applied, thereby allowing for the absorption of blacks into higher skilled employment according to the expanding technical requirements of industry.[45]

The exclusion of African workers from the industrial conciliation machinery was by no means wholly successful in smothering discontent, for unofficial strikes and stay-at-homes indicated continuing African resistance to exploitation. But following a mass strike in Durban of nearly 100,000 workers in early 1973 (when employers were at a loss with whom to treat, the strikers being fearful that nominated leaders would be subject to later victimization), the government promulgated the Labour Relations Regulation Amendment Act, which amended the 1953 law by allowing for the strengthening of works' committees and the establishment of 'liaison committees' formed by black workers to negotiate wages upon an industry-wide basis. In addition, the Act specifically conceded the right of Africans to strike, although only after the exhaustion of a lengthy and complicated official procedure.[46]

These various concessions were, in effect, an official recognition of the increasing bargaining strength of the African working class. Indeed, the Durban strikes had given a tremendous impetus to the growing black trade union movement which, while denied the advantages of registration, was by 1977 composed of some twenty-six unregistered unions with a membership of over 45,000. Such a development – especially when combined with the impact of the township uprisings of 1976 – gave rise to the spectre of potential industrial unrest on such a scale as to undermine business confidence and perhaps discourage foreign investment. Accordingly, in 1977 the government established a Commission to make proposals for changes in the legislation governing industrial relations.

The major recommendation of the subsequent Wiehahn Report was that all black workers should be enabled to join registered trade unions, these being eligible to engage in full participation in the statutory industrial relations process. However, when amendments to the Industrial Conciliation Act later appeared in Parliament, it became evident that the government had departed substantially from the Commission's recommendations, for while it allowed for the registration of black trade unions under a number of stringent criteria, it excluded migrants and 'frontier commuters' (from the homelands) from the definition of employee and thus denied them access to the registered trade union movement. In short, the new strategy had two distinct aims. First, it sought to curb the growth of militant trade unionism by linking the concept of registration (and thus access to the industrial relations machinery) to a system of supervisory control from above; and secondly, it sought to divide the working class by allowing for the incorporation of urban 'insiders' into the system of industrial bargaining, while maintaining the exclusion of migrant 'outsiders'. However, the effects of this strategy were potentially mitigated after refusal to register by unions induced the government to rule that Africans (excluding foreigners but including Africans from independent homelands) be allowed to join registered trade unions or form trade unions which would be eligible for registration.[47]

The implementation of these various measures to ensure the cheapness of black labour has been supplemented by the growing involvement of the state in the direction of labour. Thus the needs of the secondary industrial sector were early catered for by the Native Laws Amendment Act of 1952, which increased state control over recruitment by providing for the establishment of labour bureaux in the urban areas to regulate the movement of all black workseekers. Then, in 1964, powers relating to influx control were transferred from the municipalities to the labour bureaux themselves, and in 1968 provision was further made for bureaux to be established within the homelands, thus facilitating the canalization of workers to the various centres of employment directly from the bantustans.

The establishment of this comprehensive system of labour control, direction and regulation has enabled capital to overcome the constraints on labour utilization imposed by the disintegration of the reserves. In short, given the decreasing capacity of the non-capitalist mode to provide for the full cost of the reproduction of its migrant labour power, it would seem that a steadily increasing proportion of the homelands' migrant workforce was, prior to the early 1970s, probably being absorbed into the secondary sector, whose relatively flexible cost structure enabled it largely to forgo subsidization by the reserves. In contrast, because the imperatives of gold mining necessitated such subsidization by a non-capitalist base, the postwar years witnessed an increasing dependence by mining capital upon the recruitment of foreign workers and a proportionately lesser reliance upon migrant labour drawn from the internal reserves. However, in the 1970s, following the rise in the price of gold brought about by dramatic changes in the structure of international finance which enabled mining capital to employ labour at increased wage levels (more nearly approaching the cost of subsistence), this trend was to be reversed – and once again the bantustans were to assume their former prominence as suppliers of cheap labour to the mines.[48]

3. The third and final mechanism whereby capital secures cheap labour under apartheid relates to an intensification of the control measures

promulgated during the era of segregation to regulate and limit black access to the white areas of the Union. Hence in terms of the Native (Urban Areas) Consolidation Act of 1945, the existing provisions of the 1923 Act were codified, rationalized and extended to cater for the increased flow of blacks to the towns consequent upon secondary industrialization and the declining capacity of the reserves. Under apartheid, therefore, Africans residing in white areas continue to be defined as temporary sojourners, permitted domicile only upon condition that they satisfy certain minimum requirements laid down in the 1945 Act. In particular, Section 10 of this law provides that Africans shall be allowed to remain in an urban area for longer than seventy-two hours only if they have resided there since birth; if they have worked continuously in that area for one employer for not less than ten years, or have lived there continuously for fifteen years with official concurrence; or if they are wives or unmarried children (under the age of eighteen) of a qualified male resident; or finally, if they have received permission to remain in the area from a labour bureau official. Thus any African who becomes unemployed, who offends against the regulations or who generally fails to service the needs of the white economy, is subject to loss of residence rights and may in consequence be legally dispatched to his or her 'homeland'. In addition, legislative enactment has also provided for considerable further refinement, notably through the Group Areas Acts which define the actual townships or locations where Africans may actually reside – the dreary, compound-like organization of such ghetto areas (typified by the extensive Soweto complex) – also allowing for intensive political and military control.

The influx control measures have been necessarily complemented by coercive legislation which allows for the ready identification of each and every individual black. The Population Registration Act of 1950, therefore, is fundamental to the operation of the entire apartheid system in that it requires the classification of the entire South African population into discrete racial groups, while the quaintly named Abolition of Passes and Co-ordination of Documents Act of 1952 lays down that every African shall carry a reference book (or 'pass') which contains his photograph, race identity card, registered number, ethnic classification and (where relevant) official authorization to be resident in urban areas. Allowing not only for the strict enforcement of the Urban Areas Act, the system also provides for the constant surveillance of the subordinate racial groups.

Finally, if blacks have long been designated 'temporary sojourners' in white areas, then the implementation of apartheid has much increased their insecurity. Indeed, in terms of the policy of separate development, the mass removal of 'surplus' blacks to their ethnic homelands has become a vigorously pursued objective, having received particular emphasis from a General Circular of December 1967 whereby officials of the Department of Bantu Administration were instructed that all 'unproductive' Africans should be sent to 'resettlement' areas in the bantustans.[49] In practice, this has meant that (apart from the unemployed) it has been the aged, the sick, the widows and their children – in short, those least able to cope with their sorrows – who have been defined as the superfluous and deported to the reserves. But in addition, as the converse to the homeland consolidation proposals, policy is also directed towards the elimination of all so-called 'black spots' which remain to blemish the white heartland, official pronouncement having indicated in 1969 that some 3·8 million Africans would eventually be compulsorily removed to the bantustans. While in theory these 'resettlement' areas to which they are destined to be sent will become centres of vibrant industrial growth, the practice has led to widespread impoverishment and the creation of extensive rural slums. Black workers are valued for their labour alone and, under apartheid, their unproductive appendages are unhesitatingly swept aside.[50]

Postwar capitalist development under apartheid has prospered, with the South African economy having enjoyed a growth rate which in the western world has been exceeded only by Japan. Yet the white regime at present confronts a crisis of greater proportion than it has ever faced before, for in the context of the radical transformation of the entire Southern African region triggered off by the April 1974 Portuguese *coup*, the black working class has become increasingly assertive, and through such series of events as the Durban strikes and Soweto has served notice that it is preparing to assault the ramparts of apartheid.

The response of the white regime has been manifold, ranging from an increased emphasis upon defence and the conversion of South Africa into a garrison state, to its attempt to deflect external pressure by its policy of *'détente'* with western-oriented states in Black Africa. Yet what is of especial relevance here is the two-pronged strategy whereby the apartheid state has, first, accelerated the tempo of separate development through a programme of intended 'internal decolonization' and, secondly, embarked upon the urgent search for an African middle class with which white capital may forge an alliance across racial lines. Both facets of this design have hitherto received their fullest expression in the promotion of the Transkei as the model bantustan, whose significance has thus been promoted to a level it could not otherwise command. Yet before progressing to a detailed study of Transkei, it is first vital to trace out the extent to which the bantustan design has also been evolved as a pragmatic response to pressures mounting against apartheid from outside.

The evolution of the apartheid neo-colonial design

Although present-day 'independent' homelands cannot properly be regarded as sovereign states, there can be little doubt that the evolution of the bantustan strategy in the postwar years came to be regarded and implemented by the regime as a policy of quite deliberately intended neo-colonization. However, this development only occurred over time, and was in large measure a direct response to the process of decolonization which was followed by the European colonial powers elsewhere throughout the African continent.

Prior to the accession to office of the National Party in 1948, the reserves had been administered through a system of direct colonial rule, the authority of (white) Native Commissioners being tempered only by the largely advisory role of a number of indirectly elected councils, which under the Native Affairs Act of 1920 had allowed for a limited degree of popular representation. But with the passing of the Bantu Authorities Act of 1951 the government gave notice of its intention to erect a new structure of indirect rule based upon the revitalized authority of the chiefs. Existing councils were to be abolished and were to be replaced by a base of Tribal Authorities (composed of chiefs and headmen), a middle tier of Regional Authorities drawn from the organs below, and an apex of a Territorial Authority relevant to the reserve in question – these various levels of government being created in stages as the peoples concerned supposedly showed their developing political maturity. Simultaneously, the Act also abolished the Natives' Representative Council, a central advisory body established in 1936 (and drawn largely from the emergent African élite), which had constantly reiterated demands for racial equality and direct African representation in Parliament.

The Bantu Authorities system enjoyed little immediate success. Born in the year prior to the ANC Defiance Campaign of passive resistance against unjust laws, the political context was hardly conducive to its implementation; and reluctant to provoke rural resistance when its hands were fully occupied with urban protest, the government's only significant triumph came in 1955 when it cajoled the Transkei Territories General Council into abolishing itself and accepting the revived form of tribal government.[51]

In retrospect, what is especially notable about the 1951 Act was the lack of intention to introduce the Bantu Authorities as a preparatory step towards eventual internal decolonization. Thus while the National Party had already indicated in its ideological blueprint for apartheid that Africans would one day exercise control over their own affairs, it had equally assured the white electorate that African areas would remain under white guardianship and would never become independent or even semi-independent states. Similarly, Prime Minister Strijdom wrote in the *New York Times* in 1955 that although Africans might aspire to 'self-government' in their own areas, this was not as yet a practical problem for contemporary politicians: 'It will not crop up for generations to come ... [The natives] must remain under the trusteeship of the whites ... I am not philosophising about what will happen in a hundred years from now.'[52] Nor was the government yet referring to their programme of devolution in quasi-colonial terms, and indeed, it was deliberately eschewing the analogy. In 1956, for instance, Verwoerd argued thus:

> The contention ... that the reserves in terms of the Government's policy will undergo a colonial development is not correct. What is the characteristic of a colonial empire? Its chief characteristic is that economic penetration by coloniser takes place. He enters that area and establishes his economic interests there. The area becomes an area for exploitation by his state ... The United Party's policy follows precisely the same pattern ... [and] wants to bring the white colonist into those reserves in order to establish his industries there permanently ... [but] We want to help [the Africans] develop these potentialities for themselves.[53]

In addition, South Africa was at this time still seeking to achieve its long-cherished goal of *incorporating* the High Commission Territories into the Union, the Tomlinson Commission actually founding its report upon the assumption that Bechuanaland (now Botswana), Basutoland (now Lesotho) and Swaziland would eventually be absorbed. However, the British government was subsequently to maintain its insistence that the Protectorates would only be transferred to South Africa at the express wish of their inhabitants – and when this was not forthcoming, was to set each territory on the road to its own political independence.[54]

Within a brief span of three years, policy towards the reserves was to undergo a major change, for in 1959 the government promulgated the Promotion of Bantu Self-Government Act, whose immediate effect was to abolish the last vestiges of black representation in Parliament, while simultaneously making provision for the recognition of eight national units among the African people and asserting their right to 'gradual development within their own areas to self-governing units on the basis of the Bantu system of government'. But in addition, the government now began to adopt the rhetoric of national self-determination, explicitly equating what were now to become the bantustans with colonies elsewhere in Africa. Full political independence for the various territories was now proclaimed a legitimate goal, and the ultimate (neo-colonial) aim was declared the eventual formation of a South African Commonwealth, with white South Africa as its core and the emerging Bantu states as its peripheries – even though the alleged immaturity of the African peoples supposedly made it impossible to anticipate a definite pace of development.[55]

It was not until four years later, however, that any degree of authority was to be devolved upon any 'national unit'. Then, in 1963, under the Transkei Self-Government Act, the Transkei Territorial Authority was scrapped in favour of a Legislative Assembly composed of 64 nominated chiefs and 45 elected members, from which were to be appointed an African Chief Minister and a Cabinet of five other members, who would together be responsible for portfolios of Finance, Justice, the Interior, Education, Agriculture, and Roads and Works. But these powers of self-government were yet subject to considerable limitation. Not only did the white authorities reserve to themselves control over major spheres such as defence, foreign affairs and internal security, but all legislative measures passed by the Assembly were to be subject to the veto of the State President; and in addition, the reality of fiscal control was retained by the South African government upon which the new Transkeian government was to be almost wholly financially dependent. The powers devolved were in any case applicable only to African (rural) areas of the Transkei, and the white municipalities were to remain under Cape Provincial authority. Finally, the Act contained a sharp sting in its tail: all Africans deemed to be of Transkeian origin were now allotted the citizenship of their 'homeland'. In terms of internal relations, therefore, they were stripped of their South African citizenship, and those who were permanently resident in urban areas had their ideological designation as 'temporary sojourners' in the white heartland further confirmed.[56]

However limited the conception of self-government held by the South African government, the latter had clearly moved significantly beyond its position in the early 1950s when the Bantu Authorities system had been largely conceived in terms of 'indirect rule'. One factor responsible for this development, it is now apparent, was the changing external environment, for apartheid had become the butt of widespread international criticism. While the regime had felt able to brush this aside so long as it originated from the Afro-Asian nations, it was taken aback by the decision of the USA in 1958 to abandon its practice of abstaining on UN resolutions against apartheid and to vote for a motion condemning South Africa's racial policy.

More fundamentally, western policy was itself undergoing that transformation whereby political power was to be transferred to indigenous rulers, who were thereafter to be largely incorporated into the structure of dependency. The wind of change, as British Premier Harold Macmillan observed to the South African Parliament in 1960, was blowing through the continent. The Gold Coast had become independent as Ghana in 1957, and the process of formal decolonization elsewhere in British Africa was well under way, culminating in the independence of Tanganyika (1960), Nigeria (1960), Sierre Leone (1961), Uganda (1962) and with Kenya and Zanzibar destined to follow the same path later in 1963. Nearer to home, the Central African Federation had collapsed with Nyasaland's secession in 1962, and it had also become clear that Bechuanaland, Basutoland and Swaziland were destined for a future that would be politically separate from the Republic. The South Africans, stunned by the rapidity of events but unable to influence the course of decolonization upon which the colonial powers had embarked, could only lament and condemn; and by 1960, Foreign Minister Louw had correctly predicted that white rule would soon be confined to the Portuguese territories, Southern Rhodesia and South Africa itself.

It was against this rapidly changing background that there occurred the series of events which were to actuate the quickened pace of bantustan constitutional development. On 21 March 1960, crowds of Africans assembled at police stations throughout the country in a PAC campaign to protest against the Pass Laws. At Sharpeville police station near Johannesburg, the police lost control and opened fire upon the 10,000 Africans who had gathered, massacring outright 67 and injuring a further 186. A wave of black protest, in the form of stay-at-homes, riots and marches, swept the land, the government reacting with a campaign of repression that culminated in April with the banning of the ANC and PAC under the newly passed Unlawful Organizations Act and the arrest of many of their leaders.

In a rapidly decolonizing world, Sharpeville caused outcry against apartheid as no single event had done before. More to the point, it led to a loss of confidence that the white regime could continue to safeguard the interests of foreign investors, with a resulting massive capital outflow. Traditional allies were openly embarrassed, and in April 1961 Britain and the USA voted in favour of a UN resolution calling on all member states to take whatever action that was open to them to bring about an end to apartheid; and, within only a matter of weeks, diplomatic isolation appeared almost complete when, as a result of enormous Afro-Asian pressure, South Africa quit the Commonwealth and established itself as a Republic.[57]

Following their proscription, elements of both the ANC and PAC opted for a violent alternative. Umkonto we Sizwe (Spear of the Nation) formed by ANC militants went into action in December 1961. Initially eschewing direct attacks on persons, Umkonto planned to escalate resistance into full-scale guerrilla warfare, but was effectively smashed when seventeen of its leaders were arrested at Rivonia in July 1963. Meanwhile Poqo, an offshoot of the PAC, was held responsible by the authorities for the deaths of eleven policemen and informers in the Western Cape, being also linked to a number of assassination attempts on Kaiser Matanzima and other collaborationist chiefs and headmen in the Transkei, where in 1960 inhabitants of rural Pondoland had risen in armed revolt against the imposition of Bantu Authorities – only to be crushed by force in 1961. Thereafter, with the government firmly back in control, and with the African masses having withdrawn into a state of sullen acquiescence, international business confidence returned and the economy subsequently enjoyed an upswing which brought western capital pouring back.[58] None the less, the post-Sharpeville years of internal uncertainty had severely weakened South African standing with the western bloc, and had in consequence strengthened the hands of those inside the Republic's Cabinet who were arguing for the devolution of self-government to the Transkei, the most suitable reserve wherein such an experiment might be undertaken, in order to demonstrate that separate development was not merely a negative policy of repression. In the words of one spokesman, the Transkei constitution bill would remove 'one of the grievances which countries overseas have against us, namely that we are suppressing them'.[59]

Yet the issue that was immediately responsible for the actual timing of the Transkeian bill was the threat posed by Ethiopia and Liberia who, in 1960, had requested the International Court of Justice to rule as to whether South Africa had violated her League of Nations' mandate over the former German colony of South West Africa by the introduction to that territory of apartheid. The trial lasted through to 1966, and constitutional developments in the Transkei were linked directly to South Africa's campaign of defence, being accelerated so as to establish the credibility of separate development as a policy designed to further African feeedom – for the Transkeian formula was explicitly canvassed as the model for the later application of the bantustan scheme to the various peoples of South West Africa itself. Thus, somewhat reluctantly on the part of the government but in response to external pressures, the Transkei found itself launched into 'self-government' in order to impress the International Court of Justice of the sincerity of the Republican authorities' good intentions.[60]

The government had by now fully committed itself to the rhetoric of self-determination, and comparison was habitually drawn between the devolution of power to the Transkei and the process of decolonization elsewhere in Africa. Yet bantustan self-government was clearly founded upon neo-colonial premises, as became evident in the course of exchanges in debate with the Opposition United Party, which posited an autonomous Transkei as both weakening the Republic's defences and endangering white security by providing an arena for extensive communist subversion.[61] Official response was that such fears were wildly exaggerated, as political independence was but a distant prospect, and that in the meantime the Transkei would remain under very close white supervision. Nor would the strategic threat posed by bantustan self-government approach any degree of significance, for it was inconceivable that the Transkei would develop a military capacity whereby to endanger the Republic, and nor would it advance to an industrial or technological level from which it would be able to pose an economic threat.[62] But most revealing of all were the elaborations of Verwoerdian purpose as envisioned in the future creation of a regional state system of politically independent bantustans which yet remained otherwise dependent upon South Africa. Thus F. S. Steyn, a backbench Nationalist MP:

> Constitutionally, a commonwealth relationship as the Prime Minister outlined it would be nothing else but a confederal relationship in which there would be black states linked confederally with the white heartland ... In such a situation *there is nothing inherently against the Republic, as the confederal leader, keeping control over the central money, military and diplomatic powers* ... such a confederal concept, *in which certain confederal states will have no part to play in the army, and in the monetary and fiscal policy*, will not necessarily be regarded as not being sovereign internationally ... [just as] the Ukrainian Soviet Republic

and the Byeolo-Russian Soviet Republics, which are constituent parts of the Union of Soviet Republics ... have been granted international recognition as sovereign states ... [my emphasis].[63]

In short, although the conception of a commonwealth was later to be subject to alteration in the lights of changing circumstances, the bantustan scenario was from the first explicitly neo-colonial, with the Republic depicted as maintaining its hegemony as the foremost regional power.

None the less, further progress towards the creation of a subordinate state system over the following decade was slow, and the only accomplishments which remotely resembled the processes of colonial devolution elsewhere were the development of a party system and the holding of two general elections (for the elective minority in the Legislative Assembly) in 1963 and 1968 in the Transkei. The Umtata government received no increase in powers, and no other bantustan was advanced to the self-governing stage (although Territorial Authorities were constituted in six other homelands in terms of the Bantu Authorities Act of 1951).[64]

It was not until the 1970s that bantustan constitutional development was to receive a new impetus – and then it came with a heady rush that belied an officially propounded image of gradual and orderly advance. The legislative foundation for the hastened rate was laid by the Bantu Homelands Citizenship Act (no. 26 of 1970), which laid down that every African not a citizen of a self-governing Bantu territory would become a citizen of one or other Territorial Authority area, and the Bantu Homelands Constitution Act (no. 21 of 1971) which empowered the State President to establish by decree a legislative assembly for any homeland wherein power had previously been exercised by a Territorial Authority – thus relieving the government of the necessity of promulgating separate laws for the devolution of self-governing powers to each and every individual bantustan.[65] And following hard upon this enabling legislation came a plethora of other measures: the Bantu Laws Amendment Act (no. 23 of 1972) transferred control over prisons, motor transportation, traffic regulation and the licensing of road vehicles to the Transkeian government, while similar enabling legislation in 1972 and 1973 allowed for the Umtata authorities to raise loans of their own accord, and to undertake responsibility for hospitals, health and the police. Finally, the Bantu Laws Amendment Act of 1973 then made it possible for these various powers to be granted to the other homeland governments at the discretion of the Minister of Bantu Administration and Development.[66]

At the political level, legislative assemblies were created to replace existing Territorial Authorities during 1971 (except in Kwazulu where this occurred in 1972), with the Ciskei, Bophuthatswana and Lebowa assuming self-governing status, followed by Gazankulu and Venda in 1973 and Kwazulu and KaNgwane in 1977, in which year the South Ndebele were also recognized as a distinct 'nation' and allocated their own territorial homeland. Then, in the wake of these developments, general elections were held for the elective minorities in the legislative assemblies in Bophuthatswana (1972 and 1977), the Ciskei (1973 and 1978), Lebowa (1973), Gazankulu (1973), the Transkei (1973 and 1976), Venda (1973 and 1978), Kwazulu (1978) and in Basotho QwaQwa in 1975 and 1980 (see Table 2.2). In most cases, where they were not already in existence, political parties were created subsequent to the initial

Table 2.2 *The homelands: constitutional stages and political leadership*

Homeland	Establishment of Legislative Assembly	Date of self-government	Date of elections for electoral minority	Current ruling party	Current leader
Transkei	1963	1963 (independent 1976)	1963 1968 1973 1976 1981	Transkei National Independence Party	President K. D. Matanzima
Ciskei	1971	1972	1973 1978	Ciskei National Independence Party	Chief L. Sebe
Kwazulu	1972	1977	1978	Inkatha	Chief M. G. Buthelezi
Lebowa	1971	1972	1973 1978	Lebowa People's Party	Chief C. Phatudi
Venda	1971	1973 (independent 1979)	1973 1978	Venda National Party	President P. R. Mpephu
Gazankulu	1971	1973	1973 1978	No party	Prof. H. W. E. Ntsanwisi
Bophuthatswana	1971	1972 (independent 1977)	1972 1977	Bophutha-tswana Democratic Party	President L. M. Mangope
Basotho QwaQwa	1971	1975	1975 1980	Dikwankwetla Dikwankwetla	Mr T. K. Mopeli
KaNgwane	1977	1977	—	—	Mr E. J. Mabuza
S. Ndebele	1979	Not yet granted	—	—	—

Source: SAIRR, *Surveys, 1963–79.*

elections, and assembly affairs were ostensibly conducted upon a partisan basis, involving a complex pattern of chiefly intrigue and party fissure and fragmentation.[67] Finally, associated with these changes came an increased emphasis by the white regime upon the possibilities of homelands progressing to full independence. As late as 1968, the responsible Minister, M. C. Botha, had indicated that bantustans could only aspire to sovereign status if they were able to meet a comprehensive set of prerequisites (which related to administrative capacity, political maturity and a certain minimum level of economic development). But by 1970, the same Minister let it be known that it would no longer be necessary for homelands to be economically capable of supporting their populations before independence might be granted, and in 1972 Vorster himself stated that any Bantu people was welcome to negotiate independence at any time it believed was appropriate.[68]

This quickened pace of quasi-decolonization was, of course, to culminate in the grant of political independence to Transkei in 1976.[69] Yet that this had not been a completely straightforward progression is indicated by the fact that, although he had long espoused the cause of a politically sovereign Transkei, Chief Minister Matanzima was in the event to exhibit an ambivalence to independence upon the actual terms that were to be offered by Pretoria.

Matanzima (depicted by Laurence as a Xhosa nationalist) had never been troubled by the prospect of a South Africa fragmented into a multiplicity of ethnic states, but from the first he had sought to relate the goal of independence to a demand for increased land (in excess of the provisions laid down by the 1936 Trust and Lands Act, which had been adopted by the Republican government as the basis for bantustan territorial allocation). Thus the 1968 conference of Matanzima's Transkei National Independence Party (TNIP) had called for the inclusion of the border areas of Elliot, Maclear, Mount Currie and Matatiele into the Transkei – to which in 1972 was added a further demand for the inclusion of Port St Johns, a coastal outlet which was cut off from the rest of white South Africa. And in April of the same year, Matanzima tabled a motion in the TLA whereby he requested the grant of independence together with the transfer of the disputed areas – thus apparently making the pursuit of the former goal conditional upon the attainment of the latter.

But the government remained firm over the land issue, and Matanzima was thereafter to link hands with the other homeland leaders in a joint attempt to extract concessions. In November 1973, six bantustan leaders met in conference in Umtata to formulate a joint approach concerning common problems and, amid much talk of black unity, agreed to act together in dealings with Pretoria and to consult with each other over such vital matters as the merits of independence and their separate (and often conflicting) land claims. Then, in March 1974, all the homeland leaders met in summit with the Republican government in Pretoria, and raised as a major issue their dissatisfaction with the 1936 Land Act as the basis for demarcation between black and white. But Vorster refused to be moved, and reiterated earlier statements that while any homeland was free to negotiate for independence, such approaches would be ignored if they were linked to demands for more land.

It was at this point that Matanzima broke ranks with his fellow homeland leaders. Less than a week after the summit, the TNIP annual congress authorized the Transkeian government to negotiate for independence within five years, even if outstanding land claims had not been met; and by 27 March 1974 a motion to this effect had been adopted by the TLA (although not without the defeat of Opposition demands for the people to be consulted upon the independence issue by means of referendum). But thereafter the progress of events was to be dramatically compressed, for the upshot of almost immediate negotiations between the Transkeian and South African governments was that the TNIP timetable of independence within five years was dramatically foreshortened – with the final break now being scheduled for 26 October 1976, only eighteen months after the official request had been made. Thus after years of uncertainty, it now seemed that Transkei was being shot into independence with almost unseemly haste. In addition, the new move was premised upon a *volte face* by Matanzima over the land issue, for no longer was his acceptance of independence to be made conditional upon the fulfilments of his claims for the transfer of white lands along the Transkeian border.

The seeds of this rapid transformation may partly lie in a deal negotiated between Matanzima and Vorster whereby Transkei would receive more land – although within the confines of the 1936 settlement as the territorial basis of the homeland policy. In essence, the bargain would appear to have been that, in return for opting for independence (which, for reasons discussed below, was something the Republican government now wished the Transkei to do), Matanzima would be granted Port St Johns and small parts of the disputed territories – but all in conformity with the 1936 proposals (that is, that all these extra lands would come out of the total area allocated to the African population). In addition, the Republican government agreed to hand over the Ciskeian Districts of Herschel and Glen Grey (which bordered upon the Transkei) – despite the fact that the inhabitants of the latter district had already previously rejected such incorporation in a referendum held in 1971;[70] and finally, the pill was further sweetened by the provision of a few white farms in Matatiele – two of which were later to be acquired by the Matanzima brothers from the Bantu Trust at only a nominal sum.[71]

Yet the key to understanding the rapidly foreshortened timetable lies not so much in assessing the determination of Matanzima to pursue his land claims as in appreciating the contemporary requirements of the Republican government. In the first place, faced with indications – such as the Durban strikes – of a new wave of African protest, the regime sensed the necessity of launching a new political initiative to assuage discontent. Secondly, although the pace of quasi-decolonization had been accelerated to appease external critics, bantustan leaders had hitherto evinced a disconcerting hesitance to opt for independence, and South Africa was accordingly in growing need of a breakthrough to demonstrate the reality of its declared intention of 'liberating' its African 'peoples'.

Thirdly, the progression of Transkei to independence also seemed to be required by the demands of successive South African policy relations with black Africa. Initially, especially after Sharpeville, the new states of Africa had been unremitttingly hostile to the Republic and had sought to secure her diplomatic isolation. South Africa had later responded with an 'outward policy', which was based on the promotion of technical and functional contact with black states, and whose rationale was to open new markets for her products and to neutralize external criticism of her internal policies; and in particular it was hoped that were South Africa to become less repugnant internationally, then so would African states come to accept the homelands as units worthy of self-determination.[72] Indeed, in South African eyes, the case for bantustan constitutional advance was also strengthened by the accession to independence in the mid-1960s of the former High Commission Territories, whose immediate post-colonial relationships with their white neighbour seemed to demonstrate the feasibility of separate development, for so dependent were all three upon the Republican economy that they initially acted in an extremely cautious and co-operative manner, with Leabua Jonathan of Lesotho going out of his way to exhibit his alignment with Pretoria. If, so it was argued, these independent states were acting so 'responsibly', then prospects were bright that sovereign bantustans would present no greater threat, and might even function as bridge builders with black Africa to the north.[73]

South Africa's outward movement was also associated with the expansion of her economy in the mid-1960s and the simultaneous build-up of her military might. However much they might resent continuing white domination, the newly independent African states seemed powerless to overturn it, while contemporary disarray within the liberation movements fighting to dislodge white minority rule in the sub-continent did little to convince that they were capable of achieving their objective.

It was these manifest signs of failure which encouraged a number of African states to call for a new strategy, the move being led by Houphouet-Boigny, who in November 1970 urged a 'dialogue' with the white Republic. Rejecting the violent overthrow of the regime as a practical solution to apartheid, the Ivory Coast leader argued the necessity of persuading Pretoria to change her internal policies by means of peaceful interaction and discussion.

While the call for dialogue provoked a largely hostile reaction in the rest of Africa, Houphouet-Boigny did gain the support of Dahomey, Gabon, Ghana, Lesotho, Niger and Malawi, with a number of other states choosing to equivocate. For South Africa, in turn, dialogue appeared a natural extension of the outward movement, and provided a seemingly favourable environment in which to press ahead with the bantustan policy; and with the OAU divided, there were hopes that as the homelands became increasingly manifest realities, black Africa would evince a greater willingness to accept their existence at least as a basis for compromise and negotiation. However, although dialogue was to cause intense diplomatic activity in Africa during 1970-1, thereafter the furore died down – for increased contact had failed to activate the white government to change its internal policies, and South Africa had in any case become increasingly involved in the open military and logistic support of the illegal Smith regime in Rhodesia.[74]

The stalemate in Southern Africa was transformed by the Portuguese *coup* in April 1974, and the subsequent collapse of colonial authority in Angola and Mozambique. Of necessity, South Africa was forced to reassess her foreign policy objectives, and what emerged was a tentative agreement between herself and a number of other governments in the Southern African region to co-operate in seeking a transition to majority rule in Rhodesia – for with the collapse of the Portuguese empire, the former British colony now lay exposed along all its border with Mozambique, and the Republic was faced with the apparent choice of either engaging in indefinite military support for an embattled regime with no guarantee of eventual success, or of securing the assumption to office of a 'moderate' black government with which it might be able to develop functional and working relations in the future. Yet what is of importance in our context is that South Africa received open western backing for the *détente* initiative, and that previously hostile black governments (led by Zambia) had shown themselves willing to make direct contact with the white regime in order to resolve regional tensions; and in addition, it was hoped in Pretoria that were South Africa to maintain its efforts to promote a settlement in Rhodesia, the USA and other western powers would reciprocate with favourable concessions to her needs, among them the recognition of the Transkei when it became independent.[75]

The request for Transkeian independence was put forward by Matanzima in March 1974 – a few weeks *before* the Portuguese *coup*, so that any interpretation based upon a causal link between the one event and the other would be totally misplaced. Sufficient reason for the move occurring at this time can be adduced from developments internal to the Transkei itself, and the Republican government's desire to hasten the pace of bantustan change in order to promote the credibility of its policy upon the international scene. Yet correspondingly, there can be little doubt that the Transkeian issue assumed rather more significance in the official mind after the Portuguese collapse had occurred – and that this in itself may account for independence being granted well within the five years requested by the TLA.

But the Transkeian issue was only one of the more minor issues at stake in a complex and rapidly changing situation, for growing Soviet involvement in the subcontinent was to provoke an aggressive western response; and in an attempt to counter Soviet influence (which took the form of Cuban military and technical support to the MPLA), the Republic was covertly encouraged by the USA into siding openly with UNITA in the Angolan civil war to the extent of launching a military invasion deep into the heart of MPLA-held territory. But US nerve thereafter failed and South Africa was forced to withdraw, while the Soweto upheaval in June 1976 and subsequent black unrest profoundly affected the white government's image of stability and control.[76] The Republic now appeared more vulnerable than ever before, and western powers (notably the incoming Carter administration in the USA) were reluctant to cause offence to Africa (and thereby perhaps increase Soviet influence) by extending recognition to an independent Transkei.

Nevertheless, the collapse of hopes for winning recognition for the Transkei did not deter Pretoria from pressing ahead with its plans for internal decolonization. Indeed, once a date for independence had been publicly announced, it would have been impossible for the government to withdraw from the precipice without provoking international scorn. But in any case, even after the Soweto upheaval the Vorster regime was disinclined to undertake a fundamental reorientation of its internal policies, and in consequence had no hesitation in proceeding with the bantustan experiment and, in so doing, attempting to lay the foundations for a future Verwoerdian-style commonwealth composed of a white core and black peripheral states. South Africa had now irrevocably committed herself to a calculated process of self-fragmentation, and events had forced her to embark upon a strategy which was explicitly neo-colonial in design.

Notes

1. For a sophisticated sociological rationalization of 'separate development', see Rhoodie and Venter (1960). But note that the 1936 Act was never intended at the time to serve as a basis for the fragmentation of the country into a number of separate states.
2. See, for example, Lipton (1972a); Barbara Rogers (1976); and almost any anti-apartheid literature on the bantustans.
3. The approach adopted in this chapter was developed in conjunction with Bardill, Perrings and Southall (1977).
4. For a discussion of the alliance between 'gold and maize', see Trapido (1971).
5. Legassick (1974a).
6. Johnstone (1976), pp. 13–20.
7. Francis Wilson (1971).
8. On 'extra-economic' coercion, see Legassick (1974b).

9. De Kiewiet (1941), pp. 44–5; and Johnstone (1976), pp. 26–34.
10. For a detailed analysis, see Tatz (1962).
11. De Kiewiet (1941), p. 180.
12. Francis Wilson (1971), p. 128.
13. Doxey (1961), pp. 128–9.
14. On the Mines' Recruiting Agencies, see below pp. 79–80.
15. Transvaal Province (1922), para. 267.
16. See, for instance, the perspective presented in Palmer and Parsons (1977).
17. See the official comparison with the Transkei in *Financial and Economic Position of Basutoland*, 1935, Cmd. 4907, pp. 33–4.
18. For the analysis of the Transkei as a supplier of cheap labour, see below, pp. 76–80.
19. *Native Economic Commission, 1930–32* (UG 22 – 1932, Pretoria, 1932); and *Social and Economic Planning Council* (UG 32 – 1946).
20. Between 1921 and 1946, the African urban population grew from 587,000 to an estimated 1,794,212, although the impact of influx controls is indicated by a population structure in which males outnumbered females in 1946 by a ratio of 1·8:1. *The Fagan Report* (UG 28 – 1948), paras 7, 13.
21. Wolpe (1972), p. 444.
22. First, Steele and Gurney (1973); also Ann and Neva Seidman (1977).
23. Legassick (1974b), pp. 269–74; Houghton (1976), pp. 119–46.
24. *Third Interim Report of the Industrial and Agricultural Requirements Commission* (UG 40–41, Pretoria, 1941), paras 100–1.
25. Johnstone (1976), pp. 54–7.
26. The interpretation that follows draws heavily upon the recent debate concerning the nature of the South African state. See in particular Davies, Kaplan, Morris and O'Meara (1976); Bozzoli (1978); and Innes and Plaut (1978).
27. Board of Trade and Industry, Report no. 282 (1945), pp. 42–6.
28. ibid., p. 46.
29. Wolpe (1972), p. 445; and O'Meara (1975).
30. For a classic survey, see Roux (1964).
31. See Stultz (1973) for a corroboratory analysis of the shift of white working-class votes to the National Party.
32. Johnstone (1970).
33. The consolidation plans announced in 1975 (and published in detail in the *RDM*, 28 July 1975) were supposedly 'final' in the sense of their finalizing the process of land distribution and allocation between the races subsequent to the Land Acts of 1911 and 1936. However, politics is the art of the possible, and in 1978 the government of Prime Minister P. W. Botha announced that the 'final' plan was still negotiable, as the possibility remained of future exchange of land between South Africa and independent homelands. See SAIRR, *A Survey, 1978*, p. 270.
34. Tomlinson Report (UG 61 – 1955).
35. Horrell (1959a).
36. Horrell (1973), pp. 81–2.
37. Barbara Rogers (1976), pp. 30–4.
38. Dr Verwoerd, then Minister of Native Affairs, speaking in Parliament, Senate *Hansard*, 24 May 1956, cols 3866–7; *HAD*, 14 May 1956, cols 5301–3, 5508–11.
39. For example, production of maize fell between 1958 and 1968 from 252,000

tons to 151,000 tons per annum, and sorghum from 45,700 tons to 22,700 tons per annum. (Republic of South Africa, 1970, pp. J6, 8, 10).
40. XDC, *Tenth Annual Report* (1975), p. 25.
41. Beinart (1975).
42. ibid., p. 104; and Bell (1973).
43. Horrell (1973), pp. 71–2, 122.
44. For an introductory survey, see Hepple (1971).
45. Legassick (1974a), especially pp. 11–18.
46. Horner (1976).
47. Department of Labour and Mines, *Report of the Commission of Inquiry into Labour Legislation Part I* (RP 47/1979); and Cooper (1979), and SAIRR, *A Survey, 1980*, p. 169. For a useful recent overview of the history and dilemmas of black trade unionism, see Bonner (1980).
48. Satisfactory statistics pertaining to changing sectoral patterns of employment of migrant workers are extremely difficult to obtain from official sources. However, the proportion of the total classified black workforce employed in manufacturing and construction rose from 8·2 per cent in 1946 to 13·9 per cent in 1970, and in mining declined from 15·2 per cent to 10·8 per cent over the same period, and it is probable that this reflects a relative transfer of domestic migrant labour from mining to the secondary sector as a consequence of the higher wages paid by the latter. Thus, in 1973, average monthly wages of blacks as a proportion of average monthly wages paid to whites in mining were 6·3 per cent, whereas in manufacturing and construction they were 17·9 per cent and 16·9 per cent respectively. See BENBO (1976), Tables B.5.7 and B.5.9, pp. 50–1. For an elaboration of the renewed role of the bantustans as suppliers of labour, see below, pp. 208–18.
49. 'As soon as they [the Bantu] become, for some reason or other, no longer fit for work or superfluous in the labour market, they are expected to return to their country of origin or the territory of their national unit where they fit in ethnically even if they were not born or bred in the homelands.' Quoted in Anonymous (1969), p. 19.
50. Desmond (1971). It needs to be noted carefully that the 1969 prediction of a prospective 3·8 million further removals was a considerable underestimate, as the 1970 census indicated that the South African government was using forecasts of African population which have since turned out to be too low. They were estimating for 21·3 million Africans in the year 2000, while current estimates are for 35–40 million. On this, see Barbara Rogers (1972).
51. See below, pp. 97–8.
52. Tatz (1962), pp. 156–7.
53. *HAD*, 16 May 1956, col. 5518.
54. Spence (1964).
55. *Memorandum Explaining the Promotion of Bantu Self-Government Bill*, 1959 (WP3 – 1959).
56. Kahn (1963).
57. Barber (1973), pp. 143–59, 182–9.
58. Feit (1971). For the Transkei, see Mbeki (1964). For Poqo and the assassination attempt on Matanzima, see note 26, p. 143 below.
59. *HAD*, 21 March 1963, col. 3175.
60. Carter *et al.* (1967), pp. 12–13.
61. For a summary of the debate, see ibid., pp. 67–9.
62. *HAD*, 20 March 1963, col. 3099.

63. *HAD*, 19 March 1963, cols 3039–40.
64. Horrell (1973), pp. 52–3.
65. *Memoranda on the Bantu Homelands Citizenship Bill*, 1970 (WP2 – 70); and the *Bantu Homelands Constitution Bill*, 1971 (WP1 – 1971).
66. Horrell (1973), pp. 45–52.
67. D. A. Kotze (1975).
68. Horrell (1973), pp. 43–61.
69. The following analysis of negotiations preceding independence is principally reliant upon Laurence (1976), pp. 91–103.
70. 'A referendum in Glen Grey resulted in an overwhelming vote against Transkei incorporation, namely 37,842 (83·7 per cent) against and 6,634 (14·7 per cent) in favour of incorporation.' D. A. Kotze (1975), p. 162.
71. *Daily Dispatch*, 28 April 1976.
72. Molteno (1971).
73. Grundy (1973), especially pp. 133–9.
74. ibid., pp. 141–7; and Barber (1973), pp. 268–72.
75. While US foreign policy was still in the hands of the Ford administration, Andrew Young, later US Ambassador to the United Nations under President Carter, outlined a scenario whereby the United States might lift its embargo on the sale of arms to the Republic, adopt a more favourable monetary policy towards her, and perhaps recognize the Transkei in return for South Africa's agreement to increase pressure on Ian Smith to bring about majority rule in Rhodesia, and to produce a convincing timetable for Namibia's independence and to abolish the cruder realities of apartheid. (*Washington Post*, 17 May 1976.)
76. For the fullest guide to this period, see Johnson (1977).

Chapter 3
The Transkei as a native reserve

The purpose of the present chapter is to provide an overview of the way in which the Transkei functioned as a native reserve. In particular, the intention is to illustrate the manner in which the area was transformed historically from a subsistence, pastoral, pre-capitalist economy into a reservoir of cheap labour for an external capitalist sector, a process which spanned the years from the late eighteenth century to the early twentieth. Such a complex task may scarcely be attempted, let alone adequately accomplished, within the space of the few pages that are available here, so readers will have to be indulgent of the heavy reliance placed upon secondary sources and continuing studies by historians of the period and processes at work, for these provide an essential basis for an understanding of the contemporary Transkei. In particular, special attention will be paid to the factors which were eventually to facilitate the transfer of authority from the white state to an indigenous minority class; and it will be suggested that it was because this class had developed a material interest in the preservation and expansion of bantustan structures that it was prepared to proceed to formal political independence in 1976, notwithstanding the Transkei's continuing acute dependence upon and integration with the 'white' South African political economy.

Annexation and the establishment of colonial rule

The extension of direct colonial rule to the areas which today constitute Transkei began in 1879, with the incorporation of the territories of Fingoland, Idutywa and Griqualand East into Cape Colony, and ended with the annexation of Pondoland in 1894.[1] In all cases but one, the final subjection of the various tribes – known today collectively as the Xhosa – occurred without actual physical conquest, for the annexation of the Transkei proceeded piecemeal as the various peoples felt it prudent either to request or accept the 'protection' of white magistrates, behind whom lay the spectre of colonial military force, whose efficacy had been previously displayed in a series of expansionary wars.

The one exception involved the Gcaleka and Ngqika, who in the so-called Ninth Frontier War of 1877–8 engaged in battle for land use with the Mfengu (a composite group of refugees from the Hlubi, Bhele and Zizi chiefdoms from Natal who had allied themselves with white settlers in previous engagements with the Xhosa). This struggle was essentially an attempt by the Gcaleka and Ngqika (along with some Thembu factions) to regain tracts of land from which they had been previously expelled and which had subsequently been occupied by the Mfengu (who had also been admitted to his territory by Thembu Paramount Ngangelizwe to protect his southern borders from the Gcaleka). However, following the active intervention of the Cape Military in support of the Mfengu, the assailants suffered physical defeat and were thereafter brought under white rule with the incorporation of Fingoland into the Colony in 1879.[2] Likewise, Thembu involvement in the war led to their being constrained to submit to the indirect authority of the Cape, with the creation of the Thembuland magistracy in the same year.[3]

It was only Gcalekaland that was annexed as a direct consequence of immediate military defeat, yet within the space of fifteen years all the other Xhosa peoples had succumbed to colonial authority. Physically undefeated though they may have been, the various influences which had been brought to bear upon them to part with their independence – economic, political and religious – had all been underwritten by European military superiority. Ultimate surrender was preceded by a complex history of contact between black and white extending back over two and a half centuries, involving both conflict and co-operation[4] within the context of the expansion of the mercantile capitalist economy centred in the Cape. Yet the finally decisive feature of this relationship, which moved from relatively equal barter and exchange to a later and unequal struggle for land (the principal means of production), was the triumph of white arms in a long succession of bitter and hard-fought frontier wars, with the eventual submission of the Xhosa to colonial rule being brought about by their reluctant acknowledgement of their inability to resist the armed might of the Cape and British governments.

The various peoples of Transkei, the Southern Nguni, are customarily referred to as the Xhosa, but this is technically incorrect as in reality there are twelve tribal clusters, each of which has its own separate chieftaincy and its own distinctive customs and history. These clusters are the Xhosa proper (including the Gcaleka), the Thembu, Mpondo, Mpondomise, Bomvana, Bhaca, Hlubi, Bhele, Zizi, Mfengu (Fingo), Xesibe and Ntlangwini, and each (except the Xesibe) is divided into several chiefdoms, which are interrelated either through common membership of a royal lineage or through sharing subordinacy to a paramount.[5] These varied peoples have become identified together in common parlance because they all (bar a few Sotho chiefdoms located mainly along the Lesotho border) speak dialects of Xhosa – the Xhosa proper being the first cluster to come into sustained contact with whites and the first whose language was recorded, this leading to the application of the title 'isiXhosa' to the whole group of dialects spoken by the Southern Nguni.

Unlike the Zulu, Swazi and Sotho, who formed kingdoms in response to the various challenges they encountered, the Xhosa never formed themselves into a coherent political unit. Production was organized through small settlements, each controlled by headmen, which were fairly evenly distributed over the land. Each village needed sufficient suitable land for grazing throughout the entire year, a condition highly conducive to political dispute between neighbouring settlements when pasture was in short supply. In consequence, chiefs were able to contain competitive tendencies between villages only by progressing physically through their domains, a necessity which, given the coercive resources at their disposal, effectively limited the extent of their authority.[6]

Nguni political units exhibited a tendency towards *segmentation* (the emergence of divisions within a polity) or *fission* (the actual disintegration of chiefdoms into politically separate units).[7] In theory, being related to the right of the heir of the right-hand house of a chief to establish his own independent chiefdom at the death of his father,[8] fission could occur with each generation, but in practice secession tended to follow on from internal dispute. The present divisions between the Eastern and Western Pondo and between the Thembu and Emigrant Thembu are products of this process, as are numerous other examples among the Xhosa, Bhaca and Mpondomise clusters, the essential feature of such fission being the clear spatial separation of the newly established from the parent chiefdom and an unequivocal declaration of intent either by force of arms or the express consent of the paramount (who might wish to limit conflict). In addition, heirs of minor wives also had the right to locate themselves away from the chief. Encouraged to build up their own entourage following their initiation (when they received gifts of land and stock), segmentation tended to diffuse the authority of the paramount and to limit his ability to exert centralized control. Taken overall, therefore, a distinguishing feature of the pre-colonial system was that it militated against the assertion of central authority and resulted in chiefly power being subjected to considerable popular limitation.

A further distinguishing feature of Nguni society was its absorptive capacity. Related in part to the need of weaker groups to seek protection from the stronger, the tendency was also associated with the fact that political legitimacy was based upon the personal allegiance of followers to the chiefs, who were thereby encouraged to build up a clientele. It is recorded that a number of shipwrecked mariners from Europe were thus absorbed in the sixteenth and seventeenth centuries, but in later years newcomers tended to be slaves, military deserters or convicts who had fled the Cape, whence demands were periodically emitted – and raids made – for the recovery of errant bodies.[9]

More significant was the incorporation by various chiefdoms from about 1822 onward, notably by the Thembu, Pondo and Gcaleka, of thousands of refugees of mostly Bhele, Zizi and Hlubi origin from the disruptive effects of the *Mfecane* (the dispersal of African peoples westwards as a result of the rise of the Zulu state). Closely related to Xhosaspeakers in language and customs, these wanderers – who became known as 'Mfengu' or 'supplicants' – came to occupy a subordinate position in the chiefdoms in which they were absorbed. In the early 1830s, Hintsa, Chief of the Gcaleka, attempted to incorporate over 20,000 such persons,[10] but far from becoming absorbed into the host society, the Mfengu distinguished themselves by the manner in which they responded to the opportunities for enrichment provided by the expansion of mercantile economy. Accumulating wealth through the energetic trading of commodities with surrounding tribes, they also engaged in the sale of both agricultural surpluses and labour power to white merchants, missionaries and settlers in exchange for cash and kind. In so doing, they alienated themselves from their Gcaleka patrons; and given also intense competition for land, the settlement of the newcomers resulted in considerable conflict with the established population.

These various tensions developed to such a level of hostility that the Mfengu allied with the British against the Gcaleka in the frontier war of 1834–5; and thereafter, some 17,000 Mfengu moved into Cape Colony at the express invitation of the Governor, Sir Benjamin D'Urban, whose intention was to insert them as a human barrier between the white frontiersmen and the Xhosa. However, this ploy worked rather to exacerbate than to minimize conflict, for not only did the Mfengu remove some 20,000 head of cattle from their late hosts, but they were also settled on land belonging to the Ngquika, who were under white domination in the area presently known as the Ciskei. Thus the Mfengu became transformed into bitter enemies of the Xhosa. Regarded as turncoats and collaborators, they further estranged themselves by serving as military allies to the whites in other frontier wars in 1846–7 and 1850–3.[11]

The early history of the area now known as Transkei is that of the steady subjugation of its black inhabitants to colonial authority and their corresponding incorporation into the mercantile trading economy. By 1700, southern migrating Nguni had reached the Kei River, and with the Xhosa at their head had by 1750 penetrated as far as the Keiskamma. As they swept south-west, they inevitably came into more frequent contact with white society as it, in turn, progressed north-eastwards. The first recorded encounter between whites from the Cape settlement and Xhosa occurred in 1702 in the form of a skirmish, this being a fitting prelude to the uneasy and unstable relationship that later obtained upon the frontier. Thereafter, the Nguni were increasingly drawn into contact with the expanding settler-based economy, with white trading parties bartering items such as metal, beads, tobacco, liquor and (in later years) horses and firearms in exchange for ivory and cattle; and at the same time, the Nguni were equally eager for the goods which the settlers could supply, and many sought the wherewithal to purchase these by entering white employment as herdsmen or servants. By disposing of non-essential resources, the Xhosa were able to obtain those items of a more technologically advanced society that they required without affecting the basic material structure of their own society: 'In other words, participation in trade at this limited and discretionary level did not affect their mode of production nor the economic organisation of their society.'[12]

Yet the relationship between the frontiersmen and the Nguni was inherently unstable, for both were expanding societies and both were seeking to extend their land. Thus whereas the settlers had been able to deal cursorily with the San and Khoikhoi (the first peoples they had encountered in the Cape), in the Nguni they faced a far more numerous grouping, and one which – like themselves – sought a pastorally based existence. In addition, the Nguni population was growing, the increase probably not unconnected with the introduction of maize, faster growing and more suited to the environment than sorghum, hitherto the staple crop.

In the earliest days of contact, the authorities at the Cape attempted to minimize conflict on the border by limiting contact with the African peoples who lived beyond, while successive boundaries were ordained beyond which whites were forbidden to settle. Yet such regulation was ineffective, and trade between black and white increased steadily, while successive governments were unable to contain the advance of land-hungry farmers.

The passing of the Cape into British hands in 1806 presaged a marked change in the nature of trade on the frontier. An infusion of British mercantile capital, along with a swelling population of white settlers (notably following the 1820 settlement in the Eastern Cape) led to a greater volume of trade and its more formal regulation. Furthermore, control of trade passed from the hands of non-specialist Boers to those of professional, often itinerant, merchants drawn from the British settler community.

The extension of Cape mercantilism was premised upon the disruption of the self-sufficiency of the Nguni pastoral community. If merchant capital was to expand the sale of imported manufactured goods, then the prime requirement was increased production of agricultural commodities (cattle, wine, sheep and various natural resources). This in turn demanded the acquisition by white settlers of more land and the more intensified exploitation of black labour-power. Thus although African producers themselves responded more than adequately to the needs of the commercial market, African societies were none the less pressured for more land and a greater supply of labour. Hence it was that the expansion of the mercantile economy initiated an era of competition for land and resources, a conflict which culminated in the long series of frontier wars and eventual conquest of the indigenous inhabitants by the whites.[13]

Up till the early 1770s, the ruling Dutch East India Company refused to countenance settlers establishing farms east of the Gamtoos, but in 1806 the border was extended to the Fish River.[14] Typically, such annexation (of necessity accomplished by military force) involved expulsion of the prior inhabitants and the clearing of a strip of unoccupied neutral territory to serve as a buffer between colonists and Xhosa. Then, following the war of 1834–5 in which thousands of Xhosa warriors sought to reoccupy the buffer zone, Governor Sir Benjamin D'Urban annexed land as far east as the Kei River for white settlement, proposing that all Xhosa living to its west should be pushed back to allow for the establishment of Mfengu settlers as a barrier between the white frontiersmen and their late antagonists. However, D'Urban was forced to temper his design, for Lord Glenelg at the Colonial Office concluded that expulsion of Xhosa on such a massive scale would create a disturbance that would be difficult and costly to contain. Accordingly, although large numbers of Mfengu were settled between the Keiskamma and the Fish River, a new policy was implemented whereby diplomatic agents were appointed to reside near chiefs to mediate in disputes, while treaties were made with individual rulers which defined clear boundaries between black and white territory, with the frontier being patrolled by Mfengu and the military.

Yet the new strategy met with little success in stabilizing the frontier. The military too often ignored the agents, and failed to pay due deference to the chiefs. For their part, Xhosa warriors raided settler homesteads, with reprisals being launched by frontiersmen in response. It was one such punitive expedition mounted in retaliation for stock thefts that provided the spark for the so-called War of the Axe in 1846. In this the Xhosa fared little better than before, and defeat brought with it renewed annexation of territory between the Fish and Kei Rivers as British Kaffraria (incorporating the present Ciskei), with tribes falling directly under the Crown. The diplomatic agents were withdrawn, and the chiefs were turned into salaried officials and placed under the supervision of resident white magistrates.

Uneasy peace did not prevail for long. Drought and famine in 1850 formed a background to resistance to colonial authority mobilized by the prophet Mlanjeni, and the deposition of the Ngqika Chief Sandile led to a further outbreak of war in December 1850. This in turn led to a reversion to earlier policy, with Mfengu being placed between the Xhosa and whites on more land confiscated from the Ngqika.

A further device of colonial policy was experimentation with new forms of landholding for the indigenes, missions being invited to hold land in trust for African wards who might later obtain title to it when deemed fit to do so. It was this aspect of policy which was soon taken up by a new Governor, Sir George Grey. Discarding the prior emphasis on minimizing conflict by territorially segregating antagonistic groups, he now sought to establish a more lasting peace through the explicit and deliberate socio-economic integration of black with white. This was not integration in the modern, liberal sense, but was rather devised with the paternalistic intent of subordinating 'barbarians' via a master–servant relationship until such distant time as they might have become 'civilized', to which end Grey encouraged an influx of Europeans to settle among the indigenous blacks to provide them with employment, tame them through Christian teaching, and to instruct them in the various arts of industry and farming.[15]

Such paternalism, symbolizing defeat in eight successive wars, turned the subordinated society inwards. Pressure of a growing population within an ever-diminishing land area created disruption and despair, and deep frustration manifested itself in an act of mass hysteria, the cattle-killing of 1857, a millenarian reaction which was to break the Xhosa far more effectively than their having been put to the sword. Visionaries played an important role in Xhosa society, and a young girl, named Nongqause, reported to a diviner that she had been visited by strange men who had insisted that the people should consume their corn, refrain from sowing, and kill all their cattle. Were they so to do, their ancestors would rise on the appointed day and, with the help of a great wind, drive the whites back into the sea. The ancestors would themselves then be restored to the full vigour of their youth, stores would overflow with grain, and the fields would be grazed by the choicest cattle.[16]

The prophecy, versed in traditional Xhosa idiom, caused consternation and division among the chiefs, but Sarili, the Xhosa paramount, ordered that the commands of the visitors should be obeyed. In October, a date was set by which all cattle should be killed, and when the ancestors failed to return upon the appointed date, thousands of other beasts were slaughtered and further stocks of grains destroyed. Yet still the ancestors declined to appear, and by February 1857 the countryside was in the grip of a merciless, man-made famine. It was the Xhosa chiefdoms themselves that were most badly affected for theirs were the people who had borne the brunt of the white advance, and an estimated 20,000 perished, with a further 30,000 being forced to migrate to the Cape in search of sustenance and employment, while the population of the chiefdoms which participated in the self-destruction dropped from 105,000 to a mere 37,000.[17]

The cattle-killing of 1856–7, one of the most destructive millenarian reactions to colonial conquest in any part of Southern Africa, the wider continent and elsewhere, presaged the transformation of the lands of the Xhosa into a labour reservoir for the white economy. But the people rallied yet again in an attempt to turn back the white tide. The Gcaleka, languishing on their overcrowded, famine-struck lands, looked with envy upon the Mfengu, the former supplicants, who had been allowed to settle on neighbouring territory by Paramount Ngangelizwe of the Thembu. The Mfengu, having aligned themselves with the whites, were enjoying relative prosperity, having not only ignored but also having been excluded from Nongqause's call on account of their perceived treachery in collaborating with the whites. It was with the objective of wreaking vengeance upon the Mfengu that the Gcaleka (with Ngqika support) now invaded Thembu territory in 1877. As has already been told, the Cape government (which had been awaiting some such excuse to confront the Gcaleka) now intervened on behalf of the Mfengu and Thembu, and this

– the Ninth and last frontier war – ended with the outright annexation of Gcalekaland and the extension of direct rule over the Thembu. Indeed, such was white superiority at the war's conclusion that legislation was subsequently enacted to disarm all Cape Africans, including the Mfengu who had so closely allied themselves with the British for many years. Formal incorporation of Gcalekaland into Cape Colony was not merely the adoption of a new technique of control by the administration in response to a local crisis, but rather reflected the adoption of a new strategy of outright colonization, for it was feared that were white expansion to continue indefinitely, the Nguni would respond to progressive land loss by yet further wars that would be unwholesomely burdensome to the colonial exchequer; and indeed, it was to relieve such financial stress that a hut tax had been imposed on both Fingoland and the Idutywa area in 1874, a move which was then followed by their outright annexation in 1877, together with that of East Griqualand as the Cape sought to contain the rival territorial aspirations of settlers in Natal.

Thereafter Gcalekaland was divided into the districts of Willowvale and Kentani and was formally united with Idutywa and Fingoland to form the Transkei, being placed under the authority of a Chief Magistrate. Similarly, East Griqualand, which comprised the districts of Elliot and Maclear (both of which were excised in 1912), Mount Fletcher, Qumbu, Tsolo, Matatiele, Kokstad, Umzimkulu and Mount Frere, also became a Chief Magistracy, with the small Xesibe tribe being attached (although not formally incorporated until 1886). In addition, as previously related, magisterial rule was extended to the Thembu in 1877, Emigrant Thembuland being divided into the districts of St Marks and Xalanga.[18]

This left only the Mpondo independent, and they managed to cling to their autonomy for a further seventeen years, although they lost control of Port St Johns, at the mouth of the Mzimbuvu, in 1884.[19] Their incorporation was inevitable, however, and it finally came about in 1894 after their chiefs had been given an ultimatum to submit to annexation or face the consequences.[20] The various Chief Magistracies of the Transkei, Thembuland, East Griqualand and Pondoland were then subsequently welded together in 1903 as the United Transkeian Territories under a Chief Magistrate in Umtata, under whom authority was exercised in individual districts by magisterial subordinates.

Origins of the reserve economy

The transition of the majority of her inhabitants from pastoral cultivators to wage workers is necessarily a central concern of any study of industrial development in South Africa, but interpretations of the causes and dynamics of this historical process have varied considerably. While earlier historians tended to focus upon the alleged conservatism and backwardness of 'native' socio-economic structures and the consequent 'civilizing' effects of wage labour,[21] more liberal and later interpreters sought to correct the former viewpoint by stressing the destructive and dislocating impact of rapid economic change and imposed land limitation upon African societies previously well adjusted to their physical environment.[22] But characterizing both views, despite their variant emphases, is a fundamental dichotomy distinguishing between traditional (African) and modern (European) sectors of the economy, and a consequent belief that the primary task of economic development is to rationalize African economic activity. However, a considerable body of recent work has exposed the colonial myths which lie at the root of this perspective, by demonstrating that the response of African communities to the expanding economy was highly rational, resulting in the emergence of peasant communities which were commercially oriented to the market. Thus some parts of the 'Native Reserves' of South Africa and the peripheral High Commission Territories enjoyed an initial period of prosperity in the early days of their contact with the commercial economy, but were later to undergo a process of underdevelopment as a direct result of their participation in the capitalist transformation of Southern Africa on disadvantageous and uneven terms that were coercively induced by settler and mining capital, whose interests were in no way served by continuing African autonomy.[23]

Focus on the emergence and decline of an indigenous peasantry is of significance because it defines the character of the transformation of the majority of the African population from pastoralists to their present condition as a rightless, exploited and to a large extent migratory labour force. Whereas a pastoral society is principally concerned with production merely for the satisfaction of subsistence needs, a peasantry is one which is engaged in the regular production of an agricultural surplus for sale to a market which goes beyond the bounds of the immediate community. Having their ultimate security in access to land (which need not entail actual individual ownership), peasants are primarily reliant upon the use of their own and family labour and, furthermore, are involved in relations of coercion and obedience imposed by non-peasant outsiders through whom their surplus is channelled and who are economically, if not politically, dominant.[24]

Colin Bundy has located the origins of such a community in South Africa in the areas of greatest contact between southward migrating pastoral Nguni and Europeans in the early years of the nineteenth century.[25] Adapting considerably to the changes which the alien intrusion wrought in their environment, the former came to participate in market relations, such activity being initially encouraged by colonizing elements both for its inherent economic value and for the fact that such a peasantry provided a physical and moral barrier against hostile peoples in territories beyond. Thus missionaries, settlers and officials alike all sought to promote the 'civilizing influence' of trade and barter, believing that the creation of a landed class of indigenous farmers whose prosperity was dependent upon the regular sale of their surplus produce to white purchasers would serve to stabilize the insecure frontier.

In particular, Bundy isolates the Mfengu as forming the first significant peasant community after their migration into the present-day Ciskei area in 1835. Wealthy in cattle (notably after their removal of the 20,000 beasts from the Gcaleka after the 1834–5 frontier war), a crucial factor which predisposed them towards commercially oriented activity was that their enterprise was largely uncurbed by the impositions of a strong chiefly structure, the *Mfecane* having led to the death or dispersal of many of their chiefs. In addition, once having arrived in the Cape, the Mfengu became closely associated with Methodist missionaries, who eagerly espoused the cause of peasant agriculture. Indeed, Bundy argues forcefully that the mission stations served as important foci of social change, mission activity being oriented towards restructuring African societies in accordance with capitalist norms and in a manner that would firmly attach them to the expanding mercantile economy.

Increased trade and commercially oriented production being advocated as heralding a movement away from barbarism, African receptivity to the civilizing mission was enhanced, not so much by acceptance of the Christian message, as by awareness of the missionaries' role as transmitters of various skills (such as reading and writing), the acquisition of which could lead to a higher material existence. None the less, while crucial, the missionary impact should not be exaggerated, for the very example provided by such peoples as the Mfengu in turning to discretionary wage labour for whites and agricultural production for sale, equally served as a demonstration of the benefits of such enterprise to others who, by in turn attaching themselves to mission stations, were able to loose themselves from the social sanctions exercised by their chiefs upon material accumulation by commoners.

By hastening the process of annexation of the Ciskei and the extension of control over large parts of the Transkei, the cattle-killing of 1857 brought increasing numbers of Africans into unavoidable and regular contact with the agents of colonial society – the administrators, missionaries, settlers and traders. For some, this meant separation (through outright dispossession) from the land, and many were forced into wage labour for white employers on the latter's terms; but for others, such as Mfengu and loyalists who actually received land, there was the alternative of peasant production. And as such people migrated deeper into the Transkei, they dispersed knowledge and information about agricultural methods and implements (such as the plough) which were new to their recipient societies. Engaging in the production for profit of grain, stock and wool, their successful enterprise attracted an influx of European traders into both the Ciskei and Transkei, whose function was to channel such peasant produce to the external market.

If the rate of peasantization among the various tribal clusters in the middle years of the century was a relatively gradual process, the situation was transformed by the unearthing of diamonds in Griqualand West in 1867, the effects of which were intensified and multiplied by the discovery of gold on the Witwatersrand in 1886. The input of large-scale mining capital sent shock waves rippling through a hitherto predominantly agricultural economy. The export of minerals necessitated the construction of railways and roads linking centres of production to the ports; the flow of wealth to rapidly growing mining towns encouraged the development of service and secondary industries; and the expansion of settled urban populations created commercial opportunities for those who had the ability to provide them with foodstuffs. Of necessity, all these processes were themselves dependent upon an increasing manual workforce, and legislators were in no way backward in establishing a framework of coercive laws and tax measures whose design and effect was to draw out a greater supply of labour from dominated and recently subjugated African communities. Yet, at the same time, these very developments broadened the scope for participation in the market for indigenous agricultural producers, 'and the early 1870s saw a virtual explosion of peasant economic activity':

> Five hundred wagons of corn were sold by Fingoland's peasants in 1873, as well as a crop worth £60,000; and in 1875 the trade of Fingoland 'at lowest computation' was adjudged to be worth £150,000. From Gaikaland, Gcalekaland, Tembuland and East Griqualand came similar reports; peasants were selling cattle in order to invest in sheep; the number of traders across the Kei trebled; African produce in 1875 was estimated to be worth £750,000. A single firm bought £58,000 worth of African produce while a merchant's house in Port Elizabeth boasted an annual turnover of goods for the African trade of £200,000. New methods and resources rippled from tribe to tribe, and even amongst the most 'backward' tribes crop diversification and wider cultivation were common by the 1880s.[26]

In turn, as the frontier continued on its ineluctable advance, so did the process of peasantization continue, and the reverberations of the mining expansion were felt in parts previously distant from the commercial economy. Thus the 1870s and 1880s saw increasing imports of agricultural implements and other goods into Pondoland which had hitherto managed to retain its political autonomy. European traders – fifty to sixty of whom were resident in the area by about 1876 – acted as a catalyst to both the production of surplus and its exchange for cash or kind, and whereas in previous decades the major exports had been ivory and skins, by the 1880s these had been replaced by cattle and grain which found their outlet in the Cape and Natal.[27]

Yet as far as Pondoland was concerned, the peasant response reached its climax in the period following annexation until 1910. Previous to 1894, the Mpondo had been relatively insulated from cultural contact with colonizing elements, and whereas missionaries and administrators seem to have acted as something of a stimulus to surplus production in the Ciskei and Transkei, commercially oriented activity in Pondoland was initiated when European penetration was still extremely limited. Thus before annexation the Christianizing influence was muted and access to external markets was restricted by the undeveloped communications network and the bad state of repair of the few roads that existed. None the less, it is undeniable that the imposition of colonial rule brought in its wake new factors that stimulated an extension of peasant activity. The levying of a hut tax of 10 shillings per annum obligated each adult male to find a cash income, and the typical Mpondo response was to do this through the sale of their cattle or crops rather than their labour (although increasing numbers of them were forced by circumstance into wage employment after 1900). Indeed, at this time *per capita* grain production was higher in Pondoland than in other districts of the Transkei, and exports of cattle (until a rinderpest epidemic in 1897), grain, fruit, tobacco and wool increased steadily, as did the quantity and range of commodities imported by traders and sold to the Mpondo. Ploughs and implements which assisted in raising agricultural productivity were in particular demand, while – as in other areas – items such as cotton goods and blankets also rapidly became regarded as necessary items for a basic living. The road network was extensively improved (the most notable developments being the linking of Port St Johns to Umtata and Kokstad), with the result that the interior was opened up and the internal and external markets made more accessible. European administrators, soldiers and missionaries now clustered around the various magisterial headquarters, and the number of trading stores in Pondoland increased from 99 in 1903 to 119 by 1905. Thus, as had been the case elsewhere in the Transkei and Ciskei, African producers were enabled to enjoy a modest degree of economic success by commercializing their agriculture, adopting innovatory techniques and producing a surplus for sale.[28]

If peasantization was a process that was uneven in its pace and timing, it was by no means uniform in its impact. The one side of the coin was that African producers were enabled to retain a considerable measure of autonomy; the other was that peasant production simultaneously served to integrate indigenous communities into the expanding capitalist mode and to encourage a structural dependence upon the commodity markets of the mercantile economy. Similarly, just as inhabitants of each area successively turned to commercial production and came to enjoy a relative prosperity, so were there others whose condition reflected a state of steadily increasing impoverishment. Many there were who had been made landless by the colonial incursion, and there were others who had access to insufficient land whereby to provide for even a meagre subsistence. While both human and animal populations were subject to increase, they were simultaneously confined to a diminishing land area, as African territory was gradually expropriated by the incoming settlers. Thus, in the midst of plenty, there was also considerable distress, and an ever-growing stream of menfolk was forced to leave their homes and seek work on an expanding labour market; and the turn of events introduced a cycle which led eventually to social degeneracy and decay.

Just as the causes of the peasant prosperity of the later decades of the nineteenth century were located in the expansion of the mining industry, so were the origins of an increasing rate of proletarianization of the African mass, for given that an abundant supply of cheap black labour was essential to the mines, mimimization of labour costs could be achieved only through a variety of extra-economic coercive measures – such as the implementation of the contract, Pass Law and compound systems, as well as the steady elimination of competitive recruitment and the adoption of an agreed low-wages policy among the various mining companies.

Indications of such proletarianization were first visible in the Ciskei, which had experienced earlier and more intensive contact with Europeans and where a peasantry had first emerged. Exacerbated by drought in the period 1876–8, landlessness and poverty became increasingly evident in long-established peasant areas surrounding towns such as Kingwilliamstown, East London and Victoria East, even though farming yet remained a viable proposition for many of those who managed to retain access to land. By the early 1890s, a similar phenomenon was readily observable in areas of the Transkei such as Fingoland, Thembuland and East Griqualand. There were still peasants who possessed sufficient capital and enterprise who could adapt to changing circumstances, but there were growing numbers who could not and who were forced out on to the labour market. Overpopulation, overstocking, indebtedness and impoverishment became objects of official comment, and there were those who specifically noted that the districts they administered seemed to be regressing, and were enjoying less prosperity than some years before; nor was it long before such a process also became apparent in Pondoland, where by 1910 surplus production was already on the decline, with increased consumption of grain being absorbed internally by a growing population.[29]

The most important aspect of this decline in peasant prosperity was that it resulted in steadily growing numbers of Africans being forced out on to the labour market. Unable to meet their subsistence requirements on the land, they were forced to seek cash earnings by going into white employment; thus whereas in 1893 some 27,511 bodies left the Transkeian Territories and Pondoland in search of work, by 1912 this figure had increased to 96,667. This increasing flow of labour was the subject of much comment, and an Official Commission was to note in 1894 that: 'These [Transkeian] Territories appear to produce labour for work outside them somewhat in proportion to the length of time their inhabitants have enjoyed good government.'[30] Bundy's paraphrase of these words is apt: 'The Territories produced wage labourers somewhat in proportion to the extent that structural underdevelopment had been induced by the penetration of Colonial Rule and capitalist economic relations.'[31] Such indeed was the case, and the more the Transkei was integrated into the structure of the South African economy, the more it exhibited the constellation of features which we currently characterize by the term underdevelopment, notably the appropriation of its economic surplus by external capital and the emergence of stratification in the form of a wage-labouring mass matched by the development of a relatively privileged élite. It is to the dynamics of this process, and an analysis of its primary characteristics as manifested in colonial Transkei, that we now must turn.

The development of underdevelopment

> More than ever we can see how completely these territories, with all their officials and paraphernalia, are today mere appurtenances of the Chamber of Mines. The people have just so little land per family, and are taxed just so much, that they can only subsist by sending their men to the mines. And the whites simply batten on the couple of pounds brought home by each mineworker after his dreary contract has expired. – S. P. Bunting, Communist Party candidate for Thembuland in the 1929 General Election Campaign.[32]

By the early years of the twentieth century, the once prosperous areas of the Ciskei and the Transkei were displaying signs of acute economic dislocation, the most notable feature of which was that increasing numbers of their African inhabitants were flowing on to the labour market, as they were no longer able to maintain their economic independence by providing for their own subsistence through agricultural production. The most immediate cause of this transformation was undoubtedly the massive loss of land to which the African community had been subjected by the settler appropriations of the previous century, but this was in turn compounded by a set of natural disasters which weakened peasant self-sufficiency, and by the simultaneous enforced and unavoidable participation of Africans in capitalist economic relations on unequal and disadvantageous terms.

By the early 1900s the area of land under communal tenure had been reduced to critical limits and, in order to relieve the consequent pressure, Africans were increasingly seeking to purchase back land from whites which they had lost by conquest. But further encroachment by Africans upon the market was halted by the passing of the Land Act of 1913 and its subsequent amendments. In terms of this legislation, the area of the Transkeian Territories (as estimated by the Beaumont Commission in 1916) was some 13,560 square miles (35,120 square km), expanding slightly to 13,916 square miles (36,000 square km) by 1936.[33] Yet if the land area remained virtually constant, the population did not, and the same period witnessed a natural increase which was augmented by an influx of individuals who had been turned off white farms on which they had previously been squatting. Thus although the precision of almost any statistics for the Transkei in this period is open to query, the reported size of the Territories' African population over the passing years was as set out in Table 3.1. Thus although all figures are approximate, the density of population in the Transkei increased from about 67·8 persons per square mile (2·6 square km) in 1916 to 82·9 in 1936, compared with an average density increase over the same period in the Reserve areas as a whole from 50·3 to 57·2.[34] As will be demonstrated below, this increased burden led to continuous agricultural deterioration and the perpetually diminishing ability of the Territories to provide the subsistence requirement for their burgeoning population.

Table 3.1 *Estimated African population of the Transkei, 1911–41*

Year	Population	Approx. annual growth rate (%)
1911	871,602	
1916	919,781	1·1
1921	938,990	0·4
1936	1,153,975	1·4
1941	1,270,319	1·9

Sources: 1911, 1921, 1936: Census figures as used by the *Witwatersrand Mine Natives' Wages Commission*, UG 21 – 1944. 1916: *Natives Land Commission*, 1, 1916, UG 19 – 1916, Appendix IV. 1941 Fox *Chamber of Mines* and Back (1941).

The passing of the Land Act had been facilitated in order to secure the interests of white agriculture and, indeed, the immediate effect was an enforced exodus from the land of many thousands of squatters. Of necessity having to sell their stock at basement prices, many were left destitute and drifted aimlessly across the countryside, a large proportion of them migrating to the already overburdened reserves (although because the Cape already possessed a formidable collection of anti-squatter laws prior to 1913 which had already done much to erode the position of squatter–peasants, the impact of the Land Act was most heavily felt in the Transvaal and Natal). But the Act itself was a culmination of a complex of events which had already weakened peasant self-sufficiency. In the first place, while the 1899–1902 war raised prices for all foodstuffs and thus provided a favourable market for producers who were left undisturbed by the hostilities, others were looted, raided and made homeless. There was also natural disaster which struck in the form of drought in 1894–5 (the worst in living memory) and 1900–1 which ruinously affected crops and promoted consequent indebtedness, as peasants were forced to part with stock to traders in return for means of subsistence.[35] But in particular African participation on the market was undermined by the rinderpest epidemic of 1897 (which destroyed 80–90 per cent of cattle in the Transkei) and the East Coast fever of 1910–11, which likewise decimated herds and pauperized large numbers of peasants who had invested their capital in stock.[36] If natural disasters had also afflicted pre-capitalist societies in earlier times, a significant difference now was that, instead of being retained for purposes of renewed accumulation and reproduction, surplus was drained off by levies (such as hut tax) imposed by the colonial state. Peasant wealth thus plundered by disease, the labour supply was proportionately increased by the indigent.

Finally, peasant production was increasingly undermined by worsening relative access to the market. As Macmillan pointed out some time ago, 'to locate the native reserves it is no bad rule ... to look for the areas circumvented or entirely missed by even branch railway lines'.[37] While European farmers increasingly benefited from favourable legislation, state subsidies, reduced rail rates and enhanced ability to secure credit, African peasants were denied such advantages. Not only this, but within the reserves (the Transkei included) it became established principle that the costs of Native Administration should be raised from local sources through direct taxation of the African populace, and it was not until 1925 with the passage of the Natives Taxation and Development Act that any state funds for development purposes were diverted to the reserves.[38] Accordingly, the market became increasingly inaccessible to reserve peasants as the twentieth century wore on, and the incentive to surplus production was correspondingly diminished.

The basis for peasant production was thus eroded by processes both natural and deliberate. Yet it did not suit the dominant capital interests that the African population should become wholly proletarianized nor that it should become completely separated from the land, for the profitable operation of the mines (in particular) necessitated indirect subsidization by reserve agriculture, just as the imperative of cost-minimization made the mining industry reliant upon the migratory labour system. So long as migrant labourers had access to means of subsistence and remained politically rightless, wages could be fixed at the level of subsistence for the individual worker, since it could be presumed that, to some extent, his dependants were supported by agricultural production in the reserves. Thus the Mine Natives' Wages Commission of 1944 concluded that:

> ... the gold mining industry of the Witwatersrand could not have been developed, nor could the Union have reaped the consequent economic benefit which it has derived from that industry, but for the fact that the cheap unskilled labour necessary has been available through the migrant native being prepared to sell his labour at a price rendered possible by his possession of a supplementary means of subsistence from his holding in a Reserve.[39]

Yet such a system could not operate unless the workers and his kin retained their access to the means of subsistence. If the interests of mining capital were to be adequately served, therefore, it was necessary to arrest the process of creeping landlessness which had been effected by settler expansion and, to a certain extent, escalated by the individualization of tenure which had been introduced – on a limited scale – to promote the development of an African yeomanry in an earlier era. Extension of freehold and quit-rent tenures to indigenous peoples had become lawful in the Cape under the Native Locations Act of 1879, and had found considerable application among the Mfengu.[40] Individual tenure among Africans was then extended in tribal areas by Cecil Rhodes' Act of 1894, which provided for the survey of 5-morgen plots and their allotment to families, primogeniture being introduced to prevent subdivisions and transfer of such land being subject to the consent of the Governor-General. The beauty of this Act, so far as the Cape legislators were concerned, was that it not only sanctified the notion of private property but also simultaneously served as a specifically proletarianizing measure, for by making the land available to the holder of insufficient size to allow for the subsistence of an entire family, it ensured a continual supply of labour on to the market. Yet the Act was double-edged, for it also laid down the principle of one-man-one-lot, which not only made access to the means of production more widely available than under an uninhibited freeholding system, but also limited the possibilities of accumulation of land by more successful farmers and thereby undermined the competitive challenge posed by peasant farming to white agriculture.[41]

Operative at first in the Ciskei, the Glen Grey system (as it was known after the area in which it was first applied) was tentatively extended to the four (mainly Mfengu) Transkeian districts of Butterworth, Idutywa, Nqamakwe and Tsomo, later finding some application in Umtata, Xalanga and Engcobo, but was then halted, ostensibly on grounds of the prohibitive expense of survey,[42] but in actuality because of the strength of African opposition; for while wealthier, surplus-producing peasants welcomed the prospect of security of tenure, there was also widespread realization that the size of surveyed allotments would allow for little more than bare subsistence. In addition, chiefs and headmen perceived the new system as an assault upon their authority, and were able to mobilize support because of the threat of landlessness that the Act implied. Accordingly, outside the surveyed districts land continued to be allotted by the chiefs and headmen (subject to the authority of District Magistrates) under the communal tribal system, whereby access to grazing and natural products was free to all, though residential and arable land, once allotted, was exclusive to the holder so long as it was effectively utilized. Importantly, however, apart from being strictly enforced in the surveyed areas, the principle of one-man-one-lot was also applied in practice under magisterial supervision in other areas.[43] Thus the effect of the land tenure system which applied in the Transkei was to limit the extent of landlessness and to inhibit the practice of capitalist agriculture, thereby making the means of subsistence widely available.

The widespread application of the principle of one-man-one-lot is worth stressing because of the common assumption that it was tribal backwardness that was responsible for the deteriorating state of agriculture in the Transkei and other reserves. Accordingly, it was often argued that were individual lots to be extended and their size increased, encouragement would be given to the adoption of modern techniques; and indeed, the Native Economic Commission (1930–2) argued for the introduction of an upper limit of 50 morgen of land for individual tenure in the seven surveyed districts of the Transkei to allow for the development of 'progressive' farming.[44] But such a view ignored the function of the one-man-one-lot system in providing for the basis of subsidization of the mines. Thus although various officials would themselves have encouraged a transition to a more flexible land system which would have allowed scope to peasant–capitalist farming,[45] their cautious advocacy of change was always subordinated to the white economic interest. Again, the Mine Natives' Wage Commission put the point quite explicitly:

> It is clear ... that, having regard to the circumstances of the Witwatersrand gold mining industry, the migratory system of peasant labour must continue. Any other policy would bring about a catastrophic dislocation of the industry and consequent prejudice to the whole economic structure of the Union. But if that system is to continue, then the combined income of those labourers from wages and their Reserve production should provide them and their families with a proper livelihood, not only for the period during which the man is at work on the mines, but for such period of stay in the Reserves as will enable him to maintain his tribal association, keep in reasonable touch with his family, preserve his health, and retain an adequate control of the interests of his allotment.[46]

Thus the function of the reserves as suppliers of labour so cheap as to guarantee the profitability of capital (and the mines in particular) was never in doubt; and lament though there might be in plenty about deteriorating conditions in the reserves, the objects of official concern were overwhelmingly the symptoms of underdevelopment (such as soil erosion, declining productivity and so on) rather than the structural conditions which underlay them.

It was the high rate of labour migrancy which featured as the major characteristic of the reserve economy of the Transkei. By 1936, the recorded number of migrants had reached 152,392 (or approximately 13 per cent of the total African population), a figure which represented 23·5 per cent and 1·2 per cent of the male and female populations respectively. But even more critically, the male absentees as a percentage of males aged 18–54 years was 53 per cent.[47] In any one year, therefore, it may be presumed that over half the effective male workforce of the Transkei was away (the average period spent away at the mines being fourteen months), and the burden of agricultural activity was thus shifted on to the young, the women, the aged and the infirm. Moreover, such long periods of absenteeism had deleterious effects upon other aspects of family and social life.

Paucity of statistics make it impossible to relate in detail the work destinations of Transkeian migrants, but it appears that approximately a third of them found work with a variety of employers – such as mining enterprises concerned with coal, diamonds, manganese and lime, other private industry, farms and public services.[48] Significant numbers of workers were also drawn to the sugar industry in Natal, Pondoland being the main source of supply.[49] The other two-thirds found employment in the gold mines of the Witwatersrand, for which the Transkei and other Union reserves formed a major source of supply, as illustrated in Table 3.2. Available figures do not allow for its specific contribution to be differentiated, but an indication of its crucial importance to the mines can be gauged by the fact that by the late 1930s over three-quarters of recruits from the Cape were being drawn from the Transkei.[50] It was therefore the largest single supplier of labour from within the Union, providing something like a third of the mines' total requirements.

Table 3.2 *Geographical sources of black labour employed by the Chamber of Mines, 1906–43 (%)*

Year	Cape	Other Union Provinces	High Commission Territories	Mozambique	Other
1906	13·7	9·1	3·7	65·4	8·0
1916	33·0	16·2	11·6	38·1	1·1
1937	39·8	12·6	18·3	17·3	2·0
1940	37·8	13·8	20·5	21·4	6·5
1943	34·3	14·5	17·6	26·4	7·2

Sources: Francis Wilson (1972a), Table 8, p. 70; *The Native Reserves* (UG 32 – 1946), Annexure XVII, p. 79.

Given the inadequacy of the labour supply within South Africa, the gold mines had early cast their recruiting net far beyond the borders, the largest foreign supplier being Mozambique, which before and after Union offered a guaranteed minimum number of workers (themselves coerced) in return for a capitation fee for each recruit and an agreement to route sea-borne import traffic to the Johannesburg area through Lourenço Marques (now Maputo). In sum, from the earliest days, the mines remained dependent upon foreign sources of supply for over half (and often rather more) of their requirements, the importation of foreign workers offering additional advantage by effecting a downward pressure on African wage rates.

Within the Union, the availability of labour to the mines was inhibited by African economic independence and competitive recruitment by farmers, the diamond and coal mines and, increasingly, secondary and tertiary industry. As has already been seen, African autonomy was founded on peasant production and it had accordingly become vital for both the mining and white agricultural sectors that this be undermined. 'The tendency of the native is to be an agriculturalist who ... cares nothing if industries pine for want of labour when his crops and home-brewed drink are plentiful,' lamented the President of the Chamber of Mines in 1912, and it was therefore necessary for the state to implement coercive measures to force the African to earn his living by working for a wage, 'as every white man who is not a land-owner has to do'.[51] Thus, although the initial political pressure for the passing of the 1913 Land Act came from the farming interest, it gained the full support of the mining companies, which specifically advocated the policy of land dispossession in order to force labour out on to the market – and land limitation and the consequent pressures upon reserve agriculture were highly effective in leading to the intended increase in the mining workforce.

The other critical problem for the mines was the competitive pressure exerted upon the market by other employers, which not only threatened the supply of labour but tended to increase its price. Although Union Africans clearly found mine work less congenial than other employment, the imperative of cost minimization rendered the mining companies reluctant to overcome their repulsion by offering economic compensation, and accordingly the need for the 'rationalization' of recruitment procedures became obvious. The solution was therefore found in the formation of the Native Recruiting Corporation in 1912, which was designed to eliminate competition for labour between the individual mining companies (thereby reducing recruitment costs), while simultaneously enabling the adoption of industry-wide measures to increase the actual flow of labour and to order its distribution among the various mines. Thus the NRC was made responsible for recruitment of Africans from within the borders of the Union and the High Commission Territories, while the Witwatersrand Native Labour Association (established in 1896) operated in other territories.[52] Together, therefore, the NRC and WNLA constituted a monopoly buyer of labour for the mining industry, thereby greatly increasing the control of the companies over the market; and through the benefits of this centralization, the cost of recruiting Africans for work on the gold mines fell by about 20 per cent between 1913 and 1924.[53]

The NRC operated through a network of local branches, and by employing additional recruiters to whom it paid a capitation fee for every African secured for mine labour. Within the Transkei (and Ciskei) the large majority of these agents were European traders, who were located deep in the interstices of the reserve economy and formed a critical connecting link with the external market. The corporation guaranteed to take from each recruiter a certain number of labourers each month, the latter being subject to a financial penalty in cases of failure to provide a certain minimum (known colloquially as 'the quota') of able bodies but receiving compensation for every recruit not taken up.[54] In turn, traders who acted as agents stimulated recruitment by active debt inducement among reserve inhabitants. According to the President of the Chamber of Mines, speaking in 1912, it was only by 'paying out large sums to recruiters, who in turn endeavour to induce the natives to come to work by offers of loans and the wherewithal to pay their taxes and their debts to the local traders who have given them credit, that we have been able to keep up the supply of labour to what it is today'.[55] Thus by offering cash or credit loans to those in need, the latter were then encouraged to pay off their debts by signing up for the mines.

Statistics concerning black earnings on the gold mines are rare, but it is clear that while wage rates were unresponsive to rising expectations and costs of living, they were subject to a consistent downward pressure in the interests of cost minimization and profitability. 'As the result of education and increasing contact with European standards...' noted one commission, 'the wants of the Natives are becoming more numerous and diversified, while their earning power is not increasing in the same degree. The result is that they are becoming relatively poorer.'[56] Yet throughout the interwar period, the Chamber of Mines continuously justified its low wage rates by assuming that African subsistence requirements were remaining static, even though throughout this time migrant labourers and their families were needing to purchase more food and clothing, in addition to their exhibiting increased discretionary wants, such as education for their children and consumer items such as beds and lights, and foodstuffs such as coffee and sugar. Yet the Chamber remained impervious to requests for increased wages to cover rising aspirations, claiming that its provision of food and accommodation for its workers insulated them from inflation, and that dependants in rural areas were less affected by increasing costs of living than Africans upon the Rand.[57] But reserve inhabitants were involved in the cash economy through the medium of the European trader, who imported consumer goods and any accompanying inflation from the industrial areas, with the result that prices in the reserves tended to be considerably higher than elsewhere – and were subject to an overall rise in the interwar period taken as a whole. Yet wage rates varied only minimally, with total cash earnings by blacks on the mines remaining roughly constant.[58] Given increased numbers of blacks being employed, this implied a declining wage income in cash terms; between 1921 and 1934, for instance, the actual average earning per black mineworker declined from two shillings and twopence per shift to two shillings and one penny.[59]

Declining incomes found their reflection in reserve family budgets, which were subject also to the pressures of lowering agricultural productivity. Increased densities of population necessitated previously marginal land being brought into production, while simultaneously disallowing the periods of fallow required to enable soil to recover its fertility. At the same time, the migrant labour system had an adverse effect on agriculture in that it deprived households of much needed manpower, while chronic overstocking (which was related to traditional culture and economy, plus better veterinary care and lack of market opportunity to sell livestock) resulted in overgrazing and damage to the veld. In the words of the Native Economic Commission, the overall effect was 'denudation, donga erosion, deleterious plant succession, destruction of woods, drying up of springs, robbing the soil of its reproductive resources, in short *the creation of desert conditions*' (their italics);[60] and accordingly, reserve production became particularly dependent upon the elements and faltered sharply in inclement years. Thus for the Transkei in the years 1934–9, production amounted to an average of only 1·5 200-lb (90-kg) bags of grain per head per annum, compared to a minimum estimated requirement for subsistence of 2·75 bags, thereby necessitating the import of large quantities of grain for sale through the traders; and for the 1939–42 period, the average amount of grain available per head was 1·6 bags including imports.[61] 'For a number of years the Native population in the Transkeian Territories has been living very much below the bread line,' concluded the Mine Natives' Wages Commission[62] (while also reporting on similar conditions that prevailed in other reserves and Basutoland). The same body also produced detailed estimates on migrant labourers' budgets and the required cash income necessary for maintenance of their families at what it considered to be a reasonable standard of health. Calculations based upon an average family size of five and on an average absence of the adult male at the mines for fourteen months, a gap between actual income and the subsistence requirement was recorded for the Transkei as shown in Table 3.3. The social effects of such impoverishment were manifold: malnutrition was rife, there was a high rate of infantile mortality, and disease was widespread. Practically all these were associated with overcrowding, inadequate sanitation, impure water supplies and general poverty, and were to this extent considered by medical authority to be largely preventable. Simultaneously, the migra-

Table 3.3 *Budget for 2 years for family of 5 with adult male at work at mines for 14 months and living in the Transkei for 10 months*

	1939		1943	
	Surface worker	Underground worker	Surface worker	Underground worker
Expenditure	£87 17s. 0d.	£90 7s. 2d.	£111 16s. 3d.	£115 2s. 9d.
Income	£60 12s. 11d.	£65 2s. 2d.	£ 66 15s. 1d.	£ 71 4s. 4d.
Shortfall	£27 4s. 1d.	£25 5s. 0d.	£ 45 1s. 2d.	£ 43 18s. 6d.

Source: *Report of the Mine Natives' Wages Commission*, Table XXVIII, para. 242.

tory labour system was held responsible for a general instability in family life, and high rates of adult crime and juvenile delinquency.[63]

In addition, overlaid upon this chronic social decay was the asymmetric relationship between European commerce and reserve inhabitants, which raised further the cost of the latter's existence. This was particularly the case in the Transkei, where the traders had acquired for themselves a collective monopoly, after having played a vital early role in the expansion of the market economy. Thus the Land Act of 1913 which prohibited purchase of land by Europeans in scheduled native areas allowed for exceptions to the rule to be made by the express consent of the Governor-General,[64] and assurance was given at the time that the law would in no way interfere with the right of traders to sell their business sites to other whites.[65] Following this, Proclamation no. 11 of 1922 specified that no trading station should be allowed to operate within 5 miles (8 km), by the shortest route, of an existing site.[66] The effect and intention of this regulation was to defend white traders against competition, for although no reference was made to the different status of Africans, all such trading sites thus delimited had been taken up by Europeans many years previously. However, in response to the Native Economic Commission of 1930–2, which had strongly criticized white monopolization of reserve trade, concentration of such trade was restricted by Proclamation 164 of 1934 which laid down that no person who was owner or occupier of a trading site might trade at another place within 20 miles (32 km) of the former;[67] and Proclamation 244 of the same year lowered the protective radius against African traders, butchers and bakers to 2 miles (3·2 km), although competition was not to be free, and trading was to be by licence only.[68] The first measure was effective in ensuring that the European trading monopoly remained collective,[69] a primary characteristic being its family nature, with businesses being handed down from one generation to another; but the threat to white commercial domination posed by the second regulation was rendered ineffective because African traders had limited access to capital and faced considerable difficulty in obtaining credit from wholesalers in the Cape and Natal.[70]

The trader acted as a crucial link between the reserves and the external economy. Haines, writing in 1933, gave a graphic description of his role:

> More than churches, schools or magistrates, he seems to represent Western civilisation in the Territory. He penetrates every part of the country; he comes in contact with every section of the population. The witch-doctor buys alum from him, the naked baby begs sweets of him. He sells the products of Western industry; cloth from Great Britain and the United States, from Germany, Italy and Japan; iron pots from Birmingham; ploughs and saddles; Indian tea and South African sugar; American oil, Norwegian brisling. More than that, he buys from Natives to sell both to Natives and to Europeans; wool and hides for the East London market, and mealies and kaffir-corn and cattle, Native pipes and tobacco, to be re-sold to Natives. He is the Natives' chief creditor; apart

from credit sales of goods and grain and cattle he makes actual cash advances. And closely connected with this function are his activities as a recruiting agent; he is the most important direct cause of the Native 'drift' to the mines and to the towns.[71]

Yet from the outset, terms of trade were heavily slanted against reserve inhabitants – whether peasants or migrant labourers. Enjoying *de facto* local monopolies, traders were effectively the sole purchasers of agricultural produce offered for sale, while simultaneously being the single sellers of manufactured goods and foodstuffs and the only source of credit available to the average African family.

The trader was able to exploit his local predominance to make monopoly profits. Although the charge of price exploitation was commonly dismissed by reference to the willingness of Africans to walk long distances in order to make a small cash saving,[72] there is sufficient evidence to indicate that prices in the Transkei were generally higher than those operating elsewhere at the same time (allowance being made for transport expenses).[73] Yet it was through the extensive system of credit and advances which had developed that Africans encountered traders on the most disadvantageous terms, for – as has already been indicated – in his role as labour recruiter for the mines the trader engaged in deliberate debt inducement among his customers. The system became extensive during the 1890s when the mines enabled recruiters to make cash advances of £5 to each labourer, the latter making reimbursement from his wages; and accordingly, given the ease with which credit could be obtained, the amount of indebtedness was considerable. Bundy cites sixty-four traders in a single district as being owed about £100,000 in 1904,[74] and by 1933 total debts to traders in the Transkei were conservatively estimated as exceeding £500,000.[75] But credit represented good business to the traders, for cash sales realized only 50–60 per cent of the credit price, security being often offered by the debtor in the form of livestock (usually cattle) or by labourers opting to receive their mine wages under the Deferred Pay System, whereby they could receive their remuneration in a lump sum after their stay at the mines had been completed, the trader supplying their families with necessary goods during the interim. None the less, as poverty became more extensive, the amount of bad debts increased, so that the seizure of property by traders in settlement became more common; and a developing reluctance in the mid-1930s to receive wages under the Deferred Pay System may well have been linked to a desire by migrants to extricate themselves from the usurious network of credit.[76]

It was during the 1890s also that traders exhibited an increasing reluctance to purchase grain for cash, as opportunities for its resale on the open market were curtailed by cheap American imports, and the extension of the communication network brought European farming areas relatively closer to the urban areas, while leaving African producers on the periphery. There thus grew up the widespread practice whereby traders in the Transkei purchased grain by offering credit or goods in return (thereby tying the producer to their custom) and, later in the same season, reselling the crop back to the local community at a considerably higher price. Forced to sell their crop to meet tax obligations, repay debts or simply satisfy daily needs, necessity often compelled producers to repurchase grain from the traders later in the year at a cost 'never less than twice and more often three or four times the amount previously received by the Native from the trader for the same produce'.[77] In addition, by the 1930s half the total requirement of grain consumed in the Transkei was having to be imported from outside, and was subsequently sold at the Union retail price plus the cost of railage plus the margin of profit to the retailer; and by being so charged, the reserve inhabitants effectively subsidized European farmers, for whom the Maize Quota Act of 1931 secured a minimum price for grain by creating an artificial shortage on the domestic market.[78]

Their collective monopoly therefore served the traders well. Undertaking a function which could in more favourable circumstances have been readily performed by Africans, they were assured a livelihood that was financially secure and 'fairly profitable'.[79] Large fortunes made in trading were reportedly rare, but so were bankruptcies and individual traders were protected from the cold winds of competition. In turn, their good fortune encouraged their entering a paternalistic relationship with their customers, fulfilling the role of family doctor, adviser and lawyer in times of stress, while simultaneously their profit was absorbing the meagre financial surplus of those to whose needs they so carefully attended.

If the traders constituted the locally dominant commercial class, the drawing of the Transkei into the orbit of capitalist economic relations led to the development of new forms of internal stratification within Xhosa society. Class differentiation was closely related to the emergence of the peasantry in the nineteenth century. Not unconnected with the divide between 'red' (or traditionalist) and 'school' people (who adopted Christianity, sought education and wore western clothing)[80] in that the latter evinced a greater willingness to undertake production for profit, peasantization was also related to differential access to land, labour and markets. At the upper end of the spectrum, there was a stratum which can be identified as having become small-scale capitalist farmers. Often having individual title to their land, such men sloughed off communal obligations to the extensive network of kin, and replaced them with profit-seeking activity and the employment of labour on wage terms. As such, they were in a similar class position to the smaller white farmers (to whom they represented a threat), except in so far as they had less access to political power. This subsequently proved critical in limiting their subsequent expansion as a group once white capital had secured the racial delimitation of land in its own favour in 1913.

Among the peasantry proper, it is possible to identify various strata:

the relatively successful (differentiated from capitalist farmers by their continuing reliance on family labour), and successive gradations of middle and marginal peasants, the latter's self-sufficiency being highly precarious, and on occasion pushing them over into wage labour as migrants. It was at this point that the peasantry shaded off into a class of individuals composed of those who had been made landless – and these constituted a rural proletariat, having nothing to offer but their labour.

The purpose of the Land Act of 1913 was to freeze the development of capitalist class relations in the reserve areas. By limiting the availability of land to blacks it sought to block the development of African capitalist farming; and by preserving the communal land system (as adjusted by the one-man-one-lot system of individual tenure), it attempted to retard the process of complete proletarianization by maintaining the ties of migrant labourers to the land. However, in a situation of growing scarcity of resources (notably of land) traditional distributive norms of African societies were subject to erosion by new competitive tendencies, with the result that reserve populations became increasingly stratified.

Within the Transkei, class formation primarily centred around access to the means of production in terms of stock ownership and land. As early as 1894, a magistrate at Nqamakwe remarked that: 'the property is very unevenly distributed. Some natives own thousands of sheep and hundreds of cattle ... whilst others ... and these forming far the larger portion – own very little, if any stock'.[81] Although little research has yet been done in this sphere, there is sufficient evidence to indicate that stock ownership remained (if it did not become increasingly) unequal over the next half century. Thus Fox and Back calculated in 1936 that only 20·7 per cent of the family units in the Transkei owned any sheep, and that of these over 50 per cent owned less than 20; and in one particular location ('considered an average one for the Territories'), three out of one thousand stock-owners owned 70 per cent of the sheep and 50 per cent of the cattle.[82] Similarly Jokl, reporting in 1941, found that about 33 per cent of all cattle were in the hands of only 5 per cent of the people.[83]

More detailed figures relating to uneven distribution of cattle-ownership were recorded for 1942 for seven districts in the Transkei which included 'about one-third of the total cattle, sheep and goat population'; these figures are set out in Table 3.4. This survey further reported that, taken overall, 44 per cent of families had no cattle at all, 20 per cent owned from one to five, and the remaining 36 per cent had five or more; while in the same districts, 47 per cent owned neither sheep nor goats, and of the sheep-owners 13·39 per cent possessed from one to five head and 25·22 per cent goat owners from one to five.[84] Such a pattern of stratification suggests, therefore, that the burden of impoverishment lay heavily upon the majority of the reserve population.

Inequality of stock ownership was in part related to differential control and access to land. Within the limits of the one-man-one-lot policy (pursued, as discussed earlier, even in areas held under communal tennure), there remained considerable scope for unequal usage. In the first place, land was still allocated by the chiefs and headmen (although in a later era coming rather more under magisterial control). Each homestead head was theoretically entitled to an arable plot of 5 morgen for each of his wives; once a plot was allotted, the occupier had exclusive use of it for cultivation. On the death of the landholder, however, the land reverted to the chief for reallocation.[85]

Table 3.4 *Distribution of cattle ownership in 7 districts of the Transkeian Territories in 1942*

District	Owners with 5 head and less No.	%	Owners with 5–25 head No.	%	Owners with more than 25 head No.	%	Total owners No.	%
Umtata	2,855	40	3,860	53	503	7	7,218	100
Engcobo	3,064	35	5,094	57	734	8	8,892	100
Nqanduli	1,880	31	3,635	61	471	8	5,986	100
Elliotdale	895	23	2,531	66	426	11	3,852	100
St Marks	2,883	49	2,682	46	320	5	5,885	100
Tsomo	2,076	49	1,989	47	154	4	4,219	100
Xalanga	1,034	32	1,969	61	228	7	3,231	100
TOTAL	14,687	37	21,760	56	2,836	7	39,283	100

Source: Table XI, Distribution of Cattle Ownership, Native Areas, in Social and Economic Planning Council (1946), p. 23.

In a situation of land scarcity, such a system worked to the advantage of the better-off – the chiefs' favourites, those wealthy enough to support more than one wife, or simply those who could pay the largest bribe (and corruption was allegedly widespread). If when the land was in plentiful supply this meant that the wealthier strata received the pick of the best, in a situation of absolute shortage it was bound to lead to the development of landlessness among the least well off. And so it happened: as the area of land available for allotment remained practically unchanged and as the population grew in size, the number of persons without any exclusive use of land increased. Thus according to the Chief Magistrate in 1943, 16,100 of an estimated 63,750 married males in the seven surveyed districts, and 3,590 such males in the unsurveyed districts, were landless. Yet these figures cannot be taken as a wholly accurate guide, for the effect of communal tenure was to disguise landlessness from the European eye. Persons without land were usually given kraal sites on the commonages, or resided with their kin; but whereas such households were readily identifiable to official authority in the surveyed areas, they were far less evident in the unsurveyed areas, for 'one effect of surveying and granting individual tenure [was] to make visible the actual shortage of land'.[86] Accordingly, it seems highly probable that the proportion of the population that was landless in the surveyed districts (some 25 per cent) was not unrepresentative for the entire Transkei, the significance of this being that this fraction had no access to reserve subsistence and was consequently wholly dependent for its livelihood on the sale of its labour. The effects of differential stock ownership and unequal access to land were considerable, but in particular it hastened the process of underdevelopment by promoting the dependence of the Transkei upon the external economy, and reducing its capacity for self-sufficiency in the provision of foodstuffs. Sheep had been introduced into the Transkei relatively late, but by 1936 they outnumbered cattle by three to one, the reason being the profitability of selling wool on the Union market. But given the concentration of sheep ownership, it was only a relatively small minority which benefited from wool production; yet the sheep population was responsible for taking up a major portion of the grazing land, to such an extent that some commentators held that sheep farming was the main cause of overstocking in that it was driving the cattle off the land. However, whereas the return on sheep was mainly financial, cattle provided milk and oxen for draught purposes. Accordingly, given that stockowners – however large – had unrestricted access to communal grazing land, profit from wool production which accrued to a small minority was made at direct cost to the wider community, and was one factor accountable for the high level of malnutrition. What was more, there was a considerable overlap between economic and political power, with a consequent tendency for the traditional authority structure (as adapted to magisterial rule) to become increasingly oppressive of the general populace:

> a small minority, consisting mostly of Bunga councillors, headmen and chiefs are gaining a small income from wool at the expense of the food supplies of the majority ... unequal distribution is on the increase and the actual number of stock owners in proportion to the total number of family units is undoubtedly decreasing and will continue to do so as long as the system of communal grazing continues ... In this connection it is significant that any suggestions made at the General Council meetings of the Bunga in connection with the restriction of stock ownership or the use of communal grazing are always strongly opposed by the Native councillors, some of whom own as many as 3,000 sheep, and the majority at least 200 head of small stock and fifty head of cattle apiece.[87]

Thus differentiation between classes in contemporary Transkei can be fully comprehended only against the background of the emergence of capitalist class relations in the colonial past. In particular, what is stressed here is that although the reserves were transformed into labour reservoirs for the white economy, this did not entail a process of homogeneous proletarianization. Although the majority of the population became dependent upon the earnings of migrant labour, it was only a proportion of these who became fully proletarianized in the sense of being entirely separated from the means of production; a larger element retained its access to the land, even though agriculture provided a diminishing element in their subsistence requirement. However, their continuing involvement in the subsistence economy as landholders rendered them subject to the authority of the traditional political élite, the latter now bolstered by wealth derived from the production of wool for sale on the external market. There remained too, perhaps, a residual peasant element which did not rely upon migrancy for its livelihood; and there was, in addition, a small group of Africans who found employment as teachers, clergymen and low-level public employees within the Transkei. But the fundamental divide was between the migrant labourers and the élite, mainly chiefly and political; and it is to the expression of this cleavage through the colonial political institutions that we now must turn.

Administration and politics

Superimposed upon the reserve economy of the Transkei was an administrative structure of 'direct rule'. Headed by the Chief Magistrate (who answered directly to the Minister of Native Affairs), the system centred upon the white magistrates who were each responsible for supervising a wide array of government functions in one of the twenty-six Districts. Thus it fell upon the magistrates to collect taxes, supervise welfare payments and, as their official designation suggested, dispense justice according to the law to both black and white. They served also as the link between the districts and the departmental authorities in Umtata which were responsible for local engineering and agricultural matters, while simultaneously supervising the allocation of land by headmen and arbitrating in cases of boundary disputes. It was their task also to serve as political agents, quelling unrest and reporting to higher authority any disruptive elements which threatened the docility of reserve life. 'As for the Native people,' wrote S. P. Bunting in 1929, 'our general impression is that they are far more held down here than anywhere else in South Africa. By a long regime of "segregation" and congestion, all the stuffing seems to have been knocked out of them...' (although he went on to add that it was rather bottled up, 'with a very heavy official hand on the cork').[88]

The system was one of 'direct rule' because administrative authority was delegated not to the chiefs, but to officially appointed headmen. The chiefs were originally suspect in government eyes because they had been the foci of resistance to the colonial intrusion, and in the unsettled years of the post-annexation era there was no guarantee that they would not again resort to a call to arms. Consequently, policy aimed specifically at undermining the legitimacy of the chiefs by stripping them of their functions. Thus the magisterial districts were deliberately overlaid upon the formerly autonomous chiefdoms – in some cases cutting across their boundaries – and were, in turn, divided into about thirty to forty locations, over each of which was placed a headman, a non-traditional figure, whose authority derived ultimately not from popular acceptance but from colonial appointment. Although these headmen were in practice usually elected by the people of the location, such election was subject to ratification by white authority, which also retained the right to dismiss the appointee for incompetence or for otherwise incurring displeasure; and while succession was usually (although by no means exclusively) effectively based on heredity (the headman being replaced by his son), the office was always regarded as distinct and separate from the structure of the chieftaincy. Men of wealth and held in public esteem though individuals might be, they were commonly regarded as instruments of alien control, and earned themselves the title of *isibanda*, or 'poles' supporting the colonial administration.[89]

The position of the headman was not an easy one to fill. They had a wide array of functions to carry out, and at the behest of magisterial authority were expected to implement such unpopular measures as registering taxpayers, collecting dues and enforcing agricultural improvement measures, as well as being instrumental in the allocation of land. Their role was therefore essentially coercive, however much particular individuals might attempt to conform to communal notions of relatively consensual authority; and given that the accompaniment of unpopularity was a paltry financial reward, many headmen were susceptible to seeking financial compensation in the form of gifts and bribes.[90]

The chiefs, meanwhile, were excluded from the bureaucratic hierarchy. Whereas previously their role had been pivotal to the entire structure of tribal authority, their official responsibility was now reduced to merely arbitrating in civil cases according to customary law, and even then they lacked the legal right to enforce decisions, and litigants were entitled to remove their complaints to magisterial courts for a hearing *de novo*. Nor could the chief try criminal cases, a consequence of which was that they were no longer able to sanction or 'eat up' (that is, confiscate cattle of) recalcitrant subjects. Yet precisely because they were excluded from the structure of administration, chiefs were to some extent shielded from popular disaffection and did not suffer the same disrepute as the bureaucratically appointed headmen, for they were less identified with white authority. Accordingly, they managed to retain considerable backstage influence, and the integrity of chieftaincy was to prove remarkably resilient.[91] Indeed, it was upon this retention of public respect that the Bantu Authorities system – which later more than restored the authority of the chiefs – sought to capitalize. Yet such an attempt was based upon a fundamental misunderstanding, for by the 1950s the changes wrought in reserve society by the processes of underdevelopment had thoroughly eroded any bases for the re-establishment of a traditionally oriented political obligation; and official recognition was effectively to kill chieftaincy as a popularly based institution.

Parallel to the administrative structure was the Council or 'Bunga' system, which allowed for a limited measure of representation.[92] A conciliar system was originally proposed by the Cape Native Laws and Customs Commission of 1883, which urged the importance of incorporating a consultative process into the workings of magisterial rule, but the idea was not taken up until some ten years later by Cecil Rhodes, then Prime Minister of the Cape, when he introduced his Glen Grey Bill (to become Act no. 25 of 1894) into the Cape legislature. The Act, as we have seen above, introduced limited freehold tenure to the Glen Grey area, and simultaneously provided for a tax to drive out a supply of labour into white employment; but in addition it established a District Council and a lower tier of Location Boards, the latter consisting of three landholders in a location and appointed by authority after consideration of expressed local preference. The Council, consisting of six African nominees and six members elected by the Location Boards (subject to approval from on high), was to hold office for three years and to meet under the chairmanship of the Resident Magistrate, and its function was to fix rates of taxation upon the community (within strictly defined limits) in order to meet the expenses of administration, road maintenance, tree planting and other local projects. 'Children just emerged from barbarism' should be taught first to manage their own local affairs, declared Rhodes, who further outlined the purpose of the Bill as being:

> to keep the minds of the natives occupied ... If they allowed them to think of their roads and bridges, and even to deal with the appointment of scab inspectors and with the planting of forests, they would occupy their minds usefully ... Having proposed that they should form councils, so that it should not be a farce, he let them tax themselves, and gave them funds to spend in the matter of building bridges ...[93]

Yet the full thrust of the measure related to its provision that land allotted under individual tenure should be regarded as held under communal tenure for purposes of parliamentary registration, and the effect of this was to disqualify such owners from legal claim to the Cape franchise; and indeed, this was an important motive behind the passing of the Bill.

Prior to 1882, the Colony's non-racial franchise gave the vote to male adults who could show an annual income of £50 or who occupied premises worth £25 per annum, but in that year the passing of the Franchise and Ballot Act raised the occupational qualification to £75, the intention being to limit the number of African voters. However, the incorporation of the Transkei proper into the Cape in 1885 provoked white fears that the electoral roll would be swamped by so-called 'blanket votes'; and consequently this possibility was eliminated by the Parliamentary Registration Act of 1887, which barred communally held land as qualification for franchise registration. But such devices met with considerable opposition from members and factions in the Cape legislature which were dependent upon the African vote in a number of constituencies. In his 1894 Act, therefore, Rhodes opted for a compromise course and, instead of seeking to abolish the *existing* African vote, he rather sought to limit *potential expansion* of the African franchise by excluding individual tenure under the Glen Grey system as a basis for parliamentary registration; and he simultaneously introduced the Council system as an explicit compensation for the limitation on franchise rights contained in the selfsame Act.

The Glen Grey system was extended to the Transkei immediately by Proclamation 352 of 1894, whereby Councils were established in the Butterworth, Idutywa, Nqamakwe and Tsomo districts, although in these cases membership was reduced to six (four being nominated by headmen and two by the Governor), with meetings being chaired by the Resident Magistrates and being held quarterly. Decisions and recommendations were then forwarded to a further body, the Transkeian General Council (later known as the Transkeian Territories General Council), which was composed of the Chief Magistrate of the Transkei, his four white subordinates and eight African members elected by a joint annual meeting of the four District bodies. Powers and functions of the TGC were much the same as in Glen Grey.

From these beginnings, the system was extended gradually throughout the Transkei, councils being established in the seven districts of Thembuland and Griqualand by 1903, with Xalanga being the last district to join in 1925; meanwhile, a similar network of councils was inaugurated in Western Pondoland in 1911, finding an apex in the Pondoland General Council, districts in Eastern Pondoland coming to participate in the latter in 1927. The two General Councils were then amalgamated in 1931 to form the United Transkeian Territories General Council, which by Proclamation 191 of 1932 was enabled to consider any matter relating to economic and social conditions of Union Africans generally, although its competence in this sphere was purely advisory. Presiding over a population of about a million, it raised taxes which amounted to some £170,000 per annum in the 1930s and 1940s, from which revenue its task was to undertake the limited functions laid down for its predecessor bodies by Rhodes – the maintenance and construction of roads, bridges, dipping tanks and irrigation schemes – while also providing for rudimentary agricultural and medical services. While this was sufficient to impress many contemporary observers as a notable experiment in training Africans to govern themselves,[94] its advisory role and its inability to cope financially and politically with the problems of reserve impoverishment made its instrumental significance of little consequence.

However, in spite of its inherent limitations, the functioning of the Bunga is of interest because it both indicates a general African concern with exclusion from the centre of political power in the Union as a whole, while simultaneously revealing by its composition and its local concerns the nature of the Transkeian political élite.

Although the Bunga was supposed to confine itself to discussion of non-political issues, a prominent theme in its debates was dissatisfaction with the erosion of the African franchise in the Cape and its demands for extension of political rights to blacks throughout the Union.[95] In essence, the Council system was never accepted as adequate compensation for direct African influence in the Union Parliament and this rejection of Rhodes's condescending compromise as provided for in the Glen Grey Act found vehement expression in councillors' discussion. This was particularly notable in the period from 1926, when Prime Minister Hertzog first introduced a proposal to eliminate entirely African suffrage in the Cape, and in 1936, when legislation was passed which removed African voters from the common roll and established the advisory Natives' Representative Council (as well as providing for the addition of more land to the Reserves up to 13 per cent of the total area of the Union).

The Representation of Natives in Parliament Bill and the Natives Land Act (1913) Amendment Bill of 1926 had the twin objectives of abolishing the African franchise and, in echo of Rhodes, extending the council system to cater for African political aspirations while simultaneously making for a further provision of land to the reserves. Rejected by both Parliament and urban African opinion (for rather different reasons), Hertzog's proposals were also strongly opposed by the Bunga, which set up an all-African committee to formulate its views for dispatch to the government. The subsequent report was an emphatic condemnation of the entire enterprise, stating that there was no justification for depriving Africans of the vote. While extension of the council system and the addition of more land to African areas were acceptable when taken separately, they were in no way regarded as providing an equal exchange for abolition of the Cape vote, which was regarded as a fundamental right. 'In regard to the franchise we are afraid of losing the substance we have now got for a thing we have not seen,' noted one councillor.[96]

The 1936 proposals received an equally negative response. The government's intention to abolish the existing form of franchise met with the council's 'profound disapproval', and the proposal to remove African voters from the common roll was regarded as tantamount to abolishing African citizenship. Similarly, the provision of three white members to represent Africans in the House of Assembly and the establishment of the advisory Natives' Representative Council were seen as no substitute for direct representation in Parliament. In any case, three representatives could not adequately defend African interests in an Assembly of 150, and the additional land and the extension of the council system had already been foreshadowed by the 1913 Land Act and the Native Affairs Act of 1920 respectively. The proposed bargain was thus essentially fraudulent, since the government intended to take away the vote and make payment for it in coin which Africans should by right already possess.[97]

But protest was to no avail, and Fusion (the merger in 1934 of the Government and Opposition parties under Hertzog and Smuts respectively to form the United Party) was sealed by the passage of the 'Native bills'. Yet just as the African National Congress continued to call for restoration of the franchise and African representation in Parliament, so did the Bunga reiterate the same demand – that Africans be granted full political rights as citizens. Thus motions were lodged opposing segregation (1943), deploring the denial of civil rights to Africans and racial discrimination (1945), and calling for an increase in the number of members representing Africans in the House of Assembly from three to thirty (1947) and the right of Africans to sit in Parliament (1948).[98] The request for direct representation in the legislature was repeated in 1952, and was then more forcefully restated the following year when councillors resolved that Africans should be represented in Parliament by their own people in proportion to their number. Similarly, the Bunga endorsed the action of the Natives Representatives' Council when that body terminated its own sessions in protest at the government's failure to consult it about the Witwatersrand miners' strike in 1946 and also called for the NRC to be granted legislative authority with respect to African affairs.[99]

Yet despite its resolute opposition to political segregation, the Bunga cannot be viewed as anything but a largely conservative body. Indeed, as far as discriminatory legislation was concerned, it was mainly echoing demands that were being more forcefully put by urban-centred African movements. But its feelings towards the latter were plainly ambivalent. While there was sympathy with their broader objectives, there was also concern that their activities might bring African representations into disrepute or provoke adverse reaction from the government; and more particularly there was apprehension that such bodies might undermine traditional political authority. Thus in 1925 criticism was directed at the ANC for organizing a boycott of the visit to South Africa of the Prince of Wales, disparaging reference being made to 'people whose character is known to be bad in having gone to Johannesburg and organized a Native Congress';[100] and during the election of 1929, the Thembu Paramount called for immediate action to be taken against S. P. Bunting, the communist candidate, who was making 'dangerous statements' at campaign meetings in the Transkei (another councillor adding darkly that he was also preaching equality).[101]

This inherent conservatism was reflective of the Bunga's composition, for it is clear that it was a body primarily representative of the upper stratum of reserve society. Indeed, the Glen Grey Act and the council system gave political voice to the overlapping categories of bureaucrat–headmen, chiefs and richer peasants. Reference has already been made to the fact that councillors were generally men of wealth, owning large numbers of stock; and as such, they were crucially concerned with measures of agricultural improvement, a fact that was noted approvingly by many observers as a sign of progressiveness. Yet such matters were essentially the concern of a locally prominent class, for while expenditure by the Bunga on agricultural schools, soil conservation and stock breeding might indeed accrue to the general well-being, the benefits were likely to be unequally distributed, favouring mostly those who had extensive agricultural holdings. Indeed, that at times class interests overrode other considerations was plainly apparent. In 1909, for instance, when a credit system on the lines of a Land Bank was mooted in the TTGC, one councillor approved of it 'because it appeared it would not help everyone. Poor people would not reap any advantage from it. It would only raise those who already had property ... It was good that men who desired to improve their position should be given the opportunity to do so.'[102] Similarly, later recommendations that there be limits to stock ownership or that communal grazing rights (of particular benefit to large stock owners) be curbed, met with considerable opposition.

The specific class nature of the Bunga was provided for by its particular method of election and selection. The UTTGC consisted of a total of 108 members, thirty of whom were *ex officio* – the Chief Magistrate, the twenty-six Magistrates (otherwise known as Native Commissioners) and the three Paramount Chiefs of Thembuland, and Eastern and Western Pondoland. The remainder of the members were elected by electoral colleges, each composed of four elected members and two government nominees – yet the extent to which the electoral system allowed for meaningful participation was extremely limited.

When the council system had first been introduced there had been considerable opposition, as the new councils were perceived as a threat to their interests by different segments of the Transkeian élite. In Qumbu and Tsolo, for instance, resistance was led by headmen and wealthier farmers who saw the councils as encroaching upon their local influence. In Glen Grey itself (then in the Ciskei), Xalanga and Idutywa, opposition was voiced mainly by Christian, educated and relatively prosperous peasants, many of whom possessed the Cape vote, and who feared that extension of the council system would not only undermine their local prominence relative to headmen and the less well-to-do, but would threaten their participation in the colonial polity. In Pondoland, meanwhile, where chieftaincy remained strong, both paramounts feared that the councils would dilute their power in relation to the administration.[103]

The opposition to the Glen Grey system, which reached its climax in the years 1902–6, was thus led by the élite, and pressed through the established channels of protest (via meetings with officials and submission of appeals). Its effect was to delay implementation, but resistance was steadily overcome by a combination of administrative action taken against extreme 'agitators' and the grant of strategic concessions to the élite. For instance, in the earliest years of direct rule, District Councils had been made up of four members nominated by headmen and two by the Governor of the Cape, but after complaint by the Transkei Vigilance Association (a body of African ratepayers led by E. Mamba, a labour agent from Idutywa), the system was changed in 1906 to allow for wider electoral participation in the surveyed districts. Subsequently, similar reform was provided for in 1911 in the unsurveyed districts and the elective principle became operative generally in 1925 (although in

Western Pondoland councillors were nominated by the chiefs).[104]

Under the reformed system, ratepayers (landholders) in each electoral ward would meet to elect three representatives triennially. In turn, the latter would meet with similar men from other wards to select four of their number to sit on the District Council, where they would still be accompanied by two government nominees; finally, these bodies would elect three representatives from among themselves to serve on the Bunga.

The result of this tortuously indirect method of election was that councils' membership came to be heavily biased in favour of men of local affluence and influence. Thus Hammond-Tooke records that in 1955, while some 76 per cent of the 138 District Councillors were either chiefs or headmen, the majority of these (60 out of a total of 105) were elected members; meanwhile, the rest of the councillors consisted of a motley group of 'peasant farmers', 'farmers' and a handful of agricultural demonstrators, businessmen, teachers and clerks.[105] Yet even the latter were representative of a stratum which was distinguished from the mass by its access to the means of wealth within the Transkei. Migrant labourers and their dependants – the vast majority of reserve inhabitants – had no occupational representative of their own (although doubtless a number of councillors had personal experience of conditions on the mines); and at the same time the prominence of chiefs as councillors testifies to their continuing influence in rural areas, despite their playing only a limited role within the structure of administration.

The unrepresentative character of the Bunga – the fact that it was the mouthpiece of the upper stratum of contextually wealthy traditional leaders, bureaucrats and farmers – serves to explain its conservatism. All its demands were moderate; and even in the political sphere its requests for the retention or extension of the franchise and for representation in Parliament were essentially conservative in the sense that they sought to maintain (and later, to re-establish) non-racial rights allowed for by the Act of Union. At the same time, given that the overwhelming majority of Bunga councillors were effectively civil servants, deriving income from the state, their discussions and debates were understandably inhibited by the presence of white officials. Furthermore, it has to be remembered that the council was toothless; it had only the right to advise – and its motions and protests were commonly ignored.[106] It was for this reason that the Bunga was generally regarded with apathy by the mass, so that while increasing numbers of the educated came to dismiss it as an irrelevance, or a 'talking shop' (the usual epithet), popular grievance was to find alternative outlet in various movements of rural protest.

Popular discontent was early registered in the form an anti-dipping movement which followed the outbreaks of East Coast fever in 1897 and 1912–13.[107] Compulsory dipping of sheep had been implemented in the 1890s, and had not been generally opposed as many were dependent for cash upon the sale of wool. But the spread of the fever (which decimated herds within the Territories and posed a severe threat to white agriculture beyond) prompted the administration to increase taxation (through the councils where they existed) so as to finance the extension of preventive measures. At a time when the rural economy was under severe pressure (notably in 1912 when the effects of disease were exacerbated by severe drought), few could afford the extra impositions, especially when it was popularly considered that the dipping regulations were worse than ineffective (as complaint was registered, for instance, that weekly trips to dipping tanks weakened remaining animals, and that congregation of cattle at the tanks helped to spread rather than curb the disease). In consequence, East Coast fever regulations represented a major intrusion into the reserve economy which was already under strain, with the result that passive resistance to dipping in many areas was supplemented by violent actions elsewhere (notably in Matatiele, Mount Frere and Mount Fletcher districts, where in 1914 dipping tanks and sheds were destroyed, telegraph wires cut and a number of trading stores looted). Where the chieftaincy was still strong (especially in Pondoland and Thembuland), it was used to counter disaffection, but in other areas the conciliar élite was pressed into collaborating with the administration in enforcing the regulations, with the result that the councils rapidly became objects of popular dislike.

The anti-dipping movement was largely unco-ordinated, sporadic and localized, but its significance lay in its being led from outside the ranks of the élite and operating from a mass base. In general, it had found most support in districts such as Fingoland and East Griqualand which had been most thoroughly subjected to colonial penetration (in contrast to other areas which were more isolated or which, like Pondoland, still retained a measure of economic autonomy). Similarly, it was in the former districts, where the system of migrant labour was most advanced and households generally more dependent upon wage and price levels, that a popularly based movement arose in the early 1920s aimed at using the boycott of trading stores as a response to perceived exploitation.

Isolated instances of boycott had occurred before (one trader in Butterworth had been boycotted for fourteen days for his refusal to supply grain on credit in 1920), but in early 1922 an extensive boycott movement spread from Herschel (on the borders of the Territories) to other areas in the southern Transkei, taking particular root in Qumbu in East Griqualand. A notable feature of the activity was that it was centred upon the women, for it was they who in the absence of male labour were forced to bear the brunt of rural pressure; and furthermore, the movement was organized in that its grievances were articulated by the 'most advanced' women (churchgoers and the wives and daughters of mission-educated menfolk), pickets were mounted at stores to prevent trade and emissaries were dispatched throughout surrounding districts to spread the word of protest. But such activities were of little immediate avail, for the administration swiftly curbed disaffection through the headmen, and traders themselves responded to boycott by refusing to buy produce and withdrawing credit until normal business was resumed, with the result that the movement came to a swift, untimely end. Thereafter, the major response to rural distress was exhibited indirectly through a number of millenarian movements which spread throughout the Territories, the most influential being that led by Wellington Buthelezi, who adapted the ideas of Marcus Garvey to proclaim the imminent arrival of Negroes in aeroplanes to liberate those who believed.[108]

Millenarianism subsided in the 1930s, and was followed by a period of relative quiescence which may be tentatively ascribed to two factors. First, with the system of labour migrancy entrenched, the council system successfully established and dipping reluctantly accepted, the administration made no more radical demands upon the rural economy. Secondly, the extent of rural distress seems to have been eased by limited, and shortlived, agricultural recovery which centred around a remarkable increase in the number of stock to reach record levels in the 1930s, this mitigating the worst effects of rural poverty. But if this recovery served as an ultimate testament to the effectiveness of disease control measures, it also led to overstocking and further deterioration of grazing land throughout the reserve. The improvement in agriculture was therefore marginal, as indicated by its failure to provide for the re-emergence of a surplus-producing peasantry, even though the rural élite was contemporaneously much engaged in the formation of farmers' associations and joining officially sponsored agricultural co-operatives (which were first promoted in 1926 and numbered thirty-nine by 1935).[109]

The succession of anti-dipping, anti-trader and millenarian movements points to a widening gap between the rural élite and the mass of reserve inhabitants. This forms a backcloth to all that followed after, in particular the decision of the Bunga in 1955 to accept its own abolition as a body and its replacement by a Territorial Authority under the widely unpopular Bantu Authorities system, which – as has been seen – sought to re-establish the power of the chiefs in explicit denial of the demands of African mass movements such as the ANC for a wider and more meaningful participation in the central polity. Yet why did the Bunga (whose dominant element was composed of headmen who would not be able to sit by right in the Territorial Authority) accept a change which so clearly ran counter to popular African feeling and which would serve to further exacerbate the gap between élite and mass?

The answer is twofold. First, the Bantu Authorities system had not yet been accepted in any Native Reserve, and the government was correspondingly eager to see it implemented. Considerable pressure was therefore exerted upon councillors to accept the new system when a motion to this effect was put to them during the 1955 session. A bevy of white officials from Pretoria were in attendance, and the opening address was delivered by M. D. C. de Wet Nel, MP (later to become Minister of Native Affairs), who warned the members that their authority was being undermined by intrusive social and political forces, and that unless chiefs and headmen opted to stand 'in the forefront of development ... the tribe would throw them overboard'.[110]

Secondly, the Bantu Authorities system offered both chiefs and headmen substantive new powers and opportunity for material accumulation. Previously, chiefs had enjoyed only limited judicial authority, but now they were no longer regarded as a threat to colonial rule and were viewed rather as potential allies against emergent nationalism. Accordingly, they were now offered *ex officio* membership of a Territorial Authority which would have considerably greater powers of administration and taxation than had been enjoyed by the Bunga; they were guaranteed effective control over Regional Authorities; and they were promised an integral participatory role in the maintenance of law and order. Similarly, although headmen were to lose their right to sit in the Bunga, they were assured of greater local influence from within the framework of Tribal Authorities (the bottom tier of the Bantu Authorities hierarchy), which would themselves have powers of taxation.[111]

Notwithstanding these enticements, there were a number of councillors who were reluctant to abandon the long-established Bunga system; and one suggested the appointment of a recess committee to consider the matter. But the heavy hand of the officials then intervened, and indicated that such a committee would be acceptable only if the principle of Bantu Authorities received prior approval. The councillors, unaccustomed to rejecting authoritative 'guidance', accordingly accepted the motion without dissent – and in so doing (although it was by no means clear at the time) they set the Transkei on the path which led to its becoming the first politically 'independent' bantustan in 1976.

Notes

1. Saunders (1974).
2. Monica Wilson (1969), p. 249.
3. Davenport (1977), p. 102.
4. Monica Wilson (1959, 1969).
5. Hammond-Tooke (1975), p. 9. Note that chieftaincy among the Mfengu was so weakened by the emigration occasioned by the *Mfecane* that many commentators refer to them as chiefless. However, after the implementation of the Bantu Authorities system, the South African government ethnologist successfully 'found' rightful heirs to a number of Mfengu chieftaincies.
6. Davenport (1977), p. 52.
7. Hammond-Tooke (1965); and (1975), pp. 31–41.
8. The right-hand house was composed of the second wife of a chief, and her children.
9. Monica Wilson (1969), pp. 223–4.
10. Davenport (1977), p. 53.
11. Mayer (1974).
12. Bundy (1979), p. 29.

13. Monica Wilson (1969), pp. 233–8; Bundy (1979), pp. 29–32; and Legassick (1975).
14. Monica Wilson (1969), p. 252.
15. Davenport (1977), pp. 99–103.
16. ibid., pp. 101–2.
17. For the cattle-killing, see also Hunter (1936), p. 561; and Roux (1964), pp. 32–44.
18. Hammond-Tooke (1975), pp. 21–4.
19. Le Cordeur (1974).
20. Thompson (1971), pp. 278–81.
21. See, for example, Theal (1908–10).
22. See the works of W. M. Macmillan (for instance, *Complex South Africa*, 1930); and de Kiewiet (1941).
23. For a general survey, see Monica Wilson (1971). For an influential analysis of a similar phenomenon elsewhere in Southern Africa, see Arrighi (1973). And for a study of colonial Lesotho, see Kimble (MA thesis, 1979).
24. Limitations of space prohibit a more extensive discussion of what constitutes a peasant community. My definition derives from three main sources: Wolf (1966); Saul and Woods (1973); and Post (1972).
25. Bundy (D. Phil. thesis, 1976) and (1979). Abbreviated versions of Bundy's material are to be found in his articles (1972 and 1977). My discussion of the peasant factor in Transkeian development is heavily dependent upon Bundy's work, to which I am accordingly much indebted. In the next few pages, therefore, I have chosen to avoid detailed note references and readers wishing to pursue this topic should refer to Bundy's own writings.
26. Bundy (1972), pp. 376–7.
27. Beinart (1974a), p. 5.
28. ibid.; and also (1974b). See also Beinart's MA thesis (1973).
29. Beinart (1974a), pp. 21–6.
30. Cape Parliamentary Papers G3 – 1994, III, p. 5 (1894).
31. Bundy (1979), p. 124.
32. Quoted in Roux (1964), p. 219.
33. Social and Economic Planning Council, Report no. 9 (UG 32 – 1946), Table I, p. 8.
34. ibid., para. 36. Using a rather different computation to arrive at the population statistics, Table I in this report gives the 1916 and 1936 densities for the Transkei as 65·6 and 79·5 respectively.
35. Beinart (1974b), pp. 8–10.
36. Bundy (D.Phil. thesis, 1976), pp. 164–71. Beinart (1974a) calculates that cattle losses from East Coast fever in Pondoland were as heavy as from rinderpest, but that their impact was made more destructive by a drought in 1911–12 (pp. 21–2).
37. Macmillan (1930), p. 212.
38. Beinart (1974b), p. 3; and Horrell (1978), p. 242.
39. *Witwatersrand Mine Natives' Wages Commission,* (UG 21 – 1944), para. 222. In a private communication with the author, Professor Jeffrey Butler has queried whether the 'level of subsistence' was defined as the basis for wage policy, arguing that the Commission's acknowledgement of the logic of the system in 1944 is no evidence that the mines so calculated wage rates earlier in the century. Being distant from archival sources at the time of revision of

this point, it has been impossible to substantiate my approach by appropriate quotation. However, Bundy (1979, pp. 114–15) – among others – has clearly demonstrated that mine-owners on the Rand were unhappily aware of the autonomy offered to African peasants by the retention of access to land and therefore perceived a need to introduce extra-economic coercion to induce them to part with their labour. Conversely, therefore, it is no great jump to suggest that the mine-owners were aware that subsistence production on the reserve plot would not cease automatically once the able-bodied male was away, while Johnstone (1976, pp. 34–5) has demonstrated with considerable rigour the measures taken by mine-owners to secure what he terms the 'ultra-cheapness' of non-white labour, the system operating so as to secure the recruitment and employment of Africans at 'a level of subsistence and cost chosen by the mining companies' (p. 38). See also the section on the Glen Grey Act below.
40. Davenport (1977), p. 118.
41. Hammond-Tooke (1975), pp. 84–8; and Bundy (1979), pp. 135–6.
42. Pim (1934), pp. 31–2.
43. *Native Economic Commission, 1930–32*, para. 141.
44. ibid., paras 140–7.
45. Pim (1934), pp. 32–6.
46. *Witwatersrand Mine Natives' Wages Commission*, para. 211.
47. Social and Economic Planning Council (UG 32 – 1946), paras 174, 176, and Table XXXIV, p. 45.
48. Board of Trade and Industries, Report no. 219 (1936), para. 23.
49. *The Welsh Report* (1935), para. 129.
50. The Transkei supplied roughly 77 per cent, 78 per cent and 78 per cent of mine employees recruited from the Cape in the years 1937, 1938 and 1939 respectively. Social and Economic Planning Council (1946), Annexure XVIII, p. 80.
51. Speech of the President to the Annual General Meeting of the Chamber of Mines, March 1912 (quoted by Johnstone, 1976, p. 27).
52. Francis Wilson (1972a), pp. 2–5.
53. Johnstone (1976), p. 31.
54. *The Welsh Report* (1936), paras 63–6.
55. Speech of the President to the Annual General Meeting of the Chamber of Mines, March 1912 (quoted by Johnstone, 1976, p. 28).
56. Board of Trade and Industries, Report no. 219 (1936), para. 11.
57. *Witwatersrand Mine Natives' Wages Commission* (1944), para. 109.
58. Francis Wilson (1972a), Table 5, p. 46.
59. *The Welsh Report* (1936), para. 94.
60. *Native Economic Commission, 1930–32*, para. 73.
61. Social and Economic Planning Council (1946), para. 202; *Mine Natives' Wages Commission* (1943), paras 138–40.
62. Para. 142.
63. For health and social conditions, see Fox and Back (1941).
64. Native Land Act, no. 27 of 1913, section 1, subsection 2.
65. Evidence of Mr T. L. Schreiner, representative of Thembuland in the House of Assembly, to *Natives Land Commission*, UG 19 – '16, II, 1916, p. 225.
66. Hart (1972), pp. 94–5.
67. *The Native Reserves* (1946), para. 46.

68. Hart (1972), p. 95.
69. In 1942, a total of 640 trading sites were reportedly distributed among 532 traders, with 463 traders occupying one site only, and the largest concern operating nineteen stores. Social and Economic Planning Council, 1946, para 46.)
70. Fox and Back (1941), p. 55.
71. Haines (1933).
72. See evidence of the Chief Magistrate of the Transkeian Territories cited in Social and Economic Planning Council (1946), para. 45. Little consideration seems to have been given to the notion that such ambulatory tendencies might themselves have been an indicator of poverty.
73. Fox and Back (1941), p. 56.
74. Bundy (1976), pp. 180–1.
75. Pim (1934), p. 22.
76. Haines (1933); and *The Welsh Report* (1936), paras 100–14.
77. Fox and Back (1941), p. 57.
78. Act no. 39 of 1931.
79. Haines (1933), p. 213.
80. Mayer (1961).
81. Cited in Bundy (1976), p. 176.
82. Fox and Back (1941), pp. 44–5.
83. Jokl (1941).
84. *Mine Natives' Wages Commission* (1944), paras 129–31, quoting the same survey.
85. Hammond-Tooke (1975), pp. 100, 137.
86. Social and Economic Planning Council (1946), para. 236.
87. Fox and Back (1941), pp. 44–6. Jokl (1941) also reported that stock-owners were disproportionately represented among the membership of the Bunga.
88. Quoted in Roux (1964), p. 218.
89. Hammond-Tooke (1975), pp. 77–82.
90. Carter *et al.* (1967), pp. 84–7.
91. Hammond-Tooke (1975), pp. 78–9.
92. Hammond-Tooke (1968); and (1975), pp. 186–96.
93. *Cape Hansard* (1894), pp. 366–7.
94. H. Rogers (1933), pp. 43–75.
95. For an extensive survey of Bunga debates, see Carter *et al.* (1967), Chapter 5.
96. Tatz (1962), pp. 46–51.
97. UTTGC, *Proceedings* (1936), pp. 281–6.
98. Carter *et al.* (1967), pp. 98–9.
99. ibid., pp. 99–101.
100. TTGC, *Proceedings* (1925), p. 202.
101. ibid. (1929), p. 185.
102. ibid. (1909), p. xiv.
103. Beinart and Bundy (1978), pp. 2–4.
104. Hammond-Tooke (1975), pp. 89–92.
105. ibid., p. 188.
106. Hammond-Tooke (1975), pp. 191–2, records that 30 out of 54 resolutions forwarded for government consideration in the Bunga session of 1943 were rejected.

107. The following summary of rural protest is based heavily upon Beinart and Bundy (1978).
108. Edgar (1976).
109. Franklin (1942).
110. UTTGC, *Proceedings* (1955), pp. 32–6.
111. For a contemporary review, see Horrell (1959b).

Chapter 4
The transition to 'independence'

The Bantu Authorities system was formulated as a device for utilizing the indigenous chiefly élites as agents of political control in the reserves. By restoring the traditional leadership and by binding it to the state as the source of its wealth and authority, the National Party sought to counter the heightened political consciousness of the African mass by dividing the latter into its ethnic segments and subjecting it to a system of indirect rule. But as the wind of change swept across the continent, the regime found it expedient to adopt the vocabulary of decolonization and to ape the imperialists by the grant of (a limited form of) 'self-government' to the tribal homelands.

Such a programme was widely interpreted as fraudulent, as the devolution of the shadow of power and not of its substance. That it was designed to shore up white supremacy was manifest, and it was for this reason that the outside world denied its legitimacy. Yet homeland 'decolonization' was propelled by its own internal logic. The bantustans increasingly had to be presented as potential states, and – unless National Party policy were to be exposed as a hollow sham – their ultimate independence had to be placed on the agenda. Yet therein lay the dilemma, for such independence could not be allowed to pose a convincing challenge to the white state, but had to be sufficiently meaningful to confound the critics and to provide an outlet for black frustration bred of repression by diverting the aspirations of political leadership groups to the periphery. The only solution lay in a policy of intended neo-colonization, whereby a formally 'decolonized' bantustan should have all the trappings of political independence, yet should be so dependent upon the Republic that it could constitute no threat to white dominance and economic interests.

Of necessity, such a grandiose scheme demanded the co-operation of a black political élite which was willing to accept the framework of the bantustans, whether out of conviction or from a pragmatic acceptance of white supremacy. That chiefs should form a core element of such a group was essential, for it was upon their pivotal and conservative role that control over the rural areas was maintained. But it was equally clear that their authority was too narrow a foundation upon which to base the entire strategy, and that were homeland structures to gain a modicum of black support, then they should allow for the systematic incorporation of urban and commoner aspirants to power and wealth. Accordingly, the key element in the whole neo-colonial strategy became the creation of an auxiliary black petty-bourgeoisie which was dependent for its material prosperity and political privilege upon the favours of separate development, and which accordingly would co-operate with the white state in the repression and control of the migrant proletariat and its homeland dependants. By its mouthing of the slogans of independence and its willing accession to formal sovereignty, such a class would function as a subordinate ally to white capital and disguise the latter's continuing domination over the reserves under the cloak of black rule.

Verwoerd's concept of a mutually interdependent commonwealth of states under white leadership indicates that independent bantustans were conceived from the beginning as dependencies of South Africa. Yet the requirements and mechanisms of the neo-colonial strategy were not immediately apparent to a government whose only previous experience of decolonization had been to lament it. Accordingly, these were only gradually devised, and the implementation of policy was subject to a cautious but often heavy-handed experimentation, with its timing (as we have seen) as much dictated by events external as internal. But it was the Transkei which came to serve as the model bantustan, and its significance lies in that it provided the central arena for the working-out of the neo-colonial scenario – although this was not before the rural mass had first risen in revolt and challenged the very structures of chiefly rule upon which the designedly neo-colonial system was first to be established.

Bantu Authorities and the Pondo Revolt

Following the abolition of the Bunga in 1955, Bantu Authorities were established in the Transkei under Proclamation 180 of 1956, the essential features of the new system being that it reconstituted the power of the chiefs (under white authority) and subordinated to them the headmen, who had previously been formally independent of their control. The new source of chiefly authority lay in a new, four-tiered administrative structure which, by emphasizing the legitimacy of tradition, sought expressly to limit popular participation in decision-making and to place local government in the hands of a conservative élite.

The foundation of the new system was (and still is) the Tribal Authorities, which were supposedly based on the old chiefdoms which had formerly constituted the different tribal clusters. Since annexation, the individual chiefdoms had occupied an equivocal status, chiefs enjoying some judicial authority but formally excluded from the structure of magisterial rule which rested ultimately upon the officially appointed headmen. The objective of the Bantu Authorities system was now to restore the chiefdoms and to incorporate them firmly into the administrative grid. However, the *bureaucratization* of chiefly power served to disturb the shadowy and often indefinite relationship which had previously existed between different groups within the various tribal clusters, for whereas the diminution of the chiefly rule under colonial rule had meant that individuals within the traditional leadership group had been content to derive their prestige and influence from indigenous sources, they were now concerned to legitimize their positions by gaining official recognition. Accordingly, there were numerous claimants to chiefly status from small groups which since annexation had existed as *de facto* autonomous tribal entities or as tributaries to larger chiefdoms; and it was the task of government ethnologists to validate their claims, the two main criteria being proof of descent from the last known independent chief and that the area of authority should not be too small. As a result of this process, the number of recognized chiefs increased from thirty to sixty-four between 1955 and 1963;[1] and this suited the official policy well, for not only was the administrative structure thereby retraditionalized but it was also extended more comprehensively into the reserve interior.

Under the Bantu Authorities Act, Tribal Authorities were normally to be grouped into Regions, but because they had long been features of the local scene, within the Transkei (only) Districts were interposed between the Tribal and Regional levels. District Authorities (of which there were twenty-six) linked together the chiefs who headed the Tribal Authorities and a number of other nominated representatives, while the Districts themselves were grouped together into nine Regions. To some extent, the latter approximated the former chiefdom clusters: the Xhosa districts of Kentani, Willowvale and Idutywa were brought together to form the Gcaleka Region. Similarly, the Qaukeni and Nyanda Regions represented Eastern and Western Pondoland respectively, while the Sotho-speaking chiefdoms along the Drakensberg were combined to form the Maluti Authority. But political expediency also played a part, and the Thembu cluster was arbitrarily carved into two administrative regions, Thembuland (later called Dalindyebo) and Emigrant Thembuland. This division served to weaken the influence of the generally acknowledged Paramount, Sabata Dalindyebo (who did not easily lend himself to manipulation from above), in favour of Chief Kaiser Matanzima (now declared Paramount of the latter Region) whose star was rising fast in the official firmament because of his zealous support for the Bantu Authorities system and separate development in general. These Regional Authorities were composed of all recognized chiefs and heads of Districts, plus a number of other members nominated from among the pool of district councillors; and they were presided over by the cluster paramount or a senior chief.[2] Finally, at the highest level, the Transkei Territorial Authority (TTA) was composed of all regional councillors, and led by an executive formed by the Regional Authority chairmen. It was from this latter group that one member was nominated to be the presiding Territorial chief for the ensuing year, an office occupied until 1961 by Paramount Chief Botha Sigcau of Eastern Pondoland, and thereafter – until the dissolution of the TTA in 1963 – by Kaiser Matanzima.

The main function of Tribal Authorities was to serve as guide and adviser to the chiefs in the exercise of local administration. District Authorities were expected to supervise the lower tier, and Regional Authorities to supervise the former, while simultaneously serving as school and hospital boards. Thus, in practice, the key to the system was the centrality of the chiefs, whose powers (and by implication, those of the Tribal and higher Authorities) were formally defined by Proclamation 110 of 1957. Apart from being entrusted with a variety of mundane tasks such as the maintenance of location roads, water supplies, land rehabilitation and disease prevention and control, they were also made responsible for law and order, control of workseekers and unauthorized influx into urban areas, the impounding of stray stock and the dispersal of unlawful assemblies. In addition, headmen lost their judicial powers in favour of the chiefs, who also now assumed a senior role in the allocation of land within the community.

There were some chiefs, notably Paramount Chief Victor Poto of Western Pondoland, who (correctly) feared that their new powers would align them too closely with white oppression and would consequently serve to undermine their popular respect and traditional dignity. Indeed, their apprehension was quite widely shared, but even so the majority of chiefs managed to accommodate to the new situation quite readily. In receipt of an official salary (regarded as compensation for tribute they supposedly no longer exacted from their peoples), they were now located at a strategic judicial and administrative juncture from which they could appropriate financial surplus from the community, for Authorities at all levels were required to establish treasuries into which all monies raised from taxation, fines and fees collected by chiefs and headmen were to be paid, while they were all similarly empowered to impose taxes of up to £1 per annum on adult male Africans resident in their areas, these being additional to a general levy imposed by the TTA and a number of other discretionary charges. The result was that the rate of taxation following the imposition of the Bantu Authorities system increased markedly, almost doubling over the period 1955–9.[3] Legally subject to official auditing, these revenues were officially allocated to administrative and development purposes, but given that such expenditure was determined by the chiefs-in-council themselves, much of it unduly favoured their own needs, and large amounts were customarily allocated to an unascertainable 'Miscellaneous' category allowed for in Authority accounts.[4]

But it was in their judicial and directly administrative capacities that the chiefs were enabled to engage in a strategy most appropriately referred to as one of primitive accumulation.[5] In the pre-annexation period, the institution of *busa*, whereby a man received a gift in return for performance of a service, was widespread, but thereafter the pattern changed, and it became usual for gifts to be given *before* the favour was conferred, thereby radically transforming the entire nature of the transaction. Thus Hunter, writing in 1936, indicated that it had become quite common under the magisterial system for headmen to impose a charge for allocating land.[6] Following the introduction of Bantu Authorities, the extent of such abuses was markedly increased, for chiefs now became able to exact unauthorized financial levies upon an extensive scale: for instance, various social services previously administered by magistrates now fell under the Tribal Authorities, so that performance of functions such as the payment of certain allowances became subject to chiefly graft. In addition, the allocation of land now became determined by the chiefs, and few were backward in extracting fees from suppliants, while similarly, complaint became widespread that the dispensation of justice in tribal courts had now become largely dependent upon financial offerings being made.[7] In short, therefore, with an absence of checks upon abuse and the minimization of popular participation in local administration, chiefs were enabled through Bantu Authorities to appropriate increased rates of surplus from their politically subordinate populations.

Increasing dissatisfaction with the new system of administration was compounded by the government-sponsored land rehabilitation schemes which the chiefs were expected to enforce. Taken at face value, the betterment measures were necessary to the revitalization of reserve agriculture involving stock control, contouring, fencing and the introduction of preventive measures to check soil erosion. Yet within the Transkei – and elsewhere – such schemes met with bitter and widespread opposition, for as implemented under the Bantu Authorities system, 'agricultural improvement' often represented a direct attack upon inhabitants' security. In the first place, location residents were commonly expected to abandon their huts and to group together in new settlements in order to allow for a more rational utilization of the land, but from the householders' perspective this entailed the abandonment of prior capital investment – however humble – in their previous homesteads. Secondly, in a community where the accumulation of cattle represented one of the major avenues of saving and exchange, culling involved a direct attack on local wealth; and thirdly, rehabilitation measures involved the extensive use of forced labour under the supervision of the chiefs (on pain of fine or other punishment in the tribal courts). Thus the Minister of Bantu Administration boasted to Parliament in 1962 that development works in the reserves were being undertaken at less than half the cost estimated by the Tomlinson Commissioners, citing the case of a dam whose construction cost had been reduced from £15,000 to £1,000 by the use of 'community labour'.[8] Finally, while such measures were supposed to be introduced with popular consent, it is clear that chiefs – under pressure from the white authorities – often committed their peoples to rehabilitation without consulting them. In consequence, the betterment schemes further exposed the chiefs as the instruments of white power and focused widespread grievance upon the Bantu Authorities system as a cause of popular distress.

Resistance to the implementation of betterment schemes and the introduction of Bantu Authorities was by no means confined to the Transkei, for the other reserves were correspondingly oppressed, and all were linked to the urban areas – where the ANC strategy was to mobilize mass protest in campaigns such as the Defiance Campaign of 1951–2 – by the migrant labour system, which served as a transmission belt of heightened political consciousness. Thus major instances of open revolt and violence against authority occurred in Witzieshoek (adjoining Lesotho) in the late 1940s, the Bafurutse reserve (neighbouring upon Botswana) in 1957, and Sekhukhuneland in the Transvaal in 1958, with numerous smaller (but not necessarily less desperate) incidents occurring elsewhere. But it was in the Transkei that such rebellion was most extensive and caused the government most concern.

Disaffection with Bantu Authorities was manifest well before it burst into violent flame. The most evident discontent was initially in Thembuland, where the widely respected Paramount, Sabata Dalindyebo, had originally proposed acceptance of the new system thinking that it would usher in a new and benevolent era when chiefly legitimacy would be based on popular consent. However, his illusions were swiftly shattered as it became clear that the chiefs were to be utilized as instruments of white rule; and in particular he was grossly offended by the decision to divide Thembuland into two and to promote Kaiser Matanzima, originally a minor chief and widely regarded as an upstart, to a newly created paramountcy in Emigrant Thembuland. Dalindyebo's complaint was not without popular backing, and accordingly the Thembu dispatched a four-man delegation to Pretoria to protest at the manner in which Bantu Authorities were being implemented. But all such representation was to no avail, and the delegates were informed that failure to accept the new system would lead to the withdrawal of educational and social services; and when the Thembu continued to reject the new Authorities, the four delegates (who included Sabata's secretary) were deported, and the Paramount himself threatened with displacement.[9]

It was among the Pondo people that resistance to Bantu Authorities reached its climax, in a campaign of militant struggle which developed well beyond its origins in spontaneous violence to take on the characteristics of an organized revolt.[10] Sharing all the widespread miseries of reserve life, those in Eastern Pondoland suffered the added disadvantage of a particularly repressive chieftaincy. This stemmed in part from the disputed legitimacy of Chief Botha Sicgau, who in 1939 had been chosen by the government to fill the paramountcy even though his half-brother Nelson was widely regarded as the rightful heir. Whether or not the latter's claim was just, Sicgau's position transparently derived from official support, this subsequently being made manifest by his outright collaboration with white authority. An early supporter of Bantu Authorities, he openly lent himself to attempts to promote its acceptance, and in 1958 he earned his official reward with his appointment as chairman of the TTA. Furthermore, Botha totally disregarded popular feeling in the appointment of members to the various Authorities, packing them with his own supporters; and throughout his entire Region, chiefly corruption and abuse was particularly rife.

By mid-1959, tension in East Pondoland was mounting rapidly. Then, a meeting at Isikelo location near Bizana fanned the embers of discontent into flame, when the residents demanded that the local District Authority chairman, Mr Saul Mabude (a close ally of Botha Sicgau), should explain the Bantu Authority system to them at a meeting especially called for that purpose. But the chairman declined to attend, and the people were instead confronted by the local Bantu Commissioner, to whom they expressed their opposition to the new system in no uncertain terms and relayed their fears that the chiefs would deprive them of their land. However, satisfaction was not attained, the meeting broke up in disorder, and in subsequent weeks and months popular frustration found expression in acts of spontaneous violence.[11]

Yet the significant feature of the Pondo Revolt was the rapidity and manner in which it moved beyond these acts of unco-ordinated violence and developed an organization known as 'Ikongo' (or Congress) with a leadership known as 'Intaba' (or the Hill). The model for this transformation was probably provided in part by the Makhuluspani movement which had grown up in the Tsolo and Qumbu areas in the 1950s as a set of vigilante groups to protect the locations against stock thieves (then, as now, a serious problem). Led by commoner elements, Makhuluspani initially served as an extra-legal agency for raiding, assaulting and disciplining suspected thieves, but with the establishment of Bantu Authorities, it became overtly political and acted against chiefs and headmen whom it regarded as collaborating too closely with the government.[12] Similarly, the Hill Committee was popularly based and led, but it differed in that its orientation was political from the start.

The immediate objective of the Hill Committee was to harness and organize mass support against Bantu Authorities and to seek its replacement by a more open and participatory system of local administration which would be responsive to popular needs. That the movement sought to achieve this particular goal needs to be stressed, as too often the Pondo Revolt is taken to be mainly a reflection of the urban-based campaign of protest directed by the ANC. Such a diagnosis is erroneous, for it implicitly suggests that the rebellion was irrational, a violent and futile striking out against authority which was doomed from the start by its very nature. Yet the movement had its specific rationale in the local political economy. This does not mean that it was cut off from or unaware of the wider struggle (indeed, it could hardly be so, being linked to the urban areas through labour migrancy) but that its strategy was one of deliberately limited violence aimed at extracting limited concessions from the government. Certainly, as the campaign progressed it developed links with the ANC: Anderson Ganyile, an ANC Youth Leaguer expelled from the University of Fort Hare in February 1960 for political activities and thereafter detained for four months, was actively involved with the Hill Committee from about June onwards after his return home to Bizana; and links were forged through urban tribal associations, notably those in Durban and Margate, with other ANC and Congress of Democrats activists, one of whom, Mr Roley Arenstein, a white lawyer, became involved in the legal defence of arrested rebels. Indeed, it was such evident links which allowed the government, the press, the white traders and others to ascribe the unrest to the manipulation of a primitive people by outside 'agitators' and (of course) 'communists' (culminating in the eventual restriction of Arenstein and an order in November empowering chiefs to apprehend 'white communist agitators').[13] But overemphasis on such external contacts overlooks the internal basis of the revolt,[14] which was the acute and widespread popular perception of the Bantu Authorities system as the immediate cause of the recent deterioration in the standard and conditions of reserve living.

The aim of the rebels was to paralyse the operation of Bantu Authorities, establish an interim administrative and legal structure of their own and, through negotiation, to obtain redress of grievances from the government. To this end, from March 1960 well-attended meetings were held in the hillside kraals of Bizana in defiance of orders proclaiming them illegal. There rapidly emerged a district-wide, hierarchical leadership (the Hill), and the movement soon spread to Lusikisiki and Flagstaff, where local leaders were linked to the central committee but retained considerable autonomy, the principal means of communication between the different areas being only by foot or by horseback.[15]

The campaign to displace Bantu Authorities began in earnest on 20 March 1960, when the huts of Mr Saul Mabude, who was so closely allied with the unpopular Paramount, were destroyed. Thereafter, systematic but discriminatory violence was used against known supporters of Bantu Authorities. Typically, such persons were warned in advance that action was going to be taken against them, thus giving them opportunity to flee; those who stayed to defend their properties in defiance of the warning were killed. The slaughter of Chief Vukaibambe Sicgau (brother of Botha Sicgau) is illustrative. On 20 November 1960 Vukaibambe directed the police to a meeting of the local Hill committee, and gave direct aid in its violent dispersal in which one person was shot dead and four others injured. The following day he received instructions to leave a warning which he chose to ignore. In the evening a crowd of between 500 and 1,000 advanced on his kraal and dispatched both him and two of his headmen. The total toll of such deaths was some twenty-two persons, all of them in some way identified with the authorities: two were chiefs, five were police informers and the rest were headmen or bodyguards. Such methods were highly effective, and by July or August it appears that Bantu Authorities had effectively ceased to operate throughout the whole of Bizana and large areas of Lusikisiki and Flagstaff. The chiefs were frightened men. A few repudiated the government in order to retain popular esteem (and thereby laid themselves open to official deposition), but the majority fled their posts and sought protection in refugee camps in Bizana and Umzimkulu.

With the collapse of Bantu Authorities, certain judicial and administrative functions were taken over by the Hill Committee. People's courts were established which sat in lieu of the chiefs, and took upon themselves a wide array of tasks, among which were the allocation of hut sites and ploughing land. They enjoyed popular confidence and, as the movement waxed in authority, the general populace had no qualms in submitting civil cases which were judged according to customary law. But the main function of the courts was to provide coercive muscle to the struggle. They thus arraigned before them loyalists who held position under the government, forcing them to resign or face the consequences; and in particular, they sought to root out and punish informers who, in return for meagre reward, passed intelligence to the police.

The rebellion against Bantu Authorities brought the reserve masses into direct confrontation with the state. Scores of rebels were arrested, brought before the courts and subjected to judicial vengeance. Of necessity, the financial burdens of defence fell upon the Hill Committee, which sought to meet such costs by making levies upon the local community. But given the prevailing impoverishment, income from this source was limited and the movement had to seek out alternative modes of finance. One solution that it devised was to turn to the traders, and demand that they underwrite the struggle.

Although the traders occupied a dominating position within the reserve economy, their physical isolation in remote parts and their dependence upon local customer patronage made them potentially susceptible – especially at the individual level – to local pressure. Traders were not unaware of this, and accordingly they had early become alarmed at evidences of unrest, making representation to the government that they should be allowed to place armed guards to watch over their property and that outlying stations should have direct telephonic contact with the police.[16]

That their fears were not groundless was demonstrated when individuals among them were approached for donations to an 'Anti-Bantu Authorities Fund', and were prevailed upon to provide lorry transport to ferry people to meetings and to supply grain to those in need.[17] Yet such demands placed traders in an awkward dilemma, for were they to cooperate with the rebels they would earn themselves official rebuke and probable revocation of their licences; but alternatively, if they ignored the Pondo requests, they faced the threat of their stores being boycotted. It was to counter this latter danger that the Transkei Territorial Civic Association (which represented white interests) had previously requested the administration to make organized boycotting illegal.[18]

That the authorities failed to respond to the traders' plea was one indication that they doubted the capacity of the Pondo to mount an economic strike. In this their estimate was correct to the extent that, so dependent were the reserve masses upon the traders for their daily necessities that a prolonged and comprehensive boycott would have been impossible. However, this did not preclude the effective use of the boycott weapon on a selective and localized basis – and this is what occurred in Eastern Pondoland. By mid-August, one store in Lusikisiki District and three in the Flagstaff area were being avoided,[19] and each and every trader in the locality perceived his vulnerability. In consequence, there were undoubtedly a number of traders who sought exemption from attack by making discreet contribution to the funds of the Anti-Bantu Authorities Committee; and at least one affected trader appeared before a mass meeting of the Hill and agreed to offer material assistance on condition that the boycott be lifted.[20] But if the intention of the rebels was to embarrass the trading community so that it would urge the government to make concessions to the rebels, then they failed – for the traders as a bloc were not threatened, and their reaction was to urge the authorities to bring a speedy end to the revolt by taking strong, repressive action.[21]

Faced by the systematic destruction of the Bantu Authorities' structure, the government determined to quell the revolt by force, and on 6 June it precipitated an attack upon a mass meeting of rebels at the foot of Ngquza Hill in the Flagstaff area. Teargas and smokebombs were dropped by aircraft flying overhead, while armed police converged upon the assembled gathering from the surrounding hillside. The Pondo raised a white flag to indicate their peaceful intent, but with their customary penchant for self-defence the South African Police opened fire with revolvers and sten guns. The official death toll was eleven, but local residents placed it as high as thirty, with a further sixty seriously injured. At the inquest which followed, the presiding magistrate condemned the police use of sten guns as 'unjustified and excessive, even reckless', and there appeared to be grounds for indictment of those responsible under charge of culpable homicide, but the state declined to prosecute.[22]

The massacre at Ngquza Hill served only to intensify the struggle, and in the weeks that followed resistance spread over a wider area. In consequence, the government sought to defuse the conflict by establishing a Commission of Inquiry to investigate the causes of revolt. Composed entirely of Bantu Administration officials, the Commission sat in mid-July, and at public meetings the populace was induced to register their complaints; and it was to this body that the Hill leadership submitted a memorandum (under the auspices of an Anti-Bantu Authorities Committee) which outlined the major grievances: the widespread dissatisfaction with the rule of Botha Sigcau, the drastic rise in taxation under Bantu Authorities, the pervasiveness of chiefly corruption, the threat to security represented by rehabilitation schemes and the undemocratic basis of chiefly authority.²³ The most immediate demand was therefore that the Bantu Authorities system be withdrawn – but in addition there were calls for the abolition of Bantu Education, the relaxation of the Pass Laws and for representation in the central parliament.²⁴ In such a manner did the rural struggle link up with the ANC campaign at the national level.

The Commission reported its findings on 11 October. In the meantime the Hill Committee had consolidated its control over the rural areas. Many refused to pay taxes, the decennial census currently being undertaken was boycotted, and in September a petition pleading the Pondo cause was smuggled out to the United Nations. It was natural therefore that when the Commission announced to an assembled throng of 15,000 people that it found the majority of their complaints unacceptable, and offered only paltry concessions, that resistance should continue. A meeting of 6,000 Pondo on 25 October repudiated the report, and determined to continue the fight. A decision was taken that all should refuse to be taxed, and on 1 November the entire village of Bizana was subjected to a boycott (which lasted until January 1961) in protest against the collusion of the white population with the authorities. This was followed by the murder of Chief Vukaibambe Sicgau.

The government response was predictable. Police reinforcements were brought into the area, and the revolt was crushed by force. On 30 November a State of Emergency was promulgated throughout the entire Transkei under Proclamation 400 (subsequently amended by Proclamation 413), whereby provision was made for a wide array of draconian controls to be exercised by officials, including the detention of persons suspected of having committed or having intention to commit an offence without trial, and the prohibition of meetings without the express consent of the Bantu Commissioner. In addition an attempt was made to shore up the authority of the chiefs and headmen, and it thus became an offence to make verbal or written statements likely to undermine the state, to incite a boycott of officially convened meetings or even to treat chiefs with disrespect. Chiefs were also empowered to try those accused of subverting their authority and to order the removal of any recalcitrant tribesmen out of their areas of jurisdiction and demolish his hut without being liable to pay compensation.²⁵

Armed with these arbitrary powers, government forces then engaged in a campaign of massive reprisal. Nearly 5,000 Africans were arrested and incarcerated in jail for varying periods, some to be released, but a large number to be charged with committing an offence. By April 1961, 114 persons were awaiting trial for murder, 121 for arson and 289 for other less serious offences. Of these, 30 were later sentenced to death (9 being later reprieved). Under the impact of this frontal attack, Pondo resistance was crushed and the basis of the revolt destroyed.²⁶

The Bantu Authorities system was thus restored to Eastern Pondoland by force, and the populace cowed into a sullen acquiescence. The significance of the revolt lay in its genuinely mass basis, its duration and its discipline. It was, indeed, a major triumph for the unarmed people of East Pondoland to so rudely demonstrate to the world that they repudiated their renewed subservience to the chiefs; while the sophisticated techniques of struggle they employed – the boycotts, the petitions and the refusal to pay taxes – showed that the lessons of the wider nationalist struggle had been fully absorbed and that, given the link of the migrant labour system, the rural areas of South Africa could not be isolated from rising political consciousness in the urban areas. But in the short term the revolt also demonstrated to Pretoria that if its system of indirect rule was to be transformed into one of more broadly based neo-colonialism, then there could be no genuine relaxation of political control. In consequence, the four general elections that preceded the Transkei's eventual 'independence' were held under an electoral system which was specifically designed to limit the expression and impact of popular feeling; and in addition it was henceforth clear as it could be that the chiefs exercised their rule by government licence rather than by popular consent.

From indirect rule to self-government

In April 1961, Verwoerd stated to Parliament in Cape Town that, in the light of external pressure, South Africa would reluctantly but of necessity have to develop Bantu states which might eventually go on to achieve full independence.[27] This provoked a response ten days later in the TTA, when a motion was put forward that 'in view of ... the fact that the Bantu people in the Union [had] no representation in the Union legislature', the Transkei should be declared a 'self-governing state under the control of the Bantu people'.[28] The request came from certain conservative chiefs and councillors, the most prominent of whom were Paramount Chiefs Victor Poto and Sabata Dalindyebo, whose motive seems to have been not to endorse apartheid, but to rid themselves of their domination by white magistrates and to challenge the government to match its words by the devolution of a measure of genuine authority to Africans in the reserves; and coming after Sharpeville and the banning of the ANC and PAC, it indicated a despair at African failure to gain representation in the central parliament.

The motion took the government by surprise. Being sponsored by that conservative faction opposed to Bantu Authorities (as not strengthening, but undermining, the traditional basis of chieftaincy), officials sensed danger. Consequently, after consultation with the TTA Chairman, Kaiser Matanzima, the debate was adjourned; and five days later, officials submitted a new motion to the Assembly which recommended the establishment of a recess committee to examine the implications of self-government. Once this had been accepted, the white authorities resolved to ensure that any resultant devolution of power would take place within the framework of apartheid.

And so it happened. The recess committee that was formed was whisked away to Pretoria where it sat directly under Verwoerd himself. Any opposition to an apartheid-style constitution – which incorporated chieftaincy yet more firmly in the state apparatus and excluded multiracial citizenship for a self-governing Transkei – was disallowed. Acceptance of the Committee's Report was then steamrollered through the TTA by Matanzima, no opportunity being given for the expression of contrary views; and despite widespread popular rejection of the proposed constitution outside the Assembly (for instance among the Pondo and Thembu), it was subsequently adopted by the TTA in December 1961.[29] The process was then to culminate in the passage of the Transkei Constitution Act of 1963 whereby the bantustan was styled a 'self-governing' territory, with its own proto-parliament (the Transkei Legislative Assembly) and an executive Cabinet led by a Chief Minister (who was also responsible for Finance) and otherwise composed of five other Ministers responsible for Justice, the Interior, Education, Agriculture and Forestry, and Roads and Works, within which spheres the TLA was empowered to legislate, albeit subject to veto from above; and in addition, the Transkei was simultaneously granted the trappings of potential statehood in the form of a flag and national anthem.

If the devolution of power to an African government lent itself to comparison to the decolonization process elsewhere on the continent, it also bore the stamp of an explicit process of intended apartheid-style neo-colonization, whereby the reins of power within the Transkei would be handed over to a pliable élite, and the conditions of bantustan existence so circumscribed that it would have no alternative but to service the labour needs of the South African economy. This neo-colonial strategy had four main elements. First, the Constitution Act entrenched the chiefs as the dominant political group within the TLA, where they outnumbered elected members by 64 to 45. To have established an Assembly wholly composed of chiefs, at a time when other colonial powers were discarding indirect rule, would have been to endanger what limited chances there were of international acceptance of the bantustan constitutional experiment, but to have relied upon a wholly elective Assembly would have been to risk a popular rebuff of apartheid at the polls. Accordingly, the Republican government sought to resolve its dilemma by granting the franchise to those designated Transkeian citizens but simultaneously negating its effectiveness – and justifying the resultant hybrid Assembly as a unique synthesis of African tradition and western democracy.

The second distinctive feature of the strategy was the (racial) definition of all Africans of Transkeian origin (broadly conceived) as citizens of the self-governing Transkei, and the corresponding exclusion from citizenship of all whites and coloureds resident in the Territories. The significance of this was not simply that Africans of Transkeian origin were effectively deprived of their South African citizenship and hence transformed into 'foreign' workers (thereby providing legalistic grounds on which to deny them political rights in the Republic), but equally that it changed whites in the Transkei from 'settlers' into 'expatriates'. It followed from this that key groups in the reserve economy, and notably the traders, could be made subject to a process of exclusion and replacement by blacks in the interests of 'Africanization'. This then tied into the third element of strategy, namely the creation of a homeland petty-bourgeoisie based on trade and the expansion of the administrative apparatus. The rapid development of a civil service was foreseen as providing privileged employment opportunities for educated elements which might otherwise become disaffected, thereby providing them with a material stake in the structures of separate development and expanding its African support group well beyond the confines of the chieftaincy.

Finally, the entire administrative and political superstructure of the bantustan was necessarily to be financially dependent upon the Republic. Although the political élite was to be encouraged to expand the Transkeian tax base in order to shift the burden of reserve 'development' from the shoulders of the white electorate, the homeland petty-bourgeoisie was clearly to become a beneficiary of white patronage. Hence even though it might be expected that bantustan politicians would learn to kick against the pricks, their political activities would none the less be fundamentally circumscribed by the various financial and other constraints imposed by their white paymasters.

The restrictive nature of the bantustan political arena was subsequently to ensure the predominance of an emergent homeland petty-bourgeoisie. This was to take the form of the rise to hegemony of the Transkei National Independence Party, which under the leadership of Kaiser Matanzima consistently campaigned upon a platform endorsing separate development and which eventually acceded to independence in 1976 in an electorally unchallengeable position. Yet its dominance was artificially contrived and it never came to enjoy widespread popular support, for in essence the TNIP was clearly but unofficially sponsored to the exclusion of all other factions by the South African government, and this was the crucial factor in securing its political base.

There were four general elections in the Transkei prior to independence, but it was only the first of these which could be considered critical. The Transkei Constitution Act of 1963 ordained that the Cabinet should be chosen by the Legislative Assembly from among its membership, so that the necessary prior step was the election of the 45 members to accompany the 64 chiefs who had seats *ex officio*.

The ensuing 1963 general election was contested, not upon a party basis, but revolved around the campaigns of the two figures who had announced their candidature for the post of Chief Minister of the Transkei – Paramount Chief Kaiser Matanzima and Paramount Chief Victor Poto. Both automatically members of the TLA by virtue of their chiefly status, they stepped down into the electoral arena in order to gain the support of the 180 candidates who were standing for election.[30]

The issues that separated the two main contestants were clearcut. Although it was one of his followers (Lingham Maninja, a commoner from Port St Johns) who had first requested self-government in 1961, Poto strongly rejected the apartheid-style constitution which had been foisted upon the TTA. Sixty years of age, a paramount since 1918 and a member of the Natives Representative Council from 1937 until its abolition, he was a conservative who saw no necessary discrepancy between traditional values and liberal democracy. According to Mayer, he conformed closely to the model of a 'good chief' – one who enjoyed popular respect and sought to govern by consensus; and it was this basis of chieftaincy which he sought to maintain, arguing strongly that its too close identification with white authority would erode its legitimacy. Accordingly, he argued in favour of a bicameral legislature, with an upper house composed of chiefs which would review laws and check the excesses of a popularly elected lower house. At the same time, Poto strongly repudiated separate development, apartheid and all the racially divisive policies of the Republic, and accordingly argued that whites and coloureds within the Transkei (of whom there were 14,000 and 10,000 respectively) should be made eligible for local citizenship and able to participate fully in Transkeian political affairs. Poto also rejected the whole notion of bantustan independence and the fragmentation of the Republic – even though he acknowledged that his favoured policy of multiracialism could never be implemented under apartheid unless Transkei were to become a separate state.

In contrast, Kaiser Matanzima campaigned in favour of separate development, arguing that all the territory in the Transkei should be reserved for blacks, and that the 'white spots' (towns, villages and trading sites) should be eliminated. Whites should be extruded from the trading sector, the local administrations should be Africanized and European capital should be barred from the Territories. Finally, he maintained that the chiefs should take a central role in political affairs, and should be entrenched as a majority in the Assembly. In short, Matanzima wholly endorsed the apartheid line. A Fort Hare graduate, an attorney and considerably younger than his opponent, Matanzima was reputed to be ruthless, brutal and authoritarian – and certainly he was widely unpopular, requiring the constant attendance of a bodyguard to ensure his personal safety. Thus in Mayer's terms he symbolized the 'bad chief' in the popular eye; and his election programme confirmed his collaborationist role with the Nationalist government. Yet a common stooge he was not, giving sufficient indication by his tough anti-white campaign stance that he was a man from whom Pretoria should not presume too much.

The result of the election was unambiguous, with observers generally agreeing that Poto was supported by 38 out of the 45 elected members. Although there were severe limitations on the electoral process as a reflector of popular opinion (as will be enumerated below) and which consequently make it difficult to estimate the extent to which the election was actually fought on the issues, there can be no quarrel with Carter's judgement that the electorate had clearly demonstrated its support for

Poto's stand on African political rights and parliamentary representation in an undivided, racially integrated South Africa and that it had amply registered its opposition to the bantustan policy. Yet popular opinion was to be thwarted by the unbalanced composition of the new Assembly, for once it had become manifest that he lacked a basis in popular support, Matanzima had concentrated his energies on winning over the chiefs, who as paid government officials were highly susceptible to pressure from above, material inducement and the prospect of an enhanced role in political life[31] regardless of the dangers to the chiefs' traditional dignity. Accordingly, when it came to the vote in the Assembly for the Chief Ministership, Matanzima squeezed home by 54 votes to 49, gaining the support of 47 out of the 58 chiefs who were present. It thus ill-behoved him to claim in his victory address that the people of the Transkei had soundly rejected the policy of multiracialism through the ballot box. Yet however idiosyncratic his interpretation of the popular will, this initial triumph was sufficient to secure his accession to office, and to provide a basis for subsequent consolidation of control over the apparatus of the proposed neo-colonial state.

Following the election, Chief Victor Poto and his aides formed the Democratic Party, which opened its membership to all races and based its programme on a repudiation of apartheid. In response, Matanzima formed the Transkei National Independence Party which declared itself committed to the implementation of separate development; and thenceforward the Assembly was divided on party lines, with the majority party in the legislature – the TNIP – forming the government and the DP becoming an officially recognized Opposition.

For an initial period the DP seemed to constitute a genuine danger to the ruling party, for it successfully undermined the confidence of the chiefs by warning them of the severe consequences that might follow from their opposing the popular will by supporting the TNIP.[32] That this was no idle threat was underlined by Poqo (the armed offshoot of the banned PAC) in the Transkei in 1962–3, to which the murder of two government-supporting headmen and five whites had been ascribed, along with a number of assassination attempts upon the Matanzima brothers;[33] and then in November 1963 Mlizo Salukapatwa, who had been elected to the Assembly on a Poto-supporting platform but who was believed to have subsequently switched to the Matanzima camp, was shot dead at his home. With these disturbances in mind, three chiefs crossed over to the DP, one of them explicitly claiming that he had been coerced into supporting the TNIP under threat of deposition; and in the by-election caused by Salukapatwa's decease, the DP won a resounding victory in a highly competitive fight.

But thenceforward the DP experienced a steady and continuous decline and the TNIP became unchallengeably dominant, emerging victorious from general elections in 1968, 1973 and 1976. The most significant features of this process were TNIP's accession to a majority among the elected members of the Assembly, and the fact that by 1973 it had gained a popular majority of the votes cast; and to complete the picture, in the pre-independence election of 1976 when the number of elective seats was raised to 75 to equal chiefly members (now also increased to 75), the TNIP virtually eliminated all opposition and established – for all practical purposes – a political monopoly of control (see Table 4.1).

Table 4.1 *Immediate post-election party affiliations in the Transkei Legislative Assembly, 1963–76*

Year	Party	Ex officio chiefs	Elected members	Total
1963	TNIP	56	15	71
	DP	8	29	37
	Ind.	0	1	1
				109
1968	TNIP	56	28	84
	DP	8	14	22
	Ind.	0	3	3
				109
1973	TNIP	59	27	86
	DP	2	10	12
	Ind.	3	8	11
				109
1976	TNIP	72	71	143
	DP	2	1	3
	NDP	1	2	3
	Ind.	0	1	1
				150

Notes: TNIP: Transkei National Independence Party; DP: Democratic Party; NDP: New Democratic Party; and Ind: Independent.
Source: Southall (1977).

One interpretation of this phenomenon (which is obviously favoured by the homeland regime) is that the successive election victories reflect a growing popular endorsement by Transkeians of the TNIP's pro-separate development policies. Yet in view of the deep and unrelenting black hostility to apartheid and the history of struggle against Bantu Authorities in the Transkei itself (these apart from the October 1976 election being held so soon after the Soweto upheaval of June–August), such an explanation seems transparently false – and indeed, other factors suggest that the TNIP's popular base has continuously remained extremely narrow (as suggested by the fact that its later victories at the polls were gained in conditions of limited voter participation). Accordingly, the question must of necessity be put as to how and why Matanzima managed to establish the TNIP as the dominant party and simultaneously to eliminate all meaningful opposition.

It will be suggested here that the reason for the TNIP's increasing electoral achievement lay in the peculiar nature of the bantustan political framework. In particular, apart from the bantustan authorities' considerable reliance upon coercive pressures to mobilize a pro-Matanzima vote, it would seem that three broad factors underwrote the TNIP's success. First, the electoral structure discriminated in favour of the TNIP and heavily against all groupings opposed to separate development. Secondly, as Heribert Adam has pointed out,[34] in the face of total subordination black political behaviour within the confines of the apartheid system has to be defined as a technique of 'maximum survival', or a choice between political suicide or accommodation. In the Transkeian context, therefore, the system favoured Matanzima's pragmatism in contrast to the mainly ineffective and unworldly opposition to separate development adopted by the DP in the self-governing period; and thirdly, by becoming the governing party the TNIP became the centre of a considerable network of patronage and a distributor of material resources within the impoverished society of a labour reserve.

The electoral process

One of the major symbolic features of the bantustan policy has been the gradual extension of universal suffrage to the black population in South Africa. However nonsensical in geographic or economic terms the individual homelands might be, National Party spokesmen have been able to claim that they deny the vote to no group on the basis of race, and that Africans are free to participate in the political affairs of their own areas; and although turnout in bantustan elections has on occasion been embarrassingly low, it has none the less reflected (at least in some cases) the participation of sufficient numbers of voters to allow the South African government to claim an apparent (though modest) success – and to use the existence and result of such elections as propaganda in promoting the legitimacy of the homeland concept abroad. Yet bantustan elections have been far from free, and within the Transkei the electoral system utilized in the four pre-independence elections was designed and operated so as to deliberately distort popular opinion through three particular mechanisms: first, the utilization of chiefs and headmen as agents of electoral control; secondly, the restriction of electoral activity by candidates and persons opposed to the policies of separate development; and thirdly, the limitation of urban influence in the electoral process. However, as well as working to emasculate any mass-based opposition to the bantustan state apparatus, elections have simultaneously promoted tribal parochialism, and accordingly the approach adopted here will seek to realize the dual objectives of illustrating the nature of the electoral process as an instrument of political control, while simultaneously recognizing its significance in allowing for a limited degree of popular participation which has been functional in promoting the power and authority of the ruling political group.

Chiefs and headmen as agents of electoral control
Under the constitution of 1963, all the existing chiefs sat as nominated members in the Legislative Assembly, outnumbering elected members by 64 to 45 – and as has been seen above, this was critical in reversing the expressed popular preference for the Poto faction and elevating Matanzima to the chief ministership. For a number of chiefs, this negation apparently posed an acute role conflict: 'I will kill myself as soon as I come home,' one chief is quoted as saying after he had switched his vote to Matanzima at the last minute; 'I can't face the people after what I have done.'[35] Yet the majority of the chiefs accommodated themselves quite happily to their new position and influence, and all but a few drifted over to the TNIP and away from the Opposition benches. But given the accompanying increase in support for Matanzima among elected members, he has become less dependent upon the chiefs as a bloc, and under the independence constitution chiefs lost their automatic majority, the present arrangement being that 75 chiefs are matched by 75 elected members. By October 1976 there was a total of 124 recognized chiefs,[36] so that nomination to the Assembly was no longer automatic, only the five paramounts sitting *ex officio*, the remaining 70 being selected on a regional basis by electoral colleges of chiefs.[37] Yet the chiefs remain the single most important constituent element within the legislature, and their numerous presence and extra-legislative authority will continue to guarantee the TNIP majority, even in the unlikely event of electoral adversity in the future.

But chiefly influence in Transkeian elections has extended well beyond the mere ability to negate a contrary popular vote, for it has also been the single most important factor in the selection of candidates for elective seats and the structuring of the electorate's voting behaviour. It has to be recalled at this point that, under the Bantu Authorities system, the chiefs were granted a sweeping array of local powers, and that through their domination of the administrative structure they undertake such functions as the allocation of land, the payment of pensions and welfare allowances, and the appointment of teachers – in addition to their exercise of judicial authority. Furthermore, the authoritarian sway of the chiefs is but little countered by popular representation, and individuals who openly oppose chiefly predominance expose themselves to risk. Most importantly, the chiefs' authority was sustained from the early 1960s by the notorious Proclamation 400, which – introduced at the time of the Pondoland uprisings – was operative throughout the entire self-governing period, and cast a long, dark shadow over the political sphere. Investing the chiefs with a vast array of arbitrary powers, the effect of the Proclamation was to raise the cost of dissent to an exorbitant level and consequently to achieve its desired effect of smothering mass political activity; and accordingly, given that the overwhelming majority of the chiefs have always aligned themselves with the ruling party, the TNIP has been placed at a considerable electoral advantage – for the provisions for secret balloting in the Transkei have continuously been subject to manifest, systematic and deliberate abuse.

Although the electoral law formally allows for secret voting, illiterate voters are required to state their preferences to the polling officer in the presence of two witnesses. This is of major significance for the simple reason that approximately 60 per cent of registered voters are illiterate[38] – and accordingly, the majority of votes in Transkeian elections are recorded not by the actual voters but by official appointees. But the appointment of the latter is itself subject to political influence, being made by the Electoral Officer in Umtata who falls under the (TNIP) Minister of the Interior. Thus in 1968 the TNIP actually submitted an official list of nominees for appointment as polling officers, chiefs being recommended in 23 out of the 26 constituencies;[39] and in 1973 the Cabinet directed that male teachers (who have formed one of the few significant foci of opposition to the TNIP) be specifically barred from appointment – it being feared that they would influence voters against the government.[40]

That irregularities committed by polling officers are widespread is common knowledge, and has been a source of constant complaint, especially by the Opposition: 'people fear the chiefs because of certain threats, namely that they will be deprived of their rights as well as of their arable allotments and so they are not prepared to go to the polling stations', was a typical allegation,[41] while Kotze has reported that ballot boxes from polling stations supervised by headmen often display a 100 per cent return in favour of a particular political party (usually, of course, the TNIP).[42] Similarly illustrative is the appeal to Matanzima made by an unsuccessful TNIP candidate in 1968 to declare the election in Umzimkulu invalid on the grounds that the polling officer had lodged with one of the candidates; that two candidates brought large bundles of reference books to the polling stations and recorded the owners' votes in their own favour; that the complainant candidate had had to bribe the polling officer to collect votes from all stations; that the polling officer instructed voters to cast their lot for his favoured candidates; and finally that he refused the right of the literate to a secret ballot.[43]

The ability of the chiefs to influence the popular vote in the Transkei is therefore considerable – although at the same time it should not be exaggerated, for there have been quite a number of instances where voters have successfully defied the wishes of their chiefs by electing candidates of their own choice. But in general, the fact that the large majority of chiefs has always supported the ruling party suggests that chiefly authority has been systematically used to re-elect the TNIP government to office, and in consequence, all suggested reform of the voting system to allow for a genuinely secret ballot has been vigorously resisted – for this would eradicate much of the chiefly influence at the polls and endanger the hegemony of the TNIP.

In addition to their activities in determining the vote, chiefs have also played a considerable role in the selection of candidates for the elective seats. The precedent was established in the 1963 election when Paramount Chief Sabata Dalindyebo and Kaiser Matanzima called meetings in their respective regions at which certain nominees were endorsed as representing the interests of their various tribes.[44] But with the formation of political parties, nomination procedure became (at least in theory) rather more formal. With but a handful of traditional rulers supporting it, the influence of the chiefs in the selection of DP candidates has always been limited – although the role of Sabata among the Thembu was always to the fore, and in February 1971, for instance, the Thembuland Regional Committee (which was dominated by the Paramount) forced the national executive to relinquish its official candidates for an Umtata by-election in favour of its own.[45] Thus where the DP *has* enjoyed chiefly support, it has had to accommodate the party structure accordingly.

Not surprisingly, chiefly influence in the selection of TNIP candidates has always been more explicit. For the 1968 elections the official procedure was that prospective candidates were invited to submit their names to the national executive, which would then arrange for meetings of party supporters in the constituencies to choose their favourite candidates by majority vote.[46] Yet while in theory allowing for popular choice, in practice this devolved candidate selection upon the chiefs. TNIP selection meetings were held at Tribal Authority Offices, and were usually chaired by the local or a neighbouring chief; chiefs packed meetings with their own supporters; and in many cases Matanzima let his preferences for nomination be known to the chiefs concerned. Then, in 1973, the role of the chiefs was emphasized even more, for Matanzima was seeking to exorcize the influence of party dissidents, and accordingly selection was now entrusted to nomination courts in the Districts composed of the heads and members of the local Tribal Authorities (unless they were Opposition supporters), headmen and subheadmen loyal to the TNIP, plus a number of women equal in number to the subheadmen involved. The desired result was attained, for there was a consequent considerable turnover of official TNIP candidates, while ten sitting Members of the Assembly were denied the nomination – and among them was Mr Curnick Ndamse, a populist figure who was then seeking to challenge Matanzima for the party leadership; and when these ten former

Members later stood for election as independent candidates, they were unceremoniously expelled from the TNIP.[47]

Events in the Mount Ayliff constituency are highly instructive. Curnick Ndamse a former university lecturer, had been brought into the Cabinet in 1968 after Matanzima had negotiated with the South African government to lift a restriction order imposed on him under the Suppression of Communism Act for activities among students at Fort Hare. He brought to the Ministry of Education a flair and competence unusual among Transkeian ministers, and as he developed a popular following he was hastily removed to the less influential Department of Roads and Works, before being dismissed from the Cabinet in 1971. An attempt was then made to expel him from the party in 1972, but it became clear that this would create an open breach within the ruling party. Consequently, Matanzima bided his time and took his opportunity in 1973 when he worked to ensure the non-selection of Ndamse as an official candidate for the TNIP. But all his best laid plans went awry, for Ndamse then stood in Mount Ayliff as an independent candidate, and despite an intensive campaign effort by Matanzima himself to secure his defeat, was successfully returned to the TLA, largely because he received the personal backing of Chief Jojo, the local man of power.[48]

Ndamse was not to remain a threat for much longer, for he died the following year, and with the consequent by-election in view, Matanzima sought to reincorporate Jojo into the TNIP domain by now allowing him his own free choice of candidate. The available record of the selection proceedings is worth recording at length, for it may well be representative of TNIP nomination procedures that have occurred elsewhere.

Meeting, Great Place, Lubaleko on the 18th July, 1974...[49]
In attendance: Honourable Chief George Ndabankulu, Minister for Roads and Works, accompanied by G. M. Mwanda (Secretary, TNIP), Xesibe tribesmen and Chief S. G. Jojo...

Chief S. G. Jojo: welcomed the Minister ... Then the Chief advised the Xesibe of the death of Mr. C. M. Ndamse who has represented Mt. Ayliff as an independent candidate during the last general election. The Chief advised them that it is only two men who have come forward as candidates for Mt. Ayliff viz. (i) Mr. G. Nota and (ii) Mr. Jacob Jojo who is in Port Elizabeth.

Since it is only two candidates he as Chief of the Xesibes has decided on one man best known to Xesibes as Mr. G. Nota of Rode in the Mt. Ayliff district and as such his word is final and was supported by Headman Fikeni of Ndzongiseni Location.

The Headman from Dutyini Location stood up to query the decision arrived at by the Chief alone and set the whole meeting in disorder ... [Then] all the interested people were requested to come forward. They were a good number of people who were unknown to me as Secretary of the party except Mr. G. Nota, Mr. C. Mzilwa and a certain teacher old and pensioned Mr. Fikeni, best known to me as a DP candidate in 1968 and four others completely unknown to me...

> I had to tell them that Mr. G. Nota is the choice of the Chief and that of the Xesibes and has made himself known to Umtata ... I had to deny Mr. G. Mzilwa's candidature because even on that day the Chief hated him from the bottom of his heart and as such his candidature will rock this party to pieces. Why I had to stick to Chief S. G. Jojo's candidate, it is simple to reply, to improve good relations between him and the Party (meaning Leadership) as it was very much strained last year due to Mr. Ndamse's insubordination which was clearly visible that this young chief of Mt. Ayliff was under Mr. Ndamse's chains...
> The Headman of Dutyini Location had to somersault and put everything correct in favour of Chief S. G. Jojo and nobody spoke otherwise.
> Chief S. G. Jojo summarised everything by telling everybody to vote Nota who is a Xesibe...

Nota was subsequently elected in the by-election that followed and also in the general election of 1976.

In summary, therefore, the chiefly élite plays a determining role in the majority of nominations for the TNIP. Often this means that chiefs not gaining nomination to the Assembly on an *ex officio* basis have often secured entry by election – and of course many of the other elected members have doubtless been related by ties of blood to chiefly families. Yet it is not the case that the TNIP is simply the chiefly élite in disguise, for it has also embraced increasing numbers of candidates drawn from non-chiefly elements of the upper echelons of reserve society, thereby incorporating men of rural prominence into the political ambit of the ruling party. But the fact that the chiefs retain the key role in the selection of candidates serves to ensure that popular influence over recruitment into the political élite is severely limited and subject to close control from above.

The emphasis so far has been upon the use of chiefly authority as an instrument for limiting effective political action by the reserve population. Yet while popular apathy towards bantustan politics has facilitated the sway of the ruling group, the electoral process has also been utilized to encourage a controlled participation on a tribal basis. In the first place, it has been in the interest of the TNIP government to lay claim to popular favour in order to counter accusations that it is undemocratic. Secondly, and more specifically, chiefly influence has been used to mobilize popular support upon a parochial basis in pursuit of material gain. To a degree, 'tribalism' in Africa is a product of distinct (and perhaps previously separate) peoples having been brought together in a shared involvement in a colonial economy wherein they were encouraged (by administrative policies which promoted tribal differentiation) to compete on an ethnic basis for scarce goods – such as land, employment and social services – which were deemed necessary for their security. In consequence, they were induced to identify as the source of their misfortune not the colonial power (and the system of imperial domination that it represented) but other colonized and similarly exploited peoples. Yet political independence has not brought an end to such divisive tendencies, and in the post-colonial situation new men of power have been able to instigate tribal feeling in furtherance of their own particular ends by offering themselves as patrons capable of securing benefits for 'their' people at the expense of other ethnic groups; yet, time and again, these special interests can be identified as those of fractions of the locally dominant classes, and 'Tribalism then becomes a mask for class privilege'.[50] And so, it would appear, in the Transkei, where the political arena has been structured along tribal lines under the implementation of the Bantu Authority system.

The politics of patronage in the Transkei have manifested themselves in electoral terms by a constant emphasis upon tribal particularism. In the first place, for chiefs or politicans to gain access to scarce resources distributed by the state they have had to establish their political weight, and at one level this has been expressed in the Transkei in terms of a drive for voter registration, as the number of members per electoral division is proportionate to the number of voters. In 1963, therefore, 'tribal leaders, anxious that their particular region should enjoy the maximum possible influence within the new Assembly, naturally supported efforts to build up the size of their region's electorate',[51] and Sabata Dalindyebo is reported as having exhorted his people to register so that the Thembu would have the strongest possible voice in the new Transkeian government.[52] In electoral terms, therefore, chiefs have urged their peoples to identify with their 'traditional group' – as Thembu, Xhosa, Pondo and so on – and it has been exceptional for elective candidates in any particular area to come from a different region of the Transkei (and indeed, the electoral law actually requires that each candidate be a registered voter in the constituency in which he or she stands).

Thus it is the quest for immediate benefits which may in part underlie the post-1963 voting trend in favour of the TNIP, as voters have sought to locate the patron most capable of bringing home the goods. Unless there have been local factors which have intervened, this will have effectively meant voting for the ruling party – for to return Opposition candidates endangers a constituency's position in the queue for receipt of material benefit. As one observer of the 1968 election shrewdly commented, 'a vote for the opposition parties only expressed protest. Acceptance of some of the fruits of separate development, which might lead to support for the TNIP, did not necessarily imply disagreement with much of the DP platform.'[53] It is this factor which may, in part, explain increased voter participation in the election of 1976 (44 per cent of registered voters in contested seats as compared to a turnout of 34 per cent in 1973), although this increase occurred only in the context of a substantial decline in the number of registered voters (see Table 4.2, p. 141 below). Thus it was not, as Matanzima claimed at the time, that people were enthused with the prospect of independence, but rather that independence was seen as devolving new powers of patronage upon the incumbents of office, whose favour therefore had to be gained by displays of loyalty to the winning side. Certainly, such interpretation helps to explain the popular basis of the the TNIP vote and the almost total elimination in that election of the Opposition; and it follows from this that, in so far as the chiefs continue to play a central and determining role as patrons in the political arena, so will 'tribalism' continue to be a pervasive feature of the electoral process; and in turn, so will popular participation be utilized to reassert the dominance of the ruling group and to mask divisions of interest between the chiefs, the politicians and the people.

Restriction on Opposition activity

Activity by opponents of separate development has been permitted in the Transkei only in so far as it has been perceived as compatible with, or even functional to, the achievement of apartheid goals. Thus while Opposition groups have been allowed to exist and to participate in homeland politics, this has only been to the extent that they have constituted no threat to the continuing domination of the political élite.

The boundaries of the political arena in the self-governing Transkei were defined by the existing security legislation in the Republic, such as the Suppression of Communism Act, in addition to arbitrary powers exercised by the state under Proclamation 400. As has been discussed above, the latter was introduced as an emergency measure to cope with the Revolt of 1960–1, and was subsequently retained in the years leading up to independence. Thus in addition to being subject to the restraints imposed upon African political activity elsewhere in South Africa, opponents of the white regime and its TNIP satraps had to contend with the awesome authority of the bantustan regime.

The state was not backward in utilizing the repressive powers which it had at its disposal. Between 1963 and 1966, more than 900 persons were detained under Proclamation 400.[54] Thereafter, with the African mass in the Transkei (as in the Republic) relapsing into a sullen acquiescence and the threat of Poqo crushed, these powers were used rather more sparingly – but their continued presence upon the statute book served as a constant reminder of the narrow limits of opposition to the Matanzima regime.

The criterion whereby the bantustan authorities determined whether or not to tolerate political opponents of separate development was whether they threatened to subvert the homeland political apparatus. Thus the scene was set in the 1963 election when eight candidates in Qaukeni of the Eastern Pondoland Peoples' Party (the only such grouping to emerge) were arrested during the course of the campaign. This party, the remnant of the militants who had taken part in the uprising of 1960–1, was reputedly in contact with the ANC-in-exile, and presented a potential threat to the Matanzima faction if it were to channel continuing popular discontent with Bantu Authorities against the chiefly stratum.[55]

It was precisely because the Democratic Party under Paramount Chief Victor Poto and Mr Knowledge Guzana (who succeeded the former as leader in 1966) sought to counter apartheid by operating within the confines prescribed by Pretoria that it was acceptable. For all that the DP dedicated itself to multiracialism, rejected the homeland concept and reviled the repressions of apartheid, as political opponents they played directly into Matanzima's hands by accepting the TLA as their main political forum – even after the manifestly undemocratic manner in which the chiefs had negated the popular choice. Thereafter, until Guzana was deposed from the leadership in January 1976, the DP accepted the role of parliamentary opposition and operated under the ground rules of homeland politics. Yet it was manifest from its earliest days that the DP was allowed to exist only on sufferance. Guzana himself was initially subjected to official scrutiny when he was questioned by police about alleged contacts with Alan Paton, the leader of the Liberal Party;[56] and over the years that followed the DP was the victim of a host of electoral malpractices that eroded both its credibility and its representation in the Assembly. Its campaigning was consistently hampered by TNIP chiefs refusing (under Proclamation 400) to countenance DP meetings within their areas of administration; its attempt to form a party organization in the Regions similarly foundered upon the rock of chiefly intransigence; and it was subject to all the electoral manipulations and distortions which were discussed above.

The DP's response to this was to adopt the same methods of foul play – by utilizing the politics of patronage and seeking to return its own members to the Assembly by exploiting the resources of its own chiefly notables.[57] These were not large, and its major foci of support lay in Nyanda and Dalindyebo regions, where it was backed by the respective paramounts. Yet if this was its strength, then it was also its weakness, for its small chiefly following was subject to an inevitable erosion under the joint forces of administrative pressures and the inducements of patronage from the TNIP government. The major blow came in March 1976, in which month both supporting paramounts quit the party. Tutor Ndamse, who had succeeded his father to the Nyanda paramountcy when the latter died in 1972, crossed over to the ruling party supposedly because the TNIP had now adopted the DP's multiracial platform and because at a mass meeting the Pondo had allegedly resolved in favour of independence[58] – although in actuality it would seem that he was reluctant to be excluded from the spoils of government after October 1976.

Sabata Dalindyebo left for rather different reasons. Since the succession of Guzana to the DP leadership, the party had been racked by a series of disputes. To some extent, this may have been attributable to Guzana's originally having come from the Ciskei. Certainly, from early days the new leader was never close to the Paramount and, if this predisposed him to perceiving the party struggle in universalistic terms, it did not suit Sabata, who rather viewed the DP as a vehicle for advancing his paramountcy dispute with Matanzima. In 1972 the party's Thembuland and Border Regional Committees had urged Dalindyebo to oust Guzana and assume the leadership himself. This he had declined to do, but the rift in the party continued – with different factions putting up their own candidates in opposition to each other in a number of constituencies in the 1973 election and subsequent by-elections.[59] Guzana lost all authority, and the crisis culminated in January 1976 with his displacement from the leadership by the party congress in favour of the much younger Hector Ncokazi, who scorned the TLA as a pseudo-parliament, declared he did not wish to become a member and sought to reorient the DP in a radically new direction, aspiring to align it with the South African Students' Organization (SASO) and the Black Peoples' Convention (BPC).[60] Ncokazi, a Thembu, had previously been chairman of the party's Dalindyebo Region and benefited if not from Sabata's support then at least from his benevolent neutrality in the leadership dispute. But once he had successfully made his coup, Ncokazi was subjected to a bitter and prolonged attack by the Matanzima brothers on account of his alleged communistic leanings, and thereafter it required considerable political courage or conviction to identify publicly with the radicalized DP.

Meanwhile, outmanoeuvred and outflanked on the left, the handful of Guzana loyalists sought refuge in the sanctuary of a New Democratic Party, while Sabata, who was allegedly threatened with deposition were he to lend his weight to the radical elements,[61] disassociated himself from the DP and announced he would henceforth sit in the Assembly as an independent. 'When Mr. Ncokazi was made leader of the Democratic Party,' he said, 'we were not aware he was being called a saboteur. My Thembus do not want to be involved in revolutions or anything like that.' But, he added, '*As far as we are concerned there is nothing against him.*'[62] Yet forced into a corner though he was, Sabata had one more card to play, and that was to throw his weight against Guzana when the latter stood in the Mqanduli seat at the subsequent general election. Previously benefiting from the paramount's patronage, the former DP leader now found Sabata's influence used against him, and he tumbled to a crushing defeat, locating the cause of his downfall in 'tribalism', alleging that the fact that he was not a Thembu had been used against him.[63] Thus as he had sown, so did he reap.

Even apart from its leadership disputes and inchoate organization, the premises upon which the Democratic Party had operated had presented no realistic threat to the TNIP, for the DP's programme and mode of presentation of policies were impeccably liberal. Guzana, who graduated from Fort Hare in the same year as Kaiser Matanzima himself, is a lawyer of repute, a Methodist lay preacher and a highly articulate public speaker who dominated the floor of the Legislative Assembly with flowery rhetoric and appeals to classical learning. Yet while his erudite discourses upon the conceptual contradictions of apartheid theory certainly impressed a host of overseas observers, as did his steadfast advocacy of non-violence, his sheer humanity and his unfailing belief in reason, his oratory soared above the heads of his constituency, for whom he had nothing to recommend but patience and no prospect to offer but hope of a long-term improvement; and while the DP was publicly committed to universal suffrage, it was widely known that in private Guzana favoured a qualified franchise in favour of the educated and propertied as a solution to the South African dilemma. Such an opponent – and one who obviously despaired of gaining office – was but an easy victim for Matanzima's craft, graft and shrewd political pragmatism. But in addition, Guzana served the Chief Minister's purposes admirably, for as Leader of the Opposition his precisely delivered and intelligent speeches gained widespread publicity in the outside world, and promoted the image of the Transkei as a functioning two-party democracy.

Yet if one looks beyond his personal failings for the source of Guzana's ultimate demise, it becomes apparent that his politics lacked any substantial basis in a class interest. One early commentary referred to him as the 'least typical Transkeian politician' (which was true) and as belonging to 'an almost non-existent group, the Transkeian middle class'.[64] The latter verdict was only partially true, for although the petty-bourgeois stratum to which Guzana might have appealed was small in number, it was arguably more politically conscious of the oppressions of white supremacy than the rest of the reserve population; and it was from among its ranks that the towering figures of Mandela, Tambo and Mbeki had themselves been drawn. Edwin Munger, writing in 1962, noted that 'some of the most frustrated Africans were in the Transkei':

> These include 250 University graduates, many of them included among 3,000 teachers, as well as some 600 traders and numerous clerks. This is a far greater university-educated African élite than possessed by the whole Congo at the date of independence. Many of the best minds amongst these educated Africans in the Transkei are now denied expression by the tight control of the chiefs. Many of them belong to the Liberal Party which finds its broadest African rural support in the Transkei. If the bantustans are to succeed, they will have to attract and involve these African intellectuals.[65]

This was a stratum that was destined to grow in size under the homeland strategy, yet Guzana never sought to mobilize its support – probably because he realized that it was sufficiently conscientized to reject his conservative leadership. Politically ambivalent in that it sought to grasp opportunities of material advancement offered under separate development (for example, Matanzima's pursuit of Africanization in teaching and the trading sector), simultaneously it was among this group that the greatest awareness of black deprivation was to be found in rural society.

Guzana's failure to articulate the aspirations of those petty-bourgeois elements which were disaffected from the Matanzima regime was to prove his eventual undoing, for the later emergence to prominence within the DP of Hector Ncokazi was in part premised upon the support of this selfsame group (along with tribal support via Sabata Dalindyebo, whose interest is always to back promising horses against the upstart Matanzima). Ncokazi, a PAC sympathizer in his schooldays in Umtata,[66] first came to public view in 1974 when even though he was not a Member of Assembly, he sought to topple Guzana from the DP leadership. Linking together with TLA members from Engcobo who were associated with Sabata, Ncokazi played upon the dissatisfaction which many party members felt with Guzana's conservative leanings. But what finally precipitated the leader's downfall was the decision by Matanzima in 1974 to opt for independence. Although Guzana continued to speak out against fragmentation of the Republic, there were many who felt that the Opposition should take a more active and radical line against it; and importantly, much of this impetus seems to have come from urban elements from outside the Transkei who viewed independence as constituting a threat to their residential security through exposing them to greater danger of being endorsed out of white areas as non-South African citizens.[67]

As Laurence has indicated,[68] Ncokazi's triumph over Guzana at the party congress in January 1976 was a bid to inject the mood of black consciousness into the ailing DP. Indeed, Ncokazi made no secret of the fact that he had friendly relations with members of both SASO and BPC, and as early as 1973 Matanzima had accused him of acting as a front-man for Barney Pityana (the SASO general secretary).[69] Thus after his election as leader of the party, Ncokazi proclaimed his commitment to the DP not as an opposition party in bantustan politics, but (bizarre as it sounds) as a 'Liberation Movement'. And in the context of the Transkei, his rhetoric was consistently radical: the DP was to become the vehicle of the 'oppressed and dispossessed in South Africa', and the main objective was to dislodge 'white domination'. But it was not so much his discourse which concerned Matanzima (for he often made such statements himself), but his attempt to fan underlying discontent with independence in the homeland into flame and to link it with the more explicit rejection by those affected in urban areas.[70] Thus when Ncokazi called upon the DP to boycott independence celebrations and declared himself in favour of contacting the OAU and UN in order to prevent the Transkei from gaining international recognition, he placed himself beyond the limits of toleration; and when he and his associates made it clear that they intended making opposition to independence the focus of their election campaign (after first considering a total electoral boycott), they were victims of an official clampdown. Ncokazi, an accountant with a Xhosa Development Corporation-controlled bus company, was dismissed from his post; and between 25 and 27 July nine prospective DP candidates in the election (including Ncokazi and his entire executive committee) were detained under Proclamation 400, these being joined by three others at a later date. It can hardly have been coincidence that George Matanzima's car was burnt out on the very day of Ncokazi's arrest – and that this was followed by other instances of arson.[71]

The arrests left the DP in disarray. In the Engcobo Region, from where most of those arrested came, others came forward to take their place as candidates; elsewhere, others who had intended standing for election opted out rather than risk detention. The result was that the eleven members who stood under the DP banner were subject to severe constraint; and in electoral terms the 1976 election was less of a contest than ever before, Guzana's NDP putting up only fourteen candidates, the TNIP members being unopposed in sixteen constituencies, with voters being asked to choose between alternative TNIP candidates in seats elsewhere. The final result was a foregone conclusion, and only four out of the seventy-five members elected did not belong to the ruling party.[72]

The limitation of urban influence in the electoral process

In terms of the apartheid scenario, all blacks resident in urban areas of 'white' South Africa are citizens of one of the homelands; thus according to the census of 1970, 1,271,000 Transkeians out of a total of 2,997,000 live outside the territory, mostly in the larger towns. The majority of these urban dwellers have no economic link or substantial social tie with their 'homeland', and have no association with it except in so far as they are legally bound to it by official *diktat*. At the same time, it is this element among the entire population group defined as Transkeian which is most conscious of separate development as a device for entrenching white supremacy, so that in consequence urban blacks generally reject the entire concept of the bantustans and take little or no interest in homeland politics.

In addition to the urban residents, there are usually upwards of 250,000 migrants from the Transkei who work in the Republic, mainly in the mines. Oscillating at regular intervals between their place of employment and the reserve, migrants are often dependent upon a subsistence income in the homeland for the maintenance of their families, and are in consequence by no means isolated from the Transkei as are the urban residents. Yet subject to the daily indignities of life in the compounds and the operation of the Pass Laws, while simultaneously removed from the control of the chiefs, migrants are politically volatile and alienated from the bantustan establishment, which is closely identified with the interests of the mining companies through its operation of the labour bureaux. Migrants are therefore generally hostile to the Matanzima regime.

The rejection of the bantustans and their leaders by the broad mass of the urban black population has induced the Transkeian government and the Department of Bantu Administration to limit the influence of the urban vote in the various general elections in order to protect the TNIP majority in the TLA. In apartheid terms, of course, each Transkeian citizen is enfranchised and entitled to exercise his democratic right in choosing his parliamentary representative; in practice, were the urban population to be mobilized to vote in Transkeian elections (and these were free), the electoral dominance of the Matanzima regime would be extinguished; in the 1963 elections, for instance (the only contest in which returns in urban areas were made separately available), although there were considerable variations in voter preferences in regard to individual candidates when compared with the rural vote, the general trend of the urban vote was to support the Poto faction.[73] In consequence, the Transkeian government has subsequently treated the urban electorate with considerable caution and has sought to encourage only minimal voter participation.

The procedure for Transkeian elections requires that eligible persons must register their names on an official electoral roll if they wish to qualify as voters. Within the homeland itself, registration is left to the Tribal Authorities, and is generally encouraged by the chiefs; in the 1963 elections, 97 per cent of those within the Transkei who were deemed eligible registered as voters. In urban areas, Bantu Affairs Commissioners were the sole registration officials until 1976, when they were assisted by Transkeian Urban Representatives. In 1963 (again, the only election for which figures are available), some 50 per cent (or 250,000) of those eligible registered, and calculations would suggest that this proportion has remained constant over later years or subject to only a small increase: 'only a fraction of the eligible voters outside the territory actually registered as voters', writes Kotze,[74] and the majority of these would appear to be migrant workers, especially mine labourers, who are a captive population and therefore easily dealt with by registration officials.[75] Outside the mines, there would seem to be not just a reluctance, but a positive avoidance of voter registration by urban blacks, as identification with the Transkei can often lead to an enforced removal to the homeland when people are considered by white officials as not qualifying for continued residence. Thus one obstacle towards registration of voters in the Transvaal, as reported by the TNIP General Secretary in 1968, was:

> the endorsement out of Transkeian citizens after having been found out to be a Transkeian voter by the location superintendent ... One other aspect concerning the endorsement of Transkeian citizens which is totally against the Transkei set up is the uncontrolled utterances of the so-called Location Superintendent's Municipal Labour Offices that K. D. Matanzima wants you in the Transkei.[76]

Again, complaint made by George Matanzima himself to the Republican government is instructive:

> ... many widows have been endorsed out after being found that they belong to the Transkei and their houses have been sold for hard cash to other people by the Location Superintendent ... this sort of thing really happened in 1963 during the first registration of the Transkei people as voters ... the very idea of endorsing out Transkei citizens during the re-registration period has really made the Transkeians wild and even the so-called Chiefs' representatives have not registered as Transkei voters through fear.
>
> This Mrs. Constance M— [was told] to go to the Transkei because Matanzima wants her back ... Will the Republic of South Africa allow ... the name of our Honourable Leader to be used as a scape-goat in endorsing out the

Transkeians to work against the Transkei Government? Will the Republic of South Africa allow such people who have political hatred of the Transkei to work among the Bantu... Such fatal utterances against the Transkei Government should not be allowed to be carried on by the so-called, employed Influx Control Officers serving the Bantu people under the Republican Government, as this tendency will have serious repercussions amongst our midst.[77]

Such a protest is indicative that bantustan leaders are less than enthusiastic about their territories becoming dumping grounds for the unemployed and useless, for they realize that such dispossessed elements, apart from draining away meagre resources, will constitute a politically hostile element; and the Matanzima brothers themselves can hardly rejoice that people are removed from the towns in their name. In this the interests of the Republican and homeland governments obviously conflict, even though for the latter the implementation of the enforced removal policy does serve a useful purpose in decreasing urban voter participation in elections.

Yet both the South African and Transkeian political authorities seek to enjoy the best of both worlds. The Department of Bantu Administration has therefore gone to very considerable lengths in the past to promote a façade of widespread, black urban involvement in the homeland 'democratic' process. Employers have been requested to allow workers time off to vote, and polling bureaux (550 of them in 1976) have been established throughout the length and breadth of the Republic and South West Africa. Similarly, both major parties in the Transkei have sought to gain electoral advantage by structuring the small urban vote in their favour. Yet such efforts have been perfunctory, and homeland party organizations in urban areas are largely moribund even though, for the TNIP especially, small congeries of supporters in the townships have served a useful legitimizing function whenever Matanzima has wished to claim urban support for his policies.

But it has been clearly recognized that the bantustan leadership has needed to be insulated from urban political pressure, and accordingly the Transkeian electorate resident in the urban areas of 'white' South Africa has been allotted no separate representation in the homeland legislature. Instead, urban voters have had to register for rural constituencies, where any disruptive electoral impact they might have made could usually be absorbed by a chiefly-backed, TNIP vote; and in any case, given the rural orientation of the major homeland parties, nomination procedures have always worked to exclude all but a handful of urban candidates. In the 1963 election, only eight of the 180 candidates resided outside the Transkei and only one was elected;[78] and in 1973, the 'nomination courts of both parties consisted only of [rural] supporters of the respective parties and because urban candidates were mostly not known in the Transkei they could not secure a party nomination'.[79] The reverse is as a consequence also true, and Carter and her associates recorded that in many cases the urban voters had no knowledge of any of the candidates.

The net result of these various factors has been to insulate Transkeian elections from any disruptive urban impact. The precise extent of voter absenteeism in urban areas is impossible to assess, because urban voting statistics are deliberately merged with rural figures in order to conceal the low level of participation. Accordingly, it is necessary to fall back on journalistic observation. Thus in covering the 1976 election *The Star* (29 September 1976) reported that in Soweto and Johannesburg there were generally more police than voters visible at the polling stations; and John Kane-Berman, writing in the *Financial Times* (1 October 1976), reported 'an almost total lack of interest in the election'. Fewer than five voters had cast their votes at most of the Soweto polling stations, and one returning officer, patient in his pursuit of Bantu democracy, sat for thirteen hours to supervise only four voters! There seems also to have been widespread awareness that the leading Opposition candidates had been detained, that the electoral process was unfree and that the TNIP was guaranteed a majority before a single vote was cast; and accordingly, even where voting was reportedly 'brisk' (at the mines in Roodeport and Randfontein), many voters were disappointed because in areas where they wanted to vote for the Opposition the TNIP candidates were unopposed.[80] Consequently, participation by registered voters in the Johannesburg area (including the migrants who do retain ties with the Transkei) was estimated as being no more than 10 per cent in total – which one Afrikaans source reports as a repetition of 'the tendency in the 1973 elections when only 39,000 voters outside the Transkei voted'.[81]

The TNIP: a party for the patrons[82]

Detailed attention has been paid here to the electoral process in the Transkei in order to demonstrate the systematic manner in which it is structured in order to secure the return of the Matanzima regime. Yet no analysis of the control mechanisms whereby the bantustan political élite maintains its domination over the reserve masses would be complete without an examination of the structure of the ruling party, for it is through the TNIP that the leadership claims to harmonize the needs of the chieftaincy and the people, and through which it legitimizes its right to rule.

The TNIP can be characterized as an 'élite party' which, although exhibiting outward forms that might suggest that it has an independent existence of its own, is not only dominated by the chiefs but is actually inseparable from the whole structure of chieftaincy as revived under the Bantu Authorities system. Already, it has been demonstrated that the chiefs play the critical part in selecting candidates for the Assembly and securing the re-election of the ruling party to office. Similarly, the competition between the ruling party and the Opposition groupings has been characterized as principally factional conflict between local 'notables' which only external appearances have dignified as competition between parties. Only when the revitalized Democratic Party sought to take the political struggle outside the cosy confines of the parliamentary arena, prior to the election of 1976 (by involving 'the people' in a rejection of 'independence'), were there any real signs of active participation by the masses in the political process – and this, of course, was hastily quashed by the incumbent regime. All that remains, therefore, is to examine more closely the pretensions of the ruling TNIP to be a party which genuinely represents the interests of the Transkeian populace at large.

The 'Programme of Principles' which was enunciated by the TNIP soon after its formation in 1964 stressed its adherence to the principles of Separate Development, and pledged itself both to the conservation of tribal law and custom and to the preservation of the office of chieftainship and *ex officio* membership of the chiefs in the TLA. At the same time, however, the party committed itself to the maintenance of the franchise for all those defined as Transkeian citizens, 'thus linking the traditional political system with the modern concept of democracy' – and in order to achieve this synthesis, the party further sought to develop an organizational structure to accommodate popular participation and membership. Thus a network of branches (of no less than ten persons) was to be established covering every location within the Transkei as well as in every African area in the towns of 'white' South Africa, with committees elected annually whose major function would be to secure the return of chosen candidates at time of election. In turn, these branches were to be grouped together into District Committees (composed of all members of branch executives) and Districts into Regions, with the organizational pyramid culminating at the Party Headquarters in Umtata, which was to be supervised by the Leader and National Executive. Finally, the supreme organ of the party was supposedly to be the National Congress, which was (in normal circumstances) to be held annually.[83]

In practice, such ambitious plans have never materialized, nor has there ever been any major effort to activate widespread participation, for the party leadership and the chiefly élite have always appreciated that a popularly based movement would represent a threat to their hegemony. In consequence, the party organization has always remained virtually moribund, and with a minimal formal membership. Thus (the spasmodically kept) records show that by 1965–6 there were only 200 registered members within the Transkei itself, with a balance of 143 located in the urban areas of South Africa. By 1969, while still very low, the membership had increased to 5,151 (with some 1,437 of these being resident in the Republic), but by 1975 it had slumped back to 3,428 (1,720 within the Transkei and 1,708 beyond its frontiers).[84]

Yet fundamental to an understanding of how the TNIP operates is a grasp of the division of its activities between the party in the Transkei proper and the party in the urban townships of South Africa, for it is only in the latter areas that it exists in anything more but name. *Within* the Transkei, the party has been more or less absorbed by the official structure of Bantu Authorities, with branches (such as they are) usually controlled by the local chiefs. Thus Pascoe Ludidi, the Secretary-General, writing in 1975, depicted the situation as follows:

> under the present set-up the Party in the Transkei is based upon caucuses or individuals narrowly recruited, rather independent of one another and generally decentralised; these small cliques and/or individuals work loosely and very often outside the constitution of the Party. Their aim is not so much to increase membership or to enlist the masses as to recruit outstanding people and as to vy [sic] with one another for positions to which, once they are elected, they cling tenaciously. Their leadership is in the hands of their parliamentary representative or chiefs and is very markedly individual and undemocratic in form. Thus, the support of the Party in most areas is nominal and dwingling [sic] in others...[85]

In some areas, the party machinery has been used as direct supplement to chiefly authority – in Tsolo District, for instance, membership of TNIP was at one time held to be prerequisite to the right to graze stock on communal land.[86] But more usually, the chiefs have regarded the party as a rival source of authority, and have as a consequence vigorously opposed its activation: 'some chiefs who are members of the party were even working against the party and in some areas having the elected members charged or raided by detectives', lamented the Secretary-General in 1975.[87] 'Chiefs should learn to distinguish between party administration and local government administration; above all chiefs should not regard the party jealously or take it for competing with their authority.'[88] Thus the tendency is for TNIP branch organizations to be mobilized (or rather, for Tribal Authorities to assume their party hue) only during the run-up to an election, and once the need to campaign has passed, the party structure merges once more into the chiefly administration.

In striking contrast, the TNIP enjoys a more active (if intermittent) existence in the urban areas of South Africa, precisely because the absence of an administrative structure centred around the chiefs necessitates its more formal organization. Those who are active within the urban ranks of the party are usually individuals who retain familial links with the Transkei or who envisage a move to the homeland at some future date. Commonly, party officials have ties with the chieftaincy 'at home', and a number are recognized by the white administration as Urban Chiefs' Representatives, appointed to supervise the affairs of particular tribal groups within the locations. But often, activists view the TNIP as a channel whereby they may gain access to the material resources distributed by the bantustan state. In particular, aspiring businessmen perceive party membership as providing a basis for their applications for trading rights to be granted preferential consideration by the homeland authorities,[89] while simultaneously bolstering their claim to

Development Corporation loans: 'We are forming an Association to buy businesses in the Transkei,' wrote one Regional Secretary. 'The Xhosa Development Corporation has already sent me full details ... We want to start first with buses, as soon as the capital is available ...'[90]

Yet this inevitably provides the party leadership with an acute dilemma, for the resources available for distribution are limited, and expediency dictates that the more pressing claims of those within the Transkei be given first priority. At the same time, however, necessity has hitherto ordained that a formal party organization be sustained throughout the Republic in order to legitimize the government's position as representative of *all* Transkeian citizens, inclusive of those resident in urban areas of 'white' South Africa. But active popular participation by urban citizens within the party is not without its risks for, especially if fuelled by dissatisfaction with the meagre material results of support, it carries a potential threat to the incumbent, rurally based élite. The solution adopted by the leadership, therefore, has been to retain a skeletal organization which maintains a visible TNIP presence in major urban centres, but to leave it so isolated from the party proper that it is quite unable to make any significant impact on political affairs.

On paper, the organization of the party in the urban areas is not unimpressive: even if registered membership is low, there are regional committees for the Transvaal, Orange Free State, Western Cape, Eastern Cape and Karoo, North-Eastern Cape, North-Western Cape and Natal. Yet in almost all these areas the party at all levels is habitually bedevilled by factionalism and so thoroughly disorganized that it is rendered quite incapable of representing the urban interest, let alone conducting an effective electoral campaign.

In general, party affairs in the urban areas are characterized by a general condition of apathy, as members are both physically and politically cut off from the homeland. Indeed, excepting the rare occasions where TNIP branches have taken upon themselves extra-political functions such as the running of self-help burial clubs, their activities are spasmodic, ill-attended and subject to much personal intrigue by rivals for office. Perennially, competing factions claim to be in control of the party organization at regional, district or branch levels. Where elections for office are held, the result is commonly disputed by those who lose; incumbents of office pack meetings with their supporters to secure their re-election; and prominent individuals, impatient or jealous of the local leadership, form rival party bodies of their own. Quite often, disputes acquire ethnic connotations, as particular notables seek to mobilize and structure personal support along tribal lines; and most commonly of all, there are acrimonious disputes about the handling of party funds.

A few examples may suffice to illustrate the extent and nature of the factionalism which pervades the organization of the TNIP in urban areas.

... the members [were] disheartened by the utterings of the former Regional Chairman and the National Executive member, Chief C. F. F. Mdingi, who

went around the Transvaal telling the people that his election to the National Executive is a matter that is beyond their reach, because it is decided by the Honourable, the Leader of the Party ...
 In the Transvaal, I found things not working the TNIP way, the so-called Regional Chairman was not working at all that the TNIP should be united ... Secondly, the members of the party said it out that it was a Regional Committee of pals ...[91]

... There has been reckless handling of the party's finances ... most of the officials of the branch are guilty of the mishandling of the party's funds ...[92]

Mr. Mjiqiza complained that there had been meetings at Dobsonville concerning Transkeian affairs and they had been debarred from attending these meetings by Messrs. Bidli and Mlotywa, who said ... these meetings were only for Gcalekas. Mr. Mlotywa dissociated himself from Mr. Mjiqiza's allegations and said he always considered the interests of the Xhosas as a whole.[93]

Delegates of the TNIP from all over the Eastern Cape and Karoo Region met at Duncan Village Hall near East London on 25.1.76 ... The purpose of the meeting was to elect an Executive Committee of the Region. Mr. M. P. Ludidi, Secretary-General of the TNIP, conducted the elections. A small group of disgruntled supporters gave Mr. Ludidi an ultimatum to close his books before the meeting started ... They said if he did not comply with their ultimatum, there was going to be bloodshed. Mr. M. P. Ludidi asked the disgruntled group to put in a motion which was voted down by two-thirds majority of the delegates, after a bitter exchange of words and slight physical tussle which ended just before the Police came in.[94]

Such total lack of unity within the ranks of the party in urban areas, while eliminating any major threat to the leadership from below, is not without the disadvantage that it debilitates the TNIP and renders it incapable of mobilizing even limited electoral support. Even though it is in the general interest of the TNIP that the urban vote should be strictly controlled, it is none the less obviously beneficial to party fortunes if its own recognized supporters can be shepherded to the polls. Yet if the party organization is continuously paralysed by internecine conflict, it is clear that the potential favourable vote will be endangered.

To skirt around this dilemma, the party leadership has usually attempted to act as intermediary between disputants, but at times it has resorted to the use of the Urban Bantu Administration and the South African Security Police to contain intra-party conflict within acceptable limits. Again and again, available evidence points to explicit co-operation between the Transkeian and Republican authorities.

[The Secretary-General] ... we proceeded to Welkom. Here we were received with kindness by the Security Department who offered us a car driven by Segt. Porota from Matatiele, under the supervision of Captain D. Potgieter, head of the Security Department ... We addressed meetings in Virginia, Odendaalsrus, Kroonstad, and at Thabong ... In all these places the Commissioners were very cooperative including the Directors of the Bantu Townships.[95]

Mr. Mdingi, Mr. K. Mnweba, Mr. Bidli and Mr. R. Zwakala came with police from John Vorster Plein Square to stop our branch from conducting that meeting they said they were empowered or commissioned by the Transkeian Government, with the Republican Government to stop us from holding meetings. Now we want the Head Office to inform us urgently about this matter, we cannot work under a Police State, our people are tired of being questioned time and again by the Special Branch. In Alexandra Township we are no longer calling monthly meetings because of this police threat ...[96]

All what [Mr Mangqobe] did is to go around and calling caucus meetings with a group of more than six men whom he had formed with that they must write you a letter that we had resigned from the Party ... if this man cannot be expelled from our party there will be a great SPLIT and that had been proved even by the Security Branch Police who are working with me in this case ...[97]

On the 11th April 1965 the East London Branch was formed and all office bearers were sent to your office for recognition, but in or about October the same year the National Chairman Chief George Matanzima appointed his own East London Organiser against the election of the existing office ... During this juncture our Organiser Mr. W. T. Mlawu was called to the office of the Special Branch per report from the Local Authorities that he has opened an unofficial TNIP branch of Gcalekas ...[98]

In view of its incapacity to control the TNIP organization in urban areas by direct sanction from above, the leadership is thus forced to utilize Republican security forces to buttress its authority. This has suited the South African government well, for black political activity of whatever hue needs to be closely controlled, while white supervision of even so collaborative a body as the TNIP reinforces black despair.

Yet too much should not be made of the existence of the TNIP in urban areas, for its structure remains extremely rudimentary, its membership minuscule, and the conduct of its affairs chaotic. The centre of political gravity rests firmly in the Transkei – in the kraals and huts of the chiefs – and the party serves primarily to represent the interests of the petty-bourgeoisie which has emerged within the interstices of the bantustan state apparatus. Nor is the situation likely to change, for the TNIP leadership is wholly aware of the dangers of popular participation, and any attempt to provide the party with a mass base would be resisted, for Matanzima remains content to dominate his following – in Annual Congress and Parliament – by dint of his personal sway.

The move to 'independence'

Sufficient indication has been given above to suggest that Matanzima had no freely expressed mandate to lead the Transkei to political independence in 1976. Despite being assisted by all the numerous distortions of the electoral system, it was not until 1973 that the TNIP had been able to secure a majority (55 per cent) of the popular vote cast – and even this was gained only in conditions of declining participation and voter disillusion, as illustrated in Table 4.2. Matanzima was later to claim that the 1973 election had been fought on the independence issue, and that consequently the objective in 1976 was merely to allow the electorate opportunity to choose the 'Inkululeko' regime. He therefore rejected all Opposition demands for a popular referendum on independence, and when the revitalized Democratic Party threatened to stir up active resistance to his plans, simply placed its leadership behind bars. Such were the workings of the bantustan democratic process.

Table 4.2 *Voter participation in contested seats in Transkei general elections, 1963–76*

	1963	1968	1973	1976
No. of contested seats	45	45	40	59
Voters registered	880,425	907,778	952,369	847,255
Votes cast	601,204	451,916	323,092	372,098
%	68	50	34	44

Sources: D. A. Kotze (1975), Table 9.IV; and *Daily Dispatch*, 21 and 23 October 1976.

Yet however transparent the distortion of the electoral system, Matanzima was insistent that the TNIP victory in 1976 reflected widespread popular support for the bantustan regime, and to give substance to his claim he organized an unofficial 'referendum' of his own, seeking to put the independence issue to a variety of different bodies such as tribal authorities, farmers' associations, sporting clubs, women's groups, African Chambers of Commerce and urban boards. However, the results of this test, when subjected to inspection, were as dubious as the means, for while 125,000 of those polled were reportedly in favour of independence, only 14,000 were against; and of the 229 bodies polled, 148 failed to record a single vote against independence, while the total negative vote recorded by Transkeians in 'white' South Africa was only 21.[99]

But the electoral process apart, there are plenty of other pointers to the fact that Matanzima's drive towards independence in the mid-1970s was opposed by the majority of those designated Transkeian citizens. Not only did the Ncokazi-led DP pick up urban support for explicitly opposing the separation of the Transkei from the Republic, but there were reports of splits within the TNIP itself, notably in Eastern Pondoland and Maluti; and in the latter area, which is the territory of mainly South African Basotho (who constitute some 5 per cent of the Transkeian population), there was a pre-independence secessionist movement which was variously reported as wanting to join the homeland of Basotho QwaQwa, link up with adjoining Lesotho, or to stay an integral part of the Republic. Indeed, during the 1976 election campaign, Matanzima actually felt constrained to detain some of the leaders of the Maluti-Herschel South Sotho Central Committee which had delivered a petition to Chief Minister Kenneth Mopeli of the Sotho homeland, signed by 40,000 Basotho who reportedly wished to break away from the Transkei;

and similarly, resistance to independence was also registered by Basotho activists in Soweto. But most significantly of all, when Matanzima sought to extol the virtues of independence to urban Transkeians in Soweto in February 1976, his meeting attracted a meagre crowd of only 400, many of whom were present only to hoot and jeer.[100]

Support for independence was therefore minimal. The broad mass of inhabitants in the rural areas of the Transkei was cajoled into supporting the TNIP by the chiefs, while urban Transkeians (reluctant to lose their South African citizenship) were given no satisfactory means of expressing their dissent. None the less, independence came to the Transkei in 1976, and the voice of the multitude was deliberately left unheard.

Even so, Matanzima was by no means entirely without support, for independence favoured the interests of various social groups which had by this time developed within the structure of the bantustan political economy, and it was upon this internal foundation that Matanzima sought to base his regime. Created in large part by act of deliberate policy, this emergent petty-bourgeoisie was marked out by Pretoria as a future subordinate ally whose function would be to preside over the bantustan state. However, the story of the quasi-decolonization of the Transkei is still incomplete, for before proceeding to a detailed examination of the nature of this class it will be necessary first to analyse the means whereby it was given an economic base outside the narrow confines of the politico-administrative apparatus.

Notes

1. Hammond-Tooke (1975), pp. 206–7.
2. ibid., pp. 207–8.
3. SAIRR (1960).
4. This practice was to become well entrenched. See the later comments on Tribal Authority auditing by Democratic Party leader Knowledge Guzana (*Transkei Hansard* (1975), p. 134).
5. 'The so-called primitive accumulation, therefore, is nothing else than the historical process of divorcing the producer from the means of production. It appears as primitive, because it forms the pre-historic stage of capital and of the mode of production corresponding to it.' (Marx, 1977, p. 668).
6. Hunter (1936), p. 114.
7. Hammond-Tooke (1975), p. 211; Mbeki (1964), pp. 202–4.
8. *HAD*, 9 May 1962, col. 3288.
9. Tatz (1962), p. 192.
10. Fullest coverage of the revolt (albeit in unpublished form) has hitherto been given by Copelyn (BA Hons thesis, 1974). See also Baldwin (MA dissertation, 1971). More contemporary accounts are given by Mbeki (1964); and Turok (1961).
11. Mbeki (1964), p. 120; and SAIRR, *A Survey, 1959–60*, p. 41.
12. Hammond-Tooke (1975), pp. 105–7.
13. SAIRR, *A Survey, 1961*, p. 43.
14. 'For the Government, the charge of outside agitation immediately introduces the spectre of communism, of professional politicians exploiting the mass for their own personal ends. There is the further implication that the

people are content until misled by false propaganda. The magic formula thus exonerates the Government, eliminates the issue of policy, and transforms it into a problem of exorcising the devil.' Kuper (1965).
15. Copelyn (BA Hons thesis, 1974), p. 36.
16. Minutes of the TTCA Executive Committee, 7 November 1958; and TTCA Congress, May 1959.
17. Copelyn (BA Hons thesis, 1974), p. 51.
18. TTCA Congress, May 1959. One delegate: 'The natives are going to use boycotting as a weapon. The time is ripe at the moment in view of the threatened boycott by African National Congress.'
19. *Daily Dispatch*, 2 September 1960.
20. *RDM*, 30 November 1960.
21. TTCA Congress, June 1960.
22. SAIRR, *A Survey, 1959–60*, pp. 41–2; and *1961*, pp. 42, 49–50.
23. *Umtungwa*, 12 November 1960.
24. Thus Anderson Ganyile: 'Pondoland will be satisfied with nothing short of sending representatives to Parliament' (*New Age*, 17 November 1960).
25. SAIRR, *A Survey*, 1961, pp. 43–8.
26. ibid., pp. 50–1. The Pondo Revolt was matched by similar, though less coherent and less well organized disturbances in Thembuland. Beginning with an attempt to assassinate Matanzima in December 1962 (the intention of 20–30 Poqo activists being to travel from Cape Town to Qamata in Emigrant Thembuland for this purpose), opposition to the implementation of land rehabilitation led to the formation of secret village committees which launched a number of attacks on chiefs and headmen who were collaborating with the authorities. Perhaps the most important feature of the Thembuland disturbances was the manner in which local grievances became consciously political, with Poqo influence infiltrating from the Cape via migrant workers who, while destined to spend perhaps the major portion of their working lives away from home, none the less retained limited access to the means of production in the reserve, and who thus perceived the implementation of land rehabilitation as a threat to their livelihood. These disturbances reached a peak in 1963 and thereafter declined, partly because local conditions became more difficult, but also because the Pan-Africanist-inspired leadership of Poqo was not particularly sensitive to local needs. See Lodge (1977).
27. House of Assembly Debates, 10 April 1961, col. 4191.
28. *Proceedings of the TTA* (1961), p. 12.
29. For a detailed account of the procedural trickery used by the Nationalists to promote their apartheid-style constitution, see Mbeki (1964), pp. 49–64. For the authorized version, see Department of Information (1962).
30. For contemporary accounts of the 1963 elections, see: Carter *et al.* (1967), pp. 125–52; Stultz (1964); and Mayer (1966).
31. According to the London *Private Eye* (6 February 1976), Paramount Chief Botha Sicgau was presented with a farm worth £15,000 by the South African government in order to ensure that he threw his considerable weight behind Matanzima. (East Pondoland was to send a total of 23 representatives to the TLA.) Together, the two Paramounts prospered, and Sicgau later became first President of the Transkeian Republic. For his admission of receipt of this farm see *Transkeian Hansard*, 25 March 1974, p. 76.
32. As has been noted elsewhere, it was the DP which emerged as the champion of tradition, while the TNIP came to represent the bureaucratized chief-

taincy. See Vigne (1966?), p. 14; and Szeftel (MA thesis, 1970), pp. 75–6.
33. Horrell (1971), pp. 62–3.
34. Adam (1971), p. 77.
35. Mayer (1977), p. 303.
36. There were 91 registered chiefs in April 1974, and *Transkei Hansard*s for 1974, 1975 and 1976 reveal the creation of 33 more.
37. *Transkei Hansard*, 17 May 1976, pp. 325–7.
38. BENBO (1975), p. 57.
39. *TNIP Records*: 'Polling Officers: TNIP Nominations', 1968.
40. D. A. Kotze (1975), p. 207.
41. *Transkei Hansard, 1973/74*, p. 166.
42. D. A. Kotze (1975), p. 205.
43. *TNIP Records*: Z. J. R. Pamla to Chief Minister, 23 July 1968.
44. Carter *et al.* (1967), p. 129.
45. D. A. Kotze (1975), p. 123.
46. *TNIP Records*: General Secretary to W. W. F. Makaula, 10 November 1967 – 'Candidature for the 1968 General Election'.
47. D. A. Kotze (1975), p. 128; and interview, Mr Pascoe Ludidi, Secretary-General TNIP, 1975–6.
48. For the Ndamse affair, see D. A. Kotze (1975), pp. 123, 199; and for the 1973 election campaign, *Weekend Post*, 3 November 1973 and *RDM*, 14 September 1973.
49. *TNIP Records*: Report by G. M. Mwanda, General Secretary of TNIP, 18 July 1974.
50. Sklar (1967).
51. Carter *et al.* (1967), p. 127.
52. *Daily Dispatch*, 1 August 1963.
53. Saunders (1969).
54. Laurence (1976), p. 87.
55. Mbeki (1964), p. 142; and Carter *et al.* (1967), p. 129.
56. Carter *et al.* (1967), p. 156.
57. Interview, Mr Knowledge Guzana, 3 August 1976.
58. *Daily Dispatch*, 11 March 1976.
59. D. A. Kotze (1975), pp. 123–5, 127–8; Laurence (1976), p. 84.
60. *Daily Dispatch*, 3 September 1975; *Pretoria News*, 16 January 1976; Interview, Mr Knowledge Guzana, 3 August 1976.
61. *Pretoria News*, 30 August 1976.
62. *Daily Dispatch*, 30 March 1976.
63. *Daily Dispatch*, 16 October 1976.
64. *Newscheck*, 3 December 1965: 'Focus on Transkei politicians – the many faces of conservatism'.
65. Munger (1962).
66. *Pretoria News*, 16 January 1976.
67. Much of this external support came from the Cape Town area, where the organization of the DP – previously moribund – sprang to life. See *Daily Dispatch*, 5 January 1976; *Natal Witness*, 27 October 1976; and *Daily Telegraph* (London), 20 September 1976.
68. Laurence (1976), p. 84.
69. *Transkei Hansard*, 8 March 1974, p. 27.
70. See Ncokazi (1976) for one of his few written statements.
71. *Pretoria News*, 16 January 1976; *Daily Dispatch*, 31 May 1976; *RDM*, 26 July 1976, 11 August and 2 September 1978.

72. H. J. Kotze (1976).
73. For electoral and registration statistics for the 1963 election, see Carter *et al.* (1967), pp. 127, 143–5.
74. D. A. Kotze (1975), p. 208.
75. The TNIP successfully negotiated with the Chamber of Mines for an arrangement whereby party officials were to be allowed to enter the mines to enrol members. *TNIP Records*: TNIP Meeting, Sharpeville, 1 January 1965.
76. *TNIP Records*: General Report as to why TNIP did not work and my itinerary with Mr Xhelo from Orange Free State to the Transvaal, 9 December 1967 to 7 April 1968 (by Secretary General).
77. *TNIP Records*: G. M. Matanzima and G. M. Mwanda to Minister of Bantu Administration and Development, 13 March 1968. It may be noted that the fear of being positively identified with a homeland also led to a low urban vote in the first Bophuthatswana election in 1972. Indeed, so widespread was the belief that those who registered as voters might be subject to removal from white areas that the chief electoral officer was even moved to state that Tswana who were living in Soweto illegally would not be endorsed out if they cast ballots. However, this reassurance did little to promote urban participation in the election, for of the 50,000 registered Tswana voters in urban areas, only 4,661 actually went to the polls. See Butler *et al.* (1977), pp. 51–3.
78. Carter *et al.* (1967), p. 128.
79. H. J. Kotze (1973).
80. *RDM*, 30 September 1976.
81. H. J. Kotze (1976).
82. Stultz (1976).
83. *Programme of Principles of the TNIP*; and *Statutes of the TNIP as Amended*.
84. *TNIP Membership Roll, 1965–66*; *Secretary-General's Report for the National Conference of the TNIP* (1969); *Annual Report of the Secretary-General, TNIP, 1975*.
85. *List of Proposals for Strengthening Party Membership and Funds* (1975).
86. *Secretary-General's Report* for the National Conference of the Transkei Independence Party (1969).
87. TNIP: *Minutes of the 11th Congress held on 11–12 February, 1975.*
88. *TNIP Records: Annual Report of the Secretary-General, 1975.*
89. *Transvaal Interim Report*, 20 December 1964.
90. *TNIP Records*: J. L. Nkweba to G. M. M. Mwanda, 8 October 1969.
91. *Why the TNIP did not work as Expected in the Transvaal & Orange Free State.*
92. *Commission of Enquiry into a Dispute in the Springs Branch of the TNIP* (1966).
93. *TNIP Records: Meeting held at the Margaret Gwele School* (White City, Jabavu, Johannesburg), 20 October 1968.
94. Untitled, undated Report by Secretary-General.
95. *TNIP Records:* refer to note 76, p. 144.
96. J. L. Nkweba to G. M. M. Mwanda (Secretary-General), 8 October 1969.
97. Springs Branch to Secretary-General, 17 December 1965.
98. TNIP East London Branch: *Petititon to the Leader of TNIP.*
99. *Schedule of Results of Voting on Motion No. 2 of 1974: Independence for the Transkei* (mimeo).
100. *The Natal Mercury*, 26 April 1975; *The Friend*, 14 September 1975; *RDM*, 7 September 1975, 12 November 1975, 30 December 1975 and 7 September 1976.

Chapter 5
Extrusion of the white settlers

It is not widely appreciated that, just as white minorities in other parts of Africa were forced to relinquish their political dominance at the time of independence, so did the apartheid-style 'decolonization' of the Transkei involve the physical and social displacement of a sizeable settler community. Yet the 're-settlement' of these whites should in no way be portrayed as the irrational act of an apartheid government bent on achieving its purely ideological goal of racial separation, for in practice it constituted an integral and significant element in the entire strategy of quasi-decolonization. In short, the white extrusion was effected with the explicit objective of facilitating a smooth transition to bantustan 'independence' through the Africanization of the (formerly white-dominated) commercial sector in the reserve economy; and in so doing, it was intended to make provision for the emergence of a homeland-based, black petty-bourgeois stratum which would come to identify with the maintenance of separate development, and accordingly lend its political support to the conservative chiefly élite which had assumed a local predominance under the Bantu Authorities system in the 1950s. Yet the enforced removal of white settlers was not without political risk for a regime explicitly dedicated to the upholding of white supremacy, and in consequence the government was compelled to defuse the threat of a white backlash against this particular aspect of the bantustan policy, while simultaneously allowing for white capital to forge a new accommodation with the independent Transkei.

White settlement in the Transkeian Territories

The integration of the Transkeian Territories as a reserve into the political economy of South Africa was of necessity serviced by a considerable European presence, whose primary task was to oversee the interests of the settler state. The earliest whites in the Transkei had been the missionaries, farmers and pioneer traders who, all for their different purposes, had sought from local chiefs the right to establish themselves on chosen sites. But in the turbulent years preceding annexation their existence was a precarious one, and many were subject to armed raid and physical attack by local peoples who, while often valuing the material goods and benefits they had to offer, simultaneously viewed them as the advance guard of an expanding colonialism. In consequence, as Cape rule was formally extended, whites who could had sought official protection by locating themselves upon the periphery of the magisterial headquarters in each of the Transkei's districts; and in the course of time these small settlements of Europeans had developed into towns and villages as the white population swelled with the arrival of increased numbers of administrators and traders, along with others such as teachers, doctors and public employees who attended to their various needs.

As defined by the Land Act of 1913, the white settlements did not constitute a part of the reserve area. While the magistrates served as such to European dwellers, their administrative authority as Native (later Bantu) Commissioners extended only over the colonized population, for Europeans enjoyed the right of self-government in local affairs. Each village possessed its elected management board and each town its municipal council, and all fell under the aegis of the Cape Provincial Administration, forming in legal terms a part of white South Africa, even though they were physically incorporated into the Native Reserve; and this applied even to the European traders and farmers in outlying parts, whose rights of occupation had become convertible to freehold tenure after 1911.[1]

The whites were never more than a relatively small community, numbering only 17,600 compared with 1,154,600 Africans and 12,300 coloureds in 1936.[2] But neither were they totally homogeneous, an identifiable distinction existing between permanent settlers ('Old Transkeians, born and bred', as they termed themselves) and a less rooted, urban element. The former group were composed mainly of the traders in the rural areas and smaller villages, along with a handful of farmers (most of whom owned land in the border districts of Matatiele, Mount Currie and Umzimkulu, which had been administratively incorporated into the Transkei in 1895). The rural traders were a close-knit community, a number of them descended from the 1820 settlers, whose businesses were typically handed down from father to son through successive generations. The farmers, however, were a diminishing group after 1936, for the passing of the Native Trust and Land Act of that year provided for the addition of an extra 7,250,000 morgen of land to the reserves, and thereafter they were steadily bought out by the Native Trust, so that by 1963 there remained a total of only twenty-six white farmers in the Transkei.[3]

The white traders of the Transkei functioned as an important link in the chain of recruitment of labour from the reserve economy for the mines of the Witwatersrand and the white farms of the Cape and Natal. From the early days pioneer traders had served as recruiters, promoting a labour supply through systematic debt inducement among a peasantry subject to the increasing insecurities of land shortage, expanding population and the vagaries of the colonial market economy; and after 1912 the traders had been directly employed as agents of the mines' Native

Recruiting Corporation. In their role as merchants, traders soaked up peasant financial surplus through the retail of manufactured goods and other items from the urban centres of the white economy (notably Port Elizabeth and Durban), aided and abetted by the system of official licensing, which limited the number of trading stations to a total of about 650. While the rationale behind this limitation was the purported need to prevent the ruination of all commercial activity and the minimization of profit levels by 'over-trading', the effect was to promote a collective monopoly in favour of European trade and to stifle the development of African competition.

In contrast to the traders, the majority of Europeans were based in the white-zoned urban areas; and as a general rule the larger the village or town, the less the inhabitants' direct involvement with rural life. Although there was no legal bar to Europeans taking up permanent residence in the Transkei, the urban population was characterized by a higher degree of occupational and geographic mobility. Composed mostly of civil servants, public employees (railway officials, school-teachers and so on), professionals and retailers, they were not so deeply integrated into the reserve economy as such but rather serviced the needs of the local white community, the Cape provincial administration and the central government. They were accordingly less entrenched in the Transkei, which for a large proportion of them never constituted a permanent home, but merely one posting in a career which later took them to other parts of white South Africa.

The implementation of its policy of separate development by the National Party after 1948 constituted a major threat to the interests of the white settlers in the Transkei, for at the ideological level, apartheid proposed the eventual territorial segregation of the races. Thus just as blacks were to be required to move out of white areas of South Africa, so would whites living in the Native Reserves eventually have to relocate themselves in the 'white homeland'. Yet whites were not to be eliminated from the reserves (and the Transkei, with the largest European population of any, was the one most affected) merely for the sake of ideology, but because their extrusion formed a vitally necessary part of the strategy of quasi-decolonization. As the Pondo Revolt of 1960 went to show, the chiefly stratum was too narrow a group upon which to erect the political apparatus of a bantustan state and needed to be broadened out by the addition of other African elements with a material stake in the structures of separate development. Thus Pretoria embarked upon the deliberate creation of an African petty-bourgeoisie in the homelands which was to be both dependent upon and supportive of the chiefs. Yet if such a class was to be given an economic base, it was necessary first to break the stranglehold which the settler minority maintained over reserve trade, for this monopoly was premised upon the suppression and containment of African competition. This might have been accomplished in a number of ways, but the function of the exclusively racial definition of citizenship adopted under apartheid was to convert white residents of the bantustans (who were South African citizens) into 'expatriates' working in a 'foreign land', and whose extrusion could thus be justified by reference to the goal of Africanization of homeland economic structures.

The majority of Transkeian settlers were English-speaking, whose political sympathies lay solidly with the United Party. None the less, for a National Party pledged to the maintenance of white supremacy, the implementation of its Africanization strategy was open to attack from both within its ranks and without on the grounds that it constituted a direct assault upon vested white interests. Indeed, it was to become a constant refrain of the UP over the coming years that the whites of the Transkei were being treacherously sacrificed upon the altar of apartheid: 'the whites in the Transkei are the expendable forces of civilised South Africa which [the government] is preparing to sacrifice in order to carry out an ideology not necessary and alien to the principles and concepts of the South African people'.[4] In the hothouse atmosphere of white minority politics, at a time when the winds of change were sweeping through the continent, the charge that whites were being 'sold down the river' was a highly emotive one; and accordingly the extrusion of the settler community from the Transkei and the manner in which it was accomplished was of considerable significance in the implementation of government policy.

White settlers and the bantustan strategy

The white settlers in the Transkei were an extremely politically conscious and well organized element, which had traditionally enjoyed the confidence and co-operation of the Native administration. Indeed, just as the white community looked to the Native Commissioners for the continued maintenance of order and privilege, so in turn did the magistrates themselves rely upon outlying traders – in daily contact with the tribal population as they were – for intelligence concerning any 'native unrest'; and together did administrators and settlers represent the forces of western civilization and Christianity among an indigenous people regarded as primitive, backward and but recently emerged from barbarism.

The interests of the settler community were articulated through the Transkeian Territories European Civic Association (TTCA), whose origins are illustrative of the close relations which prevailed between the trading community and the Native administration. The founder of the Association was one W. J. Clarke, whose father came out to South Africa with the 1820 settlers. First trading in the Transkei when he entered Fingoland in 1872, Clarke moved to Thembuland a year later; and when Walter Stanford chose Engcobo as the seat of the Thembu magistracy, Clarke accompanied him to the new site. Thereafter Clarke prospered,[5] opening a local hotel and expanding his trading interest to encompass over a dozen stations; and in 1910 he unsuccessfully contested the Thembuland seat for the Cape Provincial legislature against the Rev. Walter Rubusana, the first African ever to seek election to a parliamentary body in South Africa. Somewhat earlier, in the late 1890s, Clarke had founded a Farmers and Traders Association which held its first congress in 1909. It was this body which in 1912 transformed itself into the Civic Association, henceforth proclaiming itself the representative of the entire European community; and it became accepted as such by the authorities, in whose eyes its respectability was much enhanced by its presidency being assumed by no less than three former Chief Magistrates – A. H. Stanford, W. T. Brownlee and Lt.-Col. R. Fyfe-King – after their retirement from the administration. The last of this trio, who was Chief Magistrate from 1935 to 1941, was President from 1946 right through to 1968; and it was under his leadership that the Association sought to meet the challenge posed to white interests by the government's bantustan policy.[6]

Although its membership was open to Europeans alone,[7] the TTCA possessed a highly developed ideology whereby it claimed to safeguard the interests of the entire Transkeian population, and particularly those of the 'natives'. 'During the years of its existence', explained Fyfe-King in 1959:

> the Association has given heed particularly to the interests of the Native people, among whom most of its members have lived in close contact and in complete harmony. Together with the officials of the Government and the missionaries, it has played its part in advancing the welfare and progressive development of the people and has watched with interest their emergence from comparative barbarism to a state of consciousness of their own future, in which they are now called upon to play a large part.[8]

Such utterances were expressive of the paternalistic attitude adopted towards the reserve community, whose dependence upon the traders for credit, food in times of need and help in times of stress promoted the image of white benevolence.

But despite its claim to be devoted to the common good, the TTCA was overwhelmingly preoccupied with defending and furthering the interests of Transkeian Europeans, and the traders in particular. In marked contrast to the Association's proclaimed espousal of African welfare was its bitter protest at the extension of Native Trading Rights in 1934 (which was in part motivated by the government's desire to 'compensate' Africans for the abolition of the Cape franchise, although this was only accomplished in 1936). The proposed change (whereby African traders would be allowed to operate within a 2-mile/3·2-km radius of existing stores) was opposed on the grounds of the alleged irreparable damage it would inflict upon the commercial life of the towns and villages, and the harm it would cause to the interests of white and black alike. The value of established businesses would be diminished, and given that the volume of trade was insufficient to support more than the existing number of stores, chronic overtrading would result; and faced with the prospect of ruin, existing traders would be forced to leave and would doubtless 'be replaced by a class that cannot be beneficial to the Government, or to the moral or industrial welfare of the Native Population'.[9] Despite these dire predictions, the amendment of 1934 affected European traders but little, for although the number of African general dealers in the Transkei and Ciskei together increased from nineteen in 1936 to 206 in 1952, in the latter year African retailers only accounted for approximately 10 per cent of the total volume of trade in both reserves.[10]

Resolutions put to the annual congresses of the Association in later years demonstrated a continuing determination to protect the collective monopoly and to defend the traders' interest. Thus at different times it was variously proposed that Africans who were not in possession of trading licences should be legally barred from purchasing goods direct from wholesalers; the 5-mile (8-km) radius rule should be reimposed for non-Europeans; and applicants for new trading licences should be in possession of a minimum amount of stock and capital. Complaint was levied at the low fines imposed by magistrates upon mine recruits who accepted advances from traders but who subsequently deserted; civil imprisonment was urged for Africans who defaulted on credit; and it was proposed that a proportion of migrants' wages should be lodged directly with traders in order that their families could be assured of material support. But not all congress demands were wholly negative, and the government was consistently urged to encourage industrial development in the Transkei and the Chamber of Mines to raise the minimum wage for its black workers.[11] If such motions convinced the Association of its concern for 'native welfare', the greater volume of trade which would result from such changes suggests that such requests were less than philanthropic. Similarly, the much vaunted racial harmony and mutual trust that supposedly prevailed between the trading and reserve communities was perceived as but a fragile protection against the wave of protest which arose against the imposition of Bantu Authorities in the late 1950s, and there was a consequent flurry of demands by the TTCA that the traders' interests should be protected by measures such as the prohibition of the picketing and boycotting of European stores and the equipping of outlying trading stations with shortwave radios.[12]

Yet the issue in the post-1948 era which concerned the settlers most was that of internal decolonization, for the bantustan policy fundamentally affected the security of the European interest. In early 1951, Dr Hendrik Verwoerd, then Minister of Native Affairs, sent shock waves rippling throughout the Territories when he warned that the days of the whites in the Transkei were numbered. It was government policy to remove all barriers on African trading, whose development would doubtless span many years but which would none the less take the form of a natural process: 'Once the Native no longer needs the European trader, the Native will by being the consumer and accepting the services rendered by his own people, force the white trader out'. Thus as Africans became more self-reliant, so would white spots in Native areas have to be eliminated, and even so large and established a town as Umtata was destined for an eventual black takeover.[13]

Initial European reaction in the Transkei to this statement was one of both hysteria and sheer incredulity. Verwoerd was roundly accused of undermining racial harmony by inciting Africans to force the white man out, and prediction was made that removal of the European populace from the reserves would lead to 'chaos, bloodshed and murder'. 'Natives' were deemed incapable of looking after themselves for nigh on 'another five hundred to a thousand years', and left to their own devices would merely relapse into the barbarism from which they had so recently emerged; and so obvious was this truth that the Minister's prophetic vision was dismissed as totally divorced from reality.[14]

In his parliamentary statement, Verwoerd had foreseen the eventual takeover by blacks of the administration 'right up to the highest posts', but there had been no commitment to an eventual grant of independence. None the less, his utterances had a profoundly unsettling impact upon the European population, undermined its confidence, and aroused a very basic concern about 'the future of the white man' in the Territories. The seeds of doubt had been sown, and they bore early fruit with the announcement by one of the country's largest building societies that it would no longer offer loans within the Transkei. The estate market was thus temporarily frozen, land values tumbled and warning was advanced that the Cape Provincial administration would be reluctant to fund local services if Europeans were destined to depart.[15] Such indeed was the level of uncertainty that Verwoerd himself agreed to visit the Transkei, and a specially convened assembly of local authorities, Chambers of Commerce, Farmers' Associations and the TTCA appointed a delegation to meet him.

Verwoerd met the delegation on 10 April 1951. His speech on this occasion was deliberately enigmatic, attempting to defuse protest by proffering reassurance, but carefully avoiding any definitive statement about the future of the whites. Government policy, he stated, was premised upon the principle of racial separation, for the alternative of integration would lead to the eventual overthrow of the white man and political domination by the numerically preponderant blacks. However, apartheid could only be successfully implemented upon the basis of 'natural development' in the years ahead whereby 'the natives would come to predominate in their own areas'. But given the general backwardness of the African population, this process would be extremely gradual, and the Europeans of the Transkei would be necessary for 'a very, very long time'.

> Everybody who knows what is going on in the Native areas will agree – how they treat their ground, and how difficult it is to educate them up to things – everybody must know that when I talk of 'a long time', I must mean it.

Experience shews I must mean it. Senator Tucker shews this when he says 'a hundred years or longer'. I cannot bind myself down to time. It is quite clear that development as it is must take a long time.[16]

There was therefore no question of policy being to 'force' the European out. It was simply the case that the need for whites would be diminished as the number of Africans in public employment and in trade increased, and the day would eventually dawn when the white spots would disappear; but in the meantime the European presence remained essential, and could not be disposed of within the foreseeable future.

The respite given by Verwoerd's soothing words was only temporary, for in the years that followed it became manifestly clear that the government was holding firmly to its course. In 1956 the Bantu Authorities system was imposed upon the Transkei; and in the same year, the Tomlinson Commission reported the need to develop African trading within the reserves. Then in 1959 the Bantu Investment Corporation, whose explicit task was to encourage African industry and business, was established; and with the passing of the Promotion of Bantu Self-Government Act, the government recognized eight 'national units' among the African population, each ethnic segment being allocated its own particular 'homeland'. But the worst fears of Transkeian whites were realized with the granting of 'self-government' to the Transkei in 1963. If this was what Verwoerd had termed a process of natural development, then it was clear that 'evolutionary change' was being deliberately hastened by official policy.

The implementation of the bantustan policy placed the whites in the Transkei in a position of continuing uncertainty. The local property market had remained depressed and settlers had become increasingly anxious about their future. But there was dissension among them as to how best to defend their interests. On the one hand, there were those who argued in favour of militant rejection of the National Party programme and appeal over the heads of the government to the sympathies and prejudices of the white electorate; and alternatively, there were those who favoured early negotiation with Pretoria in order to secure an orderly white exodus and guarantee of financial compensation. It was to become the objective of the government to exploit this divide in settler ranks, and to thereby obstruct the emergence of a united white resistance to intended Transkeian decolonization which might otherwise prove to be a major political embarrassment.

The disagreement over tactics reflected the division in settler ranks between rural and urban petty capital. It was the rural traders and those who serviced their needs in the outlying villages who, being deeply embedded in the reserve economy, faced the most immediate threat. The traders were no ordinary retailers. Long protected by their collective monopoly, few had been subjected to the cold winds of business competition; the family nature of their businesses had led to a low valuation being placed upon formal schooling, so that few had technical or professional skills which they could sell upon the open market; and many were undercapitalized, dependent for their day-to-day financial needs upon the credit of their wholesalers. In addition, the value of their stations was generally low compared with property prices obtaining outside the Transkei. Not only had the uncertainty generated by official policy depressed the local estate market, but many of the properties were relatively old and ramshackle, having been first erected in the 1890s or early 1900s. In consequence, financial compensation at market values would have been less than sufficient to re-equip rural whites for life at their accustomed material standard outside the Transkei. If the trader should apply for employment in white areas, explained the TTCA representative at a later date:

> he will be asked what his qualifications are – he will reply that he is a trader from the Transkei. The kind of work he will be offered will be that of storeman with a low rate of pay. He will be losing an income on which he has been able to live on quite a high standard ... we are the guinea pigs for the rest of South Africa and it should be the duty of the Republic to see that we do not suffer because of Government policy and become 'Poor Whites' of South Africa.[17]

It was this fear on the part of many traders of being swept from the ranks of the white petty-bourgeiosie into those of the white working class which motivated their espousal of a strident opposition to government policy.

The traders' case was taken up with vigour by the Civic Association, which early opted for establishment of a publicity committee to link up with the press 'in order to convey to the people in general that we are going to call the [government's] bluff'.[18] Such an approach blended well with the United Party's rejection of the bantustan policy (on the grounds of its supposed threat to continued 'white leadership') and accordingly the Opposition rallied to the traders' cause. In particular, there was constant invocation of the 'Kenya analogy', whereby it had become an article of faith for white politicians that the British had shamelessly 'sold the whites down the river' in pursuit of their own interests. Thus T. Gray Hughes, UP Member of Parliament who had represented the Transkei since 1948, bluntly maintained that the Nationalists 'had done a Kenya on the white people in the Transkei', and it was a cry that was taken up in Opposition circles. Once it was accepted that the days of the whites were numbered, agitators would promote a movement 'similar to Mau Mau', spurred on by the passing of the Bantu Education Act, which by removing the benign supervision of the missionaries would lead to the development of an independent schools movement such as 'the Mau Mau organisation [had] germinated' in Kenya. The Pondo Revolt of 1960 and the later activities of Poqo in the Transkei (notably the murder of five whites in February 1963) were held up as confirmation of such dire predictions, and the government was attacked for transferring power to blacks at a time when communist-inspired hatred had led to a breakdown in law and order, anti-white hostility and when 'murders of the Mau Mau type [were] being committed, with mutilation of the victims'. The 'liberalistic policy' of handing over government to 'Black nationalism' meant that 'the whites in the Transkei [would] be on the run'. Just as the Kenyan whites had been robbed of their land and told to 'get out', so would Transkeian whites suffer a similar experience, for there was no black leader able to maintain his position without becoming an extremist, and Kaiser Matanzima was unlikely to prove an exception.[19]

Such talk as this, however out of touch with reality, was potentially damaging to the government's credibility with the white electorate, and had therefore to be rejected. Thus it was argued that whereas Kenyan settlers had from the earliest times been promised permanence of tenure and full political control, whites in reserve areas of South Africa had always known that their residence was temporary, and that they would eventually have to depart when they had no function left to perform. Furthermore, while Britain had transferred power to rabid African nationalists (Kenyatta was described as 'the greatest sadist which this continent had ever known'), self-government in the Transkei was being conferred upon conservative and natural leaders who would rule in a responsible manner. Thus whites would never be 'left in the lurch', and their material interests would be fully protected. 'We are not doing what England did in Kenya,' claimed the Minister of Bantu Administration and Development.[20]

It is not necessary to focus upon the historical inaccuracies in the arguments of both government and Opposition to endorse the former's rejection of the analogy with Kenya. The fundamental point of dissimilarity, of course, was that Transkeian whites were able to withdraw to the sanctuary of the Republic, where settler privilege and dominance was undiminished (if not strengthened) by the devolution of power to black subordinates. Thus for those who were not deeply involved in the reserve economy, official policy represented only a limited threat. The urban whites – the professionals, retailers and businessmen – had marketable skills, and faced no inherent barrier to re-establishing themselves in other parts of the Republic, while civil servants and public employees faced merely the inconvenience of transfer to new postings. For these elements, therefore, extrusion could be assessed in financial terms; and once it had become clear that the Transkei was destined for self-government, the major concern of the urban whites was to realize their capital by securing right to compensation.[21]

As the division in white ranks crystallized, it found expression in institutional form. With the TTCA primarily concerned with the position of the rural traders, urban capital became represented by the hitherto lethargic Chamber of Commerce movement, which from 1957 onward undertook an active programme of expansion (although urban whites continued to be represented in the ranks of the Association). But in order to eschew the image of sectional interest, businessmen chose to operate in public under the umbrella of the Umtata Municipal Council, all of whose members also belonged to the Umtata Chamber; and as the premier local authority body in the Transkei, the Umtata Council took upon itself a leading role in representing the white community.[22]

Although the Civic Association was ostensibly 'non-political', its personal links with the UP through Gray Hughes (who often attended its congresses) and its vocal espousal of the traders' cause were a course of irritation to the government.[23] Indeed, this indirect affiliation with the Opposition was viewed as a threat by urban capital, which regarded the TTCA as endangering the white interest by exhausting official sympathy. Accordingly, after some considerable disagreement with the Association, leading businessmen developed unofficial contacts with the government through the mediation of Hans Abraham, the Commissioner-General of the Xhosa, who was the direct representative of the Ministry of Bantu Administration in Umtata; and henceforth, in order to ingratiate themselves with the government so as to secure the best deal they could, the urban representatives allowed their tactics to be almost wholly shaped by Pretoria, whose main interest was to defuse the entire white issue by removing it from the open political arena.

Retrospectively, the official influence is clear. In early 1962, the Mayor of Umtata called a meeting of the municipalities, the village management boards and the Civic Association with the object of appointing a deputation to meet the government. From the outset, there was an attempt to minimize the influence of the TTCA, which was requested to send only two delegates to the meeting (although due to a perhaps deliberate administrative error by the TTCA secretary, each branch of the Association sent two representatives). This was not all, for there was an explicit emphasis by urban representatives upon the need to suppress all open opposition to government policy and 'to avoid politics in any shape or form'. The correct approach, it was argued, was to appoint a 'Liaison Committee' to meet the government, and to make all further representations through the Commissioner-General and not through 'any other member of parliament' (that is, Gray Hughes).[24]

A committee composed of five urban representatives and three from the TTCA was elected (and empowered to co-opt other members as it thought fit); and subsequently, in June 1962, it met Verwoerd (now Prime Minister), the Minister of Bantu Administration and various officials to discuss the difficulties faced by whites as a result of the decision to grant self-government to the Transkei. In response to their representations, Verwoerd offered to appoint a Commission of Inquiry into the position of Europeans in the Transkei; and in addition, to recognize the deputation he was meeting as a permanent 'Liaison Committee' (which would retain the right to co-opt members and have the Mayor of Umtata as its *ex officio* chairman). To this body, Verwoerd entrusted the monopoly right to represent white interests, promising that the door to direct negotiations with the government would always be open – but only upon the conditions that the committee would remain 'non-political' and that it would actively seek to assist the implementation of official policy.[25]

Verwoerd's achievement was threefold. In the first place, all future representation by whites would have to be premised upon the acceptance of the bantustan principle and would thus henceforth have to focus only upon the *manner* of the European exodus. Secondly, he had outmanoeuvred the rural traders – politically the most intractable and disaffected group – by denying the TTCA the right of independent representation; and by recognizing the delegation itself (which was composed primarily of urban businessmen) as the Liaison Committee, he had ensured that the dominance of the urban interest would be secured. Finally, he had managed to neutralize the official body from the start by imposing conditions upon it which made it clear that recognition would be withdrawn were it to engage in public activities embarrassing to the government. Thus the warning was clear; compensation and favourable treatment for the whites was to be dependent upon the maintenance of political docility.

Zoning and compensation

A three-man Commission of Inquiry into the problems created for resident Europeans by the grant of self-government to the Transkei was established in August 1962. Headed by W. H. Heckroodt, it received memoranda from the various white representative bodies and visited the Territories to hear oral evidence in November of that year. But its report was never published and it was not until June 1964 that the government released a short White Paper in which it disclosed its reactions to the Heckroodt recommendations. In the meantime, in the early months of 1963, the Transkei Constitution Bill had passed through Parliament, in terms of which trading stations in rural areas lost their status as 'white spots' and European traders were brought under the authority of the homeland government (although the urban areas of the Transkei remained a part of 'white' South Africa).

The decisions of the government as reflected in the White Paper[26] were threefold. First, it was accepted that compensation should be paid to whites for any financial loss which resulted from change in the constitutional status of the Transkei (the onus of proof resting with the property owner). Secondly, a body known as the Adjustment Committee was to be appointed by the Minister of Bantu Administration to value white businesses which were on offer for sale in *black* areas but for which no buyer could be found; and thirdly, the South African Native Trust was empowered to buy such properties at prices as were approved by the Minister.

What had been offered was almost the very reverse of what whites had requested from the Heckroodt Commission. The rural traders had urgently requested that their stations remain as white spots in the belief that this would grant them protection to operate in the Transkei for some considerable period (if not indefinitely); instead, their properties had been zoned black, and there were indications that they were going to be put under considerable pressure to accept financial compensation to move out. On the other hand, the urban businessmen, who had looked for the right to immediate compensation at commercially (and not officially) assessed values,[27] found this denied them, for the towns remained zoned white and thus their properties were not to be eligible for purchase by the Trust. Clearly, such a situation was not accidental, and its explanation has to be sought in the official strategy for 'decolonizing' the Transkei.

It was argued above that Pretoria had early identified the need to break the settler hold over reserve trade in order to promote the development of an African middle class which would be supportive of separate development. Thus the decision to isolate the traders, to place them under the authority of the new black government (which took office in December 1963) and to make them, initially, the only whites eligible for compensation was deliberate strategy, for it was the expressed intention of the incoming political élite (the coterie of chiefs and others who surrounded Kaiser Matanzima) to break the traders' monopoly, which had long been an object of considerable resentment; and one of their very first legislative enactments was the Trading Amendment Act (no. 5 of 1964) which abolished the radius rule and enabled licences to be granted to blacks to trade within 2 miles (3·2 km) of established sites.[28]

Yet Verwoerd had promised that white traders would never be 'forced' to leave the Transkei and that the development of African commercial successors would take place as a result of a 'natural process'. Certainly, he was not prepared to give ammunition to the United Party by formally compelling the white traders to quit. Instead, therefore, the government opted for a policy whereby the traders were to be placed in a position of economic insecurity and declining profitability, and compensation so structured that its real value was likely to decrease the longer the trader delayed in applying for it.[29] At the same time, through the machinery of the BIC (replaced by the Xhosa Development Corporation within the Transkei in 1966), cheap loans would be offered to Africans deemed capable of becoming successful businessmen which would enable them to take over the previously white-owned stores.

A similar strategy was also to be applied to the rural villages of the Transkei. In 1964 a Zoning Committee was established whose ostensible purpose was to investigate the zoning of European towns for possible future African occupation. Visiting the Territories three months after the publication of the White Paper, the Committee received representations from white residents of urban areas, and the government subsequently issued a Zoning Proclamation on 31 December 1965.

In terms of the White Paper, compensation would be paid only to whites with properties in black areas. Thus whites were faced with a considerable dilemma; were they to continue enjoying the benefits of racial exclusivity by retaining white-zoned status, they would be ineligible to receive compensation. Given that the uncertainties of the future of the Transkei had frozen the estate market and the possibilities of selling property to other whites had thus been virtually eliminated, there was considerable pressure upon those who wished to make their exodus to request their towns and villages to be zoned black. On the other hand, were a village zoned black, those whites who wished to maintain their businesses would be exposed to unknown hazards, not the least of which was that they would become surrounded by black neighbours as other whites departed – and such a fate was considered as both socially unacceptable and fraught with financial risk, for

> ... once actual Bantu occupation takes place a depressed financial area is established ... The European owners of such properties are then faced with an immediate capital loss and due to the reluctance of European tenants to occupy such properties and the inability of most Bantu to rent such properties the owner is faced with an ever diminishing return from his investment.[30]

Yet this dilemma for the whites was in many ways a false one, for the government's policy was predetermined and unlikely to be much affected by residents' representations. In short, the official strategy was to zone the small rural settlements black first, and to leave the larger towns (notably Butterworth and Umtata) as white spots to the last. Just as the traders were to be induced to leave so as to make way for blacks, so were the white owners of small-scale enterprises in the service sector – notably in general dealing, other retailing, passenger transport and hotel, bottle-store and garage management. Characterized by a low level of technology and requiring relatively little capital input, such businesses were considered highly suitable for transfer to emergent black petty capitalists, whose initial funding would be provided by cheap loans from the XDC.

In addition, Pretoria was concerned with what it considered the orderly transfer of the apparatus of the bantustan state into black hands. Given the time required to create a reliable black intermediary class, the transfer of white properties, businesses and the administration had to be carefully regulated. A mass exodus of whites in the early years of self-government would result in disruption of the economy and a decline in confidence in the entire bantustan programme.[31] Consequently, the retention of the larger towns as fully white-zoned areas functioned to arrest the departure of Europeans in the more advanced and technical sectors of the economy (which were generally located in the larger urban areas), while after 1968 (when white investment was first encouraged in the bantustans) the maintenance of white zoning served as a necessary adjunct to the inflow of white 'expatriate' personnel from the Republic.

'Sold down the Kei River'

It was the issues of zoning and compensation which determined the variant reactions of the white petty-bourgeoisie to the bantustan strategy as implemented in the Transkei after 1962. Although the fundamental divide in interest was between urban and rural capital, it is three – and not two – groups which can be identified. First, there were the rural traders: it was their economic security which was most immediately threatened by the official policy, and accordingly it was their response which was to be the most frenetic, culminating in an explicitly political appeal to the white electorate in 1963 to save them from the 'treachery' of the National Party government; and when this failed, they were to be left with little alternative but to make their exit upon the best terms they could. Secondly, there was an intermediary group of small businessmen located in the rural settlements and smaller towns of the Transkei who came to accept the inevitability of their extrusion and who thus came to concentrate their efforts upon bargaining with the government so as to obtain the most favourable terms of compensation. And thirdly, there was a category of more highly capitalized businessmen, who were able to accommodate to the changes engendered by the implementation of separate development. Initially alienated from the official policy by the apparent threat to their interests posed by apartheid rhetoric, it was this group which had first formulated the demand for compensation and which was to emerge as the dominant element upon the Liaison Committee. Paradoxically, however, it was this fraction whose properties were destined under official policy to remain in white-zoned areas (and thus to be ineligible for purchase by the state) until almost the last; but, as will be detailed below, the inflow of capital into the most advanced sectors of the local economy which resulted from the bantustan programme was to allow this element an increased scope for profit and enable it to expand in to new areas of commerce and industry.

The rural traders
In the course of his meeting with the body which he designated as the European Liaison Committee in June 1962, Verwoerd had given notice that whites resident in the rural areas of the Transkei would, in terms of the forthcoming constitutional change, be brought under the authority of the new homeland government. Being citizens of the Republic, their rights and interests would be protected by an 'ambassador' (the Commissioner-General) just as would South Africans living in any other foreign land, although they would none the less be subject to the laws of the Transkeian 'state'.[32]

The reaction of rural traders to this information was predictable. Although it was now fully recognized that the principle of self-government was irreversible, there was strenuous protest at their being placed under a black government. Yet this was not merely an objection on racial grounds; rather, it was motivated by the realization that the new black authorities in Umtata would pose a major threat to their livelihood by seeking to undermine their collective trade monopoly. Accordingly, traders launched an urgent campaign to cajole the government into making two concessions. These were, first, that it would guarantee the preservation of the 2-mile (3·2-km) radius rule after self-government; and secondly, that trading stations should remain as white spots until such time as they were individually taken over by African owners.

The traders' cause was championed from the start by the TTCA. However, because the government had designated the Liaison Committee as the only legitimate transmitter of European opinion, the Civic Association was obliged to work through the officially appointed body. Yet composed of a predominantly urban membership, the Liaison Committee came to exhibit a marked reluctance to press the traders' case to an extent which might antagonize the government, and in consequence it was rendered ineffective as a monopoly pressure group, as it became racked by conflict between its constituent factions.

This clash of interests between rural and urban capital became explicit from an early stage. Initially, when the TTCA sought to register its protest at traders being placed under black authorities, the committee refused to forward its complaint lest such action embarrass the Commission of Inquiry then currently investigating the position of the whites.[33] But when in January 1963 it became clear that the government intended proceeding with the passage of the Transkei Constitution Bill before it had received the Heckroodt Report (in which the problems of the trading community would of necessity be dealt with at length), the Liaison Committee was constrained to meet the Minister of Bantu Administration and to request that constitutional change be delayed until after the receipt of Heckroodt.[34] But no concession was made, so that Pretoria was approached yet again and implored to make an eleventh-hour change in policy.[35] On this occasion, however, the government was clearly irritated, and responded by merely issuing a curt statement that 'native interests' in reserve areas had always been paramount, and that by the choice of their trading environment, traders had implicitly accepted the risks arising out of the 'developmental possibilities of their clientele'.[36]

At this point, the Liaison Committee lost all semblance of unity. The (minority) trading element now argued that the Committee should publish its correspondence with the government in the press in a bid to expose the latter's treachery towards the traders, while the (majority) urban representatives rejected such tactics on the grounds that they would constitute political involvement, probably resulting in the withdrawal of official recognition from the Committee, and arguing that the traders could not expect their interests to be pursued to the extent of harming those of other whites in the towns and villages of the Transkei.[37]

Matters moved swiftly to a head. Resentful of the Liaison Committee's lukewarm defence of rural interests, the TTCA Executive resolved on publicizing the traders' case themselves. 'The patience of the white minority was now utterly exhausted,' declared a circular. 'The members of this Association unanimously protest at the contemptible manner in which the Government has negotiated the white minority into an isolated corner preparatory to forcing them into a state of oblivion, and in complete disregard of the personal wishes of the white minority.'[38] Accordingly, the Association had appointed a Press Publicity Committee to put the true facts of the government's betrayal before 'a fair and rational press'; and on 1 March, some three weeks before the Constitution Bill was due to be discussed in Parliament, a statement was issued to the press about the dangers of exposing the traders to 'the avarice and administrative inexperience of an untried people':

> They know only too well the bribery and corruption which is rife and which a sense of power is likely to increase to a point where life for the traders and their families will become insupportable. Refusal to meet unreasonable demands will result in boycotts engineered to extract bribes and to force the traders into compliance or the abandonment of their stations.[39]

All the traders had asked was that they should remain under white rule until their stores were acquired by blacks, but the government had wilfully ignored all their representations. Thus no course was left to them but 'to appeal to the people of the Republic to plead with the Government to reverse that part of its policy which will subject Europeans to Bantu rule in defiance of past tradition'.[40]

The effect of the press statement was to bring about the political isolation of the TTCA. In the first place, the TTCA had ignored the government's insistence that the whites should remain 'non-political', and in so doing could not now avoid being openly associated with the parliamentary Opposition; and accordingly, precisely because their cause was taken up with considerable vigour by the UP during the second reading of the Bill, they alienated potential sympathy in National Party quarters. Secondly, and in the long run of more significance, the traders also offended those blacks who aspired to power under the bantustan state. Always resentful of the white trading monopoly, the TTCA's attack upon them now strengthened their resolve to edge the traders out; and indicative of their mood was the allegation that emanated from among their number that certain traders were actively supporting Poqo. The acrimonious exchange between the TTCA and Matanzima which followed the levelling of this rather far-fetched charge only served to estrange the white traders even further from the incoming regime.[41] Finally, the entry of the Civic Association into the political arena so polarized relations between urban and rural capital that the Liaison Committee became almost wholly a vehicle of the urban interest. Considering that the traders had jeopardized the position of all whites in the Transkei by alienating the political sympathies of the government, the urban representatives sought to placate the authorities by explicitly disassociating themselves from those they identified as seeking to hinder official policy.[42] TTCA motions were consistently defeated and its memoranda rejected, while the urban element consolidated its control over the Committee by co-opting known allies by majority vote.[43] Indeed, so naked were the tactics of the urban group that meetings degenerated into fairly frank exchanges of personal abuse,[44] and with the accession to the chairmanship by the new Mayor of Umtata (who also happened to be the President of the Chamber of Commerce) in 1965, the Committee became virtually defunct, as the new incumbent sought to minimize the influence of the TTCA by simply declining to hold meetings.[45] As a result, the Civic Association registered bitter complaint at its annual congresses, and in 1967 called for the resignation of all the Committee's members and its reconstitution by election.[46] When this call produced no result, the TTCA sought to enter into direct communication with the government in relation to certain issues concerning compensation, only to be referred back to the Liaison Committee as the official mouthpiece of the Transkeian Europeans. Ensuing negotiations came to nothing, and by 1971 even the government itself admitted that the Liaison Committee was dead,[47] and was henceforth more amenable to the TTCA's overtures – but by this time, more than half the traders had gone from the Transkei for good.

The demise of the Liaison Committee signified the defeat of the white traders as a group. Although there was no legal barrier to their remaining in the Transkei, they were thereafter subjected to sufficient pressures and inducements to ensure that they had no great reluctance to quit. In particular, there seems little doubt that, at least initially, their profit margins were eroded by an increase in competition. This came from two sources. First, the abolition of the 2-mile (3·2-km) radius rule in 1964 by the Matanzima government led to an increase in the number of African competitors. Statistics relating to the number of trading licences issued after 1964 are not available, but it is clear that it was very considerable; and although African petty traders (who gained their licences from the Tribal Authorities) suffered from a lack of capital and an inability to obtain credit from wholesalers, they made sufficient impact upon the market to become a source of constant complaint by the Civic Association.[48]

But secondly, and of more significance, was the rapid emergence of the XDC as a monopoly competitor, for the Corporation acquired stores from departing whites at a faster rate than it passed them on to the incoming blacks, so that by 1972, for instance, although it had purchased 423 trading stations, only 217 had been already handed over to black entrepreneurs.[49] At this particular time, therefore, apart from its having access to cheap capital through the state, it was able to effect economies of scale (such as bulk buying) which enabled it to compete extremely effectively with the remaining established traders; and indeed, there is considerable evidence to suggest that it used its monopoly strength to capture a larger share of the reserve trade by lowering prices, thus making the position of its competitors even more insecure. Nor did it confine its operations to simple retailing. It entered into produce buying and grain storage, and in addition, from 1968 onward, its Ploughing Unit began to compete with the established traders in ploughing the fields of the reserve community. By 1974, its operations in this sphere had come to grief, but in the meantime, it had ploughed on much easier financial terms than existing tractor owners were able to contemplate.[50]

The erosion of their monopoly was an important factor in promoting a steady exodus of white traders from the Transkei after 1964. But undoubtedly the major factor behind their departure was a knowledge that the longer they stayed, the more would pressures upon them to leave be increased. Accordingly, the majority opted for the (not ungenerous) compensation offered by the state and made their exit when they could; and by 1975, 562 white trading stations out of a total of 653 had been taken over by the XDC (474 having been passed on to blacks).[51] Of the ever declining handful of those traders who have remained, the majority are older men, insufficiently capitalized to re-establish themselves in business in the Republic, and whose continuing presence in the Transkei forms no long-term threat to Africans who are moving into the commercial sector in rural areas. It was this element, the most insecure section among the white traders, which in 1974 broke away from the TTCA and formed the White Citizens' Association, whose objective was to secure legal guarantees from the South African government that it would protect their economic interests after 'independence'. Once more openly associating with Gray Hughes, the WCA attempted to present a petition of grievances to the House of Assembly.[52] Such a request had not been allowed for some forty years and this one also was refused;[53] the only significant result of the affair was that it antagonized Matanzima, who resented the attempt to limit the 'sovereignty' of an independent Transkei. The security of the remaining white traders was thus further undermined, and their extrusion will doubtless soon be effected as the black takeover of rural commerce moves towards completion.

Urban capital

The Africanization of the petty commercial sector in the urban areas of the Transkei was the complement to the transfer of the white trading monopoly into black hands, for as one member of the homeland legislature put it, 'these towns and villages in the Transkei have played the role of nothing else but money collectors for white merchants'.[54] The extrusion of white inhabitants from especially the rural settlements was thus vital to the class interest of aspiring African businessmen who looked to a white departure as the key to their own opportunity: 'Africans find it difficult to compete with these white traders,' argued the mover of a motion in the TLA to have certain municipalities declared black.[55]

The device used for bringing about the white exodus was zoning, whereby claims for compensation would be considered only for properties in areas declared black. Given that their capital assets in white zones were more or less frozen by the generally depressed state of the local market, white residents were more or less forced into applying for their areas to be proclaimed black. However, as was indicated above, under the Zoning Proclamation of 1965 it was only certain of the smaller rural settlements which were at first declared wholly black, with the larger townships remaining mostly white, the official strategy being to zone the latter black as the white departure quickened in pace. But in the interim, those awaiting their opportunity for compensation were left to bide their time.

For whites in the smaller towns, there was little alternative but to accept the compensation that they were offered and to make their exit when they could. For their part, Matanzima and his cohorts called upon the whites to leave from an early stage: well-schooled in the rhetoric of separate development, they had no hesitation in demanding that Africans become dominant in black areas, just as whites were in their own. The same message was drummed out by the Republican officials, who constantly urged whites remaining in white areas to be zoned black: 'property transactions will be much easier in those villages zoned entirely black than in those that were zoned only partially black,' advised Commissioner-General Abraham in 1966.[56] At the same time, those in black areas who were reluctant to leave were faced with a decline in social facilities available to them (for instance, white clubs and hotel bars becoming black) and, more seriously, a number of them were faced with demands for the repayment of mortgages.[57] The general view was thus as expressed at the TTCA Congress in 1970: '... as a dwindling community with activities curtailed, we are being forced out of the Transkei'.[58] Yet, as argued above, the pace of the white departure was dictated not by the settlers themselves, but by the rate at which the state chose to offer them compensation, and this in turn was determined by bureaucratic considerations such as budgetary constraint and the readiness of the XDC to take over local services prior to passing them on to black entrepreneurs. However, by 1970 the process in the rural areas was virtually complete, and all but a residual handful of whites were destined to leave at the first opportunity.[59] A Transkeian Townships Board, which fell under the direct authority of the Minister of Bantu Administration, was established in the same year, its explicit function being to train Xhosa officials in the arts of municipal administration.

It was only the four most highly populated towns – Butterworth, Idutywa, Umtata and Umzimkulu – which retained substantial white zones right up till independence in 1976. As indicated above, it was the urban businessmen (and notably those in Umtata) who had been the earliest to take the initiative in seeking the right to compensation, yet it was they who became eligible to receive it last. There was, in consequence, a considerable amount of discontent and demands were formulated with considerable regularity that parts of these urban areas be zoned black or that compensation be paid for properties in white areas. However, unlike the case of the rural traders, such representation did not escalate into political disaffection and urban complaint always remained rather muted.

The reasons for this were twofold. First, the urban businessmen – and notably those based in Umtata – were the dominant group upon the Liaison Committee,[60] and while it remained operative, they felt that they had direct access to Pretoria. The manner in which the government had ridden roughshod over the traders offered ample evidence that open protest would in itself be unlikely to secure any change in official policy, and any ability which urban capital might retain to influence events would clearly be by eschewing 'political' involvement. In consequence, those who controlled the Liaison Committee quickly learned from the traders' mistakes, and astutely pursued their interests through a strategy of quiet negotiation which deliberately avoided publicity.

But a second – and more fundamental – reason why urban-based protest at the zoning and compensation strategy was so muted was that the larger and more prominent businessmen soon found that they were in no way adversely effected by the experience of bantustan devolution. The expansion of the homeland bureaucracy, the secondment of increasing numbers of Republican civil servants and the expenditure incurred as a result of making Umtata a centre of government all ensured that the capital town would receive a considerable inflow of state funds, much of which would percolate into the commercial sector. In addition to this, Act No. 46 of 1968 brought about a reversal of the former policy whereby white capital from the private sector was specifically barred from the homelands, as Pretoria now sought to encourage industry into the homelands under an agency or leasehold system, offering a battery of concessions which were designed to ensure its profitable investment. But importantly, it was also a feature of the new strategy that the government identified a number of 'growth points' where it would provide the necessary infrastructure for industrial development, Butterworth and Umtata being the two centres chosen to fulfil such a role in the Transkei, with the result that both experienced a period of rapid expansion and enjoyed a boom in which local commercial interests were enabled to participate.[61]

Some indication of the extent of this urban-centred prosperity can be given as shown in Table 5.1 (remembering that classified, or non-subsistence, employment is largely concentrated in the two main towns). Yet the inflow of these resources was of little benefit to the reserve community in general, for the financial advantages accrued most directly to the African petty-bourgeoisie and the owners of locally invested capital, the latter being particular beneficiaries as a result of rising land values and the expansion of commerce. In the case of Umtata, for instance, whereas the valuation of property stood at R3 million in 1964, by 1970 this had increased to R8½ million;[62] and in an expanding town where land is in short supply and the population is growing rapidly, the tendency is bound to continue. Thus, while those businessmen whose premises were located in white-zoned areas were not enabled to claim compensation, their properties appreciated in value to an extent which rapidly extinguished their former misgivings and which, by defreezing the urban land market, enabled them to liquidize their assets whenever they so wished, and thereby, rather paradoxically, relieving the pressure upon them to leave the Transkei.[63]

Table 5.1 *Some indicators of increased cash flow in Butterworth and Umtata*

	Transkeian government budget (R)	Government salaries & pensions (R)	Turnover of commercial banks (R)	Persons in classified employment
1964/5	15,510,000	1,427,100* 1,500,000†	114,100,216	32,700
1972/3	38,029,000	13,692,000* 6,258,000†	538,975,445	57,700
1975/6	87,801,000	n.a.* 7,500,737‡	n.a.	87,479

Notes: * salaries; † pensions; ‡ pensions, 1973/4.
Sources: 1964/5 and 1972/3: *TTCA/Congress, 1972*, pp. 1–2.
1975/6: *Transkei Hansard*, 1975, pp. 96–7; and Department of Interior, *Statistical Labour Report*, 1976.

As a consequence of the new expansion, it is evident that certain long-established business concerns are seeking a new accommodation with the independent Transkei. Lower-level, labour-intensive sectors of the commercial sphere are being vacated in favour of African entrepreneurs (who are financed by the Development Corporation) and their former owners are withdrawing into higher-level, more capital-intensive areas. The two main examples of this are the Sparg and Spilkin groups of companies. Both originated in rural trading and diversified with the acquisition of hotels, but in more recent years both have placed an emphasis upon the development of wholesaling, with the Spilkin companies now also including a supermarket and a clothing factory.

The reaction of Sparg and Spilkin has not been wholly typical, if only because other private firms of long standing in Umtata have remained fairly small, less highly capitalized and thus more limited in their scope for expansion and diversification. None the less, it is significant that the majority of commercial concerns operating within the main towns remain white-owned, and there seems no undue haste upon the part of their proprietors to leave. So far there has been no indication of a move towards compulsory purchase, but as the commercially oriented fraction of the African petty-bourgeoisie grows in economic stature, it is possible that it will agitate for the coercive extrusion of the remaining white retailers. If this were to happen, one element of white petty capital would doubtless opt to return to the Republic, but another would probably follow the path of Sparg and Spilkin by seeking to withdraw into wholesaling and small-scale manufacturing operations.

Finally, it should be noted that the impetus towards accommodation by white capital with the bantustan state has necessitated a further change in the structure of the white population resident in the Transkei. The majority of whites have now left for the Republic, but this has not meant that the homeland has fulfilled the Verwoerdian dream by becoming an entirely black state, for as the settlers have departed so have white 'expatriates' moved in as top-level civil servants, managers and professional advisers: 'If we are to succeed economically and get real development,' explained a top aide to Matanzima, 'we will have an influx of whites to the industrial centres of the Transkei.'[64] Accordingly, special concessions were initially made to accommodate whites where this was considered necessary, including the right to segregated schools for white children run by the Cape Education Department, white wards in hospitals and the right of social clubs to pursue a racially restrictive admissions policy. Yet such blatant remnants of the colonial era had of necessity to be removed, both because of unfavourable external criticism and the aspirations of Transkeian élites to gain the right of free access to the top social facilities. Accordingly, in late 1978, Matanzima gave notice of his intention to curtail preferential treatment for whites in both the educational and medical spheres[65] (the Cape-run schools actually proceeding to admit all races the following year);[66] and conversely, in accordance with the TNIP's espousal of 'non-racialism', token whites have now been admitted to Transkeian citizenship. Yet, as formal racial barriers have been relaxed, the benefits of formerly racially exclusive preserves have become available only to those blacks who are able to pay, and discrimination by race has been largely displaced by discrimination now exercised according to the possession of wealth. Although this is undoubtedly a significant and welcome change, the lot of the Transkeian masses remains much the same.

Notes

1. TTCA Memorandum, 1968: 'Europeans in the Transkeian Territories'.
2. Social and Economic Council (UG 32 – 1946), para. 119.
3. *HAD*, 3 April, 1963, col. 3947.
4. *HAD*, 19 March 1963, col. 3030.
5. Although not without the occasional setback, as when in 1885 his house,

store and stock in trade were destroyed 'when trouble broke out between tribes'. (*TTCA Memorandum*: 'Europeans in the Transkeian Territories', 1968.)
6. Interview, Mrs Joan Brorster (Clarke's granddaughter), 25 February 1977; and *Reports of the TTCA Annual Congress*, 1952, p. 1, 1963, p. 2; 1965, p. 9; and 1968, p. 68). These reports were kindly loaned to me by Mr Harry Mather (Secretary, TTCA).
7. The word 'European' was dropped from the Association's title in 1955.
8. *TTCA Congress*, 1959, p. 1.
9. *Memorandum by the Transkeian Territories European Civic Association re Proposed Conditions regulating the Extension of Native Trading Rights in the Transkeian Territories* (1934).
10. Hart (1972), pp. 109–10.
11. *TTCA Executive*, 7 October 1950; and *Congress*, 1956, 1957, 1959 and 1960.
12. *TTCA Congress*, 1959 and 1960; and *Executive Meeting*, November 1958.
13. *HAD*, 14 March 1951, col. 3057.
14. *Report of Meeting of Delegates from Local Authorities in the Transkeian Territories re recently Published Statement by the Honourable the Minister of Native Affairs on the Future of these Territories*, 30 March 1951.
15. *Local Authority Meeting* (1951); and *TTCA Congress* (1951).
16. *Report of Meeting on 10 April 1951 at which a Deputation from Local Authorities and Other Public Bodies was received by Dr H. F. Verwoerd*, p. 6.
17. *TTCA Congress* (1970), p. 16.
18. Statement by TTCA delegate: *Verbatim Report of a Meeting of Public Bodies, 21 May 1955, Regarding Government Policy as Affecting the Transkeian Territories*, p. 3.
19. This composite formulation of the Kenya analogy is based on the *TTCA Congress* (1955), pp. 2–3; and *HAD*, 19 March 1963, col. 3042; 21 March 1963, col. 3177; 1 April 1963, col. 3847; 2 April 1963, col. 3913; and 15 June 1964, col. 8096.
20. *HAD*, 20 March 1963, cols 3097–8; 1 April 1963, cols 3825–6; 15 June 1964, col. 6073.
21. *Meeting of Public Bodies, 1955*, pp. 13–14.
22. *Report of a Meeting of Representatives of Municipalities, Village Management Boards and Civic Associations in the Transkeian Territories*, 16 April 1962.
23. One example may suffice: in 1959 the Chief Magistrate publicly remonstrated with the TTCA for even discussing the future of the whites, on the grounds that such a debate would have only been appropriate in three hundred years' time (*sic*). *TTCA Congress* (1959), p. 3.
24. Cf note 22, p. 165a.
25. *Résumé of the Activities and Endeavours of the Liaison Committee since its Establishment* (26 February 1963); and *Meeting of the Liaison Committee*, 30 March 1963. My understanding of the issues surrounding the white extrusion owes much to interviews with a number of activists who requested not to be identified. However, I am particularly indebted to Mr Edward Sparg for both an informative interview (25 February 1977) and for granting me access to documents of the Liaison Committee.
26. *Decisions of the Government regarding Europeans in the Transkeian Territories* (WPCC – 1964).

27. *Memorandum Submitted by the Mount Frere Chamber of Commerce and the Umtata and District Chamber of Commerce on behalf of the Europeans in the Transkei, to the Commission of Enquiry Appointed in Terms of Government Notice No. 1467, Dated 7th September, 1962*, especially pp. 9–16.
28. Hart (1972), p. 94.
29. Thus valuation for compensation purposes was to be calculated according to (1) land value; (2) value of improvements which existed on 30 June 1964; and (3) 'goodwill', being profits for three years, calculated retrospectively from 30 June 1964. Traders were aware that (1) land values of their properties were low compared to white South Africa, while site values of trading stores would be eroded by the abolition of the 2-mile (3.2-km) radius; (2) if compensation would not be offered to cover amounts spent on improvements after 1964, maintenance would be neglected and stores would become declining assets; and (3) given general inflation, calculation of goodwill (based on profit levels for 1961–4) might not offer a true picture of the profitability of the stores at a time of later sale.
30. *Umata Branch, TTCA: Recommendations of this Body on Future Zoning Policy to be Placed before the Zoning Committee before the 10th June 1969*, pp. 2–3.
31. Thus Abraham, Commissioner-General: '... we intend making the Transkei ... the best administered state amongst the black states of Africa ... We have recently heard demands for the removal of European officials from highly technical and responsible civil service posts. Such demands, at this juncture of development in the Transkei, are highly irresponsible. Only a person into whose political philosophy chaos fits as an ingredient of political advancement, can propose such rash measures at this stage. When one bears in mind that the Communist ideology demands chaos as a seedbed for its noxious weed, you realise how dangerous such talk can be.' *TTCA Congress* (1965), p. 7.
32. *Résumé of the Activities and Endeavours of the Liaison Committee since its Establishment* (26 February 1963), p. 2.
33. ibid., p. 5; *TTCA Executive*, 15 September 1962; and *TTCA Circular*, 22 October 1962.
34. *Liaison Committee Meetings*, 1 February 1963 and 2 February 1963.
35. Liaison Committee to Verwoerd, 2 February 1963.
36. De Wet Nel to J. H. Abraham, 14 February 1963 (Liaison Committee Papers).
37. *Liaison Committee Meeting*, 23 February 1963.
38. *TTCA Circular*, 26 February 1963.
39. *Considered Statement issued by the Press Publicity Subcommittee of the TTCA to the Press of South Africa at Noon on Friday 1 March 1963.*
40. ibid.
41. *Daily Dispatch*, 9 March 1963.
42. At least one member of the Liaison Committee left the United Party and aligned himself with the National Party at this time (interview).
43. *Liaison Committee Meetings*, 30 March 1964–23 October 1965.
44. This culminated in the resignation of the Town Clerk of Umtata as Secretary to the Committee in 1967 following 'wild, irresponsible and quite uncalled for criticism' by the rural traders. H. Nevill to Chairman, 20 July 1967.

45. Interviews, D. F. Thomson (Chairman 1965 onward), 5 August 1976 and 26 February 1977.
46. *TTCA Congress, 1967*, p. 37.
47. *TTCA Congress, 1971*, p. 6.
48. *TTCA Congress, 1967*, p. 30; *1968*, p. 61; *1969*, p. 8; *1970*, p. 25.
49. *TTCA Congress, 1972*.
50. *TTCA Congress, 1969*, pp. 62–4; *1970*, pp. 21–4; *1974*, pp. 35–6. An XDC official in 1974: '... we have lost large sums and ... about R390,000 is still owing'.
51. *XDC Tenth Annual Report*, p. 25.
52. *Daily Dispatch*, 16 April, 19 May and 3 June 1976. Interview, Mr J. Geyer (Chairman, White Citizens' Association), 1 March 1977.
53. *HAD*, 3 June 1976, cols 7961–84.
54. *Transkei Hansard*, 1 May 1974, p. 289.
55. ibid., p. 298.
56. *TTCA Congress, 1966*, p. 4.
57. ibid., p. 19.
58. *TTCA Congress, 1970*, p. 14.
59. *Transkei Hansard*, 16 June 1971, p. 461.
60. The leading members of the Liaison Committee were E. Spilkin, C. W. Nelson and C. E. Sparg, all representatives of the largest local business concerns in Umtata.
61. 'Boom town Umtata', *Natal Daily News*, 18 August 1977.
62. *TTCA Congress, 1970*, p. 1.
63. Thus Chief George Ndabankulu (Minister of Roads and Works): 'Salaries of blacks as well as the number of salaried whites increased at a phenomenal rate ... When towns were zoned for black occupation and ownership, it provided in many cases, opportunities to exchange old properties in a weaker part of town or in a small village for new properties in a better part of town or in bigger towns. There are many examples where self-government resulted in great material benefit for those whites who stayed on.' (*TTCA Congress, 1974*, p. 3.)
64. J. H. T. Mills (Secretary to the Chief Minister), *TTCA Congress, 1972*, p. 5.
65. *RDM*, 1 December 1978.
66. SAIRR, *A Survey, 1979*, p. 510.

Chapter 6
Class formation in a bantustan

One of the ironies of South African political economy – where capitalism has developed the forces of production to a level higher than anywhere else on the continent – is the fact that the African bourgeoisie has remained relatively more backward than in the large majority of African countries which, though subjected in the past to the oppressions and expropriations of colonial rule, none the less experienced the emergence of a significant petty-bourgeoisie within the confines of colonial economy, this class in most cases heading their nationalist drive to independence. But in South Africa, even more than was the case of other territories dominated by settler colonialism, the formation of an African middle class was blocked by racial barriers deliberately erected to protect the class interests of the white population. Consequently, all possibility of the African middle class developing into a fully fledged bourgeoisie was prevented by state-imposed limitations specifically designed to inhibit, if not to totally suppress, its ability to accumulate capital, with the result that the numerically small African middle class which did emerge was primarily composed of non-property owning, non-productive and non-employing elements in the professional spheres such as law, religion and education (notwithstanding the existence of remnant peasant–farmer elements and some small-scale businessmen whose potential for expansion was hedged around by a maze of restrictive laws).

The limitations imposed by the white state upon its development had meant that, historically, the African middle class had sought to link up with the African masses in a class alliance contained within the framework of the African National Congress. Overcoming various deficiencies which had previously plagued this body in the interwar years, the forces working for the strengthening of an alliance across class and ethnic lines within the black community found their expression in a predominantly national consciousness; and it was when, in the post-1948 era, this led to mass action in the Defiance Campaigns and Anti-Pass Law demonstrations that the apartheid state felt constrained to suppress and outlaw all political resistance among the dominated. But more than this, appreciating the threat posed by such class and national combinations as the Congress Alliance – which linked the ANC to the Indian Congress and the (white) Congress of Democrats – the white ruling class now sought to fragment national consciousness by the implementation of its bantustan programme, whose objective was not merely to 'divide and rule', but also to create a collaborative African petty-bourgeoisie within each of the homelands. Indeed, as the bantustan strategy took off, the deliberate intent became to build up a set of dependent ethnic states along the neo-colonial model wherein emergent auxiliary elements would rely for their material prosperity and political privileges upon the favours of separate development and would accordingly co-operate with the white rulers in the repression and control of the migrant proletariat whose role was to oscillate between the white core and the ethnicized peripheries.[1]

The focus of the present section will be to analyse the historical roots of an auxiliary class in the Transkei, while it will be the purpose of the following chapter to illustrate that so severe are the structural limitations imposed upon the bantustan economy that the emergent homeland petty-bourgeoisie has little option but to reinforce and strengthen its ties with Pretoria. In short, it will be argued that the Transkeian petty-bourgeoisie, notwithstanding the fact of its constitutional independence, directly manages the affairs of South African capital in a subordinate capacity, and that however much it may be encouraged by events and its own immediate political interests to indulge in militantly anti-apartheid rhetoric, its situation is almost wholly constrained by its almost total continuing dependence upon white power.

The Transkeian bourgeoisie: chiefs and politicians

That the origin of the Transkeian auxiliary class lay in the Bantu Authorities system and the revival of chieftaincy has already been made clear. But, as was also indicated above, the Pondo Revolt of 1960–1 demonstrated that the traditional leadership, however much reinvigorated by expanded administrative functions, was far too fragile a foundation upon which to erect a lasting state apparatus, and accordingly it was later deemed necessary to allow for the incorporation into the latter of a significant commoner element. In essence, Pretoria identified the need for an African middle class to impart stability to its designs, and this in turn necessitated that such an element be given a permanent source of income (or, in short, an economic base). In other words, a price to the metropole of establishing a designedly neo-colonial entity was in allowing emergent auxiliaries to draw off a small proportion of the economic surplus being appropriated from the Transkei, the intention being to ease the long-term exploitability of the labour resources of the reserve in the changing conditions of South African political economy.

One of the most startling features of the bantustan project has been the particularly explicit manner in which chiefs, headmen and politicians (who generally possess few skills which they can sell on the open market) have been bound to the state through direct financial inducement. In a society where jobs are scarce and where the level of payment is generally low, appointment to official positions or membership of the Transkeian

Parliament offers a chance and scale of remuneration which few recipients can find elsewhere. Thus whereas *per capita* annual income for reserve-based blacks in the Transkei rose in monetary terms from a calculated R54 in 1960 to R169 in 1973,[2] remuneration for the chiefly administrators increased disproportionately, thereby relieving them of the necessity of migrating for work and thus ensuring their continual presence in rural areas; see Table 6.1. In addition to their salaries, chiefs also receive extra payment based on the number of taxpayers in their districts (from R360 to R1,080 in 1975), and together with the headmen receive travelling and various other allowances, as well as a pension when they retire from formal duties; and apart from these official payments, of course, chiefs and headmen are also able to use their positions of administrative dominance to extract surplus from their political subordinates through coercive and corrupt mechanisms as outlined above.

Table 6.1 *Salaries of chiefs and headmen, 1964–78*

	Paramount chiefs	Chiefs sitting *ex officio* in TLA	Chiefs not sitting *ex officio* in TLA (R)	Headmen's scale (R)
1964	£1,500	£400	—	64–112
1967			400	120–216
1971		R1,900	600	144–276
1975	R11,000	R3,000	1,000	288–456
1978	R14,000	R3,300 (est.)	1,296	348–540

Sources: *Transkei Hansard*, 26 April 1971, p. 74; 2 April 1974, p. 132; 4 March 1975, p. 97 and 10 March 1975, p. 115. *Transkei Estimate of Expenditure*, Year ending 31 March 1976, p. 7. Some newly created chiefs were apparently not yet receiving the full rate of payment for chiefs.

The escalated financial remuneration of chiefs has been accompanied by an increase in salaries for members of the Legislative Assembly from R800 in 1964 to R4,000 in 1977[3] – the latter figure being exclusive of a daily attendance allowance while Parliament is in session (which is usually rather less than three months a year); and in 1975, Ministers were receiving R12,000 per annum with Matanzima himself earning an official Prime Minister's salary of R14,000.[4] Although the actual number of politicians who receive these salaries is small (a total of 150 by 1976), it is significant in that it may be assumed that ability to secure election or appointment to Parliament denotes the possession of influence, and that in consequence men of prominence in the rural situation have been drawn into financial dependence upon the bantustan state apparatus, and are likely to use their positions to promote support for, and to suppress resistance to, separate development.

It is perhaps instructive to examine precisely the social strata from which the bantustan politicians have been drawn, focusing upon the occupational background of elected members in the Transkeian legislature, as illustrated in Table 6.2. What is significant, of course, is that the elected members of the Transkeian legislature are broadly unrepresentative of the reserve community, whose mass is composed of semi-proletarianized migrants and their dependants. Yet this does not imply – as Innes and O'Meara suggest – that it is elements of 'a stable, rich peasantry' which form the basis for TNIP rule in the Transkei,[5] for the data clearly demonstate that the politicians are typically drawn from petty-bourgeois occupations which are located on the periphery of the reserve economy. This does not mean that they are *not* engaged in direct agricultural production on their own account (for, constituting a rural élite, it is likely that they retain privileged access to landholdings), but rather that they rely for the major part of their income upon non-productive resources. The Transkeian political élite, therefore, is primarily dependent for its livelihood upon financial resources which circulate

Table 6.2 *Occupational distribution of elected members of the Transkeian Legislature*

Occupation	1963	1968	1973	1976
Professional	4	3	3	5
Educational	10	9	5	9
Clerical	3	5	4	5
Businessman/trader	6	5	8	17
Chief/headman	13	10	15	24
Commercial employee	2	0	0	2
Farmer	7	12	9	6
Diverse	0	1	1	7
TOTAL	45	45	45	75

Sources: D. A. Kotze (1975), Table 7.1, p. 134 (adapted); *Daily Dispatch*, 19 August 1968; *Transkei Gazette*, 13, 33, 20 August 1976, pp. 7–19; and private interviews.

in the bantustan in the form of salaries, loans and contracts (these often being drawn indirectly from the white state via the administration in Umtata).

Finally, it is perhaps worth noting that although the chiefly élite has been considerably leavened by the introduction of the commoner element into the Assembly in the guise of elected members, the traditional leadership remains predominant. Seventy-five chiefs sit in Parliament *ex officio* – and, as can be seen above, a number of other chiefs and headmen also secure admission through election. Yet this does not imply that tradition continues to dominate over modernity, but rather that the traditional élite, by being drawn into the financial orbit of the state, has itself undergone a transformation of embourgeoisement through its bureaucratization under the Bantu Authorities system. Thus whereas popular legitimacy was to a considerable extent still accorded to chieftaincy through the years of obscurity precisely because of its limited assimilation into the chain of command issuing from the colonial authority, it has now been largely alienated by its absorption into the official sphere: 'The chieftainship has lost its most valuable political shock-absorber – its apparent elevation above the arena of political strife';[6] and in so doing, the mystifications of its class dominance have also been exposed before the critical gaze of the reserve community. It will be argued below that this polarization between dominant and dominated classes is likely to become continuously more evident, as the commercial fraction of the petty-bourgeoisie become increasingly interlinked with its political counterpart.

The bureaucrats

The essence of the bantustan programme in the Transkei was the superimposition upon the reserve economy of the apparatus of an Africanized state. Accordingly, as Pretoria progressively devolved functions upon Umtata, so was there need for a marked expansion of the local administration; and a key feature of the project, of course, was that the new bureaux should become staffed by Transkeian bureaucrats whose material interests would lead them to identify with the autonomous existence of a Xhosa polity.

The expansion of the bureaucracy in Umtata has been perhaps the most visible and substantial aspect of the entire homeland scheme. In earlier days, the administration in the Transkei was geared to servicing only the most rudimentary needs of the reserve economy. The Bunga's responsibilities had extended to little more than the maintenance of minor roads and bridges, the running of a handful of industrial, agricultural and technical training schools, and the performance of certain very basic agricultural services. Accordingly, the number of public servants in the Council's employ was minimal, amounting to only 15 whites and 154 blacks in 1932 (100 of the latter being African agricultural demonstrators); and by 1953 the establishment had shrunk even further to a total of 117, of whom only 43 were Africans (there being by this year only 17 agricultural assistants).[7]

The Transkei Constitution Act of 1963 made special provision for the creation of a Transkeian public service, into which all existing staff of the TTA, as well as African officers of the Republican government employed in the Transkei in those fields in which the TLA was to exercise competence, were to be absorbed. Until the homeland administration could be localized, white officials were to be seconded from the Republican government, by whom they would be paid and under whose control they would fall; and the Act also laid down that such officials were to be progressively replaced by Africans 'from the lower grades upwards' according to an agreement to be worked out between the South African and Transkeian authorities (thereby generally ensuring that no white would have to serve under a black).

The expansion of the local administration had been foreshadowed by the devolution to the TTA of certain educational, health and judicial functions under the Bantu Authorities system. Thus, with the further creation of six new Departments each officially headed by a Minister in the Transkeian government, the official establishment thereafter underwent a period of extremely rapid growth, so that by the end of 1963 it numbered 2,446 posts (25 per cent of which were vacant), 455 of these then being held by seconded white officials. The subsequent development of the public service can be illustrated by Table 6.3. Not all these posts were new creations under the homeland policy, and the rapid expansion of the official bureaucracy in the latter pre-independence years in actuality reflected the takeover by the government of some twenty-one mission hospitals, the police, prisons, security, postal and border control services, along with the absorption of the Herschel and Glen Grey areas into the Transkei.[8] None the less, it can be safely estimated that there are

Table 6.3 *Establishment of the Transkeian public service, 1963–79**

Year	Fixed establishment	Increase (%)	No. of posts for seconded white officials	Rate of white secondment (%)
1963	2,446	—	455	18·6
1964	2,475	1·19	427	17·3
1965	2,821	13·98	382	13·5
1966	2,920	3·51	359	12·3
1967	3,393	16·20	365	10·8
1968	3,460	1·97	377	10·9
1969	3,576	3·35	349	9.8
1970	3,673	2·71	339	9·2
1971	3,862	5·15	314	8·1
1972	4,094	6·01	306	7·5
1973	5,594	36·64	349	6·2
1974	5,679	1·52	270	4·8
1975	10,291	81·21	258	2·5
1976	17,320	68·30	358	2·1
1977	17,300	−0·12	314	1·8
1978	17,310	0·06	232	1·3
1979	19,800	14·38	140	0·7

Note: * Excluding the police and prison services, transferred to the Transkeian government from the South African authorities in 1972.
Source: Reports of the Public Service Commission, 1963–79.

up to 10,000 *central* government bureaucrats at the time of writing, with an equal number of official employees in more outlying spheres of administration.

It is these public servants who presently form the main core of the homeland petty-bourgeoisie, and their class interests are both well defined and clearly articulated. In the first place, they are separated from the mass of the reserve community (which is largely dependent upon the meagre returns of migrant labour) by their education (which has enabled them to gain white-collar employment), by the level of their financial remuneration and by their constant preoccupation 'to better themselves'. The rapid expansion of the administration has provided for high rates of promotion, with accompanying schemes for individuals to improve their educational and technical qualifications.[9] But, more importantly, since 1963 the public service salary structure has experienced an improvement which has far outstripped the rate of inflation, and increases in one form or another were awarded in the years 1964, 1967, 1968, 1969, 1970, 1971 (twice), 1973, 1974, 1976 and 1978; and after the 1971 increases, for example, the pay scale ranged from R660 (for lower-level officials with a Junior School Certificate) to over R6,000 for the higher grades, with civil servants also being entitled to subsidized housing rented from the state at 10 per cent of their salaries within municipal areas and $7\frac{1}{2}$ per cent outside such areas.[10] All these improvements have been justified on the grounds of shortage of qualified personnel and in pursuit of the policy that homeland civil servants should be paid no less than African employees in the Republican civil service,[11] but the objective effect within the homeland has been to visibly consolidate the material privileges of the bureaucracy relative to the reserve masses to an extent considered alarming even by the bureaucrats themselves: 'The time is fast approaching when further enhancement of earnings will be difficult to justify to the taxpayer unless accompanied by notably better service to the public,' noted the Public Service Commission in 1970.[12] Comment by the same body in the following year was even more explicit:

> A stable, content, well-paid government service is, needless to say, the backbone of any country – particularly a developing homeland – but the ratio of earnings of a large, poor peasantry in such a developing area to those of a comparatively small, select, group in the pay of that selfsame public is a factor which must, presumably, eventually inhibit government service salary increases notwithstanding that disparities with the government services of neighbouring states or other homelands may thereby arise. Put succinctly, a developing and mendicant homeland must cut its suit according to its cloth and further salary increases of the order of those experienced in 1971 seem contrary to the larger public good for some years to come.[13]

It was perhaps not accidental that later improvements in remuneration were not in the form of increased salary levels, but were hidden in the guise of various 'allowances' ($17\frac{1}{2}$ per cent of basic salary in 1973 and 20 per cent in 1976)!

Apart from their official remuneration, there is evidence that some bureaucrats, like the chiefs, engage in the primitive accumulation of capital through outright corruption. By its very nature, the extent of such illicit activity is difficult to gauge, but the indications are that it is not inconsiderable. The Annual Reports of the Public Service Commission themselves point out that the level of misconduct (notably drunkenness, bribery and theft) is relatively high, but the bulk of official prosecutions tends to fall upon the lower-level bureaucrats, probably because corruption at their level is easier to detect (and possibly because they are less controversial victims for prosecution). But what does emerge from even the official statistics is that the burden of many such unofficial levies falls upon those least able to afford it. Thus, in referring to the Ministry of Justice whose officials then undertook duties in connection with labour recruitment and the issue of pensions and disability grants, the Public Service Commission (then chaired by Mr G. Bikitsha, and otherwise composed of Mr H. Nolutshungu and Mr E. Moahlohi) noted that:

> ... the highest frequency of misconduct amongst prescribed officers is to be found in one department (33 cases out of a total of 321 employed i.e. 10·3 per cent) – the one which also acts on an agency basis for others and Republican Departments – apparently because the opportunities for corrupt clerks to cheat and defraud largely illiterate workseekers, taxpayers and pensioners unavoidably abound despite every effort to strengthen control measures. In almost all these cases the offences concern bribes being offered or demanded and accepted (frequently in the form of liquor which is consumed to excess, virtually on the spot, shortchanging ignorant people and falsifications of records to cover up theft of government moneys).[14]

This official finding supplements more casual observation. Matanzima himself has deplored the high level of corruption throughout the ranks of the public administration[15] and press reports in 1975 indicated that an estimated R600,000 or more was stolen annually by Transkeian civil servants from pensioners and recipients of other benefits: 'An official confirmed that there were frequently shortages at points where money passes from hand to hand between officials and the public.'[16] A solution to this problem proffered by one Transkeian MP was to raise salaries for public servants so that they would be placed beyond the reach of temptation.[17] Yet markedly improved remuneration has not hitherto served to eliminate corruption, and has rather worked to widen further the gap between public servants and the mass of the reserve population.

Finally (and in parenthesis, as little hard evidence is available) it appears that civil servants (and politicians) are successfully acquiring wealth by a variety of other means. As Leys has noted, what the bureaucrat needs is income which can be obtained without his leaving his bureau, and in consequence his main aim must be to draw rent rather than to actively pursue profit.[18] Consequently, at the present time, given a legal bar to civil servants engaging in business on their own account, the main thrust of their investment would seem to be in housing. For the most fortunate and politically influential, pickings have been available in the form of cut-price bargains on properties acquired from whites by the Bantu Trust and later sold to blacks for as little as one-fifth of their original purchase cost by the Transkeian government.[19] But even for those civil servants who are forced to pay market rates for properties, their receipt of a regular and relatively high income puts them in a favourable position to take advantage of the housing loans and mortgages offered by the Transkei Development Corporation and local building societies;[20] and informal observation suggests that bureaucrats have been in no way backward in exploiting the acute accommodation shortage in Umtata by putting out their properties to rent. Given the South African government's policy of continuing to 'resettle' Transkeian 'citizens' formerly resident in white spots in their homeland, opportunity for such exploitation of the propertyless by the propertied can only be expected to grow over the coming years.

In accordance with the consolidation of their class position and their rapid acquisition of wealth, Transkeian bureaucrats have evolved their own distinct group consciousness. They possess their own Public Servants' Association which makes representations on their behalf about their conditions of service, and they enjoy sympathetic consideration inside the walls of the Legislative Assembly: 'The Government has been deaf to the plea for good salaries for civil servants,' one Member is reported as saying. 'The Transkei Army has learned all about coups and there would be one in the Transkei within a year if officials were not paid well.'[21] In addition, there has been constant (and wholly understandable) invocation of the need to eliminate racial discrimination in pay scales between black and white; 'when we claim independence we shall adopt the policy of equal pay for equal work', stated Cromwell Diko, a prominent parliamentarian, in 1974.[22]

Above and beyond their immediate financial interests, there is indication that the bureaucrats – and notably, perhaps, those in the higher echelons – are evolving a distinct ideological position which revolves around the twin notions of Transkei as a 'developing country' and a 'new state'. Although there is no available survey of attitudes of these civil servants towards independence, it would seem that they are recruited from a section of higher-educated Xhosa which is politically predisposed to accepting the notion of separate development. Thus, in one survey of students at Fort Hare (the ethnic university for Xhosa), it was found that only one-third of those interviewed were prepared to consider working in the Ciskei or Transkei, a major reason for rejection of such opportunity on the part of the remaining two-thirds being that they rejected the homeland concept.[23] It is therefore at least a tenable thesis that the first generation of topmost Transkeian civil servants have been drawn from the prior group.

A rather atypical but none the less interesting example of the new bureaucrats is provided by Dr Charles Bikitsha, who returned to the

Transkei in 1973 at the behest of Kaiser Matanzima, who had been his contemporary at university. Having practised medicine in Britain and Ireland for thirty-seven years, he now assumed office as top administrator (Secretary) in the Department of Health, seeing himself as following closely in the footsteps of his 'old friends' Jomo Kenyatta and Hastings Banda, who had both spoken with excitement of the independence that their countries had won. 'When it began looming up for the Transkei,' explained Bikitsha, 'I just had to see it work for myself.'[24]

Yet if, as individuals, bureaucrats are ideologically predisposed to accept the offerings of separate development even before they join the homeland civil service, it is also clear that their assumption of office soon reinforces their existing orientation. Indeed, they have been as concerned as the top politicians to gain acceptance for Transkei as an independent state, appreciating that entry into the world community of nations would both legitimize their status and open doors to career opportunities within international organizations and the prestigious diplomatic sphere.

Finally, it is perhaps worth recalling Leys's point that the significance of higher bureaucrats 'is less their class origins or ambitions than their specific function in relation to ruling alliance of classes and class strata'.[25] From this perspective, Transkeian civil servants can be viewed as fulfilling a straightforwardly 'comprador' function for South Africa. Indeed, many of the top posts in the administration are still filled by white officers seconded from Pretoria and, despite the increasing rate of Africanization, the South Africans who remain are highly influential:

> ... the category of seconded officer remaining in the Transkei is more difficult to replace by Transkeians than was that which predominated in the initial years of self-government. Put differently, the training requirements of the Transkeian aspirants to the top posts are far more comprehensive and the selection processes more stringent than was the case with the lower hierarchy and, whilst aware of the political necessity of showing constant progress, the Commission cannot too strongly emphasize the long term advantages of administrative patience in these matters.[26]

An incident illustrative of the continuing preponderant influence of South African officials was that involving the retention of a Professor J. D. Ben-Dak, an Israeli, as adviser to Matanzima and chairman of a proposed National Planning Agency in 1977. After his arrival in Umtata, Ben-Dak filed a memorandum in which he made stringent criticisms about the competence of the Republican officials who ran the Development Corporation, and advised that Mr Franco Maritz (Managing Director), his brother Mr J. P. Maritz (Industrial and Public Relations Manager) and other top aides be phased out in favour of black nationals, who should be appointed to the most senior posts. At the same time, he recommended that the Planning Agency should employ 'professionals' (the implication being that they should be non-South African expatriate) who would be able to 'cultivate foreign skill and capital' and promote an increased flow of overseas investment. But such an attack upon

Republican interests was too direct – and it was Ben-Dak who received his marching orders and not the Maritz brothers, even though it was perfectly clear from press reports that Matanzima himself would have been pleased to be rid of the latter individuals.[27] Nevertheless, it remains a possibility that all white South African officials may be withdrawn at some future date, and replaced by foreign experts from elsewhere. If such a course might conceivably enable the Transkeian regime to develop a limited degree of autonomy from Pretoria, such a prospect is none the less limited, for as will be demonstrated in the following chapter, the bantustan economy in the present era is becoming more, rather than less, enmeshed with that of white South Africa.

The teachers

Similarly dependent upon the bantustan state for their salaried income are the Transkei's teachers. In 1978–9 there were 2,380 schools and 13,984 qualified teachers catering for 681,621 pupils,[28] compared with 1,627 schools and 4,844 teachers for 270,756 children in 1962[29] (an increase in the teaching establishment of 189 per cent over the period). This considerable expansion of facilities is reflective of the relative degree of autonomy which the homeland regime enjoyed in education during the self-government era relative to other official spheres. Indeed, it was one of the first acts of the new Legislative Assembly to abandon the hated Bantu Education policy (whereby African children were to be instructed through the medium of the tribal vernacular and to be acculturated to the subordinate role of blacks in a white-dominated society) against the expressed wishes of the Republican government, and to return the Transkei to (an adjusted) Cape (European) education syllabus.[30] In addition, it was the Department of Education which was first released from the supervision of white officials, Africanization proceeding at a faster pace than elsewhere, with the first Transkeian Secretary (the most senior administrative grade) being appointed in 1975.[31]

This speedier devolution of authority to blacks in the educational sphere was not coincidental. The Republican government was wholly aware that even in the most outlying areas of the reserves there was a widespread demand for the expansion of the school system and, despite all the deliberate limitations of the electoral system which were designed to minimize the impact of popular choice over the selection of the legislature, even homeland politicians were by no means wholly immune from political pressures from below. Thus if the new Transkeian government, which had been so openly imposed upon an unwilling people, were to gain any degree of popular legitimacy, it was necessary for it to be able to offer at least some marginal, tangible benefits to its electorate; and given that both the homeland civil service and the increasingly sophisticated white

Table 6.4 *Professional qualifications of teachers in Transkei, 1978*

Qualification	No.	%
Lower than matriculation or equivalent	11,773	84·19
Matriculation or equivalent	1,938	13·86
University degree	273	1·95
	13,984	100·00

Source: SAIRR, *A Survey 1979*, p. 503.

economy would in future demand a more educated base from which to draw their recruits, an expansion of the educational system did not necessarily run contrary to National Party plans.

Teachers in Transkei are differentiated from the reserve community by virtue of both their training and their rates of remuneration. Qualifications of teachers in 1978 were as shown in Table 6.4. In like manner to the Public Servants' Association, the Transkei Teachers' Association was active in agitating for the closing of the wage gap between black and white (although within the territory the profession below the tertiary level has long been almost wholly Africanized), and by 1974 they were being paid on a scale ranging from R917 (for unqualified female teachers with a Junior Certificate of Education) to R5,288 for principals of secondary schools with more than 600 pupils, this income being supplemented by two salary increases in 1974–5 and one of 20 per cent in 1977;[32] and to the extent that the expansion of the Transkeian educational sector has allowed for rapid promotions (especially for the relatively few graduates), teachers have been beneficiaries of the strategy pursued by the Matanzima government. However, the benefits they have received have not been sufficient to guarantee their docility, and their political relationship to the bantustan state has continuously been highly ambivalent.

The teaching profession in Transkei is now employed only by the government, which since the time of independence has phased out all privately run schools (of which twenty-seven remained in 1975–6).[33] Consequently, all teachers are subject to official control, with their appointment, promotion, transfer and discharge lying within the competence of the Minister of Education; and the definition of misconduct for which they may be dismissed, as laid down by the Transkei Education Act of 1966, is extremely wide, relating to their conniving 'at anything which is prejudicial to the administration, discipline or efficiency of any department, office or institution of the government'. But this apart, as Kuper argued some time ago, following the introduction of the Bantu Education system in 1953, the African teaching profession underwent a process of downgrading and debasement in status terms: 'Previously [the teacher] was a member of the new élite, leading his people outward into the world. Today he is forced back within the group and subordinated to it. The official reference is the tribal or ethnic unit, distinct and inferior, not the dominant white group.'[34] Thus the political role of the teacher became to train his pupils for their racially allotted, subordinate role in society. In the Transkei, vigorous opposition by their Association to Bantu Education led to the dismissal of many of the best African headmasters and teachers;[35] and the degradation of their profession became so explicit that, as we have seen, the Matanzima government was constrained to revert to the Cape educational syllabus in the pursuit of racial (albeit 'separate') equality. But the relief that was offered by this reform to teachers as a group was limited and their fundamental political dilemma remained, for their new political role became to service the educational requirements of a tribal homeland, and thereby to promote the policy of separate development which large numbers of them (if not the majority) expressly rejected. It is this continuing dilemma which may be in part responsible for the widespread demoralization among teachers within the Transkei today, as is reflected in an excessively high rate of drinking and an allegedly low level of professional conduct.[36]

But teachers in the Transkei are by no means a homogeneous group, and it would be facile to conclude that they are all (at least potentially) opposed to the Matanzima government; indeed, given the increased opportunities now available for their personal advancement within the educational sphere, it would appear that many are presently reconciled to the notion of a Transkeian state and, for the most part, teachers have remained politically compliant. On the other hand, there has continuously been a degree of antagonism to the Matanzima regime which has at times flowed over into fairly open disaffection. Of course, the link between education and the development of African resistance to racist oppression in South Africa is explicit, many individuals graduating to the nationalist movement through the ranks of the teaching profession or through university; and within the Transkei this political awareness was reflected in a widespread rejection among teachers of both colonial structures such as the Bunga (which was dismissed as a talking shop) and the revival of the traditional leadership of the chiefs (many of whom were largely uneducated) under the Bantu Authorities system.

It was no coincidence, therefore, that the majority of teachers seem to have supported the Poto faction in the election of 1963. As Munger pointed out,[37] various members of the educated élite in the Transkei at that time had links with the Liberal Party, which came to be indirectly associated with the Poto set, and it can be safely assumed that the majority of teachers who stood for election (nearly one-fourth of the 180 candidates) were opposed to Matanzima.[38] Thereafter, to the extent that teachers have participated in bantustan politics, their activity seems to a large extent to have been institutionalized within the DP. Indeed, the continuing conflict between different factions within that party which culminated in the overthrow of Guzana by Ncokazi in 1976 partially reflects the challenge to 'multiracialism' posed by 'black consciousness', which was doubtless imported into the Transkei through new recruits into the homeland teaching profession who had graduated from Fort Hare. Thus teachers were forbidden by the Matanzima government to belong to the South African Students' Organization,[39] and it was the increasing influence of these radical ideas within the Opposition that led to the passage of the Government Service Amendment Act of 1974, in terms of which public employees were debarred from participating in party politics and from belonging to political organizations,[40] the objective being to cut off the dissident faction within the DP from the main impetus of its support.

The dilemmas of the teaching profession in the Transkei indicate the contradictory pressures upon the petty-bourgeoisie as a class, and its resultant political ambivalence. On the one hand, as represented by core elements such as politicians and bureaucrats whose occupational role is premised upon the very existence of the bantustan state, the petty-bourgeoisie provides the Matanzima regime with critical support. On the other hand, elements which are more peripheral to the state (such as teachers) doubt its ability to provide for their long-term class interests, which they do not perceive as necessarily being served through the pursuit of separate development.

The expansion of the tertiary sector of education, notably the Cicira Teachers Training College and the University of Transkei (both established in 1976), is likely to increase such contradictory pressures by providing channels of recruitment to the different factions of the petty-bourgeoisie. At the same time, an expanding student population is likely to provide a basis for continuous, if simmering, political disaffection. Already there have been widespread disturbances in schools throughout Transkei – in 1971, 1974 and 1976 (in the last year being a response to events in Soweto) – illustrating the impossibility of insulating the reserve population from black discontent throughout the rest of the Republic. However, students are a transitional group with no basis in the economy, and their protests are usually characterized by spontaneity rather than longevity – and hence it is unlikely that they will be able to launch any prolonged or effective challenge to political authority, although doubtless clashes between students and government will occur. Yet, for the foreseeable future, the latter will remain the major employer of graduates, and it would be unrealistic to expect that the mass of students will be prepared to risk their future careers by engaging in sustained political confrontation – although this is not to deny that they might well play a progressive role in a crisis situation.

Traders and businessmen

Expansion in the commercial and service sectors has progressed considerably and a Transkeian entrepreneurial class is being created.
– Barclays Bank[41]

An integral aspect of the bantustan process within the Transkei has been the creation of conditions favourable to the expansion of a fraction of the African petty-bourgeoisie based in trade, commerce and petty commodity production. This has been only a relatively recent phenomenon, however, and opportunity for the development of this fraction has only taken place under the impact of contradictory pressures upon the apartheid regime. Accordingly, it is only possible to comprehend the specifics of this process by relating them (albeit in cursory fashion) to general changes occurring within the framework of the broader political economy.

African participation in trading in South Africa has always been subject to severe limitation in order to protect the interests of white capital operating within the commercial sphere, and the development of a black capitalist class has been correspondingly stunted. Thus, from the earliest days, the accumulation of capital by potential African entrepreneurs was inhibited by the low wages paid to black labour by white employers; and secondly, white dominance in trading has been continuously guaranteed by a system of licensing. Thus the Native Economic Commission of 1930–2 reported critically upon the establishment of a monopoly over trade by whites in the Transkei and of a virtual monopoly in other reserve areas, and recommended that henceforth Africans should be given first option in the allocation of new licences;[42] and, as related above, Proclamation 244 of 1934 accordingly relaxed the 5-mile (8-km) radius which protected white traders in the reserves to 2 miles (3·2 km) in respect of African traders, butchers and bakers.

Thereafter, the number of licences issued to African general dealers throughout 'native areas' increased from 119 (or 9·1 per cent of the total) in 1936 to 1,199 (or 45·5 per cent) in 1952 (although these catered for only 10 per cent of the total of reserve trade). Meanwhile, outside the reserves, licensing of Africans to trade in locations was entrusted to Municipal Authorities under the Native (Urban Areas) Act of 1923. But in these urban areas African commercial expansion was generally subject to official restraint in the interests of white capital, so that although there was a steady growth in the number of African traders from the early years of the century, by the early 1930s there were only between five and six hundred African retailers on the whole of the Witwatersrand, with perhaps the majority of them making only a precarious living. However, with increased opportunities afforded by the expansion of the locations and the economy after the war, the number of African licensees had increased to 1,683 by June 1958. Yet the impact of African trading upon the monopolistic sway of white interests over the commercial sector was extremely limited. Hemmed in by the overwhelming weight of white capital, African traders suffered from a lack of education and training, capital and access to credit facilities.

It was in the 1950s, however, that official policy towards African trading underwent a considerable change. On the one hand, African traders in urban areas were increasingly subjected to greater restrictive pressures by the state, this being reflective of the progressive diminution of the rights of urban Africans under apartheid; and on the other hand, African businessmen in the homelands were provided with varying amounts of official assistance and offered a degree of protection from white competition as the Republican authorities sought to cultivate the development of a petty-bourgeois fraction based in trading and commerce.

The first move to affect urban traders was the activation in 1955 of Section 6 of the Native (Urban Areas) Consolidation Act of 1945, which provided for the removal of squatter occupants from trading sites outside the boundaries of locations, while in 1957 an amendment to the Act made it incumbent upon African businessmen (and professionals) to operate not merely under licence from local authorities, but also to gain permission from the Department of Native Affairs. Then, in 1959, the responsible Minister iterated that African traders were only temporarily resident in the locations, and that once they had acquired sufficient capital and experience they should remove their businesses to the homelands; and subsequently, in 1963, the Department of Native Affairs issued a circular laying down the harshest restrictions ever imposed upon African businessmen. Premised upon the assumption that trading by blacks in white areas was not their inherent right but was only tolerated where necessary, the circular specified (among other things) that (1) Africans were not to be allowed to form companies or partnerships and thereby to promote larger businesses by pooling their resources; (2) Africans in townships were barred from dealing in anything but day-to-day necessities; (3) Africans were denied the right to construct their own premises; and (4) the establishment of African-controlled financial institutions, industries and wholesale concerns in white areas was forbidden; and the circular encouraged municipal authorities to 'persuade' owners of existing dry-cleaning enterprises and garages to transfer their business to the homelands. Finally, as if such were not sufficient to shore up white dominance of urban commerce, further restriction was imposed in 1968 whereby no African businessman was to be allowed to operate at more than one site.[43]

The complement to the limitations imposed upon African capitalism in urban areas was the official encouragement of its development within the homelands. The Tomlinson Commission had exhorted the government in 1955 to establish a Development Corporation for the reserves, whose tasks would include the promotion of small industries run by black entrepreneurs, as well as the provision of capital and guidance to aspiring black traders. In 1959 this recommendation was given substance with the establishment of the Bantu Investment Corporation (and later the various homeland Development Corporations) which was empowered to make loans to Africans without security, and which was required to plough back any profits in the 'development of the Native'; and as indicated above,[44] although the extent of assistance which has subsequently been granted to African businessmen through the medium of the Corporations has been limited, it has been critical in allowing for the development of a stratum of African petty capitalists within all the various bantustans, this element being overwhelmingly located in the commercial and service sectors of the reserve economies which require a low level of finance and technology, and has involved the state-induced withdrawal of non-blacks.

Within the Transkei, where white settlers had dominated reserve trade since the days of annexation, the official purpose was served by effecting the transfer of the white trading monopoly into black hands. Yet the process was not mechanical, and initially involved an *attack* upon monopoly. The restrictions on African participation in trade and commerce had always been bitterly resented in the Transkei, and one of the first actions of the TNIP government was to pass the Trade Amendment Act (no. 5 of 1964) which abolished the rule operative under Proclamation 244 of 1934 whereby African traders, butchers and bakers were not allowed to operate within 2 miles (3·2 km) of an existing trading store. The measure was ostensibly designed to promote free enterprise, but it retained a system of licensing in order to allow for the protection of black Transkeian entrepreneurs against competition from the 'capital-stronger white trader'.[45] Licenses were to be issued by the Minister of the Interior or whomsoever such power might be delegated, the effect of which provision was to grant the government and its subordinate authorities an important source of patronage by which it could induce or reward support; and in practice, this has meant that the TNIP has tended to issue licences to its local supporters, much to the dissatisfaction of the Opposition and a number of traders forced out of the urban areas by the policy of apartheid.[46]

The function of licensing was delegated to the Regional Authorities, whose chiefly councillors soon found that they had acquired a new and profitable source of revenue, for it was widely alleged that applications generally needed to be graced by some form of material tribute. There was no shortage of prospective licensees, and the relaxation of restrictions swiftly led to a proliferation of retail outlets. Hawkers, whose licences officially enabled them to sell only a limited number of specified commodities (mainly fresh vegetables, fruit and so on) within a certain district, commonly resorted to the sale of other goods and travelling beyond their ordained sphere; and holders of Bantu Traders' Licences (who were formally required to situate themselves in fixed premises which supposedly complied with certain minimum standards) operated so-called 'mushroom' shops which competed directly with existing trading stores.

The extent of the commercial expansion is impossible to gauge with accuracy because of the paucity of official statistics. But whereas in 1963 there was a total of 361 African traders,[47] the responsible Minister estimated that an average of 150 licences had been granted in each later year prior to 1973.[48] In addition, it was freely admitted that there were a large number of small general dealers trading without licences, although these were balanced by the failure of many businesses which had been operating legally. Whatever the case, the white traders – fearful for their monopoly profits – were bitter in their condemnation of what they termed the indiscriminate dispensation of licences, and motions deploring 'over-trading' were regular fare at the annual congresses of the TTCA.

Yet it was not only the white traders who lamented increased competition, but also that more highly capitalized stratum of African businessmen which aspired to inherit the trading monopoly, and which had been deliberately fostered by the Xhosa (and later the 'Transkei') Development Corporation. It was one of the major functions of the XDC to purchase stores vacated by departing white traders, to train Transkeian blacks to take them over, and to advance loans to African entrepreneurs who were considered capable of running such businesses at a profit. Over the first ten years of its operations, the Corporation had acquired 562 of the Transkei's 653 white trading stations, and all had been handed over to Africans who had either a proprietary or managerial interest;[49] but heavily indebted to the XDC for loan capital, the interests of this group were closely tied up with the maintenance of the commercial monopoly.

The impact of the 'mushroom' shops upon older established trading concerns was limited because of their generally low level of capitalization, yet it is none the less clear that they made intrusion into monopoly profit. Accordingly, the larger African traders swelled the chorus of the TTCA in calling for the preservation or imposition of limits upon commercial competition, and as early as 1963 the newly formed Bantu Chamber of Commerce resolved in favour of maintaining the 2-mile (3·2-km) radius rule,[50] finding an echo in the later condemnation of 'over-trading' by its successor body (the Transkei Chamber of Commerce) in 1973.[51]

In the period immediately following the grant of self-government, the objective of both the TNIP government and the Development Corporation was to effect the extrusion of the white traders, and accordingly the erosion of the latter's commercial predominance was an act of deliberate policy. But as the XDC acquired large numbers of formerly white-owned stores, so it gained a new interest in monopoly; and given the need to secure the repayment of loans contracted by African entrepreneurs to whom it had handed over the trading stations, the re-establishment of monopoly became necessary to provide for their commercial success. Thus in September 1970 the TTCA was informed that the further issue of licences would be temporarily suspended in order to allow the Ministry of the Interior to make a detailed survey of the trading situation.[52] This decision made only a momentary impact, but in 1973 new regulations were introduced which imposed a minimum capital requirement of R2,000 upon applicants for licences to become general dealers, bantu traders (*sic*) or gristing millers or to run restaurants and garages; and a minimum of R1,000 for those applying for licences to run butcheries or bakeries.[53] The new measures led to an appreciable decline in the number of new licences issued (only fifty-three new licences were approved during 1974) and, combined with the utilization of more regular inspections to ensure that small businesses conformed with health regulations,[54] provided for stronger central control from the Ministry in the interests of the Development Corporation-supported fraction of the petty-bourgeoisie.

Table 6.5 *Financial aid from the Xhosa Development Corporation to African businessmen in the Transkei up to 1975*

Type of loan	Loans approved	Amount approved (R)
General dealers	536	3,993,705
Hotels, bottle stores	30	514,100
Garages, filling stations	25	180,950
Bus and Transport Services	57	1,346,470
Diverse	44	483,475
TOTAL	692	6,518,700

Source: XDC, *Tenth Annual Report*, 1975, p. 27.

Thus it has been the activities of the Development Corporation (and before 1965, the BIC) which have created a favourable environment for the development of a commercial bourgeoisie within Transkei. Although the major portion of the financial and other concessions offered by the Development Corporation have serviced the needs of *white* industry in the homeland, loan capital advanced to African entrepreneurs – although relatively small in absolute terms – has played a critical role in extruding white settlers from low level enterprises, as illustrated in Table 6.5. But apart from its financial and advisory assistance to African entrepreneurs, the Development Corporation has also provided other forms of aid (such as an 'after-care' service for newly installed store proprietors) and, notably, through the operation of a wholesale division by which it has sought to guarantee stocks to African traders throughout a period when other suppliers from the Republic have been reluctant to advance credit. These wholesale activities of the XDC commenced in 1967 with the acquisition of a white-owned wholesale firm (Viedge Brothers) which operated branches in Umtata, Butterworth and Engcobo, and these were later supplemented by the acquisition of other formerly white-owned stores at Cala (formerly Eli Spilkin), Idutywa (Sparg), Mount Frere and Flagstaff (both Moshal Gevisser) in 1968, and the opening up of two new branches in Bizana and Cofimvaba. The wholesale division then became the Tembalethu Wholesale Company in 1971, its main purpose being to service the needs of black traders by the provision of strategically located warehouses selling a comprehensive range of consumer merchandise at competitive prices.[55]

The interests of the commercial fraction of the Transkeian bourgeoisie are articulated through the Transkeian Chamber of Commerce (TRACOC), which links together a number of local chambers and business organizations. Since its formation in 1972 TRACOC has sought to promote the interests of African businessmen, in particular seeking to establish for them the commercial hegemony within the homeland which was previously enjoyed by the white traders. If this objective was coincident with official policy, then it also encouraged the adoption of an exclusivist attitude towards direct competitors from other racial groups, with the commercial arena inevitably coming to be viewed in specifically racial terms. Thus with the whites already being extruded from low-level enterprise under official aegis, TRACOC also lobbied for the denial of Transkeian citizenship to coloureds (of whom quite a number were in business),[56] and successfully persuaded the government to disallow Indian traders from operating within the Transkei after independence.[57]

But more important, the local chambers have sought to mobilize black capital in order to make a determined assault upon the wholesale trade, and thereby to limit the penetration of white enterprise (including the Development Corporation) into spheres where it could offer direct competition to African retailers. Through the formation of bulk-buying schemes (operative, for instance, in the Butterworth, Idutywa and Engcobo districts by 1974), African traders have sought to cut out the white middleman and to purchase their supplies direct from the manufacturers in the Republic, so enabling them to compete more effectively with white retail concerns (particularly supermarkets) still operating within the larger urban areas.[58]

Yet with the majority of the larger African businessmen still heavily indebted to the Development Corporation, TRACOC-inspired efforts to Africanize the wholesale sphere have been hampered by a critical lack of capital. In 1975, the most successful of the bulk-buying schemes was being operated by the Phambili Traders Association (Central Transkei), whose total assets amounted only to R100,000 with a working capital of R60,000. But much more typical was the activity of the Umzimvubu Chamber, which was contemporaneously engaged in persuading small groups of three to five traders to combine, and whose Trust account formed to promote the eventual formation of a wholesale concern stood at only R800.[59] Ironically, therefore, TRACOC attempts to facilitate African entry into the wholesale trade subsequently fell back upon a projected liaison with white private enterprise, discussion being held with Metro Cash and Carry (a Republic-wide wholesaling group) for the launching of a tripartite company, with the TDC holding a 10 per cent balance. However, given the Corporation's expanding interest on its own account through Tembalethu, the Metro scheme was dropped, and provision was later made for the purchase by black traders of shares in the state-run venture.[60] Both African traders and Tembalethu were then extended a degree of protection by the Matanzima government when, in 1975, it refused to countenance the establishment by a Republican concern of an extensive supermarket complex in Butterworth.[61]

During its initial years, the Xhosa Development Corporation was subjected to a constant barrage of criticism from Transkeian businessmen on the grounds that it was facilitating African exploitation rather than promoting homeland development. Complaint was levied about the limited amount of loan capital it advanced to African traders, high rates of interest, favouritism in the granting of trading licences and the employment of former white traders as supervisors over successor blacks in whose business failure they were alleged to find personal satisfaction.[62] In addition, the Chamber of Commerce was particularly resentful of the expanding XDC presence, and consequently demanded that shares in its various activities should be made freely available for African purchase.[63] In response to such calls, the XDC made certain minor concessions, allowing licensing decisions to be made by the homeland government (subject to a Corporation veto) and (as has been seen) allowing African traders to acquire a shareholding in Tembalethu.

But with the establishment of the Transkei Development Corporation in 1976, the Transkeian government was empowered to appoint five Africans to a ten-man board of directors, and effectively the choice has fallen upon individuals drawn from the Chamber of Commerce and the governing party. Thus when it was first established the board included three TNIP Members of Parliament; and by 1977, all of the African directors of the TDC were members of TRACOC, the most prominent being Mr Simon Nyamakazi, then President of the Chamber and owner of a hotel, a fashion boutique and a general store, and also upon the boards of Transkei Airways and the biggest company of hotels in the Transkei (in which both the Matanzima brothers have a substantial financial stake).[64] Such a presence within the TDC brings to the Chamber of Commerce not control over the Corporation's major activities (for the South African government continues to hold the purse strings), but a decisive voice in issues which at present most affect African entrepreneurs, notably the distribution of trading licences and the allocation of loans. Thus with developing and close contacts with the Matanzima regime, TRACOC has emerged as the vanguard of the commercial petty-bourgeoisie, and is set fair to be drawn into a close alliance (albeit as a junior partner) with white capital, to whose interests (as will be illustrated in the following chapter) the Development Corporation is primarily devoted.

Finally, it should be noted that the development of a commercial fraction of the African petty-bourgeoisie in the Transkei and the other homelands is now being paralleled by an attempt to promote a similar element within the urban areas, for following the collapse of Portuguese authority in the buffer states of Angola and Mozambique and the Soweto upheavals of 1976, the white regime has embarked upon a more intensive search for domestic allies among the subordinated racial groups.

The interests of African businessmen in the white areas of the Republic are most vocally articulated by the National African Federated Chambers of Commerce, of which TRACOC is an affiliate. It is this body which, since its foundation in 1963, has taken the lead in attempting to negotiate the removal of all the various restrictions imposed by law upon African enterprise, its central and fundamental demand being that the permanence of blacks (and hence their businesses) in urban areas of South Africa should be recognized.

Little progress was made by NAFCOC in its representations until after 1974 (the year of the Portuguese *coup*). Then, in January 1975, the government announced a number of concessions to urban blacks. The restrictions imposed upon African traders in urban areas were to be removed, and Africans were to be allowed to own and erect their business premises, to trade in an increased range of commodities, to establish more than one type of business upon the same premises and to be legally enabled to form partnerships. In addition, persons with established businesses in a homeland were to be allowed to also run enterprises in urban areas. However, there was a typical apartheid 'catch': Africans were not to be granted freehold rights, but would be permitted only a thirty-year lease, and aspiring home-owners would have to take out the citizenship of their homeland.[65]

A cautious welcome was extended to these promised reforms by the NAFCOC leadership, but hopes were dashed when revised regulations concerning urban traders were published in Government Notice R764 of 7 May 1976, for these laid down that applicants for licences would have to qualify to remain in an urban area in terms of Section 10 of the Bantu (Urban Areas) Consolidation Act; that a trader would not be able to carry on more than one business; and that no site would be allotted to any trader who had business interests outside the 'Bantu residential area'. What had been offered had almost immediately been withdrawn. But the apartheid sting was in the tail, and the reason for the change in plan became evident in a new requirement that a prior condition for the granting of a business or professional site would be that the applicant (or the partners or shareholders in larger concerns) would have to be in possession of homeland citizenship certificates.[66] In other words, with Transkeian 'independence' fast approaching (in October of that year), urban Africans (and registered Xhosa in particular) were served notice that their immediate security was to be made unambiguously dependent upon revocation of their claims to political rights in the white 'homeland'.

But the Soweto upheaval intervened. The widespread rioting was, of course, quelled with massive force by the regime, but it was by no means coincidental that a NAFCOC delegation was admitted to meet the

Deputy Minister of Bantu Administration on 20 August, and in the discussion that ensued important concessions were made. The requirement that African businessmen in urban areas would have to be homeland citizens before they could be granted business licences was dropped, and they were now to be enabled to trade in an increased range of commodities. Those in the towns would be able to establish other outlets in the homelands without losing their urban trading rights; and the promise was advanced that the government would consider the possibility of African businessmen establishing small industries in the urban areas. Finally, the Deputy Minister undertook to meet the NAFCOC executive annually and to urge all Bantu Administration Boards to co-operate and consult NAFCOC's local and regional chambers on all matters affecting black business interests.[67] All these concessions were supplementary to an announcement on 13 August that the homeland citizenship proviso had been dropped from the leasehold scheme as it applied to urban housing.[68]

More concessions to urban businessmen followed in 1977, after the second annual meeting of the NAFCOC executive with the Deputy Minister on 17 August. In particular, the government indicated that it no longer operated upon the principle that black businessmen in urban areas should be allowed to deal only with the necessities in life, so that the number of business activities open to African businessmen in black areas was to be increased from 26 to 66,[69] although (the highly profitable) ownership of hotels, cinemas, bottle stores and beer halls was to remain exclusively in white (often municipal) hands. In addition, the government indicated that it was continuing to consider the removal of prohibitions upon black entrepreneurs from engaging in industrial activities in urban areas, and that it was seeking a form of land tenure 'short of freehold' which would ease the problems faced by black businessmen in offering property as security for loans,[70] – a statement which was to culminate in a proposal made in 1978 to introduce 99-year leaseholds for urban blacks outside the homelands and the Western Cape.[71]

This relaxation of restrictions upon the development of African capitalism in urban areas has but pushed the door ajar. Many obstacles to the expansion of black business remain (notably the limited enthusiasm of white commerce for black competition), yet it is none the less clear that, especially following the 1976 riots, the regime has embarked upon a search for a black bourgeoisie in urban areas to mediate class and racial polarization, paralleled by the activities of white business which place new emphasis upon the promotion of a stable, African middle class. All this indicates that Pretoria has now identified a need to go beyond the homeland policy, and to allow for the pragmatic incorporation of an urban-based, African petty-bourgeoisie into the structures of separate development – even though bantustan neo-colonialism currently remains the central platform of the overall apartheid design.[72]

The emergent petty-bourgeoisie: collaboration, ambivalence and dependence

The development of the Transkei as a projected neo-colony of South Africa demanded the creation of a dependent African petty-bourgeoisie whose material interests would be so structured as to induce it to be supportive of separate development, the Republican government and, objectively speaking, the hegemony of white capital within the Southern African region. It remains to be elucidated, therefore, whether the domestic beneficiaries of independence which have been identified here – the chiefs and the politicians, the bureaucrats, the teachers and the entrepreneurs – will play out the role allotted to them in the bantustan scenario as laid down by Pretoria, or whether now that they have inherited a quasi-independent state apparatus they will seek to eschew a collaborationist path. This will necessitate analysis later in this study both of the structure of the bantustan economy and the direction of post-independence events.

A prior question, however, necessarily relates to the consciousness of the petty-bourgeoisie as a class and links between the various fractions which might provide the basis for class coherence. There is little doubt that the establishment of the bantustan economic and political apparatus has well served the interests of the contemporary élites, which have benefited from increased salaries, more job opportunities and greater availability of capital, and have thus been enabled to enjoy standards of living previously reserved for South African whites, who from this perspective inevitably constitute the immediate reference group. Consequently, in so far as the material well-being of the black bourgeoisie approximates to that of Republican whites, so does the gulf between themselves and the impoverished reserve masses develop.

At the same time, it is clear also that there are increasing links being forged between the different fractions of the petty-bourgeoisie, which have hitherto been relatively compartmentalized. In the first place, it appears that there is a developing overlap between chiefs, politicians and a small number of market-oriented farmers. Although few politicians seem to consider farming as their major occupation, a number of them are joining other elements in increasingly viewing small-scale commercial agriculture as an area for capital investment. In particular, they are advantaged by the state-directed policy whereby formerly white-owned farms in such areas as Mount Fletcher, MaClear and Umzimkulu which have been incorporated into the Transkei under the terms of the 1936 Trust and Lands Act are leased out to 'progressive farmers'. In a process akin to the handover of trading stations to blacks by the XDC, present policy is for all farms previously held by the South African Bantu Trust to be divided into smaller farms of 100–200 morgen capable of yielding marketable produce, and to be leased out to tenant farmers for an agreed period during which they may prove their worth, with reward of eventual freehold ownership. In practice, this is working to provide increased landholdings for the landed élite: in 1976, the Assembly agreed to the grant of personal farms to all five paramount chiefs as reward for the part they had taken in the 'struggle' for independence and provision was further made for the granting of farms 'to prospective farmers who have rendered faithful service in the development of their country'.[73] That such a formula was devised in order to allow for increased capital accumulation upon the part of the Transkeian Prime Minister and his political allies was laid bare by subsequent revelations concerning land deals between the Matanzima brothers, the South African government, the TDC and the Bantu Trust:

the exchange with the Bantu Trust by Kaiser Matanzima in 1966 of just over half a farm near Qamata in Thembuland (1961 total value R2,313) for the farm Zenzeli in the Glen Grey District (valued by the Trust at R60,110). Matanzima was also paid R10,395 in cash for the portion of his Qamata farm.

the purchase of two plots in Cofimvaba by Matanzima from the Bantu Trust on 28 December 1971 for a total of R600. Three years earlier the Trust had bought these plots from their former white owner for approximately R6,229 each.

the purchase of another plot at Cofimvaba by Matanzima for R600 on 8 December 1972 from the Bantu Trust, which had acquired it the previous month for R1,620.

the sale by the Bantu Trust in April 1973 of two plots (valued at R8,264 in March) to Matanzima for R5,520.

the rent-free lease of the farm Webbworth (value R400,236) in the Queenstown district of South Africa proper (prior to its incorporation into the Transkei) to Matanzima from early 1976 for his own profit.

the rent-free lease of a neighbouring 1,079-hectare farm ('Hafton') to Chief George Matanzima.[74]

'Farms acquired in Indwe, Bolotwa, Port St Johns, MaClear, Eliot and Matatiele will be given to black farmers near those areas,' explained George Matanzima. 'Of course, the Prime Minister, who worked so hard to acquire the land, will be among the beneficiaries.'[75] It is not unreasonable to speculate that examples of such flagrant appropriation of state land for private profit are not uncommon and form but the tip of an iceberg, and that other TNIP leaders are entering commercial agriculture via a similarly advantageous route. Certainly, press reports also indicated that Matanzima had instructed the TDC to provide a farm for his Minister of Finance, Mr Tsepo Letlaka.[76]

But agriculture is not the only sphere for investment, and observation also suggests increasing interpenetration of the political, educational and commercial fractions. Whereas civil servants tend to be based in Umtata and are thus enabled to invest profitably in real estate, teachers tend to be dispersed throughout the rural areas and small towns of the Transkei where opportunities for property speculation are more limited; and accordingly it would seem (from frequent complaints of 'unfair competition' by other businessmen) that quite a number of teachers acquire trading licences and run small shops under their wives' or other close relatives' names.[77] Such practice was facilitated by the Trading Amendment Act of 1964, which located responsibility for licensing in the hands of the Regional Authorities, and which accordingly brought the allocation of licenses into the political arena (as well as opening up the possibilities of outright graft). But more significant, perhaps, is the extent to which the political leadership has exploited the advantages it has gained as an ally in which Pretoria has made considerable political investment. Thus further disclosures concerning property transactions made by the Bantu Trust revealed that companies in which the Matanzima brothers were major shareholders bought hotels from the South African government for at least R56,000 less than the Bantu Trust had paid for them. The Masonic Hotel at Idutywa and the Coldstream Hotel at Ngqeleni were purchased by Rhoda Bantu Ltd and the Cofimvaba Hotel and the Gordon Hotel were sold to the Dalindyebo Bantu Trading Company. In addition, the Qamata Poort Hotel was sold to the Qamata Bantu Trading Company. All three companies have the same eight directors, who include Mr Simon Nyamakazi and Mr A. M. Mayaba, both of whom have served as Presidents of the Transkei Chamber of Commerce. The same directorate also serves as the board for four other companies – Qaukeni Bantu (Pty) Ltd, Maludi Bantu (Pty) Ltd, Emboland Bantu (Pty) Ltd and Fingoland Bantu (Pty) Ltd – which have been taking over other hotels from the Bantu Trust, and which now have an extensive and lucrative holding in the liquor trade throughout the Transkei, their hotels in most cases holding the only liquor licences in their respective districts;[78] and naturally enough, the board of directors is eager to maintain its favoured position.[79] However, in respect of the Matanzima brothers themselves, such an intent would not seem wholly in accord with the TNIP government's own position that Ministers should not have private business interests as this could lead to conflict between such private interests and their public duty![80]

Such data as is presently available upon links between the various fractions of the petty-bourgeoisie does suggest increasing interpenetration; in addition, evidence that children of 'upper-class Xhosas' remain in full-time education longer than pupils from less advantaged families[81] suggests that the class structure is beginning to harden. Such a phenomenon is an explicit goal of the homeland government, which sees the development of a 'responsible and stable' 'middle class' as an antidote to the revolutionary transformation of society. Thus Matanzima:

> ... in countries devoid of a stable middle class – mainly southern and eastern Europe, Russia and the Balkans – changes wrought were violent. Indeed, the violence there has never really stopped and has, in fact, spread. World War I, the Russian Revolution, World War II, Korea, Malaya, Vietnam, the Middle East are all ... part of the same epic convulsion. The continuing strife in Africa to the north must be seen in the same light. And that is precisely what people of all racial groups and political persuasions in South Africa – with the exception of terrorists and their sympathisers – devoutly wish to avoid in the Republic. To do this two great goals must be achieved. Firstly, the creation of a constitutional framework within which, particularly the Black population, can give expression to its legitimate political aspirations and, secondly, the improvement of the material welfare of that selfsame group so that a widely-based, literate middle class can arise and the violent gospel being preached in so many quarters will not prove attractive.[82]

Yet the mere creation of a black middle class does not in itself guarantee that such an element will be non-revolutionary, for this depends on the particular historical circumstance. Indeed, faced with an impoverished migrant proletariat, elements of the petty-bourgeoisie which are either upon the fringes of the class (for example, teachers) or are alienated from the state may make themselves available for alliances other than straightforward collaboration with the South African regime. Indeed, such an alliance – between the migrant proletariat and *déclassé* elements such as school pupils and unincorporated elements of the petty-bourgeoisie – seems to have underlain the re-emergence of the DP under Ncokazi as a strongly antagonistic force to the Matanzima government, although the limits to such a combination were readily exposed by the Opposition's suppression under Proclamation 400. However, the extreme degree of economic dependence of Transkei upon the South African government will continue to ensure that the core of the petty-bourgeoisie will be tied to the white regime – and such a course is likely to promote a widening polarization between the collaborationists and the Transkeian mass. However, that the primary conflict will remain as between white capital and the reserve-based proletariat will become clear only upon closer examination of the structures of the bantustan economy.

Notes

1. For a more detailed treatment, see my article (1980b). For one recent treatment of the development of African nationalism, see Gerhart (1978).
2. BENBO (1975), Table 6-4, p. 40.
3. *Transkei Hansard*, 31 March 1977, p. 119.
4. *Daily Dispatch*, 18 April 1975.

5. Innes and O'Meara (1976), p. 77.
6. Charton (1976), p. 63.
7. Charton (1972).
8. *Annual Reports of the Transkeian Public Service Commission, 1975* (para. 5) and *1976* (para. 5).
9. Promotion rates increased from 2·2 per cent in 1964 to 13 per cent in 1975.
10. *Annual Reports of the Transkeian Public Service Commission*, 1964–76; and *Transkei Hansard*, 10 June 1971, p. 409.
11. *Annual Report of the Transkeian Public Service Commission, 1971* (para. 22).
12. ibid., *1970* (para. 28).
13. ibid., *1971* (para. 24).
14. *Annual Report of the Public Service Commission, 1971* (para. 49). It would appear from other surveys that inebriation while on duty and theft by officials also pose severe problems in Kwazulu. See Barbara Rogers (1976), p. 52; and Butler *et al.* (1977), p. 49.
15. *Transkei Hansard*, 5 March 1975, p. 98.
16. *Pretoria News*, 13 February 1975.
17. *Transkei Hansard*, 31 March 1977, p. 121.
18. Colin Leys (1975), p. 194.
19. *Sunday Times*, 24 July 1977.
20. The XDC made 808 housing loans to blacks in the Transkei, totalling R2,818,244 during the three financial years 1972–5 (XDC, *Tenth Annual Report*, 1975, p. 27). Prior to this – until the end of 1971 – the Corporation had made 130 housing loans, 'mainly to civil servants and teachers' (*African Business*, June 1972).
21. *RDM*, 3 April 1976.
22. *Transkei Hansard*, 27 March 1974, p. 89.
23. C. Becker (1970).
24. *Financial Mail*, 22 October 1976, p. XXVII (*sic*).
25. Colin Leys (1975), p. 193.
26. *Annual Report of the Public Service Commission, 1971*, para. 12.
27. *Natal Mercury*, 13 February and 28 February 1978. Matanzima's eagerness to establish international links is evidenced by the retention of Ben-Dak at a salary of R75,000 per annum, paid in US dollars, to an account anywhere in the world! Some time after this, however, the Maritz brothers were removed, being replaced by an Englishman, Mr James Skinner, as Director of the TDC. But, like Ben-Dak, he attempted to remove top South Africans from the Corporation, with the result that he was deported in early 1979. Mr Ramsey Madikizela, Minister of Transport and Industry, explained Skinner's dismissal by reference to the fact that he was allegedly a 'hardened racialist' who hated South Africans, particularly Afrikaners. (*RDM*, 21 February 1979.)
28. SAIRR, *A Survey, 1979*, p. 498.
29. Ireland (1972).
30. Carter *et al.* (1967), pp. 161–2. The adjusted Cape Syllabus continued to include Afrikaans as a compulsory subject for matriculation. However, in 1979 it was announced that from 1980 pupils would be required to study English, Xhosa and Sotho (these being the territory's official languages), with Afrikaans being dropped, as the (South African) Joint Matriculation Board had agreed to recognize Transkei senior school certificates without

Afrikaans as a subject. (SAIRR, *A Survey, 1979*, pp. 509–10.) In 1980 it was announced that Afrikaans would no longer be taught in Transkeian schools. (SAIRR, *A Survey, 1980*, p. 481.)
31. *Report of the Public Service Commission, 1975.*
32. SAIRR, *A Survey, 1974*, p. 349; and *Transkei Estimates*, Year ending 31 March 1975, p. 349; and 13 April 1977, p. 170.
33. *Transkei Hansard*, 11 May 1976, p. 269; and *Report of the Department of Education, Transkei, 1978* (cited in SAIRR, *A Survey, 1979*, p. 493).
34. Kuper (1965), p. 174.
35. Vigne (1966?), p. 17.
36. *Commission of Inquiry into the Standard of Education in the Transkei*, 1973. Also *Transkei Hansard*, 6 May 1971, p. 161.
37. Munger (1962), pp. 3–6.
38. Carter *et al.* (1967), pp. 128–31.
39. Charton (1976), p. 66.
40. *Transkei Hansard*, 6 May 1974, pp. 310–13.
41. Barclays Bank (1977), p. 18.
42. *Native Economic Commission 1930–32*, para. 943, p. 137.
43. Hart (1972), pp. 103–6.
44. See Chapter 2, p. 37–8.
45. See the debate recorded in *Transkei Hansard*, 5 May to 19 June 1964.
46. *Transkei Hansard*, 6 March 1975, p. 101; *RDM*, 24 May 1974.
47. *TTCA Congress, 1963*, p. 4.
48. *Transkei Hansard*, 19 March 1975, p. 172.
49. XDC, *Tenth Annual Report* (1975), p. 25.
50. C. M. Mvumbo, Transkei Bantu Chamber of Commerce to Chief Bantu Affairs Commissioner, January 1963 (quoted in *TTCA Congress*, 1963, p. 3).
51. Minutes of the Executive of the Transkei Chamber of Commerce (TRACOC), 14 January 1973. (For elucidation of the origins and role of the African Chamber of Commerce movement in the territory, I am indebted to interviews with Mr A. M. Mayaba, former President, 4 August 1976; Mr Simon Nyamakazi, President in 1978–9, 24 November 1976; and Mr Freedman Sofute, Secretary, 26 February 1977.)
52. *TTCA Congress, 1970*, p. 27.
53. Circular no. 2 of 1973, Ministry of the Interior.
54. *Transkei Hansard*, 19 March 1975, p. 172.
55. XDC, *Tenth Annual Report* (1975), p. 25.
56. *Daily Dispatch*, 17 April 1973.
57. *TRACOC Papers*: Interview with Chief Minister, 24 February 1976.
58. ibid: 2nd Annual General Meeting (Presidential Address); and 1975 Annual Report.
59. ibid.
60. *TRACOC Papers*: Monthly General Meeting, 29 September 1974; Executive, 16 February 1976 and 15 March 1976; Ordinary General Meeting, 26 March 1976.
61. *The Star*, 24 October 1975.
62. See, for example, *Cape Argus*, 26 June 1974; *Daily News*, 30 March 1973.
63. *Daily News*, 13 March 1973.
64. *Transkei Hansard*, 26 April 1977, p. 261; *African Business*, February and April 1977.

65. SAIRR, *A Survey, 1975*, p. 83.
66. ibid., *1976*, pp. 185–6.
67. ibid.; and *African Business*, September 1976, pp. 6–9.
68. SAIRR, *A Survey, 1976*, p. 187.
69. *SA Government Gazette*, no. 5795, 1977.
70. SAIRR, *A Survey, 1977*; *African Business*, September 1977, pp. 6–10.
71. *RDM*, 26 April 1978.
72. For a more detailed analysis, see my article (1980b).
73. *Transkei Hansard*, 12 April 1976, pp. 114–22; and 13 April 1976, pp. 130–2.
74. *Sunday Times*, 17 October 1976, 24 July 1977. *Transkei Hansard*, 13 April 1976, pp. 129–30.
75. *Sunday Times*, 31 July 1977.
76. ibid., 24 July 1977.
77. *TTCA Congress, 1969*, p. 10. See also *RDM*, 23 October 1978.
78. *Sunday Times*, 3 October, 10 October and 17 October 1976.
79. Interview with director, 4 August 1976.
80. *Transkei Hansard*, 13 April 1976, p. 126.
81. *Report on Standards of Education*, 1973.
82. Address by the Chief Minister of the Transkei ... at the Opening of the Conference of the National African Federated Chambers of Commerce, Umtata, 20 June 1974 (UNISA Library).

Chapter 7
The bantustan economy

According to official South African rhetoric, the African homelands are typically backward areas, whose economies are characterized by low agricultural productivity, consequent outflows of migrant labour, a lack of industrial activity, budgetary dependence upon the 'metropolitan power', and a prevailing set of conservative and traditional attitudes among the indigenous peoples which constitute a major barrier to economic change, modernization and progress. The homelands are further viewed as akin to other underdeveloped territories in Africa, and 'independent' entities such as Transkei, Bophuthatswana and Venda are promoted as 'developing countries' whose quest for self-sustained growth requires inputs of capital investment, foreign aid and modern technology. But, so it is argued, the black nations of South Africa are distinguished from their counterparts elsewhere on the continent in that they have the advantage of a close and beneficial connection with the advanced white economy of the Republic, which provides employment, capital, skills and other assistance to the various territories now engaged in the process of decolonization.

Indeed (runs the argument), precisely because the whites in South Africa are more intimately involved with the African peoples over whom they exercise guardianship than were the other imperial powers, they are uniquely aware of the problems to be faced in overcoming their underdevelopment and backwardness, and have accordingly opted for a 'comprehensive programme of upliftment' which takes account of all the practical problems involved in the handling of the Republic's 'complex group realities'. Thus the principal aim of policy is accordingly the peaceful coexistence of the various diverse peoples 'on the generally accepted modern pattern of independent national communities', which are geopolitically based in separate nation-states and economically bound together by economic interdependence and complementarity of need. And in order to promote sound intergroup and interstate relations, the South African government is committed to the 'optimal development of the black peoples in all fields of human endeavour'. As one of the more advanced and relatively developed countries of the world – with the most sophisticated administration and infrastructure in the whole of Africa – the Republic is eminently qualified to discharge its responsibilities, and it is the intent of the whites to utilize progress in their own economy as a base for the improvement of the living standards of their black neighbours. However, rather than offering them the 'aimless and meaningless aid programmes that are applied elsewhere', the South African development programme 'is formulated upon the realistic policy of helping the economically retarded nations to help themselves'. Fully aware that 'the large-scale economic development of the Black Homelands is the key to a peaceful multinational system in South Africa', since the early 1960s the Republic has been engaged upon a 'development operation ... without peer in the entire continent of Africa', clear proof of its successful implementation being that 'the Black man in South Africa enjoys a very much higher standard of living than his counterpart in most other Black nations', this being but the first step towards assisting the various black peoples to establish as soon as possible dynamic and viable economies of their own.[1]

Stripped of the more pretentious claims made by the official propagandists, the above outline suggests that, given requisite capital investment, industrial expansion and agricultural reform, the homelands will be enabled to develop economically and to catch up with the white-dominated sector. Yet it is argued here that the bantustans can never 'catch up' with the white areas of South Africa so long as the present configuration of capitalist relations, dominated from the centre, are maintained. In short, capitalist development in South Africa remains premised upon the utilization of cheap black labour, and this it is the continuing function of the bantustans to supply, whether or not they have received 'political independence'. 'Independent' bantustans are so grossly dependent upon South Africa that they differ from the other homelands only to the extent that a degree of political autonomy and marginal economic concessions have been devolved upon a small, African bourgeoisie, whose primary function is to mediate the contradiction between white capital and black labour in the reserves. Indeed, the more such entities as Transkei, Bophuthatswana and Venda seek to 'develop', the more they become dependent upon South Africa, for limitations upon their development as 'viable' economic entities are inherent in their integral incorporation into the South African capitalist economy, and as such they are destined to remain as bantustan dependencies at least until white supremacy is destroyed (even if what will follow after must of necessity remain something of an open question). It is to elucidate this claim that we now turn to an examination of the dependence of Transkei.

Financial dependence upon South Africa

'Who pays the piper calls the tune' is a homely adage which aptly describes the relationship between Transkei and South Africa. In short, there can be no doubt but that the financial dependence of the 'independent' bantustan upon the apartheid regime is so pronounced that the limits of movement of the Matanzima government are almost wholly dictated by Republican decree. Thus analyses which argue that diplomatic disputes – notably the breaking off of formal relations between Pretoria and Umtata in April 1978[2] – demonstrate a degree of genuine 'independence' fall into the apartheid trap, and ignore the underlying structural constraints imposed upon the bantustan 'state'. In particular, they overlook the determining factor that the dominant fractions of the locally ruling petty-bourgeoisie are themselves creatures of South African government expenditure, for the entire apparatus of the bantustan state has been conjured up and remains almost wholly financed (directly and indirectly) by Pretoria. However much they may resent their dependent status (and Matanzima's verbal assaults upon South Africa do seem to display a genuine animosity), the ruling elements are well aware that the material privileges underwriting their class position are provided only upon the basis of their continuing collaboration with the apartheid state. And search though they may for increased foreign investment and 'development aid' (and this underlies the quest for international recognition), the Matanzima regime will find no other patron willing to take upon itself the costly liability of financing such a grossly dependent, client state for dubious diplomatic advantage.

The extent of Transkeian financial dependence upon South Africa is easily demonstrated. The sources of revenue of the homeland government from 1964/5 until 1975/6 (the last complete financial year preceding independence) were as shown in Table 7.1. Transkeian homeland budgets were composed of three main items: (1) revenue deriving from the administration of functions which had been transferred to Umtata; plus (2)

Table 7.1 *Sources of revenue of the Transkeian government, 1964/5–1975/6 (R'000s)*

Year	Balance from previous yr	Internal sources	Grants from SA govt	SA grant as % total	Total
1964/5	—	3,569	13,000	78·5	16,569
1965/6	4,103	3,905	13,000	51·9	21,008
1966/7	5,619	4,390	10,641	51·5	20,650
1967/8	5,479	5,069	10,805	50·6	21,353
1968/9	3,971	5,114	10,995	58·9	22,080
1969/70	3,521	5,440	15,075	62·7	24,036
1970/1	2,759	6,323	18,501	67·1	27,583
1971/2	2,192	6,854	23,517	72·3	32,563
1972/3	2,154	9,100	26,422	71·1	37,676
1973/4	2,254	9,212	45,398	79·8	56,864
1974/5	7,046	10,714	60,795	77·4	78,555
1975/6	14,741	18,730	71,800	65·7	104,551

Sources: BENBO (1975), p. 66; SAIRR, *A Survey, 1977*, p. 316 (for 1975/6).

statutory and (3) additional grants from the Republic's consolidated Revenue Fund, which were explicitly inclusive of taxes paid by 'Transkeian citizens' resident in white areas to the Republican authorities (this latter element ensuring that any subsequent rejection of non-resident Xhosa as Transkeian citizens would incur a direct financial cost).[3]

Since independence, a new financial formula has been operative whereby amounts paid to the Transkeian government fall under the Republic's annual Vote for Foreign Affairs, which now includes revenue from a bilateral trade agreement (analogous to the Customs Union between South Africa and the BLS countries) under which Umtata receives an amount estimated to be the equivalent of duty on imported goods destined for Transkei.[4] But in practice the reality remains much the same. Revenue accruing to the Transkei government in 1976/7 amounted to R155·6 million, of which the Republic provided R110·8 million (or 71·2 per cent), only R22 million coming from internal sources and a deficit of R15 million being covered by a Republican government-backed loan from the South African capital market.[5] Similarly, in 1977/8 (the first full year after independence) the Republican government provided R165 million out of a budget of R239 million (R40 million of this being estimated as Transkei's share of the bilateral Customs Union), with R37 million coming from internal sources and a balance from the previous year. The remainder (also R37 million) was financed by increases in local taxation and a R16 million loan raised on the South African capital market (a 'foreign loan').[6]

Budgeted expenditure for 1978/9 was an over-ambitious R328 million (an increase of some 38 per cent over the previous year), of which R174 million (or 53 per cent) was to be drawn directly or indirectly from Pretoria and R58 million generated from internal sources, with the deficit of R97 million being financed by tapping the South African and international money markets.[7] However, following the break in diplomatic relations with Pretoria in April 1978 (right at the beginning of the financial year), private investors were reluctant to finance such a loan, fearful that South Africa would thereafter withdraw economic backing, with the result that the bantustan government faced bankruptcy within less than three years of attaining independence. Press commentary at the time was apt:

> It is doubtful whether the South African Government [will] let the situation deteriorate beyond the danger mark. Transkei is after all 'grand apartheid's' showpiece. More likely Pretoria will let Transkei feel the pinch before coming to the rescue. From Pretoria's point of view Transkei [will] have learnt its lesson, and its economic and financial dependence on South Africa [will] have been reinforced.[8]

Subsequently, the Republic did stand back, and the Transkeian government was forced to implement drastic cutbacks in expenditure over wide-ranging spheres of administration and development. Thereafter, a much reduced budget for 1979/80 indicated that some kind of wisdom had been learned, for it proposed expenditure of only R253·38 million (a decrease of R75 million from the previous year, with expected revenue amounting to R253·5 million, providing an anticipated surplus of R120,000).[9] Even so, sources of revenue did not live up to expectation, and in September 1979 it was reliably reported that the Transkeian government was bankrupt, and would be unable to pay the November salaries of its employees. Thereupon the South African government came to the rescue with an additional financial grant, so that at the completion of the 1979/80 year Transkei had received R113·5 million as the statutory grant, R5·7 million for taxes collected in South Africa from Transkeian citizens, R88·49 million as Transkei's share of the common customs revenue pool, and R4·27 million in terms of monetary and development agreements. (The extra, unbudgeted aid was seemingly subsumed under the customs payment, which has risen from R40 million in 1977/8 to R88·49 million in 1979/80.) Not surprisingly, however, this further aid was not without strings, and South African treasury and Reserve Bank officials were sent to the territory to restore financial discipline.[10] The moral for future years was clear: Transkeian expenditure must of necessity be kept within the limits laid down by Pretoria, with Umtata's scope for bargaining being severely circumscribed.

Yet even the budgetary situation does not indicate the full extent of Transkei's dependence upon South Africa, for there remain various other services within the bantustan which are still financed by the Republic – notably the Development Corporation (for which an additional R24 million was provided in 1976/7),[11] and the salaries of white officials and judges seconded to Umtata (amounting to R6,688,000 in the same year).[12]

Transkei's increasing financial requirements have largely arisen out of the transfer to its control of services previously administered from Pretoria. Thus as the bantustan government has formally acceded to new powers so it has become increasingly dependent upon the apartheid regime. The ruling elements' aspirations for expenditure have therefore necessarily to be contained within the purview of the South African state, which under the pressure of inflation and increased defence expenditure is unlikely to augment its allocations to the homelands to any great degree.

Alternative sources of income – foreign loans and increased internal taxes – offer severely limited scope for lessening dependence upon South Africa. Given that Transkei is barred from availing itself of so-called 'soft money' offered by such organizations as the UN, FAO and ILO, it has had to resort to the private market, and – because of its ambiguous international status – to offer higher than average interest rates.[13] However, whereas the R16 million loan raised on the South African money market just before independence was financially guaranteed by the Republic,[14] that government is not politically or legally bound to underwrite similar borrowings in the future; and indeed, any threat by the Republic to reduce its subsidies to the Transkeian regime would deprive the latter of its already limited financial credibility and hence its ability to tap the capital market (as was first seen in 1978/9).[15] Correspondingly, were Transkei to receive a degree of international recognition, so would its financial image be enhanced – a result of which has been the regime's frantic efforts to break out of the present diplomatic impasse and to gain acceptance among the world community of states.

The possibilities of the Transkeian government significantly increasing its internal revenues are similarly bleak, though there can be little doubt that it is the intention of the Republican authorities to cajole the bantustan regime into accepting a greater measure of responsibility for financing its own budget. Recurrent expenditure should eventually be raised from genuinely internal sources, explained the (white) Secretary to the Minister of Finance in 1976, and this could be done if the government 'were willing to tax the peasantry far more heavily or if large-scale commercial farming were successfully introduced'.[16]

The effect of such suggestion was amply demonstrated when the 1977/8 budget abolished the annual poll tax of R2-50 (payable by all adult males), but increased both the hut tax (up to a maximum of four huts) and a general levy from R1 to R10 per annum. The burden of these taxes was to fall disproportionately upon the already impoverished Transkeian masses. In contrast, proposals to introduce a livestock tax of R10 per head on cattle and donkeys, R5 on horses and mules, and R2 on sheep and goats created such uproar among the stock-owning parliamentary clique that the rates were hurriedly reduced (the announcement being made by the Minister of Finance at the end of the second reading of the Appropriation Bill debate) to more modest levels – R5 per head on donkeys, R2 for cattle, R1 for horses and mules and 50 cents on sheep and goats.[17] (The livestock tax was then actually abolished completely the following year.)[18] Thus although urged on by its Republican advisers to increase its internal revenue (and to promote destocking simultaneously), the Matanzima government could not afford to cut itself off from its class base, and the likelihood is that future increases in taxation will fall upon those who can least afford to pay – the migrant workers, the landless and the otherwise dispossessed. Indeed, a further imposition was made on these elements in 1978/9, when the budget announced an extra Special Tax of R10 per person per annum on all able-bodied men and women over the ages of 18 and 21 respectively (with a number of exceptions which included bona-fide housewives).[19] In turn, such a process can be expected to further alienate the masses from the bantustan regime, and to lead in response to even greater political repression.

In sum, so great is Transkei's financial dependence upon South Africa and so limited the possibilities of this being significantly reduced, that the bantustan regime has no alternative but to collaborate closely with Pretoria, however much it may fulminate in public against the iniquities of apartheid in order to gain external sympathy and recognition. Although the Transkeian government may well bank upon South African unwillingness to pull the financial rug from under the feet of its foremost homeland progeny, there can be little doubt that the Republic would not hesitate to use its muscle were it to consider its interests and security to be genuinely threatened – just as it increased economic pressures upon Lesotho for its refusal to recognize the independence of Transkei in 1976.[20] Supplying well over two-thirds of the Transkeian government's annual financial requirements, it is clear that South Africa remains firmly in control; and unlike Lesotho, for whom increased international aid has been forthcoming to relieve the consequences of the Republican blockade,[21] Transkei would have no other protector to whom it could turn.

Transkei as a labour reserve

As reiterated in the previous section, the bantustan state apparatus of the Transkei is almost wholly a deliberate construct of the South African regime designed to provide for the emergence of an African auxiliary class which services the needs of white capital. In particular, its specific function is to fulfil the control functions of capital over the homeland labour force – to regulate its supply, to provide for its reproduction and to ensure its continuing political subservience. Indeed, the defining characteristic of the 'Transkeian' state is that it has no independent base in the 'national' economy (as indicated by its gross financial subordination to the Republic) and that its external dependence is incontrovertibly and irreversibly increasing year by year, thus severely circumscribing the limits of political action for the ruling elements and virtually ensuring their adherence to a collaborationist path.

Earlier discussion concerning the Transkei as an internal colony illustrated the manner in which the pre-capitalist Nguni economy had been restructured and subordinated to the dominant capitalist mode of production. It was also argued that, although the function of the Transkei was to subsidize the white economy by providing subsistence for the families of migrant workers, by the interwar period the local economy had experienced (along with the other reserves) a crisis of declining agricultural production and overpopulation such that it was no longer able to produce a surplus sufficient to ensure the reproduction of labour. But the postwar National Party government sought to prevent and even reverse any consequent movement of the reserve populations to the urban areas in the white 'homeland', and instead promoted and refined the system of migrant labour through a battery of repressive and regulatory controls. The effect has been to transform the reserves into appendages of the white economy within which the aged, the unemployable and the unproductive can be coercively interned. But the essence of apartheid is that it is designed to maintain the ultra-exploitability of black labour; and given the inability of the reserve economies to provide for the physical reproduction of the workforce, the bantustans now exhibit the starkest forms of social decay – mass impoverishment, malnutrition and among the highest rates of infant mortality in Africa. However, the outlines of this picture are by now well established, and accordingly it is the intention here to sketch out only the major characteristics and tendencies of labour dependence in relation to Transkei.

As during its period as a Native Reserve, the overwhelmingly predominant characteristic of the contemporary Transkeian economy is that it serves as a supplier of cheap labour to South Africa. Table 7.2 displays the total number of migrants *recruited* from the Transkei compared to the numbers of persons in classified (that is, non-agricultural/subsistence) employment within the homeland since 1963. It is these recruitment figures which have usually served as a basis for analyses of the bantustan economy. However, it is important to note that these are actually inaccurate indicators of the total level of migrancy, for apart from those working illegally as migrants in the Republic (and these are probably not a few), considerable numbers of workers are absent from home for more than one calendar year, and hence do not show up in the annual *recruit-*

Table 7.2 *Transkei as an exporter of labour to South Africa, 1963–78*

Year	Transkeian migrants recruited for work in Republic	Transkeian citizens in classified employment within Transkei
1963	115,777	35,507
1964	124,000	32,700(?)
1965	139,586	33,007
1966	160,093	33,663
1967	132,294	41,236
1968	155,329	41,626
1969	174,223	42,401
1970	184,788	n.a.
1971	191,600	54,751
1972	225,330	n.a.
1973	231,969	64,690
1974	256,971	74,580
1975	303,233	87,479
1976	377,760	104,560
1977	403,828	121,290
1978	425,230	140,090

Note: The above figures should be taken only as indicating overall trends, as even official sources differ as to the accuracy of the various figures.
Source: Department of Interior, Transkei, Statistical Labour Reports, 1963–78.

ment statistics. Thus Francis Wilson calculated[22] that for a variety of reasons some 32,000 economically active males did not appear in the official statistics for 1971, while an official survey published in 1978 reported the extent of migrant labour drawn from the homelands for the period 1973–5 to be as shown in Table 7.3.

Table 7.3 *The extent of migrant labour from the African homelands in the white areas of South Africa, 1973–5*

	1973		1974		1975	
	Migrant workers	% of de facto pop.	Migrant workers	% of de facto pop.	Migrant workers	% of de facto pop.
Ciskei	23,500	5·6	23,900	5·5	24,400	5·3
Kwazulu	260,100	10·6	264,500	10·4	268,900	10·3
QwaQwa	5,600	11·7	6,300	9·6	7,000	8·5
Lebowa	177,500	14·1	183,900	14·2	190,300	14·2
Venda	55,100	17·8	56,500	17·7	57,900	17·6
Gazankulu	68,100	22·2	70,300	22·3	72,500	22·4
KaNgwane	9,500	6·2	8,600	5·3	7,700	3·9
Transkei	295,400	13·4	311,100	13·7	326,800	14·0
Bophuthatswana	55,700	5·3	53,400	4·9	51,100	4·6
TOTAL	950,500		978,500		1,006,600	

Source: SAIRR, *A Survey, 1979*, p. 377 (reproduced from Buro vir Economiese Navorsing Sarnewerking en Ontwikkeling, *Statistical Survey Black Development 1978*, BENSO, Pretoria, 1979).

If these figures are correct, then it appears that many surveys of Transkeian (and by implication, other homelands') labour dependency which base themselves on *recruitment* figures have tended to underestimate the extent of male absenteeism. However, conservative though they may be, most estimates suggest that – as a rough approximation – just over half (53 per cent in 1971)[23] of the economically active male labour force are annually recruited for work in the Republic. In contrast, in 1974 for instance there were only some 74,580 persons (47,539 men and 27,041 women) in classified employment within the Transkei,[24] indicating that at least five out of every six males in wage employment were oscillating as migrants between their homes and their place of work. It should also be remembered that the official statistics disguise much effective unemployment. At the end of their contracts migrant workers are not registered as 'unemployed', but are dispatched back to their rural homes, while older men of 45 years and upwards are commonly discarded by employers in favour of the younger and more vigorous, and hence condemned to an early and unwanted retirement. An extreme case of such a preference was exposed in 1977, when it was found that certain Natal sugar estates (until earlier in that year partly owned by the British firm of Tate and Lyle) were using child labour drawn from Transkei in work conditions reminiscent of slave plantations.[25]

Nor is Transkei's labour dependence decreasing, but rather the reverse. According to Leistner, the total economically active population of Transkei is destined to grow by 125 per cent (from 810,600 to 1,825,000) between 1970 and the year 2,000,[26] and with some 46 per cent of the *de facto* population under 15 years of age, the number of new entrants to the labour market currently runs at about 41,700 (27,300 men and 14,400 women) per annum.[27] It is clear, therefore, that this burgeoning workforce will have no alternative but to migrate to the Republic. Certainly, it is scarcely credible that 1 million job opportunities will be created within the bantustan over the next quarter-century, for although the official response has been to direct excess labour to industries within the homelands, only 16,000 jobs had been provided under the aegis of the XDC (in both the Transkei and Ciskei) at the close of its ten years of operation, and the prospects of the TDC performing much better remain slim.[28] The independent Transkei, therefore, will have no alternative but to remain a supplier of labour to South Africa, and its political autonomy will consequently be constrained by the ability of the Republic to regulate the amount of employment offered.

This conclusion is supported by an official projection of socio-economic development for Transkei for the years 1980–2000. Noting that a complete restructuring of the economy was required to create job opportunities to absorb the expected increase of labour flowing on to the market, it characterized the territory as 'a labour reserve lacking at present even a subsistence economy'. Furthermore, it concluded that even if there was a massive increase in agricultural output (which we may doubt) and a twentyfold increase in industrial employment within the homeland, Transkei will still be employing 1·5 million men and women out of a labour force of 1·9 million at the end of the century *at levels of real income below those prevailing in the mining industry today* (my emphasis), in addition to about one-third of the male labour force having still to look for employment in South Africa itself.[29]

But migrant labour is not free to go where it will, for under the apartheid labour system a variety of institutions structure and regulate the flow of workers between the reserves and the centres of employment, specifically operating to prevent the emergence of a free market under whose laws employers would have to compete for labour.[30] Thus the bantustans are central to the entire process, and each reserve functions as a labour pool for different sectors of white capital. The role of Transkei as a labour supplier may be indicated by reference to data for the years 1974–8, as shown in Table 7.4. However, because comparable statistics for earlier years are not available, this table is not able to portray the major change which occurred during the postwar era; the declining proportion of Transkeian migrants going to the gold mines (although, as will be discussed below, this is a trend that has now been reversed). Thus whereas in the mid-1930s something like two-thirds of all migrants from the Territories were finding employment on the gold mines,[31] by the early 1970s (before the rise in the price of gold) this proportion had been reduced to approximately one-sixth. (In 1973, for instance, of the 231,969

Table 7.4 *Locality and sectoral distribution of male labour recruited from the Transkei, 1974–8*

Locality	1974	1975	1976	1977	1978
Cape Province	78,234	77,160	98,188	75,759	73,336
Namaqaland	1,983	2,662	2,873	11,356	9,277
Transvaal	108,781	150,232	178,414	215,427	267,832
Free State	25,262	35,097	51,522	58,772	48,790
Natal	42,711	38,082	46,763	42,514	25,995
TOTAL	256,971	303,233	377,760	403,828	425,230

Sector of employment	1974	1975	1976	1977	1978
Agriculture, forestry, fishing	41,918 (16·3%)	40,809 (13·4%)	61,145 (16·2%)	52,814 (13·1%)	46,731 (11·0%)
Mines, brickworks, quarries	97,954 (38·1%)	140,063 (46·2%)	192,939 (51·1%)	245,079 (60·7%)	273,602 (64·3%)
Factories, industries	44,846 (17·5%)	46,829 (15·4%)	50,792 (13·4%)	39,083 (9·7%)	35,574 (8·4%)
Building	26,277 (10·2%)	29,099 (9·6%)	40,129 (10·6%)	24,895 (6·2%)	27,789 (6·1%)
South African government	7,233 (2·8%)	6,912 (2·3%)	5,676 (1·5%)	5,684 (1·4%)	4,802 (1·1%)
South African railways	10,205 (4·0%)	11,169 (3·7%)	7,885 (2·1%)	5,895 (1·5%)	7,466 (1·8%)
Municipalities	9,314 (2·6%)	8,501 (2·8%)	7,215 (1·9%)	15,493 (3·8%)	14,787 (3·5%)
Provincial administrations	3,369 (1·3%)	3,055 (1·0%)	1,798 (0·5%)	2,988 (0·7%)	3,846 (0·9%)
Commerce	8,945 (3·5%)	9,633 (3·2%)	7,839 (2·1%)	8,217 (2·0%)	8,262 (1·9%)
Hotels	1,521 (0·6%)	1,762 (0·6%)	554 (0·1%)	1,634 (0·4%)	1,895 (0·4%)
Domestic service	5,389 (2·1%)	4,563 (1·5%)	452 (0·1%)	2,046 (0·5%)	2,476 (0·6%)
Other	—	838	1,336	—	—
TOTAL	256,971	303,233	377,760	403,828	425,230

Source: Department of Interior, Transkei, Statistical Labour Reports, 1974–8.

male labourers recruited in Transkei, only 46,045 were recruited for work upon the gold mines.)[32]

This growing diversification of the employment sectors to which Transkeian migrants were directed reflected two long-run tendencies within the South African economy. In the first place, the expansion of secondary industry in the Republic was calling upon increased recruitment of labour from the reserves; and secondly, this brought about a growing dependence of the gold-mining industry upon foreign sources of labour in the postwar era until conditions changed in the early 1970s resulting mainly from the rise in the international price of gold. (See Table 7.5.)

While the need for increased numbers of skilled and semi-skilled workers had relatively early led to the stabilization and urbanization of a considerable portion of the black workforce, secondary industry in South Africa in the postwar years has continued to rely upon supplies of unskilled labour drawn from the homeland-based migrant proletariat.[33] It was to serve the purpose of channelling the required numbers of workers to the various centres of employment that the government created a system of labour bureaux.

Although provision was made for these bureaux to be established within the homelands only in 1968, they were effectively operative within the Transkei from considerably earlier, having been located in the larger towns (which were, of course, legally part of 'white' South Africa until recently before independence). Given the rather higher wages and better conditions offered to black workers in secondary industry, the result was that the bureaux intruded into the recruiting monopsony which the mining organizations had for so long operated within the Transkei: thus whereas in 1961 the NRC recruited 69,237 migrants compared to 1,467 by the labour bureaux, by 1976 the corresponding figures had become 113,841 and 191,404 respectively.[34] However, although the labour bureaux recruited men who would otherwise have gone to the mines, and although there has been a very substantial increase in the number of migrants recruited from Transkei since 1961, this has been insufficient to absorb the flow of new workers on to the market. Consequently, the rate of unemployment/underemployment has remained extremely high, with Transkei and the other bantustans forming 'a chain of labour reserves where people are held in a state of compulsory unemployment until the white economy wants them'.[35] But while in the era of segregation there was tendency for the 'industrial reserve army' to remain *latent* (that is, it was still engaged in subsistence agriculture), the disintegration of the reserve base has increasingly necessitated its absolute expulsion from the land, with the result that, in the era of apartheid, surplus population has become increasingly *manifest* and 'floating'. Yet prevented from passing over to the industrial proletariat by the mechanisms of apartheid, this element is constrained to remain within the bantustans.[36]

None the less, recent changes in employment patterns in the gold-mining industry suggest that Transkei is likely to reassume some of its former importance as a supplier of cheap labour to that sector of capital (see Table 7.5). As was argued earlier, the internationally fixed price of gold had the effect of imposing a particularly rigid cost structure upon the mining industry, necessitating the ultra-exploitability of black labour, as increases in production costs could not be passed on to the consumer (although this did not prevent a rise in the distributable profits in the postwar era). But given the erosion of the non-capitalist base in the reserves, this meant that mining wages were literally starvation wages – insufficient even to allow the worker to support his family and hence reproduce labour-power; and in consequence, despite an absolute increase in numbers of black mineworkers recruited from South Africa in the postwar years, an increasing proportion of the African labour force from within the Republic moved into the expanding secondary industrial sector whose cost structure was less rigid and was therefore capable of paying higher wages. The effect of this change was therefore to increase the dependence of the gold-mining industry upon cheap, unskilled migrants from outside the Republic – labour which to a considerable extent (as in Mozambique under continuing Portuguese rule) was still subject to outright extra-economic coercion.

This increased reliance upon foreign labour carried with it an element of considerable risk, for as the labour-supplying territories became politically independent, their reliability as suppliers could no longer be guaranteed.[37] Thus following their respective dates of independence, both Tanzania and Zambia placed a ban upon their nationals migrating for work in South Africa; and in April 1974, following the crash of a recruiting company plane which killed seventy-seven Malawian miners who were returning home from the mines, President Banda ordered that the Chamber of Mines suspend all recruiting operations in Malawi, with the result that the flow of labour virtually dried up. Similarly, the accession to power of FRELIMO rendered the continuing supply of migrants from Mozambique less certain, and whereas there was an average monthly figure of 91,359 Mozambicans on the mines in 1975, the figure had fallen to 34,817 by April 1977. To compensate for these losses, the Chamber of Mines had been able to prevail upon the Smith regime in November 1974 to relax recruiting restrictions which had earlier been imposed in the interests of Rhodesian mining and farming concerns. But with the political future of the country remaining uncertain, the mining industry has no guarantee that the now independent Zimbabwe will continue as a significant supplier indefinitely; and although Malawian recruits started returning to the mines in 1978, the interruption demonstrated that mining capital can no longer take that connection for granted.

But prospects for the gold-mining industry have been transformed, not only as a result of changing recruitment patterns but also because of the collapse of the Bretton Woods system, under which the price of gold had

Table 7.5 Sources of African labour employed on the South African gold mines, 1969–80 (monthly averages)

Labour supplying territory	1969	1970	1971	1972	1973	1974	1975	1976	1977 (April)	1978 (April)	1979	1980
Lesotho	59,407	61,993	64,214	66,805	76,114	71,930	74,927	81,383	96,704	97,559	75,243	69,560
Botswana	19,595	19,549	20,511	19,864	20,339	17,037	17,432	19,863	20,982	20,731	18,350	18,826
Swaziland	5,551	6,147	5,656	4,744	4,821	5,163	7,348	9,941	10,711	9,678	11,263	9,262
Angola	6,076	4,935	4,986	4,416	2,745	2,780	3,410	2,862	1,206	182	—	—
Rhodesia	3	3	2	3	2	3	2,437	15,939	22,133	13,687	7,724	3,923
Caprivi & Kavango (SWA)	222	175	274	115	—	—	—	472	2,485	2,064	1,171	1,172
Malawi	52,901	77,329	99,397	106,379	109,723	94,728	22,875	494	163	21,893	17,843	11,491
Mozambique	88,352	92,651	95,900	80,242	83,387	80,737	91,359	67,436	34,817	32,237	25,090	37,734
SUB-TOTAL	232,107	262,782	283,940	282,568	297,131	272,378	219,788	198,389	189,201	198,031	156,684	151,968
Transkei	55,738	47,907	39,430	42,555	47,139	n.a.	n.a.	n.a.	88,733	104,181	115,579	111,114
South Africa (including Transkei)	n.a.	n.a.	n.a.	n.a.	n.a.	76,523	100,748	142,710	192,558	226,299	224,515	236,133
GRAND TOTAL	n.a.	n.a.	n.a.	n.a.	n.a.	348,901	320,536	341,099	381,759	424,330	381,199	388,101

Sources: 1969–73: *HAD*, 10 September 1974, cols. 429–30; South African totals, SAIRR *Surveys 1970*, p. 114; *1971*, p. 230; *1972*, p. 290; and *1973*, p. 239. 1974–8: SAIRR: *A Survey, 1977*, p. 258 and *1978*, pp. 211–12. 1979–80: The Employment Bureau of Africa Ltd. *Reports and Financial Statements for the year ended 31st December, 1980*.

been pegged at US$35 an ounce. Given the changing role of gold in international finance, the metal has been subject to a major revaluation; and from 1971, the price began to rise, tipping nearly $200 an ounce at the end of 1974, before taking off to reach an astronomical $850 in early 1980.

One result of the higher price of gold was a relaxation of the constraints imposed upon the industry's cost structure; and given the Republic's reduced capacity to control the flow of labour from its now politically independent neighbour territories, the Chamber of Mines has begun to seek a revision of production methods which will make it less dependent upon unskilled, migrant labour from unreliable sources of supply. In the first place, it has resolved upon the introduction of new production techniques which will reduce (in the long term) the absolute requirements of unskilled, black labour and which will require an increase in the skilled and semi-skilled components of the black labour-force;[38] and secondly, it has opted for a strategy of moving away from the utilization of foreign black labour and developing its recruitment of workers from within the borders of the Republic itself. And to accomplish this second aim the industry embarked upon a series of wage rises to enhance the relative attraction of mining employment. Thus between 1971 and 1976 African wages on the gold mines increased by some 397 per cent, compared to the national average increase in African wages over the same period of 199 per cent[39] (although these heavier wage bills were more than compensated for by increased profits). Given also a policy preference for Republican workers, the South African (including Transkeian) component of the workforce rose markedly, from some 22 per cent in 1974 to approximately 50 per cent in 1977 – with the trend being a continuing one. (See Table 7.5.)

Thus one result of the new production strategy pursued by the gold-mining industry is that it has enhanced the role of the bantustans as suppliers of cheap black labour – and the particular importance of Transkei is that it provides nearly half of all South African workers on the mines and more than all those drawn from the other reserve areas put together; see Table 7.6. In consequence of this displacement of foreign labour, the burden of unemployment will be to a considerable degree shifted to neighbouring countries, while the homelands (independent or otherwise) will become increasingly bound up with the gold industry. However, precisely because the reserve economies have now so thoroughly disintegrated that they are unable to subsidize mining production as effectively as in earlier years, the Chamber of Mines will need to pay wages more in line with the actual means of subsistence of the worker and his dependants, that is, it will have to bear an increasing proportion of the cost of the reproduction of labour. But in a situation of pervasive unemployment – as exists in contemporary South Africa – the mining companies may actually still be able to pay wages considerably below the necessary cost of labour. Indeed, that this appears to be the case at the

Table 7.6 *Employment by areas of origin of African workers from South Africa on mines belonging to the Chamber of Mines, April 1977 and April 1978*

	1977		1978	
White areas				
Cape	23,846		20,816	
Free State	14,644		17,519	
Transvaal	11,029		10,634	
Natal	5,394		4,770	
SUB-TOTAL	54,913	25·3%	53,739	23·7%
Bantustans				
Transkei	96,999	(44·7%)	104,181	(46·0%)
Ciskei	18,206		15,703	
Bophuthatswana	20,091		20,741	
Kwazulu	12,327		14,901	
Lebowa	6,543		7,306	
Venda	1,821		2,243	
Ndebele	70		52	
Gazankulu	1,657		2,062	
QwaQwa	3,725		4,177	
KaNgwane	655		1,194	
Other	83		—	
SUB-TOTAL	162,177	74·7%	172,560	76·3%
TOTAL	217,090	100%	226,299	100%

Sources: Financial Mail, 10 June 1977; and SAIRR, *A Survey, 1978*, p. 212.

Table 7.7 *Average monthly earnings of Africans upon the South African mines compared to subsistence level for an African family of 5 living in Soweto, 1977 and 1978*

Year	Average monthly wage (R) for Africans upon SA mines			Minimum living level (R) for African family of 5 in Soweto	
	Gold mines	Coal mines	Diamond mines		
1977	102	105	125	(November) 145·86	(158·43)*
1978	123	135	150	(November) 168·16	(182·31)*

Note: * 'Augmented figure which includes the cost of selected items to give a more realistic measure of living costs.'
Sources: Mine wages: SAIRR, *A Survey, 1978*, p. 213; and *1979*, p. 240.
Minimum living level (calculated by the Johannesburg Chamber of Commerce): SAIRR, *A Survey, 1978*, p. 157; and *1979*, p. 189.

moment is suggested by Table 7.7, which compares average earnings by Africans on the mines with the cost of subsistence for a family of five living in Soweto. Even if this data offers only an imperfect representation of the financial position of migrants and their families (in that it takes no account of the value of domestic production in the homelands), it does suggest that unless expansion of the economy absorbs all unemployment among blacks (thereby encouraging an overall rise in the level of remuneration), reserve migrants will continue to be employed at wage levels which are insufficient to support both them and their families, and the bantustans will necessarily continue as loci of both poverty and underdevelopment.

Thus given present circumstances – an eroding economic base, overflowing population and pervasive unemployment – it appears inevitable that Transkei will remain as an appendage of the white economy. Indeed, with the expansion of the infrastructure of the 'new state', the Transkeian regime cannot afford to risk its territory's 'privileged' position in the South African labour market, for it has a very direct financial stake in the recruitment process and the continuation of migrant labour. For each worker recruited by the mines, the bantustan government receives an attestation fee, while taxes paid by the migrants on their incomes are deducted at source and passed on to Transkei by the South African government;[40] and, of course, without remittances home dispatched by the migrant workers, the Transkeian economy – such as it is – would collapse.

In consequence, the Transkeian government – aware of the political unrest which might be generated by the high levels of domestic unemployment – has actively sought to reinforce the pattern of labour export to the Republic, and has specifically endorsed the system of preferential recruitment of homeland citizens over foreign workers.[41] In 1974, for instance, following faction fights between Xhosa and Basotho miners at the Western Deep mine at Carletonville, Matanzima came to an agreement with the mine management that in future only Transkeians would be recruited.[42] But more significantly, in order to secure the good name of the Transkeian labour force, the regime also acts as a disciplinary agent for white capital, the government-run labour bureaux seeking to enforce labourers' contractual obligations to their employers by identifying deserters and withholding offers of new employment until previous commitments have been fulfilled.[43] But as overseers of labour dependency, the Transkeian rulers can themselves be disciplined by South Africa, which possesses a potential sanction in its ability to regulate the recruitment of Transkeian migrants; and given the supply of surplus labour in the Republic, any bantustan regime is aware that it could be heavily penalized were it to step too far out of line.

The agricultural base

It was the historic function of the African reserves in the era of segregation to subsidize the workings of capital in the white areas; in other words, labour was paid at less than the cost of production and reproduction. However, under the impact of the dominant capitalist mode of production, the pre-capitalist means of production (land) became increasingly devalued and hence lost its capacity to provide subsistence for the reserve populations; yet the consequent tendency towards the expulsion from the land of the surplus population has been deliberately retarded by the controls of apartheid. The contemporary bantustans, therefore, are not simply backward areas but rather are subject to a continuing process of underdevelopment, as increasing proportions of their inhabitants are forced to sell their labour as migrant workers to the centres of production in the Republic.

The stagnation of Transkeian agriculture is starkly apparent. In the first place, consider the dimensions of poverty. According to much official propaganda, the income and development level of the homelands compares quite favourably with independent Africa. According to BENBO (1976), 'a comparison with African countries indicates that the inhabitants of the homelands nearly always have the higher prosperity level... Only countries such as Zambia, Congo, Ghana, Ivory Coast and Tunisia have a higher income *per capita*.'[44] Yet such computation is intentionally misleading, for it is based upon a calculation of homeland 'national incomes' as being inclusive of the remuneration of non-resident 'citizens'. Thus the *per capita* income figure cited for the Transkei in 1973 was R175, yet this was an average based upon the apartheid definition of the approximately 1·3 million Xhosa resident in white areas who are deemed Transkeian citizens. However, careful perusal of official data shows that the *per capita* annual income of the *de facto* population of the Transkei (including migrants) was only as little as R55 in 1973 – an income below every single one of the twenty-one African countries on which BENBO bases its extensive comparison with black Africa (including such poverty-stricken territories as Burundi, Niger, Mali, Somalia and even Lesotho). And what goes for the Transkei (whose cited *per capita* income of R175 in 1973 is the same as the average for all the other homelands put together, calculated on a *de jure* citizenship basis) will also go for the other bantustans – whose inhabitants are consequently worse off than virtually any other country in Africa.[45]

The degree of impoverishment has been repeatedly exposed in various inquiries. One very detailed study carried out in the Transkei in the late 1960s demonstrated that, within the surveyed areas, no less than 85 per cent of households received an income below the Poverty Datum Line (PDL – defined as the theoretical absolute minimum requirement of a family to stay alive in the short term).[46] Although (as the authors of the study admit) the concept of the PDL to some extent relies upon value judgements, their findings are borne out by grim reality: nearly 30 per cent of children in the Transkei's rural districts die before they reach the age of 2,[47] and 40 per cent before the age of 10[48] – as a direct or indirect result of malnutrition.

Further indication of the extent of underdevelopment in Transkei is its incapacity to support its population. Of the 3,871,287 hectares accredited to the Transkei in 1973 (that is, exclusive of the Glen Grey and Herschel areas), only 18·5 per cent is listed as arable, with fully 76·3 per cent being comprehensively described as 'grazing and non-productive land'.[49] Given that 1·5 million (if we include the landless) of the 1·7 million *de facto* inhabitants are to some extent dependent upon the agricultural and subsistence sectors, it is not surprising that productivity has stagnated at a very low level. Thus during 1972, for instance, Transkei produced 2·5 bags of maize per ha as against 20–25 bags per ha in the maize areas of 'white' South Africa.[50] 'The agricultural production of the Transkei has barely increased – if it has increased at all – during the last thirty years,' remarked Matanzima in 1970.[51] In consequence, the Transkeian population is necessarily dependent upon extensive imports of staple food for its subsistence. For instance, some 2·8 million 200-lb bags of maize were imported in 1974–5,[52] while (for those who prefer less anachronistic measurements), a net figure of 237,838 metric tonnes of maize were imported in 1976–7.[53] Thus the remittances of migrant labourers working in the Republic go to sustain the market for white agriculture. Transkei thus faces a Hobbesian dilemma: either it sells its labour to South Africa or it chooses to let its people starve. It is hardly a relationship which allows room for significant political manoeuvre.

These broad conclusions are supported by the findings of a recent survey of 757 rural households undertaken in ten locations in the Umtata, Tsolo and Kentani Districts.[54] *Per capita* income for fully 50 per cent of the surveyed population in 1974 was R25 per annum or less, and 80 per cent had an income of R55 or less. Out of a total of 3,760 people, 233 were wholly destitute (that is, were earning less than R5 per annum) and were totally dependent upon such limited communal support as an impoverished society could offer. In the short term such persons may survive: in 1970 and the preceding few years of drought, the proportions of famine were so vast that the bantustan authorities were forced to take action, running throughout the territory two Relief of Distress Schemes which employed approximately 10,000 persons per day and supplemented the feeding of 360,000 pre-school and primary school children.[55] But in the medium to long term, such persons are the inevitable victims of hunger and malnutrition. Only thirty-three of the above-mentioned surveyed households had an income above R600 per annum – and significantly, with only one exception, these drew the major portion of their income from local salaried employment (as teachers, petty traders and so on) rather than from agricultural production – and the single exception was a farmer who used his tractor to plough for cash.[56]

The structure of production is further elucidated by the breakdown of the surveyed 757 households into four categories. Sixty-two (or 8·4 per cent) households were not engaged in any farming whatsoever; these included both certain petty-bourgeois elements in local employment and the totally dispossessed – those who either scraped a living through communal support or through receipt of remittances from wage labour. Six hundred and thirteen households (or 83 per cent) farmed for home use only; and another sixty-two (or 8·4 per cent) produced for home use and sale – this meaning *not* that they produced a surplus, but that they gave their crop a financial value and at times converted it into cash. Only one household (that of the tractor owner) was actively engaged in cash crop production for the market.

Viewed from an alternative perspective, it was found that 467 households (or 61·6 per cent) were never able to produce enough to subsist or to reproduce themselves, and were in consequence largely dependent upon wage labour for survival; 165 households (or 30 per cent) could feed themselves in good years, but were also basically dependent upon the sale of labour power; and only the remainder (about 8·4 per cent) always produced sufficient for subsistence with or without a marketable surplus. Nor was the deficit in crop production compensated for by stock holdings, for the differential pattern of stock ownership is seen to continue. 45·3 per cent of households owned no cattle and 55 per cent no sheep; 50 per cent of cattle-owning households owned 5 or less cows and 50 per cent of sheep owners less than 10 sheep; and only 2 per cent (15 out of 757) of cattle-owning households owned 20 cattle or more and only 0·4 per cent (3 out of 757) reported an income from the sale of wool. The survey also corroborated earlier findings that many of the larger stockowners were chiefs and headmen.[57]

The necessary result of this reserve underdevelopment is that the heaviest burden falls upon the women. The migrant labour system dislocates the social structure so as to produce a heavy preponderance of females in reserve society (the male:female ratio in 1973 being 69·75:100);[58] and with about half the able-bodied male population absent from home at any one time, agricultural production has in the main to be undertaken by the women left behind. It is the lot of the womenfolk, therefore, not only to care for children and any other dependants and to supervise the household, but also to produce crops and to look after any stock. As has been noted elsewhere,[59] women have thus been transformed into servants of capital in a dual sense: given that migrant wages are not of themselves capable of sustaining the entire family (that is, allowing for the reproduction of labour-power), women are forced both to perform reproductory labour (child and home care) *and* to produce the means of subsistence (which subsidizes capital) at the same time.

Bantustan development strategy

The 'development strategy' pursued by Transkei, as enunciated upon various occasions by Kaiser Matanzima,[60] has the goal of transforming the present dependence of the 'new state' upon South Africa into one of 'mutual interdependence' beneficial to both countries. Investment by both private and state capital is envisioned as checking the outflow of migrant labour, while the commercialization of agriculture is seen as raising the productive resources of the 'national' economy to a level where it is self-sufficient in the provision of basic foodstuffs. Yet framed and formulated by South African policy-makers, the implementation of strategy in actuality raises Transkei's economic dependence to a new level, and is designed not to promote bantustan development, but rather to modernize and rationalize apartheid economics, for without endangering the supply of labour to white industry in the Republic, local employment is envisaged as soaking up surplus population whose subsistence will otherwise be provided by a revitalized agricultural base. At the same time, the low cost of homeland labour will provide a continuing basis for white prosperity, while the expanding commercial and industrial sectors will be oriented to the needs of the Republican economy and market. But there will be no prospect for autonomous capitalist growth, and where not facilitated by the actual physical migration of labour, the transfer of surplus from the bantustan economy will be effected by the repatriation of profit by foreign investment capital.

The policy for agriculture

It is one of the most oft-repeated aphorisms of apartheid rhetoric that the African homelands are situated in what are potentially some of the most prosperous farming areas of the Republic. According to officialdom, the reserves include 28 per cent of the most highly productive agricultural regions of South Africa, and were their possibilities to be fully realized, they would be able to provide nearly one-quarter of the agricultural contribution to the Gross Domestic Product of the Republic (that is, including 'independent' bantustans).[61] Indeed, in a common cant phrase, Transkei is posited as the future 'pantry' of Southern Africa, meeting half of the Republic's need for tea, as well as providing coffee, sugar cane, cotton and phormium tenax worth R40 million (at 1976 prices), as well as increasing its maize production from 200,000 bags to 4·5 million each year.[62] But, so the lament proceeds, the development potential of the homelands is hardly realized, and agriculture remains the most backward sector of the reserve economy and is in consequent need of a revolutionary transformation.

But if the reason for this backwardness cannot be located in the soil, then the fault must necessarily lie elsewhere, and white mythology has no difficulty in ascribing it to the inherent incapacities of African agriculture.

The Tomlinson Commission (1955) was only reflecting prevalent settler attitudes when it wrote of traditional 'Bantu' agricultural practice as 'robbing' the soil and as based upon a 'parasitic' system of land usage. With limitations placed upon their access to land, African society had not been able to adapt to arable farming, and continued emphasis upon livestock ownership – closely bound up with religious and communal values – was largely responsible for the rapid denudation of the land. The Bantu had no interest in the productive efficiency of their animals, and had taken to migrant labour as the natural course of events. They were less concerned about the progressive deterioration of the soils than about their 'stake in the land', and the primary reason for the slow progress made by official betterment schemes was the unco-operative attitude of the Bantu who feared that their traditional rights to graze stock upon the commonage might be curtailed. As a consequence, there was neither chance nor incentive for the more progressive Bantu ever to develop into a self-supporting, profit-motivated, farming class able and willing to boost the level of agricultural production.[63]

Although much work elsewhere has subsequently rendered obsolete the myth of the inherent backwardness of African farmers and their alleged inertia to change, policy-makers still castigate peasant conservatism and even plain stupidity as the greatest barrier to the hoped-for agricultural breakthrough. 'There's no real poverty in the Transkei,' insisted one white aide to Matanzima, it is just that the peasants are 'not pulling their weight'.[64] Similarly, Mr Paul Ndzumo, then the Transkeian Minister of Agriculture, simply concluded in 1977 that Transkeian farmers were 'too lazy to work for themselves'.[65]

In reality, the attitudes of African producers in the Transkei and the other bantustans are anything but irrational. Precisely because of the highly unequal distribution of land in South Africa, homeland agriculture differs in crucial respects from farming in white areas, and hence the same criteria of efficiency cannot usefully be applied to both.[66] Thus although many commentators conclude that overstocking is almost wholly a result of the important non-economic functions which stock fulfil in African society, they fail to realize that stock also represents one of the few practicable means of capital accumulation for reserve inhabitants and that in impoverished societies where only a minority can afford to hire tractors, oxen are still extensively used for ploughing. Similarly, the goal of reserve farming must necessarily be to ensure physical survival, and anything but tried and trusted methods may be correctly viewed as threats to security. Certainly, any proposed reforms whose effect would be to deprive the less advantaged of their established land-rights in order to provide for the emergence of a locally predominant class of agricultural entrepreneurs will be seen as eroding the basis for bare subsistence.

Basing itself upon the notion that African producers in the reserves were poor farmers, the Tomlinson Commission recommended a major programme of agricultural modernization, commercialization and reform. Instead of virtually every man being part migrant and part farmer, it was advised that the reserve population be divided into two classes, one wholly engaged in peasant farming and the other wholly dependent upon wage employment. The land should be divided up into 'economic farm units' (varying in size according to region but averaging about 52 morgen), which would provide for the adequate support of the full-time farmers and their dependants, while those for whom such provision could not be made should be ultimately removed to urban locations within the reserves, lose their rights to land and be found alternative employment as wage labourers.[67] Basing its calculations upon the 1951 Census, the Commission estimated that approximately 300,000 families (or 1·8 million people – about half the reserve populations) would have to be moved off the land. Given the 1970 bantustan population of 7 million, this would have meant that 5·2 million (71 per cent of the reserve population) would have been transformed into a landless proletariat.[68]

Additional recommendations made by the Commission were first, that betterment schemes – involving the resiting of dwellings and the division of land into residential, arable and grazing areas – should be immediately undertaken in order to prevent the further deterioration of the soil and thus allow for more efficient agriculture; and that these should, if necessary, be implemented without the consent of the inhabitants. Secondly, it was suggested that a portion of the agricultural population should be settled upon irrigation schemes, which would allow for more intensive and specialized types of farming and thus require smaller than average plots. Finally, it was recommended that the authorities should take the initiative in the establishment of sugar cane and fibre planting, such production where possible being undertaken by peasant cash cropping; and that these activities should be supplemented by large-scale afforestation.[69]

It is not surprising that the response of the government to the Tomlinson recommendations was less than lukewarm. In its eagerness to develop 'an efficient and self-supporting "peasant farmers" class',[70] the Commission had required the replacement of the existent tribal tenure of land by a modified form of freehold (that is, land was to be negotiable upon a cash basis although measures were urged to prevent undue concentration of holdings and the emergence of so-called 'land barons'), but – as the subsequent White Paper pointed out – this would undermine the entire tribal structure upon which the government policy of Bantu Authorities was premised. Given, too, the crescendo of African protest in the late 1950s, the recommendation to enforce widespread implementation of betterment schemes and the proposal to drive half the reserve population off the land were hardly politically feasible – especially as such wholesale displacement of people would necessarily require the concurrent provision of employment elsewhere. In addition, of course, the government also found it convenient to find reasons for paring the

£370 million expenditure which Tomlinson estimated would be required to fulfil its programme over the first ten years.[71]

None the less, abstracted from their financial and temporal framework, the Tomlinson recommendations remain to this day the government's blueprint for homeland agriculture. Betterment schemes have been widely implemented (although reportedly not in areas where the inhabitants are still opposed), and are apparently becoming increasingly acceptable as beneficial results become apparent. A small start has been made with irrigation projects, and the production of crops such as tea, fibre and sugar-cane initiated by official agencies (although usually upon a plantation rather than a cash crop basis). And now that a state apparatus has been firmly entrenched in each bantustan, so that the superstructure of repression no longer rests entirely upon the chiefs, the commercialization of agriculture and the piecemeal reform of the communal land system is being attempted with the *eventual* aim of promoting peasant capitalism upon a freehold basis; thus one source envisages the reduction of the number of small farmers (that is, households) in the rural areas of the bantustans from 500,000 to 50,000.[72] The necessary result of such a policy will be, of course, the creation of a landless proletariat in the bantustan townships which will either be absorbed into migracy or local employment or thrust into the ranks of the superfluous (thereby replicating the notorious conditions found at such places as Limehill and Dimbaza as chronicled by such writers as Desmond). In addition, in so far as the extension of freehold makes inroads into tribal land tenure, the chiefs will lose their central role in the allocation of plots and will become increasingly dependent upon bureaucratic authority delegated from above.[73]

Yet the pace of such a programme is both unbalanced and slow. Within Transkei, although the tribal tenure system (correctly or incorrectly) has been identified by advisers and official policy-makers as the main barrier to agricultural transformation, progress in reform has hitherto been constrained by the reluctance of the authorities to incur the political costs that this would involve. Compulsory enforcement of 'betterment' and 'rehabilitation' schemes which threatened communal security provided the background to the Pondo Revolt, and the bantustan government has remained reluctant to pursue a course which might lead it into violent confrontation with the rural masses. Indeed, the coercive apparatus of the 'independent' state is as yet inadequate to quell a rural insurrection on the scale of the early 1960s, and in consequence the Matanzima regime seems to have deliberately tempered the pace of change.

But of more immediate consequence is that, within the rural areas, the bantustan state still rests largely upon the foundation of the chieftaincy, but it is the chiefs who are among the most reluctant to discard the existing tenure system. Coming from the most highly capitalized stratum of rural society, it is likely that they themselves would be beneficiaries of any attempt to introduce freehold and that, in most cases, they would rapidly acquire personal rights over extensive tracts of land. Yet such a gain would be made at the expense of their contemporary authoritative role in the allocation of land from which considerable material benefits flow – and the security of the 'traditionalized' present appears to many as preferable to the uncertainties of a 'commercialized' future. In addition, the effect of displacing them from a sphere over which they now exercise considerable *autonomous* authority would further reinforce their dependence upon the central government and render their office subject to increasing bureaucratization. Finally, there is widespread appreciation among the ranks of the chiefs that freehold tenure would give rise to the emergence of an intermediary class of peasant farmers who would be *independent* of chiefly control. 'We find ourselves a society of only two sections – the peasantry and the civil servants,' remarked the mover of a motion in the TLA to introduce freehold into the Fingoland region. 'This humble motion seeks to create a vigorous class in between ...' But, as another speaker correctly indicated, 'the chiefs fear that the people might be insubordinate because of these title deeds'.[74]

Given the predominance of the chiefs within the caucus of the TNIP, therefore, outright abolition of the tribal tenure system seems unlikely. None the less, there are sufficient indications to suggest that freehold property rights will increasingly (if haphazardly) penetrate the rural areas and lead to the establishment of something of a market in land. The principle of freehold has already been accepted for Fingoland (where the chieftaincy has always been less firmly rooted than elsewhere in the Transkei) with the passage of the motion to that effect in the TLA in June 1976 (although the assembled chiefs were vociferous in their rejection of an Opposition proposal to extend the freehold system to other regions of Transkei).[75] But once established in one area, the commercialization of land values might prove difficult to stop. Then, as discussed in an earlier context, farms previously owned by whites are being handed over to blacks upon a leasehold basis and, following a successful probation of five years, such farmers will be able to convert their tenancies to personal ownership.[76] Yet the political dilemma remains, for the bantustan authorities have neither the will nor the capacity to cope with the destabilizing effects of the rural masses being driven from the land, but to leave agriculture in its present collapsed condition is similarly fraught with long-term risk.

As a compromise, resort has been made to 'group farming'. Based upon the presumption that communal land units are too small and that the management factor is lacking, groups of farmers are officially encouraged to organize themselves into co-operatives or 'corporations'. By 1977, there were eighteen registered co-operatives, which had been established to provide their members with financial credit and aids such as fertilizer, seed, insecticide and so on, as well as to undertake the marketing of produce for their members.[77] But the benefits of co-operation have not been immediately obvious, and producers have largely evinced a disinclination both to offer their labour for communal projects offering doubtful return or to abandon subsistence farming for the production of commercial crops for sale on the market.[78] As a result, it would appear that the co-operatives – which were initially supported by government financial aid – have been primarily viewed as sources of cheap loans by the rural élite, for it is only this stratum which has negotiable assets to offer as security.[79] To this extent, therefore, co-operation has assisted the official policy of encouraging the emergence of a class of contextually rich, peasant farmers.

But the ultimate objective of 'group farming' is the transformation of co-operatives into 'corporations':

> Nobody enjoying agricultural rights needs to forfeit such rights but, by combining the small units and thus enlarging the size of the business and making it worthwhile to invest capital and to find a trained manager, the yield and thus the income of farmers can be vastly increased. By appointing a trained manager individual farmers are relieved of decision-making while the separation of management from ownership, which is essential for increased production under the present system of land tenure, is also achieved. The farmers who, by combining their individual units, become shareholders in the cooperative, will also have two sources of income, viz. as shareholders they will receive a share of the net profits proportionate to their contribution in terms of land and, secondly, they can also earn a wage as an employee on the project.[80]

The effect of such a model is two-fold. On the one hand, it provides a likely basis for the development of a smallholding peasantry, for it allows for inequality of landholdings, decision-making and rates of capital accumulation; and on the other, it effectively transforms the majority of producers into landless wage labourers on land which is nominally theirs, for their rights to determine land use must necessarily be controlled and subjected to managerial control.

The extent to which such agricultural corporations have been introduced into the Transkei is as yet extremely limited, having been almost entirely confined to a small number of demonstration irrigation schemes, which have been designed to provide an experimental basis for more intensive farming methods in the future.

A case study of the Qamata project (in Emigrant Thembuland) is instructive. By early 1971, 870 families out of a target figure of 2,000 had been settled upon land irrigated from the newly constructed Lubisi Dam,[81] the settlers having been selected upon a tribal basis by the Emigrant Thembuland Regional Authority, with land being allocated by the local chiefs and headmen in consultation with the local magistrate and project superintendent. Apart from the chiefs and headmen (who received 3 morgen each), each family (which was required to relinquish all land rights elsewhere) was provisionally allocated plots of $1\frac{1}{2}$ morgen apiece. Older widows were eligible to apply for smaller garden lots (although those in receipt of the meagre old age pension of R24 per annum were barred from the land on the grounds that they were already in receipt of an income). Similarly, teachers were excluded from the scheme as they were earning a wage, while the landless unemployed from the nearby Nogate township were allocated garden lots. Land was scarce, and one objective of the scheme was to provide subsistence for as many bodies as possible.[82]

Paradoxically, however, the standard plots of $1\frac{1}{2}$ morgen were generally considered to be too small to become the 'economic farm units' so beloved by the Tomlinson Commission. Yet this was deliberate, for it was the explicit aim to separate out the 'competent' from the 'incompetent' farmers, and to gradually reallocate the land according to ability, with the successful producers with more land providing employment for the less efficient. The objective, therefore, was to create a landed peasant class of 'progressive farmers' and to transform the less able into wage labourers.

In practice, the Qamata irrigation scheme has not turned out quite as intended by agricultural policy-makers. From the very beginning, there has been continual conflict over the allocation of land. The local chiefs and headmen have from the earliest days continuously resisted the erosion of their authority over land by white supervisory staff, while the latter have correspondingly been unable to secure the distribution of plots according to the criteria and at the tempo they consider necessary ('Dishing out of lands all over the place by headmen should stop forthwith', ordered a white official).[83] Nor has the scheme yet proved an economic success. Early beset by a substantial deficit and the desertion by some farmers from their allotments, the supervisory staff have been able to impose upon the settlers neither the methods they require to be used nor the crops they demand be grown, while the farmers themselves have complained bitterly at the failure of the Agricultural Department to provide the necessary machinery for harvesting and of the inability of the Qamata Co-operative to market their crops. Yet one part of the scheme has been implemented according to plan, for so-called 'unproductive' farmers have been expropriated and their lands handed over to the more successful:

> The Paramount Chief [Kaiser Matanzima] has requested and the Department of Agriculture and Forestry agreed to increase allotments to 3 morgen per person. Secondly, he has requested that unproductive allottees be removed from the scheme, irrespective of status ... in favour of would-be diligent land users. $1\frac{1}{2}$ morgen per person is insufficient. According to reports, 484 settlers are unsuitable. (Few persons are quoted who are away at Cape Town and whose wives fail to work the land. Others are away at labour centres and loan their lands to other people. There is another lot who are too old to work in the lands and some of them receive old age pensions.)[84]

Thus the lands worked by settler families where the husband has migrated for work, as well as those 'whose allotments are neglected or farmed poorly' are now dispossessed, and the land so expropriated given to 'progressive farmers' who thus have their plots increased to 3 morgen each.[85] Similarly, it is reported that at Malenge (in Umzimkulu), where by 1975 240 ha had been settled by 144 farmers, 'good' producers have been rewarded by the allocation of second plots taken from those who have failed.[86] If agricultural experimentation must of necessity seek to encourage efficient farming, the expropriation of land is none the less a process whereby incipient class formation proceeds. Given, too, that the $1\frac{1}{2}$-morgen plots are insufficient to guarantee subsistence, it is those with initial capital who are favoured to succeed, while the families of those less well endowed, where the husband is forced to migrate in order to ensure the survival of the household, are more likely to be driven off the land – and because they have forfeited their communal land rights, they have no alternative but to swell the ranks of the burgeoning proletariat.

It needs to be re-emphasized that the impact of these irrigation schemes is likely to remain minimal. When complete, the four projects currently in operation (at Qamata, Malenge, Ncora and Glen Grey) will cover only 11,500 ha and prospects for extending irrigation are limited because of the large amounts of capital required to construct dams and provide the required infrastructure (the Ncora scheme is scheduled to cost R40 million).[87] Thus although, as Lipton has argued,[88] labour-intensive agriculture may well be the only conceivable strategy to develop the bantustans (given the present political circumstance of white supremacy in the core area), it is unlikely that irrigation projects will contribute to any significant degree in terminating the dependence of the bulk of the homeland population upon migratory labour – for the South African government (which provides for homeland budgets) has neither the will nor the capability to finance irrigation schemes at the level required to reverse the flow of black manpower to the Republic.

The remaining sphere for agricultural progress in the Transkei, as foreseen by Tomlinson, was the development of various commercial projects by official agencies. Little has yet been done to promote livestock production along modern lines, but the aim of the TDC is to promote cattle ranching with black participation: thus in 1974 negotiations were under way to establish the Co-operative Cattle Farming Society of Eastern Pondoland under an agency basis, with the XDC providing the initial capital and management, the intention being to train Transkeians so as to enable them to take the company over in due course.[89] And, as has been indicated already, the Matanzima brothers themselves are currently involved in cattle farming on the farms they have acquired from the Bantu Trust. Similarly, the Transkeian government and the TDC work together to run tea plantations at Magwa and Majola which are destined for expansion from the present 970 ha to some 5,000 ha in the future. In addition, there are two small phormium tenax projects, and experiments are being made with the production of pyrethrum, coffee, Macadamia nuts and sugar. But the longest established venture is forestry, afforestation having been pursued on quite a large scale since the early postwar years – and by March 1975 there were over 61,000 ha of plantations, producing a revenue (which accrued to the state) of some R1·7 million per annum.[90]

Yet all these projects are still in their infancy, and even though they may allow a degree of economic diversification, their expansion is unlikely to much reduce dependence upon South Africa, for all are grown to be marketed in the Republic, while their capacity for absorbing labour is limited: the tea plantations and forestry divisions together provided employment for less than 10,000 persons in 1975–6 – less than the annual increase of new workseekers from Transkei. It would also appear that the developing strategy is for such corporate project farming to provide primary products required by the white core, thereby promoting the latter's economic self-sufficiency.[91] However, there is also the objective of promoting the emergence of a Transkeian middle class: 'Xhosa ... progress from ordinary labourers to partial involvement in management, and later become partial and ultimately fully fledged owners and managers'.[92] But as plantation agriculture extends, so it erodes the basis of communal land tenure, and in so far as it brings about the dispossession of subsistence producers, and separates them from the means of production, it also increases the proportion of the population entirely dependent upon the sale of labour – that is, it completes the process of their proletarianization.[93]

The policy for industry

As a complement to its recommendations for agricultural reform, the Tomlinson Commission suggested a programme of industrialization for the homelands which would absorb human surplus from the land, reduce dependence upon migrant labour and lead to a generally higher standard of living for the African populations. Developments should initially be concentrated in 'production centres', and as far as possible undertaken by private capital. However, because the latter was unlikely to be attracted to undeveloped areas without some reasonable guarantee of success, a government-run Development Corporation should provide infrastructure and facilities necessary to stimulate private investment, as well as taking a direct lead in industrial activity itself. Finally – and most controversially as far as the Commission itself was concerned – a recommendation was put forward that, in order to achieve the desired tempo of development, European capital should no longer be barred from the reserves and should be invited to establish itself under carefully controlled conditions – with the proviso that white-run industries should eventually be Africanized as Africans acquired the requisite skills and managerial capacity.[94]

The Tomlinson recommendations, themselves echoes of earlier calls for the development of the reserves,[95] concentrated upon the establishment of light industries such as clothing, textiles and processing plants (such as meat-canning factories) linked to the output of the agricultural economy. However, even the modest suggestions that were made (entailing the expenditure of a mere £30 million over ten years) were stubbornly resisted by the government on the grounds that, if implemented, they would pose a competitive threat to established industries in white areas, and accordingly the barrier against white capital penetrating the homelands was initially maintained.[96] Nor did the state itself seek to stimulate industrial growth, and the BIC (created in 1959) mostly contented itself with the financing of African entrepreneurs in retailing and wholesale,[97] as did its offspring, the XDC, after its establishment in 1966. However, the developing tempo of the homeland programme and the consequent desire to enhance the bantustans' credibility as potential states, combined with the increasingly urgent need for the regime to check the outflow of surplus population from the reserves, was destined to bring about a major change in policy, and white capital was finally allowed to enter the homelands in 1968 under an agency or leasehold basis, the intention being that at the expiry of an agreed term (usually 15–25 years) the white investor would hand over to a black counterpart. In 1974, however, homeland governments were given increased powers over the establishment of white industries in their territories, and were henceforth enabled to conclude permanent arrangements with white investors, no longer restricted by temporal constraints.[98]

Outside capital flows into the bantustans through the BIC (renamed the Corporation for Economic Development in 1977) and the various homeland development corporations, being attracted into Transkei under the aegis of the TDC. In common with the other homelands, the TDC has sought to concentrate industry into specially designated 'growth areas', the major centres for investment in the Transkei being at Butterworth and Umtata, where the Corporation has provided the basic infrastructure necessary for industrial expansion. But in addition, in order to overcome the inherent disadvantages of Transkei as an underdeveloped region (for instance, the lack of internal demand for consumer goods and the consequent long distances from possible markets), the TDC has sought to attract capital by the provision of a battery of concessions designed to enhance the prospect of profit. In 1976, for instance, these included: the erection of factories and subsequent leasing at the low rate of 7 per cent of the construction cost, financial loans of up to 50 per cent of required investment capital at 4 per cent per annum, a 50 per cent tax rebate on wages paid to black employees for the first seven years of operation and a 30 per cent rebate on the value of machinery and equipment, the provision of housing for white staff at 3·5 per cent of construction cost, a rebate of 40 per cent on manufactured goods railed out of the area, a 50 per cent rebate on harbour dues via East London to an overseas port, a cash reimbursement of certain moving costs, and a 5–10 per cent price preference offered on all purchases by South African state authorities excepting the railways.[99] In addition, the Republican government has offered full indemnity to industrialists were their businesses to be nationalized, a possibility which is considered to be so remote as to be 'hardly worth mentioning'.[100] Finally, in November 1974, the passage of the Bantu Laws Amendment Act empowered the Minister, subject to his discretion at all points, to authorize the development corporations to indemnify an industrialist investing in a homeland against any loss provided only that it is not insurable and there is no effective right to damages. A confidential report by Sir Arthur Snelling (former British Ambassador to South Africa) upon the scope for British investment in the homelands concluded that: 'this remarkable, and perhaps unprecedented wording seems to provide the best guarantee for which an industrialist could hope'.[101]

Yet the major attraction of Transkei to white capital remains its cheap black labour power. The words of Sir Arthur Snelling make this explicit and can again be pressed into service:

> The main motive of many South African firms for moving into the homelands, apart from benefiting from the financial incentives, has been to avoid having to pay wages and offer fringe benefits which are legal or customary in the Pretoria–Witwatersrand–Vereeniging area, to be able to ignore job reservation (thereby paying Black supervisory staff much less than Whites would earn) and to escape from the legislation which in White areas lays down minimum standards, e.g. on safety, and prohibits certain practices, e.g. the employment of women and minors on night shifts.[102]

Snelling went on to say that British firms should not be discouraged from paying somewhat higher wages, yet it none the less remains clear that, in order to ensure a profitable return on capital, labour costs in all the homelands (Transkei included), are reduced to a minimum. Thus one survey found that 90 per cent of black workers in the Brits and Rosslyn Border Areas of the Transvaal and Babalegi (a Bophuthatswana 'growth point') were paid wages below the poverty datum line, as well as suffering from generally deprived working conditions;[103] and similarly, in Transkei, the highest wage paid by building contractors in 1973 came to no more than one-third of the PDL established for the Durban area:[104] 'They pay them what is termed Transkei wages – wages far below those paid to labourers in South Africa,' explained one complainant.[105] Nor has the Transkeian government sought to remedy this situation, for to do so would be to render the territory less competitive with other centres of investment in South Africa. The Matanzima government has repeatedly refused to introduce minimum wage legislation,[106] and has similarly declined to countenance the formation of trade unions, which are considered to be 'undesirable and even harmful in a developing country ... where continuing peak productivity is essential'.[107] There is, therefore, no counter to the bargaining power of employers, and given a large standing army of the unemployed, workers have little opportunity to resist their exploitation. Yet even the large surplus of labour has not been sufficient to guarantee worker docility, and strikes have broken out on a number of occasions. Seven hundred workers from at least three concerns in Butterworth struck for better pay and conditions in 1974, as did 500 workers at the Transkei Textile and Plastic Company in January

1975, and 100 workers at a biscuit factory in Umtata in December 1978.[108] In at least the first case, minor concessions were made, but elsewhere strikes have on occasion led to outright reprisal by employers, as when 160 women employees of Transkeian Hillmond Weavers were fired after they downed tools after a pay dispute in May 1978.[109] This action had a precedent in the treatment of 1,300 workers who went on strike at Pep Homeland Industries in 1976. According to management, the strike was the handiwork of agitators and intimidators, but press reports indicated that workers – who were employed at well below the PDL[110] – were striking for higher wages. Yet their plea was bluntly rejected, and the strike was terminated by the dismissal of all the strikers, who were instructed to reapply for their jobs, while the bantustan police were called in to root out the 'ringleaders' and 'troublemakers'.[111] However, the workforce (now 1,500 strong) struck again in January 1978, this time because promised pay increases had not materialized; but again the factory was closed and the workforce paid off – with half the workers later being re-employed, but only at basic rates of pay irrespective of the rates they had been paid before the strike.[112]

In place of trade unions, the Transkeian government has established a Wage Board under the Wage Act of 1977 whose purpose is to make wage determinations for industry.[113] Yet such a body will scarcely promote the interests of employees, for its composition is heavily weighted in favour of the state and employers – and with Matanzima's explicit determination to crush 'unrealistic and militant wage demands' which might result in 'the disengagement of foreign investors',[114] the primary function of the Board will be to service the needs of capital. In addition, public employees are expressly excluded from the provisions of the Act – yet wages paid to labourers employed by the Transkeian government itself are generally even lower than those paid to industrial workers in Butterworth and Umtata. Thus Leeuwenburg's judgement can hardly be condemned as too harsh: 'Freed from the "shackles" of industrial legislation and immune to the "evils" of strike action, the industries of the Transkei are little more than small-scale sweat shops.'[115]

Under these circumstances, conditions for the expropriation by white capital of surplus generated by homeland labour-power are highly favourable (although there are other cost features which have hitherto discouraged many firms from transferring their operations to Transkei or to other bantustans).[116] In the first place, by far the major proportion of official aid offered by the Development Corporation accrues not to the various 'ethnic' peoples, nor even to black proto-capitalists, but rather to white firms; up to 1975, for instance, while loans advanced by the XDC to African businessmen amounted to no more than R$7\frac{1}{2}$ million, capital aid to white undertakings under the Agency system (under which the Corporation is often a shareholder) amounted to R$28\frac{1}{4}$ million.[117] Although these figures may not be strictly comparable (as it may be argued that African businessmen have hitherto only been able to absorb small amounts of capital), it does indicate that a considerable proportion of the resources into black development are in practice channelled direct to white industry.

Again, the fact that the concessions offered to industrialists by the TDC preclude the government from collecting taxes from new enterprises for a number of years after their establishment provides for the free and unhindered expatriation of profits, while competition between the different homelands will remain highly favourable to capital for the foreseeable future. In addition, of course, given that investment will only be attracted to Transkei under the auspices of the TDC, which remains financed and thus effectively controlled by South Africa, veto power over how much and what type of capital will be drawn into the 'independent' homeland will remain with the Republican authorities. To this extent, the bantustan policy represents a modernization of apartheid, for the migration of labour in the service of capital is now complemented by the migration of capital to the sources of labour under conditions laid down by Pretoria.

The web in which Transkei is enmeshed can perhaps be most striking portrayed by a dissection of the direct involvement by white capital in the bantustan economy; and for the sake of convenience this will be classified according to its place of origin – whether it is South African or 'international' capital.[118]

The direct stake of South African capital in the Transkeian economy remains considerably larger than that of international capital at the present time, if only because of the predominance of the public sector and also because initially, the agency system did not extend to firms which had connections with foreign interests.[119] Writing in the early 1960s, Govan Mbeki identified the non-commercial sector of the Transkeian economy as almost the exclusive preserve of Nationalist capital, citing in evidence the transfer of the Territorial Authority's investments from the portfolios of non-Nationalist town councils to the BIC.[120] Although subsequent changes in policy have now rendered this judgement obsolete, it remains the case that the public sector of Transkei is almost entirely controlled by Afrikaner interests and South African state capital. When the Transkei Townships Board took over the running of the Village Management Boards in 1973, the latter's financial reserves were transferred from Barclays Bank to Volkskas.[121] Three years later, when Volkskas withdrew from the Transkei, its branches and business were taken over by the newly established *Bank of Transkei Ltd*, in which it had a majority interest, the rest of the issued share capital of R2 million having been subscribed by private (Transkeian) investors and the Transkei Research and Development Fund (a government agency).[122] The latter body also initially financed the *Transkei Meat Industry*, which is managed and controlled by South African Meat Producers (Central Co-operative) Ltd, profit being shared equally with the government.[123] A similar agreement was one concluded in 1977 whereby the Transkeian authorities appointed the *South African Wool Board* as the bantustan's sole marketing agent for wool,[124] and another whereby the *Transkei Tea Corporation* is managed by the South African-based company of Lugg Harrison & Associates.[125] Also in the agro-industrial sphere, the Development Corporation is a 40 per cent shareholder in the *Umtata Timber Development Company*, in partnership with (the South African-controlled) Sappi and Hans Merensky Trust, the consortium having taken over 19,000 ha of pine and gum forest along the Matiwane Mountains between Umtata and Engcobo.[126] A rather different enterprise is *Transkei Airways Corporation*, which now operates a regular service between Umtata and Johannesburg in association with South African Airways[127] while, rather more vitally, all electricity flowing into Transkei is supplied by ESCOM, the South African electricity corporation. In addition, of course, the TDC penetrates almost every aspect of industrial 'development', having a stake (through the financial aid it offers) in the profitability of almost every firm which has been drawn to Butterworth and Umtata. Most firms operate in buildings leased from the Corporation, which also has minority shareholdings in a number of them, as well as having a more direct interest in its wholly owned subsidiary, *Transkei Decorticators*, which processes the phormium tenax produced on the government plantation.[128] Other industries actually owned by the TDC are *Hilmond Weavers, Transkei Quarries* and the *Vulindlela Furniture Factory* – apart from a number of small concerns which are destined for transfer to Transkeian entrepreneurs (garages, stores and so on) in the future.[129]

Turning to the role of private capital, the principal beneficiaries of the bantustan programme have undoubtedly been the construction firms who have undertaken public works projects on behalf of the authorities. First and foremost is *Murray & Stewart (Transkei)* (a subsidiary of the massive Murray and Roberts Group which when formed in 1967–8 ranked twelfth in the *Financial Mail*'s survey of top South African companies).[130] Awarded a R15 million contract before independence to build new government offices and extensions to the technical college, Murray & Stewart were later contracted to build the first phase of the planned R80 million Transkei University, while also being called upon to participate in a number of other potentially lucrative projects.[131] *Grinaker Construction* has also been substantially involved in Transkei, having – among other projects – been responsible for the building of the R6 million Umtata Dam;[132] and with a lavish public works programme envisaged for the near future (including the building of a Free Harbour on the coast at Umngazana and the upgrading of K. D. Matanzima Airport to international standards), the prospects for the construction companies remain set fair for the future.

The single largest industrial venture by a South African firm at present is the R10·8 million investment by *Pep Homeland Industries* (a fully owned subsidiary of Pep Stores), in a blanket and clothing factory at

Butterworth. Attracted to Transkei by the low cost of labour (and a loan of R2·5 million from the TDC), when complete the enterprise will employ 2,000 workers (most of them women). Mr Renier Van Rooyen, Chairman of Pep, expresses political commitment to the 'new state', and is a prominent director of the Development Corporation.[133]

Involvement by other Republic-based firms is on a smaller scale, all enterprise being essentially light industrial undertakings which are oriented to the South African market. Glenjohn Holdings of Edendale run three operations on the Butterworth industrial estate: a R1·5 million (1973) tartaric acid factory under the rubric of *Butakem*; *Atlas*, producing Epsom salts; and *Glenjohn Chemicals*, which manufactures fire extinguishing powders.[134] H. Lewis & Co. of Kempton Park, through their subsidiary *Tanda Milling*, process grain from the Free State and produce maize meal, animal feeds and flour for the local Transkeian market, while *Transkei Wire Industries*, makers of metal products such as nails, wire and fencing, operate as a subsidiary of Wispeco Holdings Ltd.[135] More exotically, it was reported in 1976 that the XDC had signed a contract with Taurus Chemical Manufacturing for a R1 million investment in a seaweed-processing factory.[136]

Also in co-operation with the Development Corporation, C. J. Fuchs, manufacturers of electrical and household applicances, plan to decentralize their activities to Transkei with an investment of R5·5 million with the establishment of a subsidiary *Johannesburg Metal Pressings*, which will make a wide range of articles such as paraffin stoves, bicycle lamps and fishing tackle,[137] while *Dorbyl* have opened a R2 million factory for the production of commercial vehicle and bus bodies.[138] *Jabula Foods*, a subsidiary of Premier Milling, has contracted to open a R1 million factory for the manufacture of instant foods.[139]

Other industrial firms from South Africa operating in Transkei are mostly small privately owned concerns, for whom the cheap loan capital made available by the TDC has acted as a major draw. *Transkei Textiles and Plastics*, a subsidiary of a small private firm in Paarl, uses the phormium tenax extracted by Transkei Decorticators to make grain bags for farmers' co-operatives in the Republic. *Highflies*, employing some 220 workers (mostly women), produces fishing flies for a market that is highly specialized and reputedly worldwide, while the *Hercules* shoe firm, the first to open at Butterworth, markets footwear to Lesotho under a special non-loss agreement with the TDC. *Xhosa Clothing*, a subsidiary of the private firm of Dux Uniforms of Natal, manufactures protective clothing, while *Chet Industries* makes matches. The small *Franco Group* produces wigs and packages foodstuffs for Tanda Milling, also having an interest in *Butterworth Electrics*, which deals in car vehicle wiring. The latter activity complements *Roadmaster*, which specializes in automobile suspension; and finally, *Dawol Knitwear*, an enterprise established with the help of the TDC and operating on a 25-year lease, makes soft toys and knitwear which it markets in East London.[140]

Tourism is also seen as a sphere for profitable investment, and the natural attractions of Transkei's famed Wild Coast are now set to be exploited by the construction of a massive R35 million 'Las Vegas-style' casino complex by the *Holiday Inn Group* (subsidiary of Rennies Consolidated Holdings), who already rent a R2 million hotel from the TDC in Umtata. (In this case, a property company in which the Transkeian government will hold at least 51 per cent of the shares through the TDC will own the land and buildings.)[141] Designed to draw tourists from Durban and to compete with casinos in Botswana, Lesotho and Swaziland, the long-term objective is professedly to transform Transkei into 'the biggest tourist playground in Southern Africa'. Whether or not such a venture will promote the genuine socio-economic development of Transkei seems not to have been questioned, even though the very nature of such a project will be such as to intensify the dependence of the local economy upon white patronage.[142]

As can be seen from the foregoing analysis, apart from Pep Homeland Industries most of the South African firms which have been attracted to Transkei as manufacturers are relatively small, both in terms of their capital input and their potential for growth. Indeed, what is demonstrated is that, although offering a constant supply of extremely cheap labour, Transkei's distance from the Republican market (East London excepted) constitutes a major disadvantage for the established firms – and in consequence it is mainly companies which are oriented to the limited Transkeian market (for example, basic foodstuff suppliers), or for which the marketing factor is not crucial (for example, the Pep factory produces mainly winter goods thus allowing for off-season transportation), or which process locally grown materials, which have been drawn to Butterworth and Umtata. Otherwise, the Transkeian growth points cannot compete with industrial locations in other homelands (such as Babalegi in Bophuthatswana or Isithebe in Kwazulu) which border upon the major conurbations.

In startling contrast, compared to South African industrial investment, the involvement of foreign capital in Transkei is relatively heavier, and is likely to increase markedly. There are a number of reasons for this. In the first place, the CED and the different homeland Development Corporations – as well as the bantustan political leaderships themselves – have been responsible for a concerted advertising effort throughout the industrial west eulogizing the homelands as havens for foreign investment, with the repatriation of profits guaranteed, offering a plentiful supply of cheap labour and immune from any political threat to private enterprise. Secondly, speculation suggests that major western interests, while not necessarily openly supporting separate development, are keen to stimulate the industrialization of the homelands in order to stabilize the core area, and thereby protect the heavy western stake in South Africa. Thus reputable pre-independence rumours indicated that the European Economic Community was seriously considering granting

Transkei all the privileges which it extends to developing countries (although political pressure from the Third World subsequently rendered such a proposition politically untenable).[143] In Britain, meanwhile, UKSATA and the pro-South Africa lobby within the Conservative Party have been particularly active in endorsing the penetration of British capital into the bantustans.[144]

But the major advantages of the homelands to western capital are twofold. In the first place, the availability of labour at a lower price than in the Republic is a major attraction. 'The Transkei apparently appeals to European industrialists,' concluded the *Financial Mail*, 'because of the basic concessions and because it is reckoned that with current European labour costs and inflation levels it could be cheaper to manufacture in the Homelands and export to Europe.'[145] Secondly, a number of firms have been drawn to the bantustans by the desire to duck below the tariff barriers which have been erected to protect South African industry, this being borne out by the fact that little foreign capital *already* resident in the Republic has been drawn to Transkei, and the major foreign firms now operating in the territory are enterprises which previously had no manufacturing base in South Africa.[146] In addition, of course, there is a potential advantage for foreign companies that if Transkei were to gain any degree of international acceptance, investment within its borders would not necessarily incur the odium that attaches to capital involvement in South Africa itself.

Two of the first major foreign investments in Transkei were made by two large Italian textile groups. *Keitex*, a subsidiary of Zegna Baruffa, is a scheduled R3 million project which will eventually employ more than 1,000 workers in the production of acrylic and mixed yarns for the knitting industry. A much larger investment is that of R12·5 million in *Transkei Fashion Yarns* by the Bertrand Group, which when complete will employ about 1,500 workers and will reportedly almost fulfil South Africa's need for acetate blend fancy yarns. Both companies calculate not only to undertake production at a lower cost than possible in Europe, but also to expand their share in the South African market by avoiding import barriers.[147]

K. Braun Woodworking Machinery, established by Machinenfabrik Bernhard Braun of West Germany in co-operation with South African firms Stuttkor (a timber-processing company which later went into liquidation) and Seligson & Clare (machine distributors), has operated a R760,000 factory at Butterworth to make sawmilling machinery since 1974–5. However, using highly automated equipment, it has little employment to offer to Transkei (thirty workers in 1976). More recently, however, an agreement between the TDC, EDESA (the Corporation for Economic Development for Equatorial and Southern Africa, established by Afrikaner magnate Anton Rupert) and the parent company has provided for Braun to expand in order to manufacture exhaust systems for Mercedes Benz cars, the equipment for the new factory coming from

Germany.[148] The other German manufacturing firm currently in Transkei is *Laborbau*, which makes laboratory fittings and furniture. A relatively small concern employing less than a hundred persons (and a third of these are whites), the firm is ultimately controlled by the Federale Volksbeleggings Group.[149]

West Germany is also involved in Transkei through the innocuous-sounding *Transkei Commercial Promotions (Pty) Ltd*, subsidiary of an unnamed Berlin-based company. In terms of a contract signed in 1977, the German firm was given sole fishing rights in Transkeian territorial waters for ten years for a royalty of R30 a tonne of processed fillet (a price described as ridiculously low by incensed South African fishing companies), no provision being made for an increase should the world price go up. After ten years the contract will then either be renewed by mutual consent or Transkeian concerns will then have priority to buy the fishing fleet, so long as the distribution of fish and fish products on the world market remains in company hands. In the meantime, the company will also carry out a feasibility study on the possibility of establishing a processing and harvesting plant in Transkei.[150] This remarkable contract, signed by the Minister of Agriculture, was reportedly branded as 'a shocking example of foreign exploitation of a developing country' by official South African advisers.[151]

Before independence, there were no directly owned US companies operating in Transkei, but following a promotional campaign by Sydney Baran & Co., a New York-based public relations firm engaged by the South African government, American interest has increased. The first substantial result of this was the establishment of *Intermagnetics Transkei*, a R1 million investment venture by the Intermagnetic Corporation for the manufacture of tapes and tape casettes. In this case, the attraction of Transkei was very definitely the low price of labour, the explicit intention of the firm being to compete with tapes imported into South Africa from Hong Kong.[152]

Other foreign investments in Transkei have included an input of R5 million by a company in Buenos Aires, backed by the Central Bank of Argentina, for the manufacture of Zanella motorcycles for marketing in South Africa;[153] and a R12 million loan for infrastructural development advanced to the TDC by the UK merchant bank of *Hill Samuel* and the *Dow Bank* of the United States.[154] In addition, other investments are reportedly in the pipeline from West Germany, the USA, France, Australia, the Scandinavian countries and Britain, while in the first two months after independence the TDC had concluded agreements with nineteen industrialists for the establishment of new projects involving total investments of more than R13 million and providing jobs for 1,700 workers.[155] Israeli interests are also studying the possibilities of establishing a shipping concern and a salt plant, while a French consortium headed by *Grands Travaux de Marseille* is undertaking preliminary investigations into the construction of the harbour on the Mngazana river mouth.[156]

The above survey demonstrates that the TDC is not being wholly unsuccessful in attracting industry to Transkei. Even so, the development strategy has hitherto failed to provide sufficient new jobs to absorb the annual increase in the labour force, and given that South African industry remains to a large degree reliant upon migrant labour, it is unlikely that the Pretoria-financed TDC (or any other homeland Development Corporation) will operate to reverse the migrant trend. At the same time, while industrial decentralization and regional development are in principle praiseworthy objectives, in practice the benefits of the homeland growth centre programme do not seem to have much extended to the reserve population. Thus the labour force in Transkei has hitherto been subjected to conditions of severe deprivation, suffering from an absence of protective legislation and barred from resorting to industrial action. Certainly, there is an emergent core of skilled and semiskilled workers which, while drawing wages below those paid for equivalent work by industries in urban areas of South Africa, is able to enjoy the luxury of a stable family life, uninterrupted by the oscillations of migrancy. But the major portion of the homeland industrial workforce is clearly remunerated at below the rate of subsistence – this being facilitated by the fact that the majority of those employed are women, who are mostly supplementing the incomes of their migrant fathers or husbands.[157]

Finally, it would appear that under present conditions there is little opportunity of Transkeian entrepreneurs embarking upon a path of autonomous industrial development, for not only have they been channelled into commerce and trade but they are almost wholly dependent for capital upon the good offices of the TDC; and with virtually every industrial project directly or indirectly owned by foreign or South African capital, there is no bar to the continuing transfer of surplus away from the bantustan economy. In short, the pattern and structure of the industrial programme have done little to decrease Transkei's dependence upon the white economy, and would seem to have little capacity for encouraging its self-sustaining development in the future.

Notes

1. Bantu Investment Corporation (1975), pp. 7–13.
2. On the break in diplomatic relations, see pp. 268–70 below.
3. SAIRR, *A Survey, 1975*, pp. 121–2.
4. *South African Government Gazette*, 136, 5320, 22 October 1976.
5. *Financial Mail*, 24 September and 22 October 1976; *Daily News*, 18 November 1976.
6. *Transkei Hansard*, 23 March 1977, pp. 67–70; *RDM*, 12 November 1977.
7. *Estimate of the Expenditure to be defrayed from the Transkeian Revenue Fund, Year ending 31 March 1979* (TG 2 – 1978); and Appropriation Bill 1 April 1978 to 31 March 1979, Second Reading Speech by the Minister of Finance the Honourable T. T. Letlaka (mimeo).

8. *The Times* (London), 26 October 1978: 'Reckoning after a spending spree'.
9. SAIRR, *A Survey, 1979*, pp. 350–2.
10. ibid., p. 337; and *RDM*, 11 June 1980 (quoting figures given by Mr Pik Botha, South African Minister of Foreign Affairs, to the House of Assembly).
11. *Financial Mail*, 22 October 1976.
12. SAIRR, *A Survey, 1978*, p. 303.
13. *RDM*, 13 October and 26 October 1977. Commented the earlier edition on the effect of Transkei's limited financial credibility on future loans: 'Transkei will effectively be competing more with debentures than with other semi-gilt rates.'
14. *Financial Mail*, 24 September 1976.
15. The lack of international credibility has attracted a number of dishonest international financiers to Umtata. Prominent among them was Mr Salim el Hajj, who represented ISCOR in several Arab countries until December 1979 and who after Transkeian independence was retained as an unofficial Middle East ambassador. In 1978 it was reported that he had arranged an agreement for a R440 million loan (*sic*) whereby a Middle East consortium, Medi Dupic, would finance Transkei's budget deficit and eight proposed development projects (*RDM*, 23 August 1978). Later, the projected loan seems to have been reduced to R185 million, an agreement being signed in December 1979 with el Hajj's own consortium, Middle East Commercial and Investment Services, to be employed to finance and build a new international airport and construct an international free port at Mazeppa Bay on the Transkeian coastline (*RDM*, 7 December 1979). (el Hajj also concluded a R100 million deal on similar terms with the Venda government in November 1979). However, after downpayment of R9 million by the Transkeian government, el Hajj was lost to public view, with all of his firms (bar one) going into liquidation. (*Sunday Times*, 30 March 1980.)
16. *Financial Mail*, 22 October 1976.
17. See the debate on the second reading of the Transkei Appropriation Bill for 1977/8, *Transkei Hansard*, 23–8 March 1977, pp. 70–93.
18. *Transkei Hansard*, 19 April 1978, p. 117.
19. Appropriation Bill, 1978–9, Second Reading Speech by the Minister of Finance, T. T. Letlaka (mimeo).
20. See 'Lesotho: A State of Siege', *Africa*, 64, December 1976, pp. 42–4. Note also that in January 1977 South Africa withdrew a subsidy of R2·5 million on wheat and maize imported into Lesotho under the Customs Agreement. (*RDM*, 13 January 1977.)
21. Hirschmann (1979).
22. Francis Wilson (1972b), p. 98.
23. Wilson (1972b), p. 98. See also Rutman (1971).
24. *Transkei Calendar, 1976*, p. 63; and Table 7.2 above.
25. *RDM*, 19 December 1977. The practice had apparently been going on for some time – see Quarterly Meeting of Chiefs and Headmen and People of Libode District, 28 June 1973 (UNISA): 'Headman S. Mfunzwana complained that a European was taking school-going children and recruiting them without their parents' consent and sending them to the sugar estates.'
26. Leistner (1976).
27. BENBO (1975), p. 31.

28. XDC, *Tenth Annual Report, 1975*, p. 57.
29. Republic of Transkei, *The Development Strategy, 1980–2000* (Umtata, 1979), cited in SAIRR, *A Survey, 1979*, pp. 372–4.
30. 'The accession of the National Party to power in 1948 marked ... another new era in the history of Black labour ... characterized above all else by three aspects: immediate attention had to be paid to the political and economic development of the homelands, essentially by the creation of employment opportunities for Blacks in or near their homelands in such a way that they could live there instead of in White areas; control of the movement of Black workers to White areas had to be intensified; the employment and accommodation of Black labour in White areas had to be achieved in such a manner that it would not lead to increasing integration between White and Black or to friction on the labour front. To implement this, the authorities had to intervene in the unimpeded functioning of the market mechanism by instituting administrative apparatus through which economic activities were decentralized and control of the movement and use of Black labour could be accomplished.' (BENBO, 1976, p. 39.)
31. See pp. 77–8 above.
32. Transkei Government, Department of Interior, *Statistical Labour Report*, 1973.
33. Unfortunately, the paucity of official statistics prevents systematic analysis of this phenomenon here: '... there is an almost total blank in our information as to how many of the 800,000 Africans employed in industry, commerce and other urban employment are migrants and how many are urbanized' (Houghton, 1976, p. 90). Note, however, the tentative conclusion drawn by Francis Wilson in his survey of industrial (that is, not mining) centres that 'roughly one-half of all the African men working are oscillating migrants living in town on a single basis and with their families elsewhere' (Wilson, 1972b, p. 77).
34. Transkei Government, Department of Interior, *Statistical Labour Reports*, 1961 and 1976.
35. *RDM*, 18 August 1973.
36. Legassick and Wolpe (1976).
37. Roger Leys (1975); also Bardill *et al.* (1977).
38. SAIRR, *A Survey, 1974*, p. 284. The Surveys for 1971–7 carry a wealth of detail upon changing employment patterns in the mining industry.
39. SAIRR, *A Survey, 1977*, p. 261.
40. 'Transkei gets labour and tax pact', *Sunday Times*, 22 February 1976.
41. Statement by Minister of Interior, *Transkei Hansard*, 20 April 1977, p. 215.
42. *Natal Mercury*, 4 May 1974; *Transkei Hansard*, 3 May 1974, p. 307.
43. Statement by Minister of the Interior, *Transkei Hansard*, 11 May 1971, p. 190. The Transkei government assumed greater control over the recruitment process with the passage of the Labour Act of 1977.
44. BENBO (1976), p. 196.
45. ibid., p. 195. Actually, this figure also includes the incomes of whites working in the Transkei. *Per capita* income for blacks works out at R169 (inclusive of incomes of urban 'citizens'). See BENBO (1975), p. 40, Table 6.4.
46. Maree and de Vos (1975), p. 11 and p. 20 (Table 4).
47. *Sunday Times*, 25 December 1977 (quoting report in the *South African Medical Journal*).

48. Maree (1973).
49. BENBO (1975), p. 42, Table 7.1.1.
50. Anonymous (1976b), p. 256.
51. Quoted by Kirby (1976), p. 17. For the same conclusion see *Transkei Annual, 1968*, p. 63.
52. Transkei, *Department of Agriculture and Forestry Annual Report, 1974–1975*, p. 72, Table 34.
53. ibid., *1976–1977* (cited in SAIRR, *A Survey, 1978*, p. 308).
54. Leeuwenburg (1976), p. 7. This survey was completed under the auspices of the Anglo-American Corporation.
55. *Transkei Hansard*, 11 May 1971, pp. 189–90.
56. Leeuwenburg (1976), pp. 13–15.
57. ibid., pp. 15–17.
58. BENBO (1975), p. 31.
59. Innes and O'Meara (1976), pp. 72–3.
60. See in particular Matanzima's annual Budget speeches when he held the portfolio of Finance prior to independence. Note that in early 1980 it was announced that Transkei was formulating a comprehensive five-year development strategy which would be ready for consideration by March 1981. Professor Gustav Van Beers from the University of Guelph in Canada, the Transkei government's economic adviser, announced that it would have a 'strong spiritual affinity', and would be based on knowledge, love, loyalty, truth and integrity. Elaborating on what he meant by a spiritual affinity, he said that it was unfortunate that God had been replaced by financial institutions and that man's relationship with God, culture and nature had been destroyed. Transkei's first five-year plan would essentially be geared to making Transkeians happy and, he added, 'it's no good expressing happiness in terms of *per capita* income'. (This is, of course, most appropriate in the context of Transkei.) Professor Van Beers also stressed that South Africa was Transkei's only major donor and friend: 'Cooperation with South Africa must be the key word.' (*RDM*, 24 January 1980.)
61. Department of Information, *South Africa 1974* (cited by Kirby, 1976, p. 17); BENBO (1976), p. 79.
62. *To The Point* (Supplement), 8 October 1976.
63. *Tomlinson Report*, pp. 72–7.
64. *Financial Mail*, 22 October 1976.
65. *RDM*, 19 July 1977.
66. Lipton (1972b).
67. *Tomlinson Report*, pp. 117–19.
68. Lipton (1972b).
69. *Tomlinson Report*, pp. 117–29
70. ibid., p. 77.
71. Nieuwhuysen (1964).
72. *Financial Gazette*, 20 July 1973.
73. For one survey of agricultural policy, see Horrell (1973), pp. 80–3; and for the implementation of such policy in Bophuthatswana and Kwazulu, see Butler *et al.* (1977), pp. 179–201.
74. *Transkei Hansard*, 26 April 1976, p. 176 and 27 April 1976, p. 185.
75. ibid., pp. 176–87.
76. ibid., 12 April 1976, p. 115.

77. Interview with official, 25 February 1977. (The acquisition of Herschel and Glen Grey by Transkei provided a further eleven co-operatives, bringing the total to twenty-nine, by the end of the year 1976–7, SAIRR, *A Survey, 1978*, p. 308.)
78. *Farmers Weekly*, 20 October 1976; interview with Transkei Director of Agriculture, 3 August 1976.
79. Agriculture and Forestry, *Annual Report 1974–75*, p. 71, Table 33. Interview with official, 25 February 1977.
80. *Transkei Hansard*, 10 April 1974, p. 175.
81. ibid., 12 May 1971, p. 214.
82. Minutes of the (Special) Meeting of Emigrant Thembuland Regional Authority, 18 September 1969.
83. ibid.
84. ibid., 15 May 1975.
85. ibid., 29 August 1975.
86. Department of Agriculture and Forestry, *Annual Report 1974–75*, p. 13.
87. Barclays Bank (1977), p. 9. On group farming as applied to The Ncora scheme, see 'Transkei Farming: Bold New Projects', *Financial Mail*, 19 October 1979.
88. Lipton (1972), pp. 266–7.
89. *Transkei Hansard*, 7 May 1974, p. 319.
90. BENBO (1975), p. 47.
91. For example, Venda, christened the 'Ceylon' of Southern Africa, is also expanding the production of tea. Similarly, the Transkei forest areas of Umzimkulu reportedly provide about one-third of Natal's total timber requirements. However, this aspect of bantustan policy needs more detailed research.
92. BENBO (1975), p. 45.
93. Thus the *Sunday Tribune*, 20 February 1977: 'With 80,000 hectares of new forest land being sought, a socio-economic survey is needed to determine what must be done for families displaced from their tribal allotments.'
94. *Tomlinson Report*, pp. 131–44.
95. For example, Board of Trade and Industries, Report no. 219 (1936).
96. Thus Verwoerd: 'I think it would be catastrophic for the present economic development of South Africa to establish subsidised white industries in Native areas in competition with the existing white industries.' (*HAD*, 28 March 1957, col. 3749.)
97. Adendorff (1962), p. 68.
98. Horrell (1973), p. 72; SAIRR. *A Survey, 1974*, p. 215.
99. TDC: 'Information for Potential Investors in Transkei', April 1976, Umtata.
100. *Eastern Province Herald*, 2 June 1976.
101. Snelling (1974).
102. ibid., pp. 8–9.
103. Survey by University of Witwatersrand Wages and Economics Commission, reported in *Sunday Tribune*, 2 February 1975.
104. *Daily News*, 12 March 1973.
105. *Natal Mercury*, 23 April 1977.
106. *Transkei Hansard*, 11 March 1975, p. 122; 2 April 1976, pp. 70–1.
107. Statement by Matanzima to businessmen and industrialists in Johannes-

burg, reported in *Natal Mercury*, 23 April 1975. For government views on the alleged 'communistic' role of trade unions, see *Transkei Hansard*, 4 May 1977, p. 323.
108. *RDM*, 9 October 1974; *Natal Mercury*, 30 January 1975; *Imvo Transkei*, 23 December 1978.
109. SAIRR, *A Survey, 1978*, p. 260.
110. Male operators were earning R9 a week or approximately R36–40 a month. The PDL for the Transkei in December 1968 was calculated by Maree and de Vos (1975, p. 21) as amounting to R54 a month.
111. *Daily Dispatch*, 6 August 1976; interview with manager of Pep Homeland Industries factory in Transkei, July 1976.
112. SAIRR, *A Survey, 1979*, p. 287. Basic weekly rates of pay were now R8 for women and R10·12 for men.
113. *Transkei Government Gazette*, 2, 55, 30 September 1977.
114. *The Times* (London), 17 April 1973. See also the *Guardian* (London), 23 April 1975.
115. Leeuwenburg (1977), p. 8.
116. See p. 237 below.
117. XDC, *Tenth Annual Report* (1975), pp. 27–8.
118. The survey that follows, while not comprehensive, seeks to present a broadly accurate picture of industrial investment as at the end of 1978.
119. Horrell (1973), p. 72.
120. Mbeki (1964), pp. 89–91.
121. *TTCA Congress*, 1972.
122. *Eastern Province Herald*, 7 April 1977. Similarly, after the South African authorities had provided technical advice, it was announced in late 1979 that the Transkeian government would underwrite a R7 million share issue (to be floated by the Rand Merchant Bank and Jeanne Sterianos, a Johannesburg stockbroking company) to attract South African investors to provide funds for a Transkei Building Society. (*RDM*, 11 September 1979.)
123. *Transkei Hansard*, 25 May 1971, p. 279.
124. *Natal Mercury*, 1 December 1977.
125. *RDM*, 19 August 1977.
126. *The Star*, 29 May 1976; *Daily Dispatch*, 1 June 1977.
127. *Commercial Transport Freight*, August 1977.
128. Survey of industrial concerns at Butterworth undertaken by the author in July 1976 (henceforth cited as Survey, 1976).
129. *Daily Dispatch*, 1 June 1977.
130. *Financial Mail*, Special Survey, 'Top Companies', 29 March 1968.
131. *Daily Dispatch*, 2 June and 1 September 1975; *Financial Gazette*, 24 June 1977.
132. *RDM*, 19 January 1978.
133. *Cape Argus*, 25 June 1974; *RDM*, 17 May 1977; Survey (1976).
134. *Sunday Times*, 6 May 1973; *Imvo Transkei*, 20 November 1976. Butakem is now 50 per cent owned by Associated Engineering (AE & CI), the South African-owned chemical giant.
135. Survey (1976).
136. *RDM*, 11 February 1976.
137. *Germiston Advocate*, 11 July 1975.
138. *Daily Dispatch*, 24 February 1977.

139. *The Star*, 14 June 1977.
140. Survey (1976).
141. SAIRR, *A Survey, 1978*, p. 315.
142. Press release (undated): 'Gigantic new hotel/casino development on northern Transkeian coast'. It is not irrelevant to note that the number of South African tourists going to Transkei dropped following the April 1978 break in diplomatic relations.
143. *The Star*, 14 June 1976.
144. Snelling (1974); and Blausten (1974). See also his article (1976).
145. *Financial Mail*, 1 August 1975.
146. Survey (1976).
147. *Weekend Post*, 25 July 1975; *Daily Dispatch*, 12 September 1975; Survey (1976).
148. *Financial Mail*, 26 July 1974; *New Equipment News*, April 1977.
149. Survey (1976).
150. *Daily News*, 15 February 1978; *Evening Post*, 18 February 1978.
151. *Pretoria News*, 15 February 1978.
152. *Home Goods Retailing*, February 1978.
153. *Financial Gazette*, 21 November 1975; *Daily Dispatch*, 1 November 1975.
154. *Sunday Times*, 6 June 1976.
155. *RDM*, 1 February 1977. The TDC reportedly established thirty-three new industries in Transkei during 1977–8 (representing a current investment of R41 million) and leading to the creation of 3,500 new jobs; but not all these developments were mutually exclusive of many of those projects detailed above.
156. *Pretoria News*, 21 October 1976; *RDM*, 18 February 1978.
157. The survey undertaken in July 1976 was not able to ascertain wage rates for all firms or to determine the exact numbers of men and women employed at the different factories. However, generally it seemed that at that time skilled workers were generally employed on a scale of 45–65 cents an hour, while unskilled workers generally received from as low as 11 cents to 42 cents an hour. The survey also confirmed Leeuwenberg's finding (1976, p. 18) that a substantial majority of those employed in these industries are women, who are consistently employed at cheaper rates than men.

Chapter 8
The politics of bantustan 'independence'

When Transkei became 'independent' on 26 October 1976, it was *officially* transformed from an African homeland to a discrete nation-state, the Republic devolving formal political sovereignty upon an auxiliary petty-bourgeois class, while simultaneously maintaining the economically exploitative relationship that tied the reserve satellite to the core. The political objectives of the two main contracting parties, the South African and Transkeian governments, to the transfer of power were closely related, yet they were by no means wholly symmetrical. Thus the aims of the Republican authorities would seem to have been, *inter alia*: to promote long-term white supremacy by further entrenching political divisions among the subordinate African majority through the grant of sovereign independence to one tribal group; to impress external observers with the solid gains that Africans might make by following the path of separate development; and, hopefully, to encourage evolutionary as opposed to revolutionary trends in black politics by granting concessions to the Transkeian middle class, thereby holding out the prospect to the growing African petty-bourgeoisie in the Republic that a significant distribution of power might be negotiated peacefully in their favour within the framework of the existing order.

For the Transkeian government, on the other hand, the declared objectives of accepting independence were, principally, to take advantage of the possibilities offered by separate development to enlarge the area of freedom (territorially and politically) for South African blacks; to reduce the number of Africans under white minority rule; and – by easing the fears of the racially dominant majority – to contribute to an atmosphere in South Africa wherein whites would come to perceive their interests as being to bargain with blacks as equals, and thereby to work towards a racially just and equitable political order.[1] In addition, it may well be argued with Laurence that elements among the Transkeian political leadership avowed an exclusive Xhosa nationalism, with Kaiser Matanzima's own intention being to restore 'Xhosa hegemony in the lands historically occupied by the Xhosa people'.[2]

The emphasis in the present work has been upon the advantages that have accrued to the Transkeian petty-bourgeois class as the bantustan programme has advanced, these predisposing it to an acceptance of the goal of ethnic separation from blacks in the rest of the Republic. In other words, it has been proposed that material gain was a significant factor in motivating privileged elements in the Transkei to opt for political independence. Yet it was necessary for this petty-bourgeoisie to clothe its material interests in a political ideology that was both believable and believed; and it would be unduly cynical to suggest that the majority of the Transkeian political élite who espoused independence did so in anything but the terms of the officially propounded justification – for implicit in the Transkeian authorities' acceptance of independence is the notion that it is possible for a politically autonomous, but economically dependent, territory to redefine its relationship to the metropole in its own favour. It is necessary, therefore, to take this claim seriously; and accordingly an attempt will now be made to examine the politics of independence in Transkei by posing the following questions: to what extent has the devolution of political authority genuinely extended the area of human freedom? What is the degree of political autonomy that has been devolved upon the leadership? And has independence increased Transkei's bargaining power relative to the white core state? There does, of course, exist a considerable danger that misplaced conclusions will be reached by searching for generalizations based upon the experience of the few years that have passed since independence, and caution must be exercised lest matters of temporary importance are treated as matters of more lasting moment – but it is only upon the basis of empirical survey that the significance of homeland quasi-sovereignty may be assessed. However, it is necessary first to focus upon the independent Transkei's quest for international legitimation, for this was the major preoccupation of the Matanzima government after the handover of office by Pretoria in 1976.

The search for recognition

Unlike former African colonies which had previously emerged to independence with the consent of the decolonizing power, Transkei – as a bantustan – was denied acceptance as an independent entity into the world community of states. The question of recognition was only *one* of those crucial factors which were to determine whether Transkei was to be regarded as an independent state, yet its denial was critical in that it is only widespread international acceptance of a state as a state (especially in the case of small countries) which legitimizes the standing of a territory's rulers. Hence the Transkeian authorities were particularly active in their efforts to gain recognition, for not only would this facilitate the homeland's access to international aid, but it would also legitimize the class interests of the ruling petty-bourgeoisie, which otherwise rested only upon the ultimately precarious foundations of South African sponsorship. In addition, the ruling elements were doubtless aware that, given the long-term uncertainties of Southern African regional politics, recognition (or perhaps even widespread *de facto* acceptance falling short of recognition) might impart to Transkei a potential permanence robust enough to enable it to outlast a revolutionary upheaval in the Republic, while at a less momentous level international acceptance might increase Umtata's weight and influence (however marginal that might be) in shaping the course of future events throughout the entire region.

If for the South African government the independence of Transkei demonstrated its good faith towards its subordinate African peoples, the argument most favoured by Transkeian policy-makers was that independence validated the TNIP's claim to having liberated the homeland from colonial domination. Posing as conventional African nationalists who had rolled back the tide of white supremacy, the bantustan regime suggested that colonial Transkei, which was initially ruled by the Cape, was a separate politico-legal entity akin to the former Higher Commission Territories, but one which had had the misfortune of being absorbed into South Africa when the Colony had joined the Union in 1910, whereas 'the conspiracy of history' (*sic*) had earlier decreed that these other lands should become British Protectorates (after Basutoland and British Bechuanaland had earlier been annexed by Cape Colony and Swaziland by the Transvaal Republic). Had it not been for this 'accident of fate', so it was argued, Transkei would have been decolonized by Britain rather than by the apartheid regime, and would thus have been accepted without demur into the international community of states.[3]

Recognition of Transkei was also urged upon a variety of other grounds. Thus the new republic was cited as meeting the criteria generally demanded of a state: defined boundaries, a settled population, a stable government in effective control of its territory, absolute sovereignty over its own affairs, and so on. Secondly, it was argued that Transkeian citizens had been the unwilling victims of apartheid, should not be further penalized and that international ostracism would reinforce dependence upon South Africa. Thirdly, with an eye to western favour, it was hinted that as Transkei favoured a free enterprise system it would serve as a bulwark against communism; and finally, reference was often made to 'the struggle' which 'the freedom-loving people of the Transkei' had urged for independence. Although revolutionary violence had been eschewed in a circumstance where it was both militarily inappropriate and politically unnecessary, the homeland leadership now proclaimed that the 'oppressed people of the Transkei' had never once abandoned their idea of regaining self-determination and the right to rule themselves.[4]

Whatever the merits of such arguments (and they will not detain us here),[5] their initial impact upon the international community was minimal. Though all were invited, no heads of black African states attended Transkeian independence celebrations;[6] the United Nations called upon its member governments to deny Transkei any form of recognition; and the Organization of African Unity was unanimous in following suit (with Transkeian officials who flew to Gabon to attend the annual conference of the OAU being expelled from that country by the host government).⁷ It was only the South African government that extended to Transkei the diplomatic acknowledgement that it sought, with admission to the International Tug-of-War Federation being otherwise the major instance of international acceptance!⁸ In addition, neighbouring Lesotho received aid and sympathy from the international community in response to Maseru's refusal to recognize Transkei and its insistence that the border posts along the common frontier with the independent homeland had now been closed as points of access to the Republic in violation of an agreement signed in 1973.⁹ Again, although there were certain western interests which were outspokenly sympathetic to Transkei, western governments – notably those of the United States and the United Kingdom – were careful not to give any hint of recognition (although neither did they explicitly rule out that possibility for the future). Unwilling to give offence to black African trading partners or to upset remaining hopes for an internationally acceptable settlement in Rhodesia, they cautiously followed the OAU line, none of them willing to endorse the potential fragmentation of the apartheid Republic into a white heartland and a series of black, peripheral states.¹⁰

The refusal of the UN to admit Transkei was condemned unanimously by the territory's National Assembly, and during his speech to the motion Kaiser Matanzima roundly accused the world body of applying double standards towards the concept of Transkeian self-determination. In particular, he singled out the United Kingdom for attack, arguing that its refusal to acknowledge Transkei was consistent with its historical role in suppressing blacks in South Africa; and he concluded by accusing the UN of having become dominated by leftist and communist ideologies.¹¹ Yet such bitter attack (repeated at regular intervals during following years)¹² was of no immediate avail, and no single country (bar the Republic) proved itself willing to defy the international ban; and Transkei remained barred not only from the Southern African Customs Union with Botswana, Lesotho and Swaziland, but also from joining other regional organizations such as the Southern African Regional Tourism Council.¹³ Paradoxically, the few contacts that were made with foreign governments seemed to illustrate the extent of Transkei's isolation rather than the reverse. An official delegation from Ecuador was received in Umtata in April 1977, and a similar group from Transkei visited Taiwan later in the same year, but while both these minor countries expressed willingness to co-operate in matters of mutual interest, neither indicated that they were considering recognition.¹⁴ Kenya reportedly granted Transkei permission to use Nairobi as a base for a so-called 'roving ambassador', but otherwise referred the territory's officials to the OAU.¹⁵ And although the Transkeian Foreign Minister, Mr Digby Koyana, visited the Ivory Coast as a guest of the Ivorian government in August 1978,¹⁶ the African initiative received a setback with the accession to power of the Mugabe regime in Zimbabwe in April 1980, for friendly overtures had previously been made to (and apparently not disdained by) the predecessor government of Bishop Abel Muzorewa.[17]

Apart from these few direct contacts with governments, there were continuing efforts by the Transkeian Department of Foreign Affairs and Information to promote Transkei's image abroad. Direct representations were made to political or other interested parties that would listen (as when Koyana spoke in 1977 to a group of British Conservative MPs), and by early 1978 Transkei information centres had been established in Washington, New York, London, Copenhagen, Zurich, Beirut, Bulawayo and Salisbury. There were, in addition, increasing numbers of foreign visitors, journalists and potential investors to Transkei and, importantly, officials (and others) seemed to experience little difficulty in travelling on Transkeian passports.[18] However, after four years of independence, Transkei remained in international quarantine, with little apparent prospect of making diplomatic advance in the immediate future; yet despite this failure to make progress, the Transkeian attempt to gain recognition assumes significance in that it provides the background against which political developments evolved at home.

The deracialization of Transkei

From the time of the 1963 elections onwards, the key ideological difference between the major political parties in the Transkei related to their varying approaches to race relations and the associated separationist/integrationist political alternatives for the future of South Africa. Thus from the beginning the Democratic Party explicitly rejected National Party policy and argued for the goal of a racially mixed and unified Republic, where there was no differentiation between persons on a basis of colour or creed. In short, the DP objective was the attainment of a liberal democratic society, a goal which in the context of apartheid was versed in terms of a philosophy of 'multiracialism', this being most eloquently voiced by the (then) Leader of the Opposition, Mr Knowledge Guzana:

> ... if interests between the different racial groups happen to differ then they must be the subject of consultation, not the subject of antagonism. As this side of the House has repeatedly said, adjustment of race relations in South Africa is based on a spirit of give and take, and the White man who has all should give some to the Black man who has none, but neither shall give up all so that the other has all, and that what we have we will enjoy because we share with what they have, and what they have they will enjoy because they have it with us.[19]

But multiracialism was condemned as unrealistic by the TNIP, which under the helm of the Matanzimas was from its earliest days adamant in its support of separate development as the only practical method for achieving black advance.

Separate development, as advocated by the TNIP, consisted of two main elements. The first was an emphasis upon the right of ethnic groups in South Africa to maintain their identity by opting for political independence. The territorial separation of diverse peoples were thus perceived not merely as a tactic for eroding white supremacy, but as a goal whose attainment was in itself naturally desirable. As voiced by Matanzima in March 1974, the objective (which was happily coincident with Republican government policy) was therefore to deliberately unscramble South African history:

> Apartheid is segregation. I've long been opposed to it; I've been opposed to segregation of any kind. I regret that this has ever been a policy in South Africa, because it has complicated matters now. I feel that if we lived as South Africans, and at the same time retained our areas where we lived without any restrictive laws about the movement of our people, relations in this country would have been very good. I don't think anybody would like to see integration of races in any way. It has not happened anywhere. It has not happened in America, in Great Britain. The national identity of all groups has been maintained. You find the Chinese people by themselves, the Jews by themselves and so on. That is the position which you find in this country. You find the Tswana people. You find the Sotho people. You find the Zulu people. Therefore I don't think it was necessary to pass legislation to maintain this national identity of groups.
>
> I am opposed to apartheid. I am opposed to segregation. I think the people should enjoy human rights equally. Nevertheless, I also subscribe to the policy of territorial independence of people. That is the policy of the National Government of South Africa, of the Afrikaners ...
>
> In any event, we find ourselves in a situation where we have to seek independence because of the South African situation. It is the only way in which we can live happily in this country.[20]

This emphasis upon ethnic self-determination was then complemented by the second major strand in TNIP philosophy, namely a black exclusivism which consisted both of a rejection of inherent white supremacy and an insistence upon the advance of Africans within their own areas. At times, this aspect took on an advocacy of 'racial integrity', with Kaiser Matanzima himself going on record as being a firm believer in 'racial purity', favouring an absolute bar on cross-racial sexual contact.[21] Consequently, during the earlier days of the self-governing period, the TNIP leadership evinced considerable ambiguity about the desirability and possibilities of future racial mixing within the territory, while the Minister of Justice, Mr George Matanzima, was wont to argue that what was denied to blacks within South Africa should for equality's sake be denied to whites within the Transkei:

> ... the disabilities suffered by our people in the Republic must be suffered in the Transkei by the white people ... We have long pleaded with the white people that we want to be on the same level and enjoy the same privileges as they enjoy in the Republic ... they do not even want to hear of it and they tell us straightforwardly that we shall never get that ... It is my wish ... that, as envisaged in our policy, when we get our independence in the Transkei all the

hotels in the urban areas will be owned by Africans and when a white person wants to stay at a hotel he will occupy a back room. A tooth for a tooth.[22]

Yet such a preference was politically insensitive to the need of the Transkei to secure international support and recognition, so that with the approach of independence, racial attitudes expressed by the party leadership became more moderate, even though they remained rather equivocal in regard to wholly unobstructed integration. Thus Kaiser Matanzima, in his policy speech for the year 1975–6, expounded upon separate development as a means

> ... to restore personal dignity to Black and Brown South Africans and gradually to condition Whites to the equality, in every way, of Black and Brown people who meet the requisite norms. In this way the social intercourse between the various population groups will, in time, assume a profile acceptable to all population groups here and, more importantly, to the rest of Africa and the world. Re-admission of White South Africans to the world society from which they are increasingly isolated and a prosperous contented Southern Africa is the prize.[23]

Such a position, versed in quasi-apartheid, pluralistic terminology as it was, did not yet conform to internationally accepted norms, yet it none the less indicated that Matanzima was becoming rather more pragmatic towards the issue of race. However, this increasing flexibility was not immediately reflected in either the Transkei's Constitution Act (1976) or in South Africa's Status of the Transkei Act (1976) which together devolved independence upon the homeland, for neither law repealed the Prohibition of Mixed Marriages Act (no. 55 of 1949) or the Immorality Act (no. 23 of 1957). Whether this was because the Vorster government was reluctant to offend *Verkrampte* elements within the *volk*, or whether the Matanzimas themselves were wary of footloose whites from the Republic swarming over the borders to engage in otherwise illicit sexual delights (and certainly, prostitution has become a severe social problem in the independent Transkei), the omission was highly prejudicial to the already limited prospects of Transkei gaining recognition at independence, for the retention of such discriminatory laws (regarded by the world community as among the most offensive under apartheid) was sufficient to mark the homeland as an unacceptable offspring of Pretoria.[24]

Yet in virtually every other sphere, the racially discriminatory prohibitions of apartheid were swept aside, for if homeland independence was to increase its internal support it was necessary for white privilege to be visibly displaced. Thus bars (which profited greatly), restaurants, hotels, swimming pools, schools and hospitals (the latter two with minor exceptions) and other such facilities were immediately thrown open to persons of all race at independence (if not before), with income replacing colour as the primary determinant of who might enjoy the fruits of integration, while multiracial elections took place in 1977 when towns throughout the homeland elected municipal councils. Racially mixed local governments were chosen by predominantly black voters in most of the larger towns, with four Africans and four whites being elected in Idutywa, and six whites and two Africans in Engcobo, while five whites and five blacks running as a team were returned in Umtata.[25] Finally, after some delay and following the passage of a motion favouring their abolition in the National Assembly in 1977, the Immorality and Prohibition of Mixed Marriages Acts were repealed in 1978.[26]

Of necessity, the abolition of discriminatory measures required a transformation in the outlook of the ruling party; and increasingly aware of the need to expunge all manifestations of racism from the statute book if external credibility was to be attained, the TNIP did not hesitate to resort to the time-honoured practice of stealing the Opposition's clothes. But rather than singing the praises of DP-style 'multiracialism', the ruling elements now resorted to a vociferous exhortation of what it termed 'non-racialism', and simultaneously linked such a policy to the claim of having done more to advance the cause of black freedom in South Africa than any of the established liberation movements. Thus Miss Stella Sicgau, Minister of the Interior, argued in London in early 1976 that:

> The Transkei has ... liberated 18,000 square miles with the nation thereon from the grips of apartheid – the pass laws, job-reservation, apartheid at our post offices and segregation at the numerous beaches along our 200-mile beautiful coast. All these were the order of the day in the Transkei until they were gradually eradicated from the surface of our soil by the activities of the ruling Transkei National Independence Party and its Parliamentary majority over the last few years.[27]

Non-recognition of Transkei as advocated by 'so-called anti-apartheid forces' was now depicted as wholly displaced, for TNIP policy was dedicated to the creation of a racially open society throughout the whole of Southern Africa. 'Transkei's total rejection of apartheid is clearly expressed in its declared policy of non-racialism,' declared the official line. 'The people of Transkei share no responsibility for the apartheid policy';[28] and with an eye to the international stage, Transkei was now presented as a haven of interracial peace.

If apartheid is viewed from a narrow perspective whereby it is defined as white-ordained racial discrimination, then it has clearly been abolished within Transkei. Yet from an alternative and broader perspective, the elimination of racial segregation may be viewed as a *deracialization* rather than a dissolution of apartheid. In other words, while the incorporation of the bantustan as a supplier of cheap labour to the South African economy is in no way affected, the subordinated Transkeian population is no longer subjected to racial humiliations within the restricted confines of the homeland territorial area. If this is an advance, it objectively functions so as to make apartheid more tolerable to the dominated, thereby imparting stability to the broader political economy.

Furthermore, given that their relative wealth ordains that they are the primary beneficiaries of the racial relaxations, the homeland petty-bourgeoisie is co-opted in greater measure into the system of domination. Thus although homeland independence may indeed have widened the scope of African political autonomy, it has not necessarily weakened white control over the core area, for by adding to the complexity of the polity and obscuring the cheap-labour-centred nature of apartheid, it may rather serve to divert popular grievance away from the real power holders in South Africa on to their financially beholden subordinates in Umtata.[29]

Change and continuity in Transkeian politics

While the purely social arena within Transkei has been freed from overt racial constraints, the deracialization of apartheid has been further advanced, not merely by the Africanization of the homeland state apparatus but also by the indigenization of the processes of political control, this being most critically operative within the sphere of security.

It was the hope of many observers that an independent Transkei would seek to create a liberal and open society by ridding itself of all the various repressive encumbrances associated with apartheid. Furthermore, the repeal of South African security legislation was widely deemed as being essential to the quest for recognition as such laws had come to symbolize the repugnant nature of the white supremacist regime. But the response of the bantustan leadership was to change only the symbols of apartheid and not the substance, for although all security measures applicable in South Africa were repealed under the Transkeian Public Security Act of 1977, the major provisions of the Suppression of Communism Act, the Internal Security Act, and Riotous Assemblies Act, the Unlawful Organizations Act and Proclamation 400 were incorporated into the new law. Thus although the state of emergency existing since 1963 was formally lifted after independence, the Minister of Justice was empowered to reimpose it if he deemed such action necessary and to ban gatherings of more than ten persons or to prohibit individuals from attending them. Provision was also made for the banning of persons, detentions without trial and arrest without warrant, while the State President was similarly enabled to authorize chiefs to expel individuals from their area of authority, either permanently or for a specified period. It was also made illegal to belong to any organization declared unlawful, or to make statements or commit acts likely to cause hostility between population groups; and finally, it became an offence to help or harbour terrorists or to disseminate the view that Transkei should form part of another state (the maximum penalty for such a clearly political offence being death).[30]

The Public Security Act was accompanied by the passage of various other measures designed to bolster the repressive powers of the independent government. Censorship along the South African pattern (with all publications already banned by Pretoria remaining outlawed in Transkei) was adopted under a Publications Act (1977), while the Aliens and Travellers Control Act (1977) provided for the registration of all aliens and for the expulsion from Transkei of all persons deemed undesirable, adopting the South African device of allowing the issue of one-way exit permits to Transkeian citizens whose removal might be considered politically inconvenient. Secondly, the Intelligence Service and State Security Act of 1977 made provision (in George Matanzima's words) for 'the continuation of the activities previously exercised in Transkei by the South African Bureau for State Security'.[31]

When these draconian measures were first published, a number of critics warned that the adoption of quasi-South African security legislation would damage Transkei's prospects for international recognition; and indeed, probably as a result of this criticism, the government dropped a clause in the Public Security legislation which would have maintained the banning of organizations prohibited in South Africa (notably the ANC and PAC). However, the gap left by this omission was plugged in May 1978 by the passage of the Undesirable Organizations Act, whose primary objective was to enable the authorities to take action against bodies which could not be appropriately dealt with under the provisions of the Security Act, but whose activities were none the less deemed prejudicial to the interests of the state. Ironically, it was not any doings of any established protest or liberation movement which spurred the passage of this Act, but rather a report that the annual conference of the Methodist Church of South Africa in 1977 had decided that it would terminate an existing practice whereby messages of goodwill would be sent to the Republican President, as this would also necessitate sending a similar message to the President of Transkei, an action which ran counter to the views of Methodist clergy who were opposed to and did not recognize Transkei. Subsequently, in January 1978, Matanzima (himself a Methodist) announced his intention to ban the Methodist Church of South Africa in Transkei; and on 17 February, a day after meeting the Reverend Abel Hendricks, the President of the Methodist Conference, he banned all foreigners from attending a gathering of Methodist ministers and lay representatives which was scheduled for 21 February (this ban obviously being aimed at preventing Hendricks's attendance). The meeting later rejected by 70 votes to 40 Matanzima's threat to ban the Church; but in May, the Undesirable Organizations Bill became law, and in early June the Methodist Church of South Africa was ordered to cease all its activities in Transkei and to hand over all its property within six months. The process of exclusion was completed on 15 June, when a private Bill passed through the Assembly granting legal status to the Methodist Church of Transkei, which had been established on the second day of that month. Most lay persons and ministry went along with the new arrangement, but seventeen clergymen departed from Transkei in protest, with one (the Reverend P. Shone) being deported.[32]

The objective of Transkeian security legislation was clearly to define anew the limits within which opposition was to be tolerated. Thus the only groups which were to be extended unhindered freedom were those which neither questioned the sovereignty of Transkei nor posed a significant political threat to the government. An immediate victim of the Public Security Act, therefore, was the Democratic Party, which despite accommodating to the new law by altering its pre-independence constitution by deleting a statement defining Transkei as an integral part of South Africa,[33] was subject to perpetual harassment, with various of its leaders being almost continuously shuttled in and out of detention. By May 1978, 33 people had been detained in terms of the Act, of whom 27 had been released;[34] but of the six remaining in detention, one was Hector Ncokazi, who was charged with subverting the sovereignty of Transkei. (He was later released, but was redetained in January 1979.) Meanwhile, others who feared prosecution under the security legislation fled the territory, these including a group of students who sought asylum in Botswana, and Dr J. Mlanda, a medical practitioner, who crossed the border to neighbouring Lesotho.[35]

Within the National Assembly, the official Opposition to the government after independence was the Transkei People's Freedom Party, led by Mr Cromwell Diko, a former office-holder in the TNIP, whose breakaway from the ruling party after the 1976 election was widely construed as having been encouraged by Matanzima himself (in order to promote the image of Transkei as a functioning multiparty democracy). With four supporters in contrast to two each for the DP and NDP, the TPFP was the largest Opposition grouping within the parliamentary arena. Yet the entire performance was never convincing, for Diko consistently lent over backwards in support of the government he was allegedly opposing; and indeed, so encompassing was the scope of his eulogies that once a more virile Opposition party emerged, Diko was hastily retired to the government benches in the capacity of a TNIP whip.[36]

If the TPFP was clearly artificially contrived, the breakaway from the TNIP of Pondo and Sotho members of the Assembly in March and April 1978 had not been anticipated by the government. The immediate origins of the split lay in the coerced resignation from the Cabinet of Miss Stella Sicgau (daughter of Botha Sicgau, who had assumed the ceremonial State Presidency at independence). The ostensible grounds for her departure lay in her falling pregnant as a widowed but unmarried woman, but in actuality it is more likely that the Matanzimas were keen to rid themselves of a threat from one of their more able ministers who had been covertly associated with the challenge to their leadership made by Curnick Ndamse in 1973.[37] Following her departure from the government, Sicgau crossed the floor accompanied by five members from the Qaukeni Region of Eastern Pondoland; and by 4 April she had been joined by a further nine members, including Chief Jeremiah Moshesh (the traditional leader of the Transkeian Basotho along the border with Lesotho), who at the time of independence had been demoted from a long-held place in the Cabinet to the more lowly post of a 'roving ambassador'. The new grouping then emerged as the Transkei National Progressive Party (TNPP) under Mr Caledon Mda as leader, being recognized as the official Opposition in early May.[38] Remaining TNIP links with the Pondo were then further weakened by the deaths of Botha Sigcau in December 1978, and the assumption of the vacant presidency in February 1979 by Kaiser Matanzima. (In the interim, the latter had resigned as leader of the TNIP, with his brother George being elected in his place. George Matanzima thereafter stepped into his shoes as Prime Minister and assumed executive authority, with Kaiser withdrawing to a less active but still highly influential role.)[39]

The importance of the realignment was not simply the re-emergence of party competition, but rather that it continued the tradition of tribally oriented politics, for the new Opposition was in large measure based upon the dissatisfaction of the Pondo and Sotho rural élites with being excluded from the political centre.[40] This became clearer still in March 1979 when the three Opposition parties (DP, NDP and TNPP) combined to form the Democratic Progressive Party under the leadership of Matanzima's old rival, Paramount Chief Sabata Dalindyebo.[41] Strengthened by the Basotho support brought by Chief Moshesh, the significance of the new grouping lay in its bringing together dissidents from Thembuland and Eastern Pondoland, two regions with a tradition of resistance to the Matanzimas. But in addition, by the incorporation of the Ncokazi DP, the new Opposition sought to broaden its popular base by appealing to all those who had been opposed to Transkeian independence, the influence of the radicals being registered in the manifesto issued at the time of its formation, in which the party pledged itself:

> to help fight for the overthrow of the exclusive white minority regimes in Southern Africa in alliance with other progressive forces so as to establish non-racial democratic governments based on the will of all the people of South Africa; to develop political awareness and promote and project black pride and black solidarity; and to become a platform for the expression of black opinions and represent these internationally.[42]

Fearful of the potential of the new alliance to mobilize broad support, the government moved swiftly to counteract Opposition political activity. Thus following the detention of Mr B. C. Pikashe (the former national organizer of the now extinct DP), Sabata Dalindyebo himself was detained in early July on the capital charge of undermining the dignity of the State President, and disseminating views subverting Parliament and the sovereignty of Transkei. His chieftaincy was suspended pending the outcome of his trial and his brother (a TNIP MP) appointed as acting tribal head of the Thembu in his place, while access to his village was cordoned off by the security forces. However, the effect of the detention was the opposite of what had been intended, and when Sabata made a preliminary appearance in court, he was greeted by a massive demonstration of 5,000 supporters protesting against his arrest, while Brigadier Cwele, a Thembu and the first Commissioner of Police, was retired from his post for having refused to effect the initial arrest.[43] Subsequently, the defence lawyers subpoenaed Sabata's nephew (who is none other than Nelson Mandela, the imprisoned leader of the ANC) to give evidence in the trial. This immediately raised the political costs to the government of prosecution, for although it was unlikely in the extreme that Mandela would be allowed by the South African authorities to make an appearance in court, his enormous prestige (and that of the ANC) could now be symbolically associated with the detained leader of the TNPP.

Meanwhile, the Transkeian authorities retained Dr Percy Yutar (who had previously appeared for the State in the South African Treason and Rivonia trials) to lead the prosecution. On 19 September, the date set for the trial, thousands of pamphlets were distributed throughout Transkei attacking the territory's independence, calling for Sabata's release, and labelling the Matanzima government a puppet of South Africa. However, the immediate dangers of what was increasingly turning out to be a major political embarrassment to the Transkeian authorities were defused when the defence asked for a postponement of the trial, a request that was readily granted.

Previous to this, the security clampdown had continued, with the arrest of leading members of the Opposition, including Stella Sicgau, Jeremiah Moshesh, Chief Mpondombini Sicgau and Chief Ntzihayesizwe Sicgau (both sons of the late President, and the former the most popular claimant to the vacant paramountcy).[44] They were soon to be released, but arrests were again made in February 1980 when, in order to contain further protest, Security Police detained almost the entire executive of the DPP, together with leaders of its Youth League.[45] Subsequently, in April, in a trial held at Port St Johns (away from Umtata where previously there had been public demonstration in his support), Sabata was found guilty on just one charge of violating and injuring the dignity of the State President, and not guilty on the other charges of subverting the sovereignty of Parliament and the constitutional independence of Transkei. In response to the warning of the Transkeian Attorney General that imprisonment would make the Leader of the Opposition a martyr, Sabata was sentenced to a fine of R700 (or eighteen months' imprisonment), with R200 or six months of the sentence suspended – and he chose the financial penalty.[46] The Matanzima government thereby sought to defuse popular protest; Nelson Mandela had made no appearance in the witness box; and in the event, the trial had been in measure depoliticized. However, even if the authorities had gravely miscalculated the depth of popular opposition that the attack on Sabata would arouse, warning had none the less been given of the severe consequences which might befall those who dared to challenge the regime.

These were to become manifest in the months that followed, as further dramatic changes were registered in the political spectrum. When he returned to his home after his conviction, Sabata Dalindyebo was subject to further harassment, being barred from reassuming his paramountcy. He soon fled from Transkei and disappeared. It was generally speculated that he had sought political asylum in Botswana, Lesotho and/or Swaziland,[47] but all knowledge of his whereabouts was officially denied by these countries' governments until in early December 1980 Sabata appeared at a press conference in Lusaka with Oliver Tambo, Acting President of the ANC, and publicly pledged his support to the liberation movement.[48]

Meanwhile, in a closely related development, Mr S. K. Ndzumo, now the Minister of the Interior, was sacked from the Cabinet after alleging that an attempted *coup*, engineered by dissident police, had been thwarted by the authorities after leading army officers had refused to cooperate.[49] (The reliability of the police had earlier been questioned in Parliament, and in June eleven policemen had been charged with refusing to carry out orders, while several members of the defence force had been detained for allegedly selling firearms and ammunition to civilians, with Kaiser Matanzima further alleging that arms caches had been discovered in Pondoland.)[50] Initially, revelations about the *coup* attempt were dismissed by George Matanzima as untrue, but after further details had been published in the press, the authorities detained Mr Ndzumo and Brigadier Cwele, the former Commissioner of Police who had earlier refused to effect Sabata Dalindyebo's arrest. A few days after he had been taken into custody, Mr Ndzumo (a diabetic) was found dead in his cell, the cause of his death being not immediately established (although probably due rather to negligence of his medical condition than any deliberate intent).[51] Brigadier Cwele, meanwhile, was reported as having been behind a coterie of dissidents who had sought to overthrow the Matanzimas and install the Leader of the Opposition in their place. This grouping was said to be drawn from the military, the civil service and the public as well as from the police; was said to be largely Thembu; and was furthermore alleged to have been spearheaded by a 'Group of Eight' which consisted largely of former members of the ANC and PAC who had returned to Transkei and now worked within the administration (the most prominent of them in Foreign Affairs). However, suggestion that either of the liberation movements was directly involved in the *coup* attempt was discounted, especially as somewhat earlier, in July, a gunman had assassinated Mr Tennyson Makiwane, a former member of the ANC executive who had defected to the Matanzima regime in 1979 (and who was now revealed to have been one of the Group of Eight), and whose violent demise was taken by many to be a warning delivered by the ANC to those who would betray their movement.[52]

Faced with these major cleavages in its institutional and ethnic support, it was therefore something of a triumph for the regime when the Matanzimas enticed Stella Sicgau – who had been in opposition since November 1977 – back into the fold of the TNIP and reappointed her to the Cabinet in Ndzumo's place,[53] her move signifying dramatically the fragility of Opposition activity based largely on ethnic alliance between disparate élite groups which have been excluded from power.

The rise of the DPP had presented the Matanzima government with the gravest threat it had faced since its accession to power. Riding high on a tide of initial popularity, élite groups who were united by a common objection to Emigrant Thembu dominance at the centre had been able to mobilize widespread popular opposition to the TNIP by linking their activities to the wider liberation struggle in South Africa. However, even though the party may continue to provide a focus for continued discontent, the possibility of its providing any fundamental challenge to the bantustan regime is limited. Within the parliamentary arena, the Matanzimas (or whoever follows them) will doubtless deploy patronage sufficiently widely to head off any critical threat to their predominance; and without, they will apply the rules of the bantustan electoral game to guarantee the continuing hegemony of the TNIP. (An Electoral Law Amendment Act passed in 1979 enables the Electoral Officer to refuse to register political parties, while simultaneously raising candidates' deposits from R50 to R400). In any case, the likelihood of a Transkeian Opposition promoted by disaffected members of the chiefly élite developing mass support on anything but a temporary basis is remote, for the chiefs (especially in Eastern Pondoland) remain highly conscious of the disruptive potentialities of popular revolt (as is perhaps illustrated by the return of Stella Sicgau to the government fold). In short, an Opposition chiefly élite will be wary of its becoming politically involved with the liberation movements, for which (as the Dalindyebo trial incident suggests) there is a groundswell of support waiting to be trapped. Indeed, Dalindyebo's now explicit alignment with the ANC may well entail guilt by association for the DPP, which may as a result either dissolve or be directly suppressed by the government as a stalking horse for declared external opponents of the regime. But whatever the immediate fate of the DPP, party competition within Transkei would appear to be doomed to continuing limitation, as the parliamentary Opposition is unlikely to gain sufficient muscle to form a major threat to the TNIP leadership so long as the latter retains its hold over the apparatus of the bantustan state.

Complementary to the moves taken against Sabata Dalindyebo and the DPP has been a concerted attack upon the press. Newspaper offices have been raided on a number of occasions, and reporters have been variously detained, deported and interrogated by the Security Police, so much so that on two occasions ten Umtata-based journalists felt constrained to issue public protests decrying persistent police harassment.[54] More serious, however, was the banning of two Xhosa-language newspapers, *Isaziso* and *Isizwe*, whose editorial policies were hostile to the homelands system. After having been detained twice by the police, their editor, Mr Vuyani Mrwetyana, fled from Transkei and took out political asylum in Lesotho.[55] Then, in April 1980, George Matanzima announced in the Assembly that the East London-based *Daily Dispatch*, the newspaper with the largest circulation in Transkei, had been banned because of 'its long record of persistent false reporting'.[56] The more immediate reason, however, was its publication of a rumour that twenty-five tribesmen had been arrested in connection with an assassination attempt upon Kaiser Matanzima (and indeed, one of the paper's journalists, Mr Richard Wickstead, was subpoenaed by the state to appear as a witness at an *in camera* inquiry into a charge of attempted murder). Subsequently, after representatives of the newspaper met Kaiser Matanzima, the ban on the *Dispatch* was lifted, but not until after Brigadier Martin Ngceba, Chief of the Transkeian Security Police, had summoned Umtata's journalists before him and warned them to report in a 'patriotic' and 'responsible manner.[57]

Of greater long-term significance than the moves taken against either the official Opposition or the press has been the utilization of the security laws to contain other elements perceived as posing a more explicit subversive threat to the bantustan regime. Five blacks were sentenced in 1977 to terms of imprisonment under the Suppression of Communism Act for allegedly establishing communist cells in the Umtata, Cala, Idutywa and Xalanga districts in the pre-independence period, despite claims by the defence advocate that the law was not applicable in Transkei after independence.[58] In addition, there was a security clampdown upon all manifestations of the black consciousness movement, with Kaiser Matanzima advancing vague allegations that SASO and BPC were training soldiers to attack Transkei – and when these organizations were later prohibited in the Republic, the action met with the express approval of the Transkeian government.[59] But most symbolically of all, after an initial period when the ANC and PAC had not been specifically outlawed, they were later included among a motley group of thirty-four political, religious and journalistic organizations (including the South African Council of Churches, Chief Buthelezi's Inkatha movement, SWAPO, the South African Communist Party and the South African Congress of Trade Unions) which were banned under the Public Security Act of 1977.[60] Thus although the Matanzimas have at times made play with the notion of Transkei as a base for the liberation movements, the bantustan authorities have in practice closely aligned themselves with the apartheid regime.

For all the panoply of official power, popular resistance to the bantustan government is mounting, with local grievances becoming increasingly linked to the broader struggle against apartheid. On New Year's Day 1977, two Pondo were shot dead during an attack upon a police station,[61] and in September the police and army were reported to have invaded an obscure rural location and arrested over 200 men. Stories circulated about arms being smuggled into Bizana from Natal, while a police sergeant was hacked to death near Flagstaff in November 1979, police later scouring the local hills and effecting the arrest of 162 people. In April 1980 several people were arrested close to Kaiser Matanzima's Qamata home. The police attempted to suppress the story and, when they failed, announced that those arrested were only common stock thieves, yet suspicion remains that this was yet another assassination attempt upon the unpopular Paramount.[62] This was followed in May by an ambush of police in the Lusikisiki district, and in September army and police rounded up 300 men at Ilinge, near Lady Frere, and ordered them to report to the local police station.[63]

That much of the violent resistance was centred in Pondoland did not go unnoticed, and in a frank speech on the occasion of the installation of the successor to Botha Sicgau as Paramount, Kaiser Matanzima made reference to the rebellion of the early 1960s, and warned that the Security Act would be utilized to deal with people who associated with 'subversive elements'.[64] Subsequently, in May 1980, the Security Act was tightened up so that people accused of sabotage or terrorism need not be brought before the Supreme Court;[65] and the need to contain the mounting challenge to its rule suggests that in future the Transkeian government will become increasingly reliant upon the security forces.

Sporadic violence has been accompanied by widespread unrest in the schools and tertiary educational institutions. Indeed, so widespread were the disturbances in early 1980 that in June the Transkeian government declared a state of emergency, the enabling proclamation restricting the movement of scholars or students so that they might not leave a municipal area without the permission of a magistrate or the local police.[66] Earlier, at the official opening of the new university, the principal, Professor B. van der Merwe, had given strict warning that the university had to operate within the Transkeian system of law and order, and that political militants would not be tolerated.[67] However, this was not sufficient to curb student dissidence, which was soon after to result in the expulsion of nine and the rustication of a further six students, the latter including Kaiser Matanzima's own daughter, together with the son of Tsepo Letlaka, now the Minister of Justice.[68]

The significance of such widespread unrest is that it has been officially ascribed to the increasing influence of the ANC and PAC, both of which, according to George Matanzima, have been 'strongly resuscitated' within Transkei.[69] This is not merely scapegoating, for it seems certain that one or both of the liberation movements have been active in Transkei since independence. In late 1978 the Transkeian authorities apprehended members of the PAC within Transkei and handed them over to the Republic security forces,[70] and in April 1980 Brigadier Nceba confirmed that detainees held in Transkei included 'foreign-trained African National Congress and Pan-Africanist Congress insurgents intent on overthrowing the governments of South Africa, Transkei and Bophuthatswana'.[71] Then, in July 1980, came the assassination of Mr Tennyson Makiwane, a former senior official of the ANC and member of its executive, who had defected to the Transkeian government in mid-1979, accepting a post in the Department of Foreign Affairs. Shot dead at his home in Umtata, it was widely accepted that his death was the work of the ANC who were serving notice that similar treatment would be meted out to others who betrayed them.[72]

With its record of repression since independence, and the fact that it would now seem to be being brought into direct confrontation with the liberation movements, the Transkeian government is inevitably cast into the role of adjutant to Pretoria. Although the dismantling of institutionalized racial discrimination within Transkei may have been welcomed by the majority who live there, the process of deracialization has otherwise been accompanied by, if anything, an intensification of political repression, as the security functions of apartheid are now devolved upon the government of the bantustan. By granting the appearance of fundamental change, deracialization may lighten the frustrations of the African petty-bourgeoisie; but in so far as the bantustan authorities counter the activities of those who are potentially or actually subversive of white supremacy in the neighbouring territory (whether or not their repressive actions are largely designed to protect their own political safety), so will they become yet more clearly aligned with the apartheid regime.

Relations with South Africa

At the time of independence, there were a number of commentators who suggested that, if Transkei were to be shunned diplomatically and economically, then its dependence upon South Africa would be reinforced, thereby rendering doubts as to its lack of political autonomy self-fulfilling. Thus *The Times* of London argued:

> to prove its independence of South Africa the Transkei will necessarily have to be seen to do things inimical to South Africa ... Such a change in policy will obviously be difficult if the Transkei is to remain dependent for ninety per cent of its revenue on South Africa. Yet its only hope of diminishing that dependence is not only to define its citizens in terms of what the state can support, but also to win access to other donors and to international financial institutions from which non-recognition debars it. The world can ensure that Transkei shall remain the prisoner of South Africa, and as such remain rejected and unrecognised.[73]

At the economic level, as suggested in the previous chapter, such an argument is probably overstated, for the amount of international aid and assistance that would be forthcoming for Transkei if it were to be recognized would be unlikely to be sufficient to extricate the homeland from Pretoria's current stranglehold.[74] But to the extent that the political level is separable from the economic, it is more credible that, as proposed by another writer in the *Daily Telegraph*, Transkei might become an unpredictable catalyst in the South African political scene:

> As independence ... approached, Chief Matanzima [became] more and more critical of South Africa's 'unjust society' and outspoken in defence of all its blacks. No one can foresee what might happen if the head of a successful black State, itself a focus for pride among South Africa's black citizens, were to intervene on their behalf in South African politics.[75]

Regardless of the accuracy of this report and the likelihood of its particular forecast, the basic thesis emerges that independence may impart to a homeland government increased bargaining power relative to South Africa. It is the purpose of the present and the following sections to review the extent to which the independent Transkei has been successful in realizing such potential.

Prior to independence, the major strains in relations between the Transkeian and South African governments revolved around the issues of land and citizenship. In neither case did Matanzima advance to independence upon a basis that he considered fully satisfactory. As far as his land demands were concerned, a claim for the incorporation of East Griqualand into Transkei remained outstanding, but he unilaterally reserved to himself the right to bargain for more land later. As regards the citizenship issue, the dispute revolved around the problem of Africans resident in the white areas whom the Republican government wished to designate as Transkeian citizens, thereby depriving them of their South African citizenship. The practical implication of the South African intent was that up to 1·5 million Africans living in the Republic would be legislatively transformed into foreigners in the land of their birth, this being instrumental to the fulfilment of the apartheid dream whereby whites would eventually become a numerical majority within their 'own' territory, with all blacks having allegiance to their ethnic states.

There can be little doubt that the Matanzima government was genuinely reluctant to accept the apartheid definition of citizenship, for aware that the latter was bitterly opposed by the mass of urban blacks as a threat to their security (because of the Republic's resettlement policy), it recognized the issue as one likely to create major difficulties in the future. Accordingly, during the negotiations leading up to independence, Matanzima made a considerable show of standing up to Pretoria by denying that bantustan citizenship was being conferred upon registered Transkeians in the Republic, and stating that they would be offered the option of Transkeian citizenship. However, this interpretation was rejected out of hand by the Minister of Bantu Administration and, when it came to the test, the Constitution Bill (which contained the apartheid definition of citizenship) sailed straight through the TNIP controlled TLA with only one minor amendment. As a result: (1) all Africans born within Transkei; (2) all persons born outside the homeland of Transkeian fathers (or mothers in the case of those born out of wedlock); and (3) all persons who were registered as Transkeians in terms of any law prior to the passing of the Status of Transkei Act (1976) by the Republican government and the Republic of Transkei Constitution Act (1976) by the TLA, were declared Transkeian citizens and were henceforth to be denied title as South African nationals. The key clause was (3), for the Self-Government Act of 1963 had in any case wrapped up the citizenship issue by declaring every African deemed to be of Transkeian origin to be a Transkei national for internal purposes. Thus apartheid citizenship was imposed upon the homeland as the price of its independence; and given that the TNIP was dedicated to the pursuit of sovereignty, it acquiesced on the citizenship issue as the necessary, if unwelcome, cost.[76]

The disputes concerning land and citizenship apart, the independence settlement was otherwise based upon amicable relations between the Matanzima and Vorster governments, with the mutual intention being to pursue a policy of good neighbourliness, which would be formalized by the exchange of diplomats at ambassadorial level. In particular, the independent Transkei was to remain explicitly militarily aligned with Pretoria. Since its creation in 1975, the Transkeian army had been trained and equipped by the South African Defence Force, its role being defined as being primarily concerned with counter-insurgency.[77] Minuscule though it was (plans were announced by Matanzima in 1978 to bring its one and only battalion up to a full strength of 720 men),[78] the army was pledged by the Chief Minister not only to the defence of Transkei, but also to that of the Republic to which the Xhosa allegedly owed their 'renaissance as a people'.[79] Accordingly, military links with South Africa were forged at independence by a Non-Aggression Agreement whereby both governments revoked the use of armed force against each other, forbade the use of their territories as a base for military, subversive and hostile actions against each other, and allowed for the free use of air space and territorial waters by military and naval craft of the other state.[80] It was not surprising, therefore, that the Transkeian army was readily identified as being intended to form a first line of defence against guerrilla incursions by the liberation movements from the north.

For many critics, Transkei's apparently wilful subordination to Pretoria constituted a major reason for ostracizing the independent homeland internationally. Accordingly, there were those who argued that Transkei's best hope for gaining recognition would lie in provocatively dissociating herself from Pretoria by belligerently attacking apartheid after independence. Yet initially, the Transkeian government chose not to follow such a course, and indeed, it rather reinforced its alignment with the metropole when it extended recognition to the politico-geographic curiosity that constitutes Bophuthatswana, when that homeland also became independent in December 1977 (although formal diplomatic ties between the two 'new states' were not established).[81]

However, as time wore on, and no progress was made towards achieving international recognition, the Matanzima government became increasingly receptive to those voices which urged the necessity of distancing itself from South Africa in order to assert its autonomy. But in the event, rather than having to foment a cause for disagreement, the Transkeian regime had merely to follow its nose, as diverse circumstances now ran together to provide grounds for genuine conflict between Umtata and Pretoria.

In the first place, a dispute arose concerning the application of the Republic's population resettlement policy. In early 1977, the South African government expressed its determination to demolish the Crossroads and Unibell squatter settlements in the Cape Peninsula, where it was estimated there were between 120,000 and 180,000 coloureds and approximately 30,000 Africans living in thousands of shacks and shanties.[82] Many of the Africans were wives and children who had accompanied migrant workers to their place of employment and under apartheid law were there illegally, and in consequence these persons were now expected to return to their 'places of origin' which, as the majority were Xhosa-speaking, were deemed to be the Ciskei and Transkei. Meanwhile, male contract workers were to be reaccommodated in single-sex hostels, while the small minority of African families recognized as being together legally were to be given other emergency accommodation. Coloured squatters were to be catered for under a variety of other housing schemes.

Starting in January 1977, local authorities embarked upon a co-ordinated campaign to combat what was termed the 'squatting evil', and as the bulldozers and police moved in, officials made rail tickets available to African wives and children who were in the area illegally to transport them either back to their homeland areas or, in a number of cases, to a resettlement camp on land near Queenstown which was destined for incorporation into Transkei in the near future under agreed consolidation plans.

Between 1960 and 1975, some seventy-four of these townships or resettlement camps had been built in the homelands to accommodate Africans driven out from the Republic. A number of them were designed to function as commuter zones from which workers could migrate on a daily or weekly basis to border industries in white areas, but more often they were (in the words of a BENBO publication) 'without any economic stimulus or opportunities for employment'.[83] But this township development programme had hitherto been considerably more limited in Transkei than in the other homelands (and the resettlement programme in consequence pursued at a slower rate), because of the existence of formerly white towns which were scheduled for complete black takeover. In addition it would seem that, prior to independence, the Transkeian government was able to resist relatively successfully a large influx of repatriates in exchange for the leading role which it was playing in promoting separate development. After October 1976, however, this restraint no longer applied, and the South African government was moved to implement the resettlement of the Cape squatters without further delay.

According to one estimate, nearly 70 per cent of the African squatters were marked out for dispatch to Transkei.[84] But the response of the Transkeian authorities to the evictions was to shift all responsibility on the South African government, on the grounds that Transkei did not have the resources to house or provide work for a large influx of squatters, with Professor M. Njisane, Ambassador to Pretoria, ingenuously doubting the wisdom of having opted for independence. Then, after further heated exchanges between the two governments, the crisis culminated in a top-level meeting between Vorster and Matanzima, with the latter reportedly 'insisting' that Transkei should not be used as a dumping ground for surplus blacks from the Republic. Yet for all Matanzima's protest, negotiation was of little avail, for although a face-saving formula was devised whose main feature was that a September 1977 deadline for the departure of the squatters was extended to 1978 (while arrangements were made for Transkei to receive the repatriates), the end result was much the same, with Transkeian officials having little alternative but to reluctantly advise the homeless to accept the rail warrants offered to them and to remove themselves to their 'homeland'. However, when the Crossroads resettlement issue hit the international headlines, the Transkeian government was encouraged to renew its fight; and following a meeting between the South African Minister of Foreign Affairs, Mr R. F. Botha, and Prime Minister Matanzima on 5 October 1978, it was announced that the Republican government had agreed to move elsewhere the township being built near Queenstown to accommodate the repatriated squatters. Yet this concession was more apparent than real, for it was also announced that Transkeians living in Crossroads would still be resettled in their districts of origin (that is, Transkei) and that a list of these people had been forwarded to the Transkeian Department of Foreign Affairs (although a statement by Matanzima that most of the squatters were Ciskeian suggested that the burden of resettlement might in large part be shifted sideways on to the other Xhosa homeland).[85]

The resettlement dispute was then followed in April 1978 by Transkei's decision to break off diplomatic relations with South Africa. The immediate cause of this was a decision announced by the Republican government that East Griqualand, which had long formed part of the Cape but which had been cut off from the rest of that Province by Transkeian territorial independence (see Map 3), would be transferred to Natal on 1 April 1978. However, Kaiser Matanzima had long claimed East Griqualand as historically Xhosa territory, on the ground that it had been annexed as white land only in 1913 which, coming after the Act of Union, he felt constituted a breach of faith with the people of the

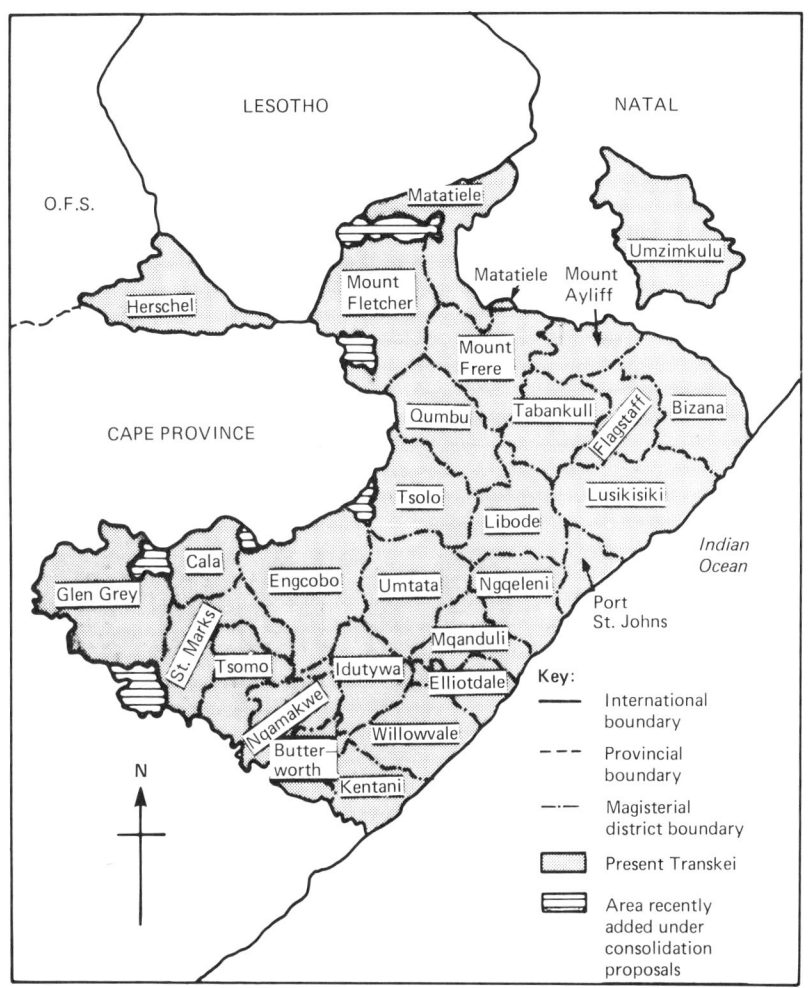

Map 3 *The Transkei at 'independence'*

Transkeian Territories. He had accordingly demanded the handover of East Griqualand (which consisted of the Districts of Elliot, Matatiele, Maclear and Mount Currie) in 1972, at that time protesting his inability to proceed to independence without the return of the disputed land to the Transkei. In the event, of course, he had later accepted independence upon a deal which rested upon the concession of the white towns of Port St Johns and Umzimkulu, plus the additions of Herschel and Glen Grey for Ciskei, but which still denied him possession of East Griqualand. However, when the latter area was separated from the rest of Cape Province in 1976, the South African government had established a Commission of Inquiry to investigate its future status, and when the subsequent report recommended that the enclave be transferred to Natal, Matanzima objected on the grounds that the land in question was not rightly South Africa's to transfer.[86]

Matanzima had informed the TNIP Congress in 1977 that were East Griqualand to be placed under the aegis of Natal, a negotiated settlement of the land issue with South Africa would become impossible.

> The normalisation of harmonious relations between our state and the Republic of South Africa will depend on the transfer of the said land [that is, East Griqualand] to us and no time must be lost in arriving at an amicable settlement ... And since the officials of the Republic of South Africa have embarked upon an abominable campaign by endorsing [Transkeians] out of the Republic of South Africa's cities and farms, the severing of relations between the two countries will be precipitated and by means of an armed struggle for which we will have to prepare, we shall take the land aforesaid under any circumstances for a settlement of our landless population.[87]

Thus when South Africa proceeded with the incorporation of East Griqualand into Natal on 1 April 1978, Matanzima followed up his words of fire by breaking diplomatic relations nine days later, accusing the Republican government of having 'callously slaughtered and butchered millions of blacks in enforcement of their obnoxious apartheid laws', and warning that Transkei would henceforth train its army for a future military confrontation with the whites: 'We have been compelled to join the liberating movements and claim the whole of South Africa as belonging to whites and blacks, with blacks controlling the majority. Henceforth this will be the fundamental policy of our struggle for liberation.'[88]

That Matanzima had given advance warning that Transkei might sever relations with South Africa over East Griqualand is beyond dispute, as the transcript of his speech to the TNIP Congress in 1977 demonstrates. Yet on many occasions past – and notably his bluff that Transkei would never proceed to independence without full settlement of its land claims – Matanzima had failed to match his words and threats with deeds. So, while accepting that the East Griqualand issue formed a genuine bone of contention, it would appear that there were additional factors which underlay the decision to break off diplomatic relations with the Republic.

These other reasons are not difficult to discern. In the first place, there was need for Matanzima to head off further disaffection from the TNIP in favour of the newly formed TNPP. Internal Transkeian politics had long rested on an informal coalition between Thembu, Pondo and Sotho parliamentary élites, and the formation of a tribally oriented Opposition threatened to strike at the heart of this alliance. As it happened, the East Griqualand issue seemed particularly appropriate for retaining the Pondo support that was left for the TNIP, for in Matanzima's own words, 'that land, namely Mount Currie and the Matatiele farms, belongs to Paramount Chief Faku of the Pondo nation'.[89] In addition, of course, the transfer of East Griqualand to Natal coincided temporally with the Stella Sicgau defection from the TNIP, and might thus be exploited by Matanzima to good advantage.

The second factor, so it would appear, would be that with all existing hopes for international recognition dashed, the break was intended to improve Transkei's external image. After fully eighteen months of independence, the 'new state' remained suspended in diplomatic limbo, and unless circumstances were to change substantially there appeared little prospect of reducing this isolation within the foreseeable future. Accordingly, by means of the dramatic action of breaking off relations with South Africa, Matanzima sought to give notice that Transkei would refuse to be cowed by the overbearing weight of its powerful neighbour. And were Pretoria to take any firm retaliatory action, Matanzima clearly hoped that the world community would be put in a position where it would feel under an obligation to come to Transkei's assistance. The breach was therefore a largely symbolic move, whose intent was to enable the bantustan to break out of its diplomatic impasse; but its instrumental value in combating white supremacy was less clear to see, for subsequent moves served only to re-emphasize the image of Transkei as an artificial creation of the apartheid regime.

The limits of 'independence'

The break in diplomatic relations could do nothing in itself to change the structure of Transkei's dependence upon South Africa, and its practical consequence was to lead to a clearer definition of the limits of bantustan political independence. Indeed, it was only a matter of weeks before Transkei was constrained to call for Republican emergency aid in coping with destructive floods which swept along its coastline in the later part of April 1978; and then the following November, after a meeting between Matanzima and R. F. Botha, the South African Minister of Foreign Affairs, an agreement was promulgated which provided for an exchange of trade representatives between Pretoria and Umtata.[90]

None the less, although there was continuing collaboration in many spheres, business was not carried on quite as usual, for South Africa was quietly working to reimpose its unambiguous political control. In the first place, the diplomatic break was followed on 10 May by an announcement by the South African Defence Force of its refusal to train further Transkeian soldiers until relations between the two governments had been normalized.[91] Somewhat speculatively, Matanzima thereafter called upon the OAU to take over the task in order to assist him to combat apartheid;[92] but denied international legitimation, he was in practice forced to resort to the black market for a supply of arms and ammunition, this being provided by a group of French mercenaries and financiers formerly associated with the fascistic OAS and a number of other dubious causes.[93] Transporting the supplies in an unmarked Dakota, it was later revealed that the plane had carried out a number of trips between Umtata and Salisbury, and that small groups of Transkeian soldiers were being trained by the Rhodesian military.[94] Yet such stop-gap measures were scarcely adequate to remedy the considerable threat posed to Matanzima's internal political position by the withdrawal of the SADF's logistical support for, lacking popular acclaim, the security of the TNIP government was in last resort dependent upon its ability to wield sufficient military clout.

Yet South African discipline was more forthrightly exercised at the fiscal level, as Transkei now plunged into an acute financial crisis. The presentation of the record 1978/9 budget of R328 million (of which nearly R100 million was scheduled to be obtained from the international money market) had more or less coincided with the break in diplomatic relations and, as outlined in the previous chapter, Transkei was only enabled to avoid outright bankruptcy through South Africa opting to sustain its client even after the severance of formal ties. Indeed, the break in diplomatic relations immediately denied Transkei of its only claim to financial credibility, so that all hopes of securing private and foreign loans to finance its deficit were immediately lost. Accordingly, the budget for 1979/80 reflected less ambition and renewed penury, being cut back to R253 million.[95] Yet by now the habits of spending were deeply ingrained, as was later to be disclosed by the Transkei Sessional Committee's Report on Public Accounts for 1977/8 (which was published in September 1979).

This report revealed a general breakdown in financial administration. With Transkei's national debt by then having increased to R39·5 million, the report disclosed that in the year under review, unauthorized expenditure by five departments exceeded R4·7 million,[96] and in addition that there was indication of financial appropriation on a considerable scale by a number of ministers and top officials. Inevitably dubbed 'Kaisergate', the scandal was of sufficient proportion to earn the passage of a vote of censure of the five departments concerned in the Assembly, even though further investigation was subsequently to be hampered by its reference to a Committee of Inquiry dominated by the TNIP.[97] Ironically, however, at the very time that this report was being publicly debated the Matanzima government was having to go cap in hand to Pretoria to beg a further R74 million for the 1979/80 financial year, this being the amount required to award civil servants a pay increase to enable Transkei to match salary increases granted to black civil servants in the Republic (for, as indicated in the previous chapter, without the extra grant Umtata would not have been able to pay its civil servants in November 1979).[98] Subsequently it was announced that South Africa intended phasing out direct budget aid, moving instead to a system whereby it would finance individual projects, thus allowing for a greater measure of fiscal control.[99]

As if to emphasize the degree of Transkei's dependence upon the Republic, the 1979/80 financial crisis was played out against the background of bizarre events concerning Humphrey Berkeley, a former British Conservative MP of liberal sympathies whose past activities had earned him denial of the right to enter South Africa. Appointed an adviser to Matanzima in late 1977, his advice was generally thought to have been instrumental in propelling Transkei towards the breach in diplomatic relations – and certainly, his influence in Umtata was viewed with concern by the Republican government.

Later events, if correctly told, were to illustrate how far South Africa was prepared to go in ensuring that Transkei remained within its orbit. Acting together with Liston Ntshongwana, a senior official from the Ministry of Foreign Affairs, Berkeley claims to have negotiated a large loan from Nigeria, having been allegedly able to persuade the Nigerian government that Transkei was no ordinary bantustan. According to Berkeley, the Nigerian loan would have been used to help finance a harbour, to train the army and police, and to establish a military presence in Transkei to protect it from external aggression. The loan was reportedly agreed in principle, although the Nigerians first wanted to convince themselves that Transkei was more than simply a stooge of South Africa; but (again, according to Berkeley), at the very moment a Nigerian emissary was waiting in Umtata to clinch the deal, South Africa sabotaged the plan by payment of R118 million in budgetary aid, thereby notifying its refusal to permit Transkei to acquire large-scale finance from what was regarded as a hostile source.[100]

Whether or not Nigeria was so prepared to be party to such an arrangement (and there must be considerable doubt), later events certainly suggested that South African advisers resented Berkeley's usurpation of their role. Just as earlier the services of foreign appointees to the TDC had been abruptly terminated, so now was the former Tory MP dismissed, although in his case he was dragged from an Umtata hotel by Transkeian police, badly beaten up and later dumped in Komgha over the South African border. Forewarned was forearmed, and Liston Ntshongwana did not wait his turn for similar treatment. Instead he fled to London, alleging that the Security Police wanted to kill him, although in his case the bantustan authorities countered with charges of large-scale embezzlement. Not surprisingly, Matanzima denied any official intention to maltreat Berkeley, and seemed little worried by the latter's declared intent to sue the Transkeian government for unlawful termination of his contract. Ntshongwana, meanwhile, having threatened to testify in court as witness to the assault on Berkeley, returned to Transkei two months after he had left, having apparently made a personal deal with Matanzima (with whom he had previously enjoyed a close relationship).[101]

Given these diverse events, it was not wholly unexpected that Transkeian foreign policy rhetoric should once more come to praise the merits of South Africa; and following the leak of information that Transkei would soon be awarded at least a portion of East Griqualand under new homeland consolidation proposals, Premier George Matanzima soon announced that diplomatic relations and the non-aggression pact would be restored,[102] this being confirmed by the arrival of a new South African ambassador to Transkei in April 1980.[103] Certainly, Transkei may thus have gained part of what it had previously demanded. Yet this may be attributed less to the Matanzimas' political skills than to a desire by the Republic to salve their pride, for the renewal of official harmony is more likely a consequence of the Republic's assertion of its financial control. Transkei had attempted to unloose the shackles which had bound it hand and foot to the apartheid regime; yet the effort had ended in ignominy, with her captive status plain for all but the wilfully blind to see.

The politics of 'independent' Transkei

The politics of bantustan 'independence' are of necessity a politics of dependence. That is, given an overall harmony of interest between the South African state and the dominant elements of the Transkeian petty-bourgeoisie, the process of government is fundamentally oriented towards the consolidation of that alliance. In particular, the Transkeian authorities are reliant upon 'metropolitan' support for continued maintenance and expansion of a (contextually) strong state machinery (police, army and bureaucracy) to contain the various class and ethnic tensions generated within the bantustan by the developing contradictions of apartheid. Yet while the interrelationship between the South African state and the auxiliary elements in Transkei is basically complementary, it is also one of lower-order conflict, for not only do the material needs of the latter demand that they bargain continuously for increased resources, but their simultaneous search for internal and international legitimacy requires that they must eschew the appearance of collaboration with apartheid. Indeed, not only must they project an image of manifest antagonism to continuing white racial domination within South Africa, but they must seek to demonstrate that the path they have chosen (of opting for independence within the framework of separate development) represents a viable mode of promoting change and one which allows blacks to extract meaningful concession from the apartheid regime. Essentially, therefore, the politics of bantustan 'independence' constitute a precarious balancing act: the South African government must be continuously abused, but not to the extent that it withdraws its material support, while internal and external critics and allies must be appeased by a display of actions and rhetoric which apparently distance the Transkeian ruling elements from the ultimate source of their own power and authority.

In his *The Eighteenth Brumaire of Louis Bonaparte*, Marx suggests that a smallholding peasantry may provide a basis for a centralized and heavy-handed government, with the expansion of the state bureaucracy enabling such a regime to maintain itself in power without relying too directly upon a particular class or classes.[104] In the case of Transkei, communal tenure today provides the foundation for extensive chiefly repression, with the emerging core of the ruling petty-bourgeoisie being located precisely within the expanding civil service; and while the Umtata regime may be seen to be *representative* of the Transkeian bourgeoisie, it is at the same time independent of that class in the sense that the ultimate source of its power lies in Pretoria.

Yet if the Transkeian government is ultimately dependent upon the neighbouring white regime (and the interests it represents), the ruling élite does possess a limited degree of autonomy which it may use to bargain for political advantage. Concessions have been made to Transkei since independence, but they have hitherto all been highly marginal. What is of greater import is that, paradoxically, the freedom of political manoeuvre allowed to the bantustan has the practical effect of furthering the interests of the apartheid state, however contrary the results of its actions (such as the promotion of non-racialism and the diplomatic break) may appear to be at first sight. Thus the class situation of the dominant elements within Transkei necessitates that they be seen to be pushing for political change within South Africa; yet those same class interests dictate that the direction and pace of that change should be both evolutionary and conservative, of such a nature as to entrench, rather than undermine, their present elevated position in relation to the broad mass of homeland inhabitants. It is for this reason that it is likely there will be a continuation of anti-apartheid posturing by the Transkeian government. But even when this irritates, it will probably be tolerated with relative calm by Pretoria, for to the extent that Transkei or any other independent homeland is allowed to develop its international credentials, so will it likely strengthen the black associates of the South African regime.

Notes

1. For one statement, see Matanzima (1976), pp. 19–38.
2. Laurence (1976), p. 8.

3. Letlaka; and Koyana (both circularized to African governments before October 1976 and kindly released to the author by the Lesotho Ministry of Foreign Affairs).
4. ibid. Note also that Letlaka has claimed the Pondo Revolt as part of the 'independence movement': 'Transkeians had fought for freedom. The Pondo established a government in the mountains during their struggle for freedom.' (*Daily Dispatch*, 2 August 1976.) Official populist rhetoric may yet be claiming the Pondo Revolt as 'The Transkeian War of Independence'.
5. See, *inter alia*, Berkeley (1978/9); Stultz (1977); and my paper (1976).
6. According to one source, President Bokassa of the Central African Federation was the only black head of state willing to attend the celebrations, but the South African government, cognizant of his controversial international image, decided that it would be counterproductive for him to come. (*RDM*, 16 August 1976.)
7. SAIRR, *A Survey, 1977*, p. 347.
8. *Natal Daily News*, 2 May 1977.
9. The Lesotho government took advantage of Transkeian independence to validate its anti-apartheid credentials, and to use the alleged blockade of its borders as a means for increasing the flow of foreign aid. For contemporary press reports, see Legum (1977); and Gordon (1977). Summary accounts are carried in SAIRR, *Surveys* for *1977* (pp. 346–7) and *1978* (pp. 286–7). For an academic treatment, see Hirschmann (1979).
10. Hill (1976); and Seiler (1976).
11. *Transkei Hansard*, 16 March 1977, pp. 25–7.
12. For example, the policy speech of Foreign Minister Digby Koyana, *Transkei Hansard*, 8 May 1978, pp. 242–6.
13. *RDM*, 18 May 1977.
14. SAIRR, *A Survey, 1977*, p. 345.
15. *RDM*, 28 November 1977.
16. SAIRR, *A Survey, 1978*, p. 286; confirmed by interview with Digby Koyana, 23 March 1980.
17. SAIRR, *A Survey, 1979*, p. 345.
18. Speech by Koyana in the Assembly, *Transkei Hansard*, 8 May 1978, pp. 242–6. In April 1980, a further bid for international attention was made when the Prime Minister, George Matanzima, invited the deposed Shah of Iran to take up permanent sanctuary within Transkei. See *Sunday Times*, 13 April 1980.
19. *Transkei Hansard*, 3 May 1971, p. 121.
20. Matanzima (1976), p. 97.
21. *RDM*, 9 January 1973.
22. *Transkei Hansard*, 28 April 1971, p. 103.
23. ibid., 12 March 1975, p. 129.
24. Dugard (1976a).
25. SAIRR, *A Survey, 1977*, p. 339.
26. ibid., *1978*, p. 281.
27. Sicgau (1976) (mimeo).
28. 'The Emergence of a New State, 26 October, 1976'. (Mimeo – released to author by courtesy of the Lesotho Ministry of Foreign Affairs.)
29. This theme is also explored in my contribution (1980a).
30. SAIRR, *A Survey, 1977*, p. 336.

31. *Transkei Hansard*, 17 May 1977, p. 413.
32. SAIRR, *A Survey, 1978*, p. 283; and *Transkei Hansard*, 17 May 1978, pp. 328–32.
33. *RDM*, 29 August 1977.
34. Statement by George Matanzima, Minister of Justice, *Transkei Hansard*, 16 May 1978, p. 321.
35. SAIRR, *A Survey, 1977*, pp. 338–9.
36. ibid. The extent of support for the party may be gauged by the fact that its first Annual Congress had to be postponed when only three people turned up.
37. This interpretation of motives was suggested by Mr Pascoe Ludidi, former Secretary-General and Chief Whip of the TNIP, who after crossing the floor of the Assembly to found the Transkei United Party fled to Lesotho in April 1977 to escape arrest. The United Party (alternatively known as the Pan-Africanist Party) was extinguished by his flight. Mr Ludidi subsequently became one of my students at the National University of Lesotho, and I am indebted to him for a number of extended discussions about Transkeian politics.
38. *The Post*, 11–13 May 1978; and *Transkei Hansard*, 3 May 1978, p. 234.
39. Interview, Mr Digby Koyana, 23 March 1980. Note also the report in the *RDM*, 22 January 1979: 'Chief Matanzima said he would still rule Transkei even if he were elected State President, as he would act with the Cabinet as President-in-council.'
40. The Pondo élite were further alienated by central government involvement in a dispute over who was to succeed Botha Sicgau as Paramount, as Kaiser Matanzima (as State President) at first refused to accept the result of elections which gave the appointment to Chief Mpondombini Sicgau (a supporter of the Opposition) over his half-brother Chief Zwelidumile Sicgau. History seemed bent on repeating itself, as Botha Sicgau himself had been appointed Paramount by the South African government in 1939 over the head of his more popular brother, Chief Nelson Sicgau. However, Kaiser Matanzima's opposition was later overcome, and Mpondombini Sicgau was subsequently installed as Paramount in March 1980. For details of the dispute, see SAIRR, *A Survey, 1979*, p. 339.
41. *RDM*, 28 March 1979.
42. *Daily Dispatch*, 28 March 1979.
43. SAIRR, *A Survey, 1979*, pp. 340–1. Anonymous pamphlets urging students to boycott classes and workers to stay at home were also distributed in November, a few days before the expected date of Sabata's delayed trial (which was again postponed because of the defendant's ill-health). The leaflets made a special appeal to Transkeian youth: 'Let us involve ourselves totally to [*sic*] the Liberation struggle. We have been quiet for so long that KD thinks all Transkei students are afraid of him. Let us correct this mistake.' (Quoted in *The Post*, 7 November 1979.)
44. *Daily Dispatch*, 31 August 1979; *The Voice*, 2 September 1979. After being convicted of offending against the security laws and receiving a suspended sentence, Jeremiah Moshesh left the Opposition and rejoined the TNIP. In July 1980 his rehabilitation was acknowledged when he was appointed the territory's consular representative in Durban. (SAIRR, *A Survey, 1980*, p. 417.)

45. Those detained were the deputy leader of the party, Mr C. S. Mda; the treasurer, Mr S. A. Xobololo; the national secretary, Mr W. M. Dweba; the chairman, Mr J. Nndika; the national organizer, Mr B. Pikashe; and a committee member, Mr J. Kati. Executive members of the Youth League detained were the president, Mr Zola Dunyawa; the chairman, Mr Mazwi Yako; the secretary, Mr S. Saliwa; the treasurer, Mr M. Mbete; and a committee member, Mr Monde Mnyande. (*RDM*, 1 February 1980.)
46. *The Star*, 2 April 1980. The prosecution was headed by the Attorney-General, Mr George Muller, as Dr Percy Yutar had withdrawn from the case.
47. *Sunday Post*, 7 September 1980.
48. *Africa Contemporary Record*, 1980–1, p. B876.
49. *RDM*, 27 August and 2 September 1980.
50. *Daily Dispatch*, 7 May and 3 July 1980; and SAIRR, *A Survey, 1980*, p. 419.
51. *RDM*, 11 September 1980; *The Star*, 12 September 1980.
52. On Makiwane's assassination and the Group of Eight, see *The Star*, 9 July 1980; and *Sunday Times*, 31 August 1980.
53. *RDM*, 2 September 1980.
54. *RDM*, 29 April 1980.
55. *RDM*, 16 July and 30 July 1979.
56. *RDM*, 18 April 1980.
57. *RDM*, 19 April, 30 April and 6 May 1980.
58. *The Citizen*, 3 September 1977.
59. *RDM*, 9 November 1977.
60. SAIRR, *A Survey, 1979*, pp. 341.
61. *Daily Dispatch*, 4 January 1977.
62. Anonymous (1980). The assassination attempt was the one for whose report the *Daily Dispatch* was temporarily banned.
63. *The Star*, 12 September 1980.
64. *Daily Dispatch*, 13 March 1980.
65. *RDM*, 1 May 1980.
66. *RDM*, 6 June 1980.
67. *RDM*, 12 April 1980.
68. *RDM*, 9 June 1980.
69. ibid.
70. *Daily Dispatch*, 21 December 1978; and *RDM*, 28 March 1979.
71. *RDM*, 30 April 1980.
72. *The Star*, 8 and 9 July 1980.
73. 'Transkei starts in Limbo', *The Times* (London), 25 October 1976. See also Taylor (1976); and Hahn (1976).
74. As in the case of Lesotho, the receipt of international aid might well grant an increased flexibility in terms of political relations with South Africa, but it would hardly allow for the fundamental transformation of Transkei's base from its present status as a captive economy and a labour reservoir. Thus Hirschmann (1979): 'Numerous projects, large and small, governmental and parastatal, agricultural, industrial, educational and infrastructural, have been initiated amidst fast-growing donor interest in Lesotho. While it will take time to assess the overall impact of these undertakings, those trends which are apparent manifest the continuation of all the major elements of a captive economy.'

75. O'Sullivan (1976).
76. See Laurence (1976), pp. 114–18, for a masterly analysis of the negotiations surrounding the citizenship issue prior to independence.
77. See statement by the Commanding Officer, Brigadier Philip Pretorius, as reported in *The Cape Times*, 3 December 1976.
78. *Transkei Hansard*, 27 April 1978, p. 182.
79. *RDM*, 14 April 1976.
80. ibid., 9 June 1976.
81. On Bophuthatswana, see Butler *et al.* (1977). For an assessment of the independence settlement, see Ashford (1977).
82. SAIRR, *A Survey, 1977*, p. 448.
83. BENBO (1976), p. 124.
84. SAIRR, *A Survey, 1977*, p. 343.
85. ibid., pp. 448–54; and *1978*, pp. 285–6. International publicity later led to a concession in that the Republican government reversed its policy on the abolition of the Crossroads camp, and in early 1980 it announced that a new township was to be built to house certain Crossroads residents, these being (1) those who qualified to reside in white areas under Section 10 of the Blacks (Urban Areas) Consolidation Act; (2) contract or migrant workers and their families; (3) other families otherwise earning a 'legitimate' living; (4) those deserving special consideration. However, persons who were offered jobs and housing in Transkei were specifically excluded. (SAIRR, *A Survey, 1979*, p. 425.)
86. Laurence (1978).
87. Speech by Kaiser Matanzima to the Fourteenth Congress of the TNIP, 1977 (mimeo).
88. *Transkei Hansard*, 10 April 1978, pp. 69–70.
89. ibid., p. 69.
90. *RDM*, 18 November 1978.
91. *Transkei Hansard*, 10 May 1978, p. 264.
92. *RDM*, 27 October 1978.
93. *The Guardian* (London), 28 September 1978; and *Sunday Express*, 17 September 1978.
94. *Daily News*, 22 September 1978.
95. *Financial Mail*, 16 November 1979.
96. The Commissioner of Police ingenuously stated that the reason why the police overspent by R522,800 was because of the widespread opposition to independence. 'Many more people were detained than originally anticipated and the cost of maintaining prisoners became very high.' (*RDM*, 13 October 1979.)
97. The financial crisis was most thoroughly treated by the *Daily Dispatch*. See its editions for 21 August, 4 September, 20 September, 21 September and 24 September 1979.
98. 'Transkei civil servants face no pay as financial crisis looms', *The Cape Times*, 6 December 1979. See also *RDM*, 10 October and 16 October 1979.
99. *Sunday Times*, 18 November 1979.
100. *The Spectator* (London), August 1979; and *Financial Mail*, 31 August 1979.
101. *Daily Dispatch*, 7 July 1979; *The Guardian* (London), 28 August 1979; *RDM*,

3 August and 4 October 1979; and *Sunday Post*, 2 September and 7 October 1979.
102. *RDM*, 8 February 1980.
103. *RDM*, 25 April 1980.
104. Marx (1970).

Chapter 9
The bantustan strategy – prospects and possibilities

It has been a central thesis of this study (as demonstrated by detailed reference to Transkei) that the bantustan strategy implemented by the South African government has represented not merely a continuing device to ensure that the reserve areas service the labour needs of the white economy, but a specifically political response to the internal pressures of African nationalism (which in its postwar resurgent form was itself a reflection of underlying economic tendencies and notably the increasing proletarianization of the African mass) and to the international pressures generated, *inter alia*, by the decolonization of the African continent. In particular, because of the lack of acceptability in the post-Second World War era of justifying a cheap labour system in terms of an ideology of racial domination, the National Party leadership evolved towards a strategy of apartheid which, at the *political* level, espoused three key elements. These were, first, the fragmentation of the African majority population into eight (later ten) groupings along ethnic lines so as to achieve the objective of 'divide and rule' while simultaneously diverting nationalist focus away from achieving power at the political centre, this policy being justified by reference to the right of diverse peoples to achieve self-determination through national states. Secondly (and following closely on from the first element), the strategy entailed the actual grant of self-determination to the resulting ethnic states via a constitutional progression through various stages of self-government leading eventually to 'independence', this entailing the political partition (or, more accurately perhaps, division)[1] of South Africa into a white core and black peripheral states (this in turn requiring the nullification of the African right to citizenship in the central Republic). And thirdly (less commonly stated yet obvious in intent), the Nationalist goal was to promote political and economic opportunities in the bantustan peripheries which would be sufficient to entice an emergent, African beneficiary class into collaborating with Pretoria in the control and suppression of the subordinated population, without simultaneously providing it with sufficient muscle to become a significant competitor for power.

So it was that the bantustan strategy evolved into a caricature of the decolonization process carried out elsewhere, to the point where it is not inaccurate to portray the official intent as one of the active neo-colonization of the artificial 'states' that the very policy was attempting to create. Yet for all its glaring lack of viability as a process of decolonization, and for all its limitations in satisfying black aspirations for power, the homeland policy was much more than a fraud and an irrelevance, for it performed a crucial function in satisfying the historically specific needs of the South African political economy in the apartheid era until conditions changed dramatically in the mid-1970s. 'The bantustan policy conceals continued white control over development under the guise of cunning examples of pseudo-independence,' summarized Adam, further proposing that it was pragmatically oriented towards 'the smooth, frictionless and tolerable domination over cheap labour and political dependants as a prerequisite for privileges of the minority'.[2] Hence from this perspective, the overall strategy not only sought to fragment non-white consciousness by the devolution of authority to black intermediaries within politico-geographically defined spheres, but it was also directed towards the incorporation of emergent petty-bourgeois elements in the bantustans into a racially compartmentalized class alliance with the white rulers, yet in a clearly subordinate and dependent capacity. In turn, the entire policy was located in the broader context of the complete and largely effective repression of black protest and representation at the national level.

The significance of Transkei was that, historically, it served as the model for the officially propounded strategy of internal decolonization. Yet the inability of South Africa to gain international recognition for the 'independence' of Transkei (and for Bophuthatswana, Venda and, doubtless, Ciskei, after) clearly denotes the failure of the major political objective of the bantustan strategy. If, in short, the intention of that strategy was to *externalize* South Africa's race conflict (and the process of exploitation that racial domination represented) by the creation of a set of dependent neo-colonies, then the adamant refusal of the world community to endorse the 'independent' homelands as separate states has shattered the chimera of the bantustan policy as a process of legitimate decolonization. Accordingly, given the context of post-Soweto South Africa wherein exclusive white rule is today subject to mounting black challenge both internally and externally, the bantustan policy has reached a critical impasse, requiring major adjustments if its essential functions (so critical to the needs of the apartheid economy) are to be incorporated into an updated structure of racial domination appropriate to the (perhaps now conflicting) needs of the white ruling class and international capital in the 1980s. It is therefore necessary to conclude this study by attempting to locate the 'independent' Transkei in the broader South African framework.

Transkei in the context of contemporary policy towards the bantustans

The experience of Transkei in being subject to a process of quasi-decolonization has been, to a greater or lesser degree, replicated in every other homeland. Although the various bantustans are differentially spaced along the ladder of constitutional development, all have been (or are currently being) equipped with legislative assemblies, cabinets (or executive councils) and the other paraphernalia of 'political development'. Popular influence everywhere has been constrained by practices similar to those which have skewed elections in Transkei: chiefs or their nominees have regularly formed a majority in the legislatures;[3] the disruptive potential of urban voting has been minimized; and there has been the habitual use of administrative coercions and security legislation to intimidate voters or to harass individuals or political parties opposing incumbent governments.[4] In each and every homeland, the authority of the traditional chieftaincy has been revived, corrupted and bureaucratized, while otherwise the apparatus of the state (or proto-state) has been expanded and simultaneously indigenized by the devolution from above of a host of administrative and municipal functions (influx control, health, education, social services and so on). Importantly, too, especially in the more constitutionally advanced territories, the police and security services are being handed over to the bantustan governments, with the creation of an army becoming a customary adjunct of bantustan independence.[5] The essence of the homeland strategy, therefore, has been the creation of an auxiliary petty-bourgeoisie to preside over a dependent state machinery in each ethnic territory.

All the different homeland governments remain critically dependent upon South African financial support, which generally accounts for 70–80 per cent of their budgets.[6] Without direct subventions from the Republic, therefore, the bantustan authorities would be unable to maintain either present employment rates or the (limited) levels of social and administrative services that they provide. Although there is some prospect of the governments of Bophuthatswana, Lebowa, Kangwane and Kwazulu being able to raise tax revenues from mining ventures within their borders, the other homelands are generally lacking mineral resources,[7] and the potential for generating internal revenue is otherwise extremely limited, as the rate of agricultural and industrial development is everywhere outstripped by the rapid increase in their populations.

In every case the homeland economies are in a state of stagnation and decay. *Per capita* incomes are low compared to all but the most poverty-stricken countries of independent Africa, with the major portion of the gross 'national' income of each territory being derived from the remittances of migrant labourers who oscillate between the ethnic peripheries and the core area according to the requirements of white capital.[8]

The lack of internal economic capacity, entailing the provision of infrastructure, goods and services from outside, meanwhile operates to drain the flow of income spent within the homelands into the white areas of the Republic. Although the bantustan and South African governments are together undertaking a variety of agricultural and industrial enterprises via the development corporations, these efforts are too late and too limited to stimulate self-sustaining growth, and are in any case largely designed to soak up black population surplus to the needs of the white economy. Homeland development projects impart a veneer of progress to economies which have otherwise lost all hope, and serve a useful propaganda function for the apartheid regime, which claims to be extending impressive development 'aid' to its black peripheral states.[9] At present, however, the latter remain much divided, inland archipelagos of territorial fragments scattered upon the face of white South Africa, their potential for unity, administrative centralization and economic development little improved by consolidation proposals which leave the largest, most populous and significant homelands (notably Bophuthatswana, Kwazulu and Transkei) still separated into a number of discrete units.

Despite these major limitations, Chief Lucas Mangope of Bophuthatswana was to follow Matanzima by leading his homeland to independence in 1977, despite the evident opposition of the majority of his homeland's designated citizens. However, the failure of either of these entities to gain international recognition, together with the strong resistance from the mass of their populations to the bantustan scenario, served to make the leaders of the remaining non-independent territories rather more circumspect towards the independence issue. In late 1978, the leaders of these homelands issued a statement rejecting both the notion of bantustan independence and the three Parliament constitutional arrangement being proposed for the non-African minorities (which would exclude Africans from the political process in the 'common area').[10] Chief Patrick Mpephu of Venda (whose Venda National Party had just fought – and lost – an election on the independence issue the previous August, being returned to office only with the support of *ex officio* chiefs) subsequently disassociated himself from the statement and proceeded to lead his territory to formally sovereign status.[11] But the actions of other leaders were less cynical and more cautious. Thus in April 1976 Dr Cedric Phatudi of Lebowa had requested his legislative assembly 'to review their long-standing objection to sovereign independence',[12] but was soon referring to independence as 'fatal for blacks'; and, given considerable difficulty in retaining his domestic political position in an election in 1978, Phatudi thereafter strongly rejected the idea of independence for Lebowa, attacked Transkei and Bophuthatswana for making their citizens foreigners in the land of their birth by accepting independence, and argued that the Republic itself was the only homeland for Africans. In addition, he accused the South African government of giving substantial development funds to those territories which opted for independence while denying investment to others.[13]

Professor Hudson Ntsanwisi of Gazankulu was rather more ambiguous, remaining opposed to independence so long as his territory continued to be economically dependent upon South Africa,[14] but he attended meetings as an uncommitted observer of the South African Black Alliance (successor to the Black Unity Front) which is headed by Chief Gatsha Buthelezi of Kwazulu. This organization, which links together the Kwazulu Inkatha national–cultural liberation movement with the Coloured Labour Party and the Indian Reform Party, is formally committed to united resistance to apartheid across racial and tribal lines.[15] Although various homeland leaders and parties have at times expressed interest in or support for SABA, only Kenneth Mopeli of QwaQwa and Enos Mabuza of KaNgwane have joined the movement, the others apparently suspecting it as being dominated by Inkatha. None the less, the other non-independent homeland leaders (except Mpephu) were able to join Buthelezi in December 1978 in proposing to the Republican authorities the notion that those homelands which choose not to opt for independence should be permanently incorporated into a structure of government which would allow for 'the maximum degree of self-government in homelands, but with an overriding connection in the form of a federal or confederal level'.[16]

In response to such misgivings, Pretoria soon gave indication that it was prepared to modify its strategy in order to cater for those homelands which might refuse independence. Commenting after Inkatha's near-clean sweep in the first election in Kwazulu in March 1978 (Buthelezi's movement being explicitly opposed to independence), Dr Connie Mulder, the Minister of Plural Relations, stated: 'There is no way of forcing a homeland leader to accept independence. Naturally we hope the final stage of their development will be independence. But depending on how many homelands are not independent, the whole situation will have to be reconsidered and a new dispensation worked out' – adding that this would not involve any form of direct power-sharing with whites.[17]

The Minister's statement was reflective of the Bantu Homelands Amendment Bill of 1977 which was then before Parliament, whose purpose was to allow for a substantial increase in legislative competence to self-governing homelands, including potential to repeal certain racially discriminatory laws such as the Immorality and Mixed Marriages Acts (although such changes would be accomplished only with the express consent of the Minister of Plural Relations). Hailed at first by Phatudi and Ntsanwisi as a means for abolishing discrimination within the homelands, it was simultaneously rejected by Buthelezi and Mopeli as a dangerous and seductive ploy designed to induce the homelands into co-operating with Pretoria;[18] and certainly, the interpretation of the latter leaders seems plausible, for were the promotion of non-racialism to be explicitly linked with constitutional advance, the various homeland petty-bourgeoisies might well be tempted to press for independent or quasi-independent status.[19] Subsequently, however, the 1977 Bill was dropped, being replaced by Proclamation R150 of 1979 which, while granting the legislative assemblies of self-governing territories certain greater powers,[20] did not provide for the development of non-racialism within non-independent bantustans. None the less, it is clear that the Republican authorities may yet seek to utilize the carrot of non-racialism as an inducement to homeland governments to collaborate with their plans.

This links into a further point that, to the extent that bantustans accept greater autonomy or advance to independence, it is Pretoria's hope that restoration of a politically united multiracial South Africa will become more difficult.[21] Thus while progression by a homeland to independence need not in theory constitute an irreversible step, it is trusted that the bureaucratic momentum of the various state apparatuses, as reflecting the entrenchment of the class interests of the locally dominant strata, will lead to the bantustans acquiring a permanence not easily dislodged. The reluctance of the bantustan ruling groups to surrender their political autonomy, once gained, is obviously a factor upon which the Republican authorities place much weight, and one which underpins their eagerness to devolve even an unrecognized independence upon the homelands. Established over their ethnic territories, bantustan regimes are perceived as conservative and stabilizing elements which, unlike in other African states that had a significant settler presence, are prepared to share power with local whites within a fragmented polity, while leaving the structure of white domination in the core area undisturbed; and to the extent that they seek to retain their political independence, they will in consequence be explicitly aligning themselves against the liberation movements whose philosophy remains predicated upon the notion of a united and undivided South Africa.

Thus pressures upon homelands to accept independence remain. Even so, the contemporary crisis facing apartheid (urban discontent and industrial protest among blacks, post-Information Scandal cleavages within the National Party, and the increasingly unfavourable international environment) has generated considerable uncertainty in ruling circles, this being reflected in a number of *verligte* proposals, all of which seek to modify apartheid, making it more tolerable for blacks, while leaving its fundamentals undisturbed. One such idea features the creation of 'dual cities', whereby white towns and cities would be linked to their adjoining black townships in a common metropolitan area, municipal functions being shared but exercised separately by both blacks and whites within.[22] Another such concept proposes the recognition of the larger conurbations such as Soweto as 'city states', with the devolution to them of powers akin to those presently delegated to the homelands;[23] and a third idea advocates the incorporation of the less viable homelands (identified as too small, fragmented and dependent upon the Republic) as provinces in a union of regions within South Africa.[24]

Elements of these ideas are incorporated in the most far-reaching and apparently most influential set of recommendations, which have been offered by Professor P. Roelf Botha, a member of the Prime Minister's Planning Advisory Council and the National Party's Transvaal Executive. These proposals advocate a far-reaching consolidation of the homelands, the extension of powers to black municipalities, and the scrapping of discrimination within certain socio-economic (but not political) spheres of the white heartland. In particular, Botha argues for a substantial consolidation with land allocation in excess of the 1936 Land Act limits, and the maximum incorporation of ethnic townships and population concentrations presently located in the Republic; and in addition he advocates a more thorough zoning of the migrant labour force by strengthening the linkages between homelands and their nearest white employment areas, and the social accommodation of Africans in economic activity, higher education, culture and sport. But Botha holds to the key principle that Africans should realize themselves politically in their own areas. Although Africans resident in white areas should be enabled to administer their own affairs through urban councils operating alongside white municipalities (with some machinery for liaison and possibly the development of a city state for Soweto), Africans should otherwise continue to exercise their political rights through the black states. They would thus be excluded from the franchise in white South Africa by virtue of their being foreigners, but once the principle of exclusion had been established it would be possible to do away with discrimination in the (white) host country on grounds of race and nationality.[25]

Roelf Botha's plan did not find favour when it was presented to the Transvaal Congress of the National Party in 1978, but statements and policies of the government of P. W. Botha (who succeeded Vorster as Prime Minister in October of that year) suggest that the proposed strategy has been highly influential. Thus the widely publicized reformism of Premier Botha includes the extension of the Community Council concept, such bodies exercising increased municipal powers (as compared with the forerunner Urban Bantu Councils, now discredited and abolished) to accommodate African (principally middle-class) aspirations in urban areas; the continuing relaxation of racial restrictions on black businessmen to encourage the development of an African capitalist stratum; and the deracialization of certain social facilities (such as hotels and restaurants) within the white core. If such measures are arguably designed to incorporate the African petty-bourgeois in urban areas within the existing framework of order, there are complementary devices intended to divide the African working class by encouraging the formation of a relatively privileged labour aristocracy in urban areas. Thus while the Industrial Conciliation Amendment Act (no. 74 of 1979) clothes an attempt to supervise more clearly the developing black union movement by subjecting it to a host of restrictions imposed from above, the ostensible deracialization of the labour process seeks simultaneously to relieve manpower shortages and to allow for absorption of African workers into higher skilled levels. But although there is now more flexible legislative provision for the relaxation of discriminatory job reservation, this is linked to a tightening of existing controls to separate urban 'insiders' from migrant 'outsiders', with concessions being made to Section 10 Africans in job advancement and training, the extension of residential leasehold to those who qualify, and the more specific linking of urban rights to both jobs and housing. In addition, while greater mobility is to be allowed for blacks qualified to be in urban areas, there is increased administrative and legal pressure to strengthen influx control and to prevent the employment of black labourers illegally resident in urban areas.[26]

In addition to these measures, Botha-style reformism lays renewed emphasis upon the implementation of the bantustan policy. Yet because of the non-recognition of the independent homelands, the strategy now has to be given a more attractive outward form so as to convince (or at least, suggest to) both external observers and participant governments that significant changes are afoot. The new image thus revolves around two issues: first, the Botha government now holds out the prospect of more meaningful consolidation of the homelands, while secondly, this is linked to the notion of a 'constellation' or 'confederation' of states.

The standpoint of the National Party government under Vorster was that the 1936 land division was historically inviolable, sacrosanct and non-negotiable. Yet faced with the near exhaustion of land for allocation under the 1936 settlement,[27] P. W. Botha announced in January 1979 his intention to appoint a Commission of Inquiry into the consolidation of the homelands, simultaneously indicating that the government might be prepared to grant land over and above the 13·7 per cent quota for blacks laid down by the Trusts and Land Act. A Central Consolidation Committee under the chairmanship of National Party MP Hennie Van der Walt was duly established later in the year, with Botha confirming at its first meeting the government's new preparedness to go beyond the 1936 allocation, arguing in justification that each generation has to provide the solution to its own problems.[28] The draft recommendations of this committee were presented to the Cabinet in August 1980, with Botha announcing that the proposals would be referred to six Cabinet committees for further study, and that interested parties – such as homeland leaders and affected landowners – would be consulted before the release of the final plans.[29] In the meantime, the government appeared to adopt a more flexible policy with regard to consolidation, both allocating a somewhat increased budget for that purpose,[30] and allowing for certain previously excluded white towns to be incorporated into neighbouring homelands (most notably Mafeking into Bophuthatswana).[31]

The indications are that the final outcome of this policy process will seek to combine the offer of more land with financial inducements and pressures, together with the prospects of greater internal autonomy, as a bargaining device to coax homeland leaders into accepting independence or a constitutional status that is not so very far removed. However, the potential magnitude of the financial cost of realizing any far-reaching consolidation exercise, together with other political and economic considerations, resulted in an apparent policy shift even while the Consolidation Committee was sitting, for in May 1980 Van der Walt himself publicly pronounced that the economic development of the homelands now required that the economic structure of South Africa would have to be examined on a regional basis, in which case a given portion of land might fit neatly into a regional economic structure without being consolidated into a homeland. Furthermore a redistribution of power on a regional level might lead to future confederation; and 'in the framework of the constellation of states, the whole question of land might not be all that important'.[32] This new approach was later confirmed by Piet Kornhoof, who in October announced that new guidelines adopted by the government might well deviate from the Van der Walt Commission proposals, as henceforth the primary criterion regarding consolidation would be in terms of whether ground that is transferred is economically and productively used, and whether border changes would best serve a national state's development needs. White owners might be allowed to remain on transferred land if they and the governments of the black states so wish; all transfer of assets would be made in a way to ensure that 'the cash flow connected with the deal is limited'; and transfers of land to national states would be 'coordinated with the programming and identification of functional economic regions'.[33]

The new approach to consolidation is seen as integrally related to Premier Botha's initiative towards a constellation of states, an imprecise concept but one clearly descended from H. F. Verwoerd's aspiration towards a Republic-centred Southern African Commonwealth. The constellation was initially proposed not as a formal international organization but rather as a voluntary and spontaneous association of independent and non-independent states based on mutual interest, in which political freedom and regional stability would be promoted by the maximization of material welfare via co-operation in economic, technical and other functional spheres; and while the prospect of a constellation developing into a federation is officially discounted (for this would imply power-sharing within the white state), the confederal option was left open as a possible future development.[34]

For black African states bordering upon the Republic, the constellation of states proposal, ostensibly proffered in a mood of pragmatic realism and good neighbourliness following the collapse of white rule in Rhodesia, raised in renewed form the spectre of South African neo-colonial domination of its hinterland.[35] Accordingly, the Botha initiative met with a sturdily negative response; and in early 1980 leaders of the five

Front Line States conferred with colleagues from Lesotho, Swaziland, Zimbabwe and even Malawi with a view to strengthening regional relations so as to lessen their dependence upon South Africa. Meanwhile, faced with lack of viable options, the independent homelands each expressed interest in the constellation idea, which was also greeted favourably by leaders of non-independent bantustans.[36]

Subsequent report indicated that the constellation idea might take a concrete form in the shape of a confederation in terms of the government's plans for a new 'constitutional dispensation'. Originally, the government had planned to introduce separate parliaments for whites, coloureds and Indians, but in late 1980 a high-level leak suggested that the present all-white Parliament might instead be extended to include the coloureds, Indians and Chinese groups, whose representatives would be elected by separate voters' rolls. Africans, meanwhile, would still be represented politically through their homelands, but would now maintain links with the core area via a single nationality (whereby blacks belonging to even independent homelands would retain their South African passports) and an overarching central chamber which would control all factors of the confederal framework and which would include representatives from urban blacks as well as from the homelands. The latter would retain their separate citizenships within the concept of the single South African nationality, but the confederation would include both fully independent as well as 'self-ruling' states. The new plan was said to be still in a formative stage and would be subject to whatever emerged from the new President's Council (installed in October 1980), whose designated function was to be to advise the government on constitutional and other matters referred to it. However, the Cabinet was reported to be anxious for those homelands which had not done so to accept independence in order to round off the proposed confederal system.[37]

The proposal for confederation was rejected outright by leading spokesmen for urban blacks, but one significant obstacle was overcome when it was announced in 1981 that the Ciskei would become independent on 4 December of that year. Dr Connie Mulder, the Minister of Plural Relations, had indicated in 1978 that negotiations for independence had begun with a fourth homeland, and speculation was rife that Chief Lennox Sebe (whose Ciskei National Independence Party had only months previously won an election conducted in the stifling atmosphere of a State of Emergency) was the leader concerned.[38] This was subsequently confirmed when Sebe, who had previously expressed support for independence providing certain 'non-negotiable' issues could be resolved, appointed a Commission (composed of various South African and international figures under the chairmanship of Professor George Quail) to review the practical feasibility of independence for the Ciskei, and to consider especially the prospects of achieving international recognition and obtaining substantial progress on consolidation.[39]

If Sebe was hoping for the backing of distinguished advisers in progressing to immediate independence, he was to be disappointed, for when the Commission reported in February 1980 it urged the Ciskei government to hold its fire: 'the status quo, unsatisfactory as it may be to the government and people of the Ciskei, is preferable to independence on present terms, that is those accepted by Transkei, Bophuthatswana and Venda'.[40] Significantly, one of its major reasons for offering this recommendation was that an opinion survey conducted among Ciskeians both in the homeland and outside suggested that 90 per cent favoured one-man-one-vote in a unitary system of government (with 70 per cent of the survey's respondents being prepared to accept a federal structure as a second best option). Accordingly, the Commission recommended that the Ciskei should not opt for independence unless (1) the majority of Ciskeians both inside the territory and in South Africa voted in favour of independence in a carefully supervised referendum; (2) non-resident Ciskeians were given a choice of either Ciskeian or South African citizenship or both, and the South African government relinquished its right to expel, deport or otherwise remove from the white area Ciskeians who had chosen South African citizenship; (3) an enlargement of the Ciskei, agreeable to the territory's administration, was negotiated with the South African government; (4) the rights of Ciskeians to seek and retain employment in the Republic were explicitly preserved; and (5) South Africa agreed to provide equitable financial support.[41]

Despite the loopholes left open by these conditions, an apparently chastened Sebe subsequently rejected independence on what he termed 'the Transkei pattern',[42] but in March 1980 proceeded to spell out the conditions under which Ciskei would accept it. These centred upon land consolidation, citizenship and finance, with Sebe demanding (*inter alia*) a written undertaking from the South African government that it would buy and transfer to the Ciskei all the land proposed for it under the 1975 consolidation proposals; that the Ciskeian and South African governments should 'investigate' (*sic*) the possibility of a confederation within which all Ciskeians and South Africans would enjoy associate citizenship, with an undertaking that both governments would remove all racial discrimination within their territories; and that South Africa would pay certain funds to an independent Ciskei on an annual basis, with provision being made for Ciskeian membership of the Rand monetary area, the Southern African Customs Union and development aid for assistance with resettlement projects.[43] Then in April he further clarified his stance when, at the CNIP Congress, he stated that the Ciskei claimed all land between the Fish River and the Great Kei River extending from the Indian Ocean to the Stormberg Mountain range, adding that whites living in the area could either remain in the enlarged Ciskei or have their properties purchased by the South African government and handed over to the territory.[44]

Subsequently, after negotiation with the Republican government, it was announced that the Ciskei had agreed in principle to accept independence, Dr Piet Kornhoof indicating that the Ciskei and surrounding areas of Berlin, East London, King William's Town, Mdantsane and Zwelitsha would be promoted as an area of common economic development. In addition, it was further announced that the South African government would not remove Ciskeians resident in the Republic except after consultations between the two governments.

At a meeting attended by some 8,000 in the Zwelitsha township (outside East London) in October, Chief Sebe indicated that Ciskeian independence would be located within the confederal framework. The key aspect of the envisaged deal – whereby Ciskeian independence would be favourably distinguished from that of Transkei, Bophuthatswana and Venda – would be that member states of the confederation would share a common nationality (so that all individuals would retain their right to a South African passport), but would none the less possess sovereign status and would each retain their own citizenship.[45] Sebe further revealed that the South African government would allocate increased funds for the greater consolidation of Ciskei before the end of the year, and that it had also indicated that it would agree to the other demands set out in his proposed package deal. A show of hands by those attending the meeting was then interpreted as an acceptance of the proposed independence agreement for the territory, with a referendum being pledged for 4 December. The result of this referendum, when announced, purported to show that the strong antipathy against independence had now been dissolved, with 295,891 voting in favour and only 1,642 against independence in a 59·5 per cent poll of the territory's 503,000 registered voters. However, as Chief Sebe had issued a threat that those who voted against independence might be incarcerated, there were those who evinced doubt as to the fairness and accuracy of the referendum as an impartial measure of opinion.[46]

The confederation idea, and the advance of Ciskei to independence within that framework, demonstrate both change and continuity in the theory and practice of separate development. On the one hand, the official design of propelling the remaining non-independent homelands into accepting quasi or formally sovereign status is intended to complete the removal of their black populations' claims upon the South African polity. Indeed, while much emphasis is currently being laid upon Africans' right to retain their South African nationality within confederation, the proposed dispensation would in practice be merely a refinement of the situation laid down by the Bantu Homelands Citizenship Act of 1970 whereby every African was declared a citizen of a self-governing territory or a territorial authority area, so that only in terms of international status did they continue to retain the citizenship of the Republic itself. Thus when the governments of Transkei, Bophuthatswana and Venda obliged official policy by acceding to independence, all that was left to do was to remove their citizens' claim to South African citizenship in the international arena, for domestically they had been bantustan citizens all along; and while the independence settlements did not deprive existing residents of their Section 10 rights whereby they legally remained in urban areas, the Bantu Laws Amendment Act, no. 12 of 1978, laid down that children born to parents from independent bantustans after independence would not be eligible for Section 10 status.[47] The envisaged scenario, therefore, is that as each bantustan proceeds to independence, and with the eventual passing away of the pre-independence generations, the number of Africans with legal claim to permanent residence in the urban areas of white South Africa will dwindle away.[48] The constellation/confederation initiative, which has combined an official change in nomenclature for the homelands so that they are now referred to as 'national states',[49] now seeks to further this long-term scheme by blurring the distinction between the independent and non-independent bantustans, thus more subtly but none the less explicitly identifying both as separate 'countries' and their *de jure* populations as citizens of a foreign land, with no legal claim upon the white South African polity.

In turn, the continuing obligation of Africans to assume a homeland citizenship articulates with the renewed emphasis upon influx control and the resettlement/relocation policy, whose objectives remain as the 'correction' of the increasingly unfavourable black/white population imbalance in the large urban centres, the removal from white areas of all Africans who are superfluous to the needs of the economy, and the retention of the bantustans as labour reservoirs and compounds for the unemployed.

The total number of Africans affected by the relocation policy is a complex one because of the inscrutability of official statistics and numerous changes in policy. For instance, whereas (as mentioned above)[50] the government had forecast in 1969 that some 3·8 million Africans remained to be relocated to the bantustans, a statement which followed the 1970 census by Mr Ferdie Hartzenburg, Deputy Minister of Bantu Administration, estimated that by the year 2000 72 per cent of all Africans should be resident in the homelands (compared to 47 per cent in 1970). According to this estimate, the bantustans would at the turn of the century thus have to accommodate 25 million of the expected 35 million Africans in South Africa as a whole (that is, including the independent 'national states'); and if it were further assumed that the figure of 7 million Africans resident in the bantustans in 1970 will experience a normal increase to about 16 million by 2000, the implication is that up to 9 million Africans will be relocated in the interim.[51] Certainly, while the African townships of South Africa are burgeoning and contain countless thousands of illegal residents, official policy claims to have effected a major population shift of Africans away from the urban areas to the homelands over the last decade, preliminary results from the 1980 census indicating that while the numbers of Africans in white areas had increased by 13 per cent during the 1970s, the increase in the homelands' population was 59 per cent for the same period.[52]

The extent to which such a demographic redistribution is more apparent than real and has been achieved by redrawing homeland boundaries so that urban townships have been newly incorporated into the bantustans; and how much relocation policy will be affected by both the recommendations of the Van der Walt Consolidation Committee and the new regional planning approach being adopted by the Botha government, it is impossible to say. Yet, whatever the result, there is no indication that official policy will reorient its emphasis away from population removals on a massive scale; and even though future proposals may yet offer increased land area to the bantustans, the process of consolidation (or rationalization) is of necessity (and has always historically been) associated with the widespread use of coercion to remove African people from wherever their presence is unwanted. Correlatively, the implementation of the relocation policy will necessarily require the continuing collaboration of the leaders of the homelands to which large numbers of Africans will be removed.[53]

Yet the continuity in separate development strategy evinced in the confederal idea is matched by a major change in that the government now appears to have accepted the inevitability of an African population permanently resident in white areas. In marked contrast to the Verwoerdian masterplan which envisaged the physical return of the vast majority of Africans to their homelands, a mood of greater realism now suffuses the latest policy initiatives. Broadly, this is demonstrated at two levels. First, there is now official acknowledgement that efforts to stimulate economic growth in the bantustans so as to soak up 'surplus' African population have failed. Accordingly, current government thinking would appear to be about to reorient homeland development strategy within the context of regional co-operation transcending political (that is, confederal) boundaries.[54] And secondly, while at present the confederal idea suggests that urban Africans will remain linked politically to their homelands, new developments such as the creation of community councils and *verligte* suggestions that urban Africans should have an independent voice in any body co-ordinating a constellation of states, open the door to new possibilities whereby the government might seek to incorporate urban Africans into the central political structure. Such a strategy would doubtless be based on efforts to co-opt the urban African petty-bourgeoisie, but whatever the case, it would clearly signal the end to Verwoerdian-style separate development, while simultaneously inaugurating a new era of domination under apartheid.

Such a scenario, aimed at stabilizing the core, might well have disastrous consequences for the periphery as, for all the talk of locating homeland development within a regional framework, the urgent need for the apartheid regime to contain unrest and revolt in the urban areas demands that the latter be accorded immediate financial and political priority. Accordingly, the contradictions and chronic underdevelopment that characterize the bantustans (which have been the focus of this book) are likely destined to increase rather than decline, and the problem thus remains acute for the government as to whether or not the bantustan policy may backfire. In short, will not the political strains of containing South Africa's surplus and migrant African population undermine the very alliance with the bantustan leaderships which the government has been forging for so long? Is it not possible that, alienated by an approach which favours urban leadership at their expense, the homeland governments might seek to overcome their dependence and become instrumental in winning significant changes for the African majority? And may not the bantustans, teeming with the desperate and unemployed, become bases from which a revolutionary challenge might arise to confront the apartheid government? It is to a final consideration of such questions that the concluding section of this study will now turn.

Perspectives and possibilities

In their pioneering study of South Africa's 'domestic colonialism', Carter, Karis and Stultz concluded that, in establishing the Transkei as the first self-governing territory under the policy of separate territorial development, the Republican government had failed to meet the challenge posed by internal and external criticisms of and pressures against apartheid. They argued that, although the developments in the Transkei were insignificant in themselves, both in the number of persons affected and the extent of change, they might have provided a strikingly attractive alternative for Africans to opportunities in the urban areas if sufficient economic resources (jobs and capital investment) had been devolved. 'Taken together with the imminence of independence for the former High Commission Territories – Bechuanaland, Basutoland, and Swaziland – the Africans' opportunities in their own areas in South Africa might have dulled the edge of African resentment at overt discrimination and restrictions elsewhere.'[55] In practice, however, the South African government had been unduly parsimonious in terms of its expenditure devoted to the Transkei and the other reserves, where the lack of jobs remained a critical problem, little diminished by the implementation of the border industries and industrial decentralization policies. In short, the Transkei remained overwhelmed by economic problems, and existing government policies were too limited to suggest that a serious effort was being made to overcome them.

On the credit side, however, the three American authors felt that Transkeian developments had opened the way for certain constructive opportunities. For the first time in South African history, Africans had been enabled to participate in officially sanctioned electoral and party political activity. In addition, the acceptance of the principle of one-man-one-vote for Africans – even within their limited territorial spheres – was an advance and one which might have an impact on national politics (Carter *et al.* correctly predicting that it would undercut any hope the then Progressive Party might have in persuading Africans to opt for a restricted, qualified franchise in the broader sphere). Furthermore, a 'small, but not unimportant' group of Africans was now being given the opportunity to exercise limited legislative and administrative responsibilities which, even given the continuing influential role of white officials, would serve to provide valuable and necessary practical experience if Africans were to realize their potentialities for political maturity. None the less, given the Transkei's extremely limited resources and the territory's almost total dependence upon South Africa, any future grant of independence was likely to be meaningless 'except, perhaps, to its small group of leaders and local inhabitants'. As far as the majority of Africans were concerned, it could hardly be expected that what would be 'virtually a unilateral settlement by whites for a small, impoverished area would compare with the progressive extension of political, social and economic rights for Africans within the present boundaries of South Africa'.[56]

A decade later, a further trio of American observers was rather more impressed with the potentialities offered by the homelands. Following their detailed study of Bophuthatswana and Kwazulu, Butler, Rotberg and Adams concluded in 1977 that, within a context of international insecurity in Southern Africa, 'the homelands provide new and potentially beneficial leverage for Africans on the otherwise rigid politics of the dominant power', this proposition implying the possibility of an 'evolutionary, not a revolutionary, future for South Africa, a radical redistribution of power, and the use of some of that power in favour of Africans'.[57]

From this perspective, the independence of Transkei and other bantustans 'is meant to provide a recognisable means of muting, if not resolving, the struggle for power between blacks and whites in South Africa', and to buy time for whites.[58] Despite the very considerable constraints imposed by economic underdevelopment and dependence upon South Africa, the independence of Transkei (and by implication of the other bantustans), 'offers a range of options that have hitherto been available to black and white South Africans only in theory'.[59] In deciding whether to opt for independence, homeland leaders will calculate carefully whether it will increase their leverage in and on the overall South African system; and in so far as it is successful, accelerated development of the homelands will lead to an elaboration and deepening of connections between the peripheral economies and the core which will necessitate a machinery to reconcile differences (although hitherto official policy is viewed as having rather maintained economic and administrative dependency).

For Butler, Rotberg and Adams, homeland leaders are pragmatic realists who recognize both their powerlessness and the fact that the homelands have been designed to serve the domestic and international needs of South Africa, yet they have nevertheless sought to take up constructive potentialities of separate development. In practice, despite their origin and clear benefit to whites, the homelands have proved useful to Africans as political and administrative training grounds, while their very existence has given to African leaders a new institutional base and a legitimate platform to articulate the grievances of the African masses, and not merely those of the ethnic groups they represent. Given that the leaders have access to their citizens in the cities, there is a genuine possibility of their developing a mass base within urban areas wherein ethnic division will play a lesser part, while the protection offered by their participating in official institutions has enabled them to criticize and even embarrass the Republican government, their new assertiveness perhaps indicating 'the beginning of a move from hierarchical towards political relations'.[60] However, if (and only if) they can successfully achieve the difficult task of ameliorating living conditions for blacks, securing a relaxation of petty apartheid, and obtaining accretions in political power, will urban, student and radical hostility to homelands subside.

Butler and his co-authors consider that the homeland policy has succeeded in that it has brought forward leaders of distinction and moderation who have not yet given up hope of evolutionary change. In the latter cause, they are now assisted by the chain of events which has followed the Portuguese *coup* which has brought revolutionary-oriented black governments to the borders of South Africa. This may well impart to homeland leaders either greater potentiality for internal leverage, or possibly for leverage outside the present framework in that independent homelands could provide sanctuary for guerrillas of the ANC or PAC. The test of independence, therefore, will be whether it improves bargaining power, with various future options flowing from whether it does or does not. However, dependent upon the price that the homelands and their allies can compel whites to pay:

> South Africa could conceivably use the present homelands as a nucleus of an arrangement of institutional power-sharing or as the core of some form of partition that is not against the interests of Africans now or in the future. If it does, the homelands may constitute a way station, useful to blacks as well as to whites, on the road to a restructuring of South Africa.[61]

This is a conclusion that is echoed by Newell Stultz, one of the trio of earlier authors who, as noted in the introduction to this text, has returned to the further study of Transkei. But rather than adopting a political economy perspective (as has been pursued here), Stultz's contribution is located within a determinedly conservative mould that argues that revolution in South Africa is neither likely nor welcome. Indeed, so pessimistic is Stultz about the prospects for liberal democracy (which he regards as the most preferable but unlikely outcome in South Africa), that his study is premised upon the viewpoint that a majoritarian political solution to the country's problems would probably be productive of continuing injustice, for in a plural society of diverse subcultures (such as he takes South Africa to be), majority rule would likely result in the oppression of the racial minority (the whites) by the blacks. His overriding concern, then, is to elucidate the potential of Transkeian independence for increasing or decreasing racial justice and to assess what contribution it might make to resolving or minimizing conflict in the future.[62]

After an empirical examination of 'Transkei's share' of economic resources, Stultz concludes that, materially speaking, Transkeian independence represents a highly unfavourable separation from South Africa. Furthermore, he argues that independence has been drastically compromised by the removal by Pretoria of Republican citizenship from those Xhosa-designated Transkeian who are permanently resident in the cities. However, because this denial of citizenship to urban Xhosa is manifestly unrealistic, Pretoria will eventually undoubtedly have to adjust its policy, so that (paradoxically) the citizenship issue should not in itself constitute an insurmountable barrier to Transkei's acquiring a politically viable separation. Consequently, notwithstanding Transkei's impoverishment (which is no worse than that of a number of sovereign Third World states), he contests that Transkei is no less objectively independent than other of the international community's smaller states, and that despite its continuing dependence upon South Africa, it is free to undertake those mundane tasks – such as collecting taxes, making laws and allocating resources – which is the principal occupation of most states most of the time. However, although he disputes my own contention that the majority of Transkeians were pressurized into accepting independence against their will through the distortions of the electoral system, he does concede that 'the meaningfulness of Transkei election results can be questioned by fair-minded persons'. Accordingly, he argues that the political separation of Transkei from South Africa 'lacks that critical and widely accepted legitimacy a more democratic decision-making process might have provided',[63] especially as the political process within the homeland is so clearly dominated by Kaiser Matanzima's personalized and centralized leadership.[64]

Stultz goes on to elaborate, in line with my argument presented above, that the material benefits resulting from independence have accrued disproportionately to a tiny percentage of the territory's population, and notably to an élite of chiefs, MPs, managers and local entrepreneurs. However, he regards the drawbacks of this differential impact to be greatly offset by the abolition of racial discrimination within the territory which, while perhaps affecting little the daily lives of ordinary Africans, has fostered individual equality in a legal and symbolic sense that has contributed significantly to the advance of human dignity.[65] And while he goes on to deplore the erosion of civil liberties that took place during the first year of independence, he argues that the Transkei government's conflicts with South Africa over the citizenship issue (Crossroads) and land (taken together with the Republic's own interest in ensuring that Transkei be perceived as fully independent politically), suggest the potential for beneficial political manoeuvre even within the severe limits set by the territory's continuing economic dependence upon South Africa.[66]

In summary, therefore, Stultz concludes that: (1) at present, Transkeian independence does not constitute a genuine partition of South Africa because it does not lessen the reality of white privilege or power, and is blatantly unfair to African interests; (2) even though South Africa has sought to characterize the grant of independence to Transkei as an exercise in decolonization, the historical incorporation of Transkei into South Africa involved the creation of opportunity costs for Transkeians in relation to their legal claims upon the wealth and resources of the Republic which did not hold in the case of the peoples of genuine colonies *vis à vis* their metropoles; (3) despite the moral ambiguities of Transkei's status, it none the less exists as a *de facto* state, and is digging deeper institutional roots with the passing of time; and (4) functionally, Transkei now serves as the equivalent of a black-run provincial government in a highly decentralized confederal political system, and may therefore serve as a pointer to future evolutionary change in South Africa as a whole. Thus it seems plausible, he suggests, to view Transkeian independence as a step towards federation, not in the sense that white South Africans have yet accepted this implication, but rather with reference to the fact that the homeland's separation has objectively promoted power-sharing by exposing whites to the vision of independent African political power. Meanwhile, (5) the elimination of legal apartheid from the territory and the emancipation of 2 million Africans from direct control by the South African authorities constitute a significant achievement by the Transkeian political leadership, while the termination of legal apartheid within the homeland will presumably contribute to an undermining of at least petty apartheid in the Republic by the power of successful example. Finally (6), he proposes that if conflict in South Africa were at some future date to arrive at a situation of politico-military stalemate, the constructive relations which the white rulers have forged with the Transkeian state might well provide a positive demonstration of the beneficial potentialities of a partition as an alternative to revolution or endless civil war.[67]

Stultz's assessment of Transkeian independence is undoubtedly a thoughtful piece which reflects a clearly humanitarian motivation, yet its political premises are so profoundly conservative (and many would use unkinder terms) that there is little point in confronting his analysis here. That task has already been undertaken elsewhere,[68] and readers may themselves prefer to make their own judgements as to the relative merits of his own and the present author's widely contrasting approaches. Suffice to say, therefore, that although there are significant differences between the studies of Carter *et al.*, Butler *et al.* and Stultz, they all conform to an approach which tends to argue that, although designed to entrench existing patterns of political and economic inequality, the bantustan policy has unintended consequences which may contribute to the eventual undermining of racial domination. Thus according to an analysis offered in similar vein by Michael Savage in 1975, the dynamics of interaction between the bantustan leaders and the South African government had up till then at least four major unforeseen results. These were first, that conflict had propelled homeland leaders into taking radical political positions against apartheid. Secondly, confrontation with the white government had unified the bantustan leaders on a number of critical issues, so that black solidarity was now challenging the strategy of divide and rule. Thirdly, the homeland politicians had raised issues in public (such as the allocation of resources and the forms of black and white contact) which the Republican authorities would have preferred to have swept under the carpet; and fourthly, political interaction between black and white leaders had stimulated the growth of political awareness among the population outside the homelands. Accordingly, concluded Savage, while the flexibility of the system of white rule had enabled it to make marginal adjustments to rationalize the system of domination, the very machinery of apartheid had simultaneously worked to foster 'a political consciousness amongst blacks that separation can be used as a strategy to create an organisational base from which to challenge and to change the structural bases of existing inequalities'.[69]

If such an analysis should not be lightly dismissed (for it does seek to spotlight the dynamics of South African politics), the rapid pace of regional and domestic events since 1975 suggests that the approach is now manifestly outdated. For instance, not only have any pretensions to a wide-ranging unity between the homeland leaders been broken down as they have gone their separate ways but, more importantly, post-Soweto black politics are now less oligarchical and more mass-based than they arguably were before the mid-1970s. Indeed, it is also probably the case that even at the time that Savage was writing the supposed politically progressive effects of the bantustan policy were exaggerated, for as Heribert Adam commented, many of the 'unintended consequences' of the strategy were largely rhetorical and were even carefully calculated by the more sophisticated apartheid engineers. From Adam's perspective, therefore, rather than reflecting a growing political polarization between black and white leaders, the working out of the bantustan policy indicated an increasing *institutionalization* of racial conflict, with the whites still dictating the tune. In contrast, the alternative prediction that Adam offered was that given developments internal and external to the Republic as well as the latter's military might, 'the outdated racial hierarchy in South Africa will be gradually undermined by an evolving class structure, in line with western societies, in which a small élite of the subordinate strata increasingly participates in the economic rewards and political status of the system'.[70] The implication to be drawn from this analysis, therefore, is that as the bantustan scenario proceeds (whether or not each and every homeland is propelled into independence), the effect will be to draw the emergent African petty-bourgeoisie into more explicit, and more dependent, collaboration with the white state.

It is the aspect of class alliance and collaboration that has been emphasized in the present study of Transkei. Whereas the authors considered above tend to focus upon the homeland leaders as in actuality or potentiality representing African interests, the argument here is that the bantustan state apparatuses are principally coercive instruments through which ruling homeland petty-bourgeois elements preside over South Africa's migrant workforce and surplus population. Rather than articulating their grievances, the homeland leaders are manifestly involved in the political control of the African mass, actively participating in the subordination of black labour in the peripheries to white capital in the core. Although the leaders may at times voice mass grievances and rail against the oppressions of apartheid, in practice their governments represent the interests of a small African intermediary class whose material existence has been to a great extent summoned up by, and remains directly dependent upon, the support of the South African state. And although it has been suggested by sympathetic commentators that bantustan leaders have on occasion extracted gains for Africans, it cannot convincingly be argued that these have yet brought significant advantage to the African majority. The resettlement of countless Africans continues; administrative policy and legal enactments contrive to eliminate Republican Africans' effective claim to South African citizenship and their right to participate in the central polity; the economic and financial dependence of the homelands shows no prospect of declining; and political repression, in the form of structured elections and official intimidation (as in Transkei) would seem to be replicated throughout all the bantustans. Outspoken criticism by bantustan leaders of apartheid may indeed have been a contributory factor leading to the relaxation of petty apartheid, but the desegregation of limited social facilities in the white areas (for example, hotels and restaurants) tends to benefit only a few, while the advantages of non-racialism as implemented in the independent homelands accrue mainly to a petty-bourgeois minority, and have hitherto been achieved only at the cost of loss of South African citizenship for homeland citizens. Only if homeland leaders were able to mobilize mass urban support would they be able to develop a political base from which to make a significant challenge to the South African government. Hitherto, only Chief Gatsha Buthelezi has sought to employ this strategy by the extension of his Inkatha movement to the towns; but while he enjoyed some considerable initial success, recent developments – notably his post-Soweto alienation from such contemporary urban leaders as Ntatho Motlana, Bishop Desmond Tutu and the Committee of Ten, together with its continuing rejection by younger militants – suggest that Inkatha is losing whatever mass base it might once have had. Indeed, Buthelezi has now moved significantly to the right of the black political spectrum, and his now expressed willingness to involve Inkatha in elections for the Community Council system and the Kwazulu homeland in a Botha-style South African confederation clearly indicates that he is being drawn into a more explicitly collaborative relationship with the apartheid regime.[71]

Butler *et al.* suggest that, through accretions of power, the bantustan leaders may be able to exert leverage upon the white state for meaningful concessions. Such a perspective, however, overlooks the dynamics of settler colonialism (as exhibited in South Africa), whose political economy needs to be understood in relation to the historic expansion of western imperialism and in the light of the notions of underdevelopment and dependency. Thus Kenneth Good has suggested[72] that one of the overriding characteristics of settler states in Africa has been their political rigidity, and that given settler societies have displayed a capacity for relatively autonomous capitalist development (based upon the coercive exploitation of African land and labour, combined with policies of economic nationalism externally), 'the long-term problem for a *colon* society is the containment of the new African classes brought forth "inadvertently", albeit as a necessary component of their development path'.[73] The relevant point is that significant concessions cannot be made to the forces of emergent African nationalism, for such would threaten the very material basis of settler existence. In South Africa, as Robert Davies puts it, all three elements of the dominant bloc, 'the settler bourgeoisie, which runs the state apparatus, the white workers who depend for their economic advantages on the use of political power, and the international capitalists', gain from their racially exclusive access to the means of production and the coercive direction of African labour.[74] Historically, therefore, as in other settler societies in Africa, while the whites have exhibited capacity for pragmatic manoeuvre, they have been intransigent on the fundamentals of political control, the postwar years having seen the complete emasculation of the popular African leadership. And while the apartheid regime is attempting to generate a 'legitimate' bourgeoisie with its associated political leadership in the homelands (and, we might now add, in the urban centres as well), 'this new element is conspicuously presented in dependent collaboration with white power, or obliged to act as guardedly critical spokesmen for their people's misery'.[75]

It is precisely because of this political rigidity of the settler state that we should be wary of the interpretation of contemporary South Africa that suggests that the white state may be prepared to offer major concessions to blacks, and thereby to engage in a quasi-American politics of bargaining and compromise at a pace which would give homeland leaders 'a hold over their legally defined populations sufficient to ensure the preservation of order' and whereby 'the redistribution of power and resources, though limited and slow, was genuine and progressive'.[76] Rather, meaningful bargaining by the white regime is likely to begin only when it is placed in a position of weakness, when the white state (and the unity of the white ruling class) is severely threatened by revolutionary forces from within and without, by which time (as was Muzorewa in Zimbabwe–Rhodesia) it is also probable that the homeland leaders will long have been overtaken as claimants to popular trust. This is not to argue that a revolutionary end is necessarily determined for South Africa's future, for the western powers will undoubtedly seek to protect their vested interests and may well at some critical political juncture seek to compel the apartheid leadership to make a deal with any credible internal leadership (which would necessarily have to be able to draw upon significant mass support) or, more likely, to reach a political settlement which fulfils the minimum demands of the revolutionary forces themselves.

Such a scenario is based upon the recognition that mounting assaults inside South Africa upon the white state by the ANC indicate that the process of liberation war has begun. And from a perspective which argues that the prospect of political gradualism in South Africa is remote, the 'independence' of Transkei (or any other bantustan) appears extremely fragile, for tied to the apparatus of the white state through their abject financial dependence, the subordinate bantustan regimes are likely to exhibit little capacity for autonomous survival. Yet, in spite of everything, the will to survive on the part of the locally ruling elements will be there, and the bantustan governments will likely respond to their own crises in a number of different ways, according to their own particular circumstances. If faced with the threat of guerrilla activity within their own borders, they may well throw their armies into the fray against the forces of subversion in defence of their political 'integrity'. Alternatively, it is conceivable that bantustan regimes may in certain cases (for instance, especially those such as Kwazulu which border upon neighbouring states which might be harbouring guerrillas) seek protection by covertly or overtly attempting to align themselves with the forces of liberation.[77] The response of the liberation movements might conceivably be more pragmatic in the long run than they would at present care to admit, but the crux of the matter would be that the bantustan authorities would have to have something substantial to offer, this probably being the freedom for the movements to operate within their territories. But such a possibility should not be exaggerated. For a dependent bantustan regime which probably would not retain popular support, such an alignment would be a high-risk strategy, and whether it would be able to successfully straddle the fence separating the white state from the liberation movements without falling off can only be regarded as doubtful in the extreme.

What is more likely is that widespread disaffection in the townships (itself encouraged by successes of the armed liberation movements) may spread to the homelands themselves, and rural resistance to apartheid (whose potential was most dramatically demonstrated by the Pondoland Revolt of 1960–1), may well take the form of direct attacks upon the bantustan leaderships and symbols of their authority. If in most cases the bantustan security forces are able to suppress such militant activity, the fragmentation of the homelands may also work to ensure that pockets of resistance are able to survive in isolation from the authorities; and if contained directly by the intervention of the white state, either ethnic 'sovereignty' will have been violated, or (if under the guise of mutual defence) any ambiguity about the collaborative role of the bantustan regimes will be finally removed. Even if popular revolt within the bantustans is unlikely to feature as a critical feature in the crisis that faces white South Africa, it is very possible that it will undermine the already fragile authority of the bantustan leaderships and thrust them into yet closer alliance with the white government, while simultaneously at least stretching the capacity of the latter to survive.

In conclusion, therefore, the prospect is that the bantustan policy is beset by its own limitations. Far from being possible way stations on the road to a restructured South Africa, those bantustans which opt for or are cajoled into independence are likely to enjoy only a finite existence as separate political entities. As grossly dependent regimes with minimal popular support, their very existence would seem to be predicated upon the continuance of white power. It could be, as Stultz suggests, that longevity may improve the prospects for survival and that an 'independent' Transkei will become a feature of the Southern African landscape for a considerable period of time to come; yet the prognosis here is that, given its dependence upon and alignment with the apartheid regime, the Transkeian state apparatus has little capacity for autonomous being, and that in time to come it will likely be reabsorbed into the body politic of a liberated South Africa.

Notes

1. For an extended discussion of the concept of partition as applied to South Africa (which he takes to involve the notion of not just racial division but of a 'just' separation), see Stultz (1980), *passim* but especially Chapter 6. For my own assessment of Stultz's contribution, see pp. 297–300 below.
2. Adam (1971), pp. 69, 53.
3. Although the emerging pattern (exemplified in all three existing cases) is for independence constitutions to reduce the proportion of chiefs and traditional leaders to equality with directly elected members.
4. Two examples, both of which fit into the analysis below, may suffice. (1) Proclamation R252, which makes provision for detention without trial, was in full operation during the 1978 election in the Ciskei; and during that electoral contest, a number of Opposition meetings were banned and Opposition leaders detained, with others leaving the Ciskei or going into hiding. The Ciskei National Independence Party won all twenty-two elective seats, with Chief Minister Sebe thereafter refusing to recognize the three *ex officio* chiefly members of the Assembly who opposed the CNIP as the Opposition. (2) Similarly, Proclamation R276 was used to reverse the result of the 1978 election in Venda, where the Opposition Venda Independence

THE BANTUSTAN STRATEGY – PROSPECTS AND POSSIBILITIES 305

Party (which, despite its nomenclature, was at this time opposed to independence) won 31 out of 42 elective seats, only to have eleven of the successful candidates detained before the meeting of the legislative assembly whose purpose was to select a government. Thereafter Chief Patrick Mpephu, reputedly the most conservative of the bantustan leaders, was re-elected Chief Minister with the support of the *ex officio* chiefs and led his homeland to the independence which the electorate had rejected. (SAIRR, *A Survey, 1978*, pp. 287–8, 297–8. Also 'Venda government snuffs out VIP victory', *RDM*, 22 July 1978.)

5. Most of the self-governing homelands operate their own police services, with all three independent territories developing an army. It is also on public record that the Ciskei runs its own intelligence service, headed by Chief Sebe's brother, which operates directly under the authority of the Chief Minister. (SAIRR, *A Survey, 1979*, p. 327.)
6. The only exception is QwaQwa, which derives nearly 60 per cent of its revenue from internal sources. The reasons for this are not wholly clear to the author, although it needs to be noted that QwaQwa is the most peculiar of all the African 'homelands', with in 1970 only 24,200 (or 1·7 per cent) South Sotho residing there out of a *de jure* population of 1,451,800. QwaQwa has since then been the recipient of massive numbers of resettled Africans, the *de facto* population having increased to 232,226 in 1980 (SAIRR, *A Survey, 1980*, p. 191). In fact, so overcrowded has this tiny homeland now become that the Benso *Economic Revue: QwaQwa* (Pretoria, 1978) advocated that the territory should be transformed into a 'city-state'.
7. The value of mineral production (excluding platinum) in the non-independent homelands was in all cases less than R1 million in 1978, except in Lebowa (R66 million), KaNgwane (R14 million) and Kwazulu (R6 million). The estimated value of Bophuthatswana's total mineral product was R245 million for 1980. (See SAIRR, *A Survey, 1979*, p. 376.)
8. In 1973–4 migrant workers contributed 64·8 per cent of the Gross 'National' Income of Lebowa; 77·5 per cent of Gazankulu; 78 per cent of Venda and 41 per cent in Kwazulu (in 1973). (SAIRR, *A Survey, 1977*, p. 375.)
9. Eschel Rhoodie, then Secretary for Information, claimed in 1977 that the transfer of wealth in South Africa from whites to blacks 'is on a *per capita* basis, very much higher than any of the world's nations attains via foreign aid programmes', while Dr Connie Mulder similarly compared UN expenditure on developing countries with South African expenditure on 'the eight developing countries in our subcontinent'. Both quoted in Kane-Berman (1978), p. 246.
10. *RDM*, 15 December 1978.
11. SAIRR, *A Survey, 1978*, p. 268; and on Venda at independence, Duff (1979). For the official version, see the feature articles in *Informa*, vol. XXVI, 6, June 1979; and Anonymous (1979).
12. *RDM*, 6 April 1976.
13. SAIRR, *A Survey, 1977*, p. 316; and *1979*, p. 319. The financial weapon is an important one in inducing homelands to move on to independence. In early 1980, Hudson Ntsanwisi protested at what he perceived as discrimination in favour of Venda at the expense of Gazankulu, pointing out that although the actual population of the two territories was similar and the *de jure* population of Gazankulu was much larger, Venda's budget for 1980–1 was more

than double that of Gazankulu (R104m as opposed to R49m). Professor Ntsanwisi ascribed this discrepancy to the fact that Venda had chosen to opt for independence while Gazankulu had remained a self-governing territory. (SAIRR, *A Survey, 1980*, p. 396.)
14. ibid., *1979*, p. 316.
15. *RDM*, 27 January 1979.
16. *RDM*, 15 December 1978.
17. *RDM*, 21 December 1978.
18. *RDM*, 15 April 1977, and 13 September 1978.
19. Thus Mangope: 'We deliberately chose independence for Bophuthatswana in the faith that the example we have committed ourselves to, namely of non-racialism and tolerance and democratic freedoms enshrined in a Bill of Rights, would help to soften the political rigidities and serve as a catalyst for accelerated, creative change in the whole subcontinent.' (*RDM*, 22 December 1978.)
20. Basically, this amendment made permanent all those arbitrary powers of detention, prohibition, banning and restriction previously operated under separate Emergency Proclamations (such as R400 in Transkei and R252 in Ciskei).
21. Reporting upon discussion with the Vorster government and various homeland leaders in 1974, Sir Arthur Snelling commented: 'Some of [the homeland leaders] say they want a federation, or confederation, of Homelands, as recommended by the United Party. But in my view, based on [British] decolonisation experience, these leaders underestimate the pressures both to take independence soon after a neighbour has acquired it, and to retain full sovereignty once it has been obtained.' (Snelling, 1974.)
22. See statement by Moolman (Director of the African Institute in Pretoria) (1977).
23. Krause (1976).
24. 'Verligte blueprint for SA's future', *RDM*, 27 May 1977; for the full text, see Olivier (undated).
25. Botha (1978).
26. See *inter alia* Bonner and Webster (1979), and Cheadle (1979), pp. 1–12 and 12–26 respectively. Also Cooper and Ensor (1979); Mare (1979); and Duncan (1979). For a useful overview of the new strategy, see Price (1980).
27. 'Blacks' land is running out', *RDM*, 14 December 1977. According to Dr P. Kornhoof, Minister of Co-operation and Development, only 494,689 hectares of land remained at the end of 1980 to be acquired for Africans for the 1936 quota to be achieved.
28. SAIRR, *A Survey, 1979*, pp. 302–4.
29. ibid.,*1980*, pp. 390–2.
30. In his budget allocation for the 1981 tax year, Senator Owen Horwood, Minister of Finance, proposed an additional R15 million be added to the R74 million already set aside for consolidation, the total of R89 million representing a 41 per cent increase on spending for the same purpose in 1980. (*RDM*, 27 March 1980.)
31. *RDM*, 27 February and 29 March 1980.
32. SAIRR, *A Survey, 1980*, p. 390.
33. *The Star* (weekly), 1 November 1980.
34. SAIRR, *A Survey, 1979*, pp. 2, 647–51.

35. At a 'summit meeting' with 250 of South Africa's top financiers and industrialists in December 1979, Dr Piet Kornhoof, Minister of Co-operation and Development, said that the constellation proposal required agreement on (1) a security pact in terms of which the participating countries would not threaten each other and would present a unified front to any threat from outside; (2) the creation of a wider customs union in which goods would flow freely across national borders; (3) creation of markets in each territory for agricultural and industrial goods produced in the member countries; and (4) the establishment of sound transport links. (*South African Digest*, 30 November 1979, p. 2.) None of these requirements is likely to appeal to states within the region which are attempting to reduce their dependence upon South Africa.
36. On a state visit to Bophuthatswana in October 1979, President Kaiser Matanzima welcomed the call for a constellation of Southern African states, provided that such a grouping consisted only of independent states with sovereign constitutions. (*RDM*, 11 October 1979.)
37. *The Star* (weekly), 20 September 1980.
38. SAIRR, *A Survey, 1978*, p. 289.
39. The Commission was composed of certain prominent South African academics (Professor Quail, Professor Ernst Marais and Dr Martin Van den Berg) together with Professor Robert Rotberg and Professor Peter Kilby from the USA, Sir Arthur Snelling and Professor Coax Lolandle.
40. *RDM*, 13 February 1980.
41. SAIRR, *A Survey, 1980*, pp. 404–5.
42. *RDM*, 26 February 1980.
43. *RDM*, 31 March 1980.
44. SAIRR, *A Survey, 1980*, pp. 405–6.
45. *Guardian* (London), 7 October 1980.
46. SAIRR, *A Survey, 1980*, pp. 406–7.
47. ibid., *1978*, p. 321.
48. Note that such a scenario is not necessarily inconsistent with the new willingness to concede the acceptance of the notion of a permanent African population in white areas (referred to below), for one aspect of the government's 'new deal' for urban Africans seeks to forge a stronger link between permission to reside in urban areas to the availability of approved employment and housing. In other words, the right to reside in urban areas will remain conditional and will not become an unqualified legal right.
49. In November 1979 the Department of Plural Relations and Development (formerly Bantu Administration and Development until 1978) was transmogrified into the Department of Co-operation (between South Africa and its 'black' – now 'national' – states) and Development.
50. See p. 44 above.
51. Kane-Berman (1978), pp. 242–3.
52. SAIRR, *A Survey, 1980*, p. 68.
53. For important surveys of the relocation policy, see Desmond (1971); Baldwin (1975); Nash (1980); and especially Mare (1980).
54. 'Homelands: PW talks of facing reality', *The Star* (weekly), 25 October 1980.
55. Carter *et al.* (1967), p. 176.
56. ibid., pp. 180–1.
57. Butler *et al.* (1977), p. 219.

58. ibid.
59. ibid., p. 220.
60. ibid., p. 225.
61. ibid., p. 231. For a detailed critique of Butler et al. see my review (1978).
62. Stultz (1980).
63. ibid., p. 56.
64. ibid., p. 66.
65. ibid., p. 94.
66. ibid., pp. 98–129.
67. ibid., pp. 130–59; see also Stultz (1979).
68. Southall (1980c).
69. Savage (1975).
70. Adam (1975).
71. Southall (1981).
72. Good (1976).
73. ibid., p. 610.
74. Davies (1973), p. 45.
75. Good (1976), p. 609.
76. Butler et al. (1977), p. 229.
77. There has already been suggestion that the return of a number of former PAC exiles to Transkei (headed by T. T. Letlaka, formerly Minister of Finance and now Minister of Justice) indicates the beginning of a rapprochement between the bantustan government and the PAC. Thus according to *Africa Confidential* (5 November 1976, vol. 17, 22) the Transkeian administration is staffed with a substantial number of former PAC–Poqo members, which suggests that Motanzima is trying to build up some sort of relationship with the PAC leadership abroad. Given, however, the attempt by Poqo activists to assassinate Kaiser Matanzima in 1962 (see Horrell, 1971, pp. 62–3), as well as a host of other reasons, this report should be treated with considerable scepticism.

Postscript

Like many authors who today write on contemporary Southern Africa – where events move so fast – I have fallen prey to the temptation to update the manuscript before it goes to press. However, being at present resident in Canada rather than based in neighbouring Lesotho, my sources on Transkei are now second-hand, and my analysis of the latest developments has inevitably to be conducted from long distance.

Since I completed the revision of my concluding chapters in June 1981, Kaiser Matanzima has declared his intention to retire from the Presidency of Transkei. He announced this decision on the fifth anniversary of 'independence', within a week after the TNIP had consolidated its hold over the Bunga in a general election which, even more so than in 1976, it had won handsomely before the first vote was cast. By retaining the allegiance of 72 out of 75 chiefs when the Assembly was dissolved, the ruling party faced contests from the Opposition DPP in only six of the elective seats.[1]

Matanzima's decision came as a surprise, for he has clearly enjoyed power, and it may be speculated that his resignation may have been prompted by the ill-health from which he is known to have suffered for some time. Whatever the case, now that Stella Sicgau is back in the government, the presidential succession will likely facilitate the restoration of the balance between the Thembu and Pondo chiefly élites, which was upset when Kaiser Matanzima assumed office as President after the death of Botha Sicgau in 1979. Thus the man now tipped to succeed to the Presidency is Paramount Chief Tutor Ndamase of Western Pondoland, although it is predicted that the Matanzimas will ensure that the office of head of state will revert to the purely ceremonial function it fulfilled before Kaiser Matanzima's own occupancy effectively transformed it into an executive role.

Whoever succeeds to the Presidency, it will not effect the nature of the regime, whose repressive powers have been supplemented during 1981 by the passage of a bill, aimed principally at the press, making it illegal to publish anything about the Transkei Government without ministerial approval, and requiring people who publish such information to disclose their sources.[2]

In these depressing circumstances, it is hardly surprising that the DPP should be able to call upon only six candidates foolhardy enough to challenge the regime in the latest election, and this suggests that opposition is being increasingly directed through extra-parliamentary channels in the form of a resurgence of support for the ANC. Evidence for this is not only the continuation of school boycotts, attacks and protests directed at the regime (including a hand-grenade assault upon the home of Major-General Martin Ngceba, Commissioner of Police, in December 1980),[3] but the reimposition of (yet another) State of Emergency in June 1981 which was justified by George Matanzima by reference to a resuscitation of activity by the exiled Congress Movements, and followed the detention the previous month of Brigadier Keswa, Commissioner of the Defence Force, and two other high ranking officers, for alleged contacts with the ANC.[4] Certainly, the decision of former Opposition leader, Dalindyebo, to throw in his lot with the liberation camp may well facilitate the further penetration of Transkei by the ANC among his supporters. Finally, it is perhaps a pointer of things to come that in August 1981, five guerrillas who had successfully planted bombs in East London and Port Elizabeth should withdraw to Transkei where they killed two local policemen before two of them were later shot dead and three captured by a combined South African, Transkeian and Bophuthatswana security force. If, as is supposed, the insurgents were attempting to make their way to Lesotho, it raises the possibility that they chose their route through Transkei in expectation of receiving succour and support from the local population.[5]

If, as would seem likely, disaffection continues to develop, the regime will become increasingly dependent upon the security forces, whose loyalty it will need to retain. It is therefore significant that, following the arrests of former Police Commissioner Cwele for suspected involvement in the 1980 coup attempt, and the more recent detention of Brigadier Keswa, Matanzima has appointed Major-General Ronald Reid-Daly, former commander of the *Selous Scouts* (the crack anti-guerrilla unit of the white Rhodesian regime), to head the Defence Force. His mission, apparently, together with the six former *Scouts* he has taken with him, is to re-organize the bantustan military, a task which will be oriented to combatting the ANC threat and which will involve an extension of the already close liaison between the Transkei and South African security services. Indeed, Reid-Daly has already stated that one of Transkei's key roles will be to prevent neighbouring Lesotho from being used as a springboard for insurgency against South Africa.[6]

Despite continuing collaboration with the Republic in the security sphere, there are continuing strains as Transkei now reaps the increasingly bitter harvest of bantustan independence. The Matanzimas have been particularly angered by recent South African efforts to control their government's erratic handling of finance and the economy, and have sought to assert their autonomy by replacing South African expatriate bureaucrats with white Rhodesian emigrés, about 30 of whom have been imported to fill key civil service and security positions.[7] Even more so, however, Transkei–South African relations have soured over continuing deportation of squatters from the Western Cape. Police raids on the Nyanga squatter camp outside Cape Town in August 1981 resulted in about 1,000 workers, deemed by the police to be illegal migrants, being transported to Transkei. While a number of squatters (many of whom had been forced to leave families and possessions in the Cape) stubbornly insisted on making their way back to Nyanga by attempting to elude road blocks in South Africa established to contain them, about 600 camped out in church halls in Umtata, refusing to go back to their villages and demanding that they be returned to the Cape. Although the South African government presented a cheque for R35,000 to the Transkeian authorities with which to compensate those who had been 'repatriated', the Matanzimas declared their intention to assist squatters to return and to evict those who were not Transkeian citizens (of which it was alleged there were a number). Angered because the relocation exercise had taken place only a week after Kaiser Matanzima had paid a state visit to Cape Town (which made it look as though he was acting in collusion with the Republican authorities), Chief George accused South Africa of violating an understanding about the humane treatment of Transkeians in the Cape.[8] But as both Matanzimas must know, the scene for this entire relocation tragedy was set when they accepted the definition of Transkeian citizenship laid out in the 'independence' settlement.

The relocation issue has overlaid growing differences between South Africa and Transkei concerning the proposed constellation of states. Thus at a meeting with Prime Minister Botha in July, George Matanzima insisted that his government could not participate in the constellation unless the Republic took prompt action to clear bottlenecks holding up aid and committed itself to the genuine development of Transkei.[9] But more critically, the Matanzima Government has taken offence at the notion of 'independence' for Ciskei on the grounds that this will destroy the Xhosa national unit. Arguing that the Sebe Government has deliberately eschewed an amalgamation of the two Xhosa units, the Transkei authorities claim to be the sole national representatives of the Xhosas and now maintain that they will refuse to sit with the Ciskeian Government at any meeting of a constellation of states.[10] How the enacted grant of 'independence' to Ciskei in December 1981 will affect Transkei's willingness to enter any formal confederal arrangement with the Republic therefore remains to be seen – but whatever the case, the limited autonomy of the Transkei Government will continue to be bound by the severe constraints of its dependence upon South Africa.

Notes

1. *Africa Research Bulletin*, October 1–31, 1981, p. 6214; and Patrick Laurence, 'Transkei poll will confirm Chief Kaiser's rule', *The Guardian*, 8 September 1981.

2. *The Times*, 14 April 1981.
3. *The Star* (Weekly Airmail Edition), 20 December 1980.
4. *Focus* (News Bulletin of the International Defence and Aid Fund), 35, July–August 1981, p. 2.
5. Laurence (1981).
6. *Africa Research Bulletin* June 1–30, 1981, p. 6087; and Laurence (1981).
7. *The New York Times*, 11 August 1981.
8. *Daily Telegraph*, 22 August 1981; 26 August 1981; *Guardian* 25 August 1981; *Times* 26 August 1981; *The Star* (Weekly) 10 October 1981.
9. *Africa Research Bulletin* August 15–September 1, 1981, p. 6145. Matanzima accused two top-level South African advisers of having more power in his own country than himself, and stated that because of the hold up in capital aid projects, there would be little to show the people of Transkei on the fifth anniversary of independence.
10. *Daily Dispatch*, 4 February 1981; *Rand Daily Mail*, 5 February 1981.

Bibliography

Official publications

South Africa
Cape Hansard, 1894.
Cape Parliamentary Papers G3 – 1894, *Report of Commission on Labour Supply*, III.
Report of the Natives' Land Commission (Beaumont), I, II, 1916 (UG 19 – 1916).
Transvaal Province, *Report of the Local Government Commission* (Stallard) (TP 1, Pretoria, 1922).
Report of the Native Economic Commission 1930–32 (UG 22 – 1932).
Report of Departmental Committee appointed to Enquire into and Report upon Certain Questions Relating to Native Labour in Zululand, the Transkeian Territories and the Ciskei, 1935 (Welsh).
Board of Trade and Industries, Report no. 219: *Establishment of Industries in Native Territories* (1936).
Third Interim Report of the Industrial and Agricultural Requirements Commission: Fundamentals of Economic Policy in the Union (UG 40 – 1941).
Report of the Witwatersrand Mine Natives' Wages Commission on the Remuneration and Conditions of Employment of Natives on Witwatersrand Gold Mines and Regulations and Conditions of Employment of Natives of Transvaal Undertakings of Victoria Falls and Transvaal Power Company Limited (UG 21 – 1944).
Board of Trade and Industry Report no. 282: *Investigations into Manufacturing Industries in the Union of South Africa* (1945).
Social and Economic Planning Council, Report no. 9: *The Native Reserves and Their Place in the Economy of the Union of South Africa* (UG 32 – 1946).
Report of the Commission Appointed to Enquire into the Operation of the Laws in Force in the Union relating to Natives in or near Urban Areas; the Native Pass Laws; and the Employment in Mines and other Industries of Migratory Labour (Fagan) (UG 28 – 1948).
Debates of the South African House of Assembly (1951–76).
Debates of the South African Senate (1951–76).
Report of Commission for the Socio-Economic Development of the Bantu

Areas within the Union of South Africa (Summary) (Tomlinson) (UG 61 – 1955).
Memorandum Explaining the Background and Objects of the Promotion of the Bantu Self-Government Bill, 1959 (WP3 – 1959).
Department of Information, *The Transkei: Major Steps on the Road to Self-Determination* (1962), Fact Paper no. 102.
Decisions of the Government in Regard to the Important Recommendations of the Commission of Enquiry regarding Europeans in the Transkeian Territories (WP CC – 1964).
Explanatory Memorandum on the Bantu Homelands Citizenship Bill, 1970 (WP2 – 1970).
Republic of South Africa, *South African Statistics*, 1970.
Explanatory Memorandum on the Bantu Homelands Constitution Bill, 1971 (WP1 – 1971).
South African Government Gazette, 136, 5320, 22 October 1976.
Economic Revue: QwaQwa (Pretoria, 1978).
Department of Labour and Mines, *Report of the Commission of Inquiry into Labour Legislation* (Part I) (RP47/1979).

The Transkei

Transkeian Territories General Council, *Proceedings and Reports of Select Committees* (various, 1908–30), King William's Town: The King Printing Company Ltd.
Annual Report of the Transkei Public Service Commission, 1964–79.
Transkei Government, *Debates of the Transkeian Legislative Assembly*, 1964–76.
Transkei Government, *Commission of Enquiry into the Standard of Education in The Transkei*, 1973.
Transkei Government, *Debates of the National Assembly*, 1976–8.
Transkei Government, *Department of Agriculture and Forestry Annual Report* (various years).
Estimate of Expenditure to be defrayed from the Transkei Revenue Fund, Year Ending 31 March 1979 (TG 2 – 1978).
Transkei Government Gazette (various).

United Kingdom[1]
Financial and Economic Position of Basutoland (1935), Command 4907.

Other primary sources

Fox, F. W. and Back, D. (1941). *A Preliminary Survey of the Agricultural and Nutritional Problems of the Ciskei and Transkei* (Report to the Chamber of Mines).
Jokl, E. (1941) *A Labour and Manpower Survey of the Transkeian Territories* (mimeo, copy in SAIRR library).
Report of Meeting of Delegates from Local Authorities in the Transkeian Territories re recently Published Statement by the Honourable the

Minister of Native Affairs on the Future of these Territories, 30 March 1951 (mimeo).
Report of Meeting on 10 April 1951 at which a Deputation from Local Authorities and other Public Bodies was received by Dr. H. F. Verwoerd (mimeo).
Verbatim Report of a Meeting of Public Bodies, 21 May 1955 for the purpose of considering recent statements issued by the Department of Native Affairs Regarding the Government Policy as Affecting the Transkeian Territories (mimeo).
Minutes and other documents of the *Transkeian Territories Civic Association Executive Committee* (1951–76, spasmodic).
Proceedings of the Transkeian Territories Civic Association Annual Congress (1951–76) (mimeo).
Report of a Meeting of Representatives of Municipalities, Village Management Boards and Civic Associations in the Transkeian Territories, 16 April 1962.
Memorandum Submitted by the Mount Frere Chamber of Commerce and the Umtata and District Chamber of Commerce on behalf of the Europeans in the Transkei, to the Commission of Enquiry Appointed in Terms of Government Notice No. 1467, Dated 7th September, 1962, especially pp. 9–16.
Resumé of the Activities and Endeavours of the Liaison Committee since its Establishment (26 February 1963); and Liaison Committee Executive Committee Meetings and correspondence.
Xhosa Development Corporation, *Annual Reports*, 1966–75.
Transkei Development Corporation, *Information for Potential Investors in Transkei*, April 1976 (mimeo).
Statement by Miss Stella Sicgau, Transkei Minister of Interior, in London on 11 February 1976 (mimeo).
Koyana, D. S. (1976) 'A New State: The Republic of Transkei – Why and How Transkei Becomes Independent' (mimeo).
Letlaka, T. T. (1976) Transkei's Independence: The Historic Breakthrough for a people – the Path to Freedom and Self-Determination in South Africa (mimeo).
The Emergence of a New State, 26 October 1976 (circular, mimeo).
Schedule of Results of Voting on Motion No. 2 of 1974: Independence for the Transkei.
Appropriation Bill 1978–79, Speech by Minister of Finance (mimeo).
Records of the *Transkei National Independence Party*, collected by author.
Transkei Calendar (various years).
Snelling, Sir Arthur (1974) 'The Scope for British Investment in the South African Homelands' (Report to Members of the United Kingdom South African Trade Association, December, mimeo).
Various Bantu Authority records kept at the library of the University of South Africa (UNISA).
Various Bantu Authority records collected by the author.

Newspapers and journals

Africa Confidential
Africa Magazine
African Business & Chamber of Commerce Review
Africa Research Bulletin
The Citizen
Comment and Opinion: A Weekly Survey of the South African Press and Radio (for Afrikaans sources, *Die Burger, Die Vaderland, Hoofstad*).
Commercial Transport Freight
Daily Dispatch
Daily News
Eastern Province Herald
Farmers Weekly
Financial Gazette
Financial Mail
Focus
Guardian (London)
Home Goods Retailing
Imvo Transkei
Natal Mercury
New Age
Newscheck
New York Times
Pretoria News
Private Eye (London)
Rand Daily Mail
South African Digest
Sunday Times
Sunday Tribune
The Star
The Times (London)
To The Point
Umtunywa
Washington Post (Washington)
Weekend Post

Theses and Dissertations

Baldwin, Alan (1971) *Rural Administration and the Response of the People in South Africa, 1948–60: An Analysis of the Pondoland Revolt and other Rural Uprisings* (MA, School of Oriental and African Studies, University of London).

Beinart, William (1973) *Peasant Production, Underdevelopment and the*

Traditionalist Response in Pondoland, c 1880–1930 (MA, University of London).
Bundy, Colin (1976) *African Peasants and Economic Change in South Africa, 1870–1913, with Particular Reference to the Cape* (D. Phil., Oxford University).
Copelyn, J. A. (1974) *The Mpondo Revolt, 1960* (BA Hons, University of the Witwatersrand).
Kimble, Judy (1979) *Towards an Understanding of the Political Economy of Lesotho: The Origins of Commodity Production and Migrant Labour, 1830–c1890* (MA, National University of Lesotho).
Szeftel, Morris (1970) *Emerging Conflict Themes in the Transkei* (MA, University of Zambia).

Secondary sources

Adam, Heribert (1971) *Modernising Racial Domination: The Dynamics of South African Politics* (University of California Press, Berkeley and Los Angeles).
Adam, Heribert (1975) 'Internal Constellations and Potentials for Change', in Leonard Thompson and Jeffrey Butler (eds), *Change in Contemporary South Africa* (University of California Press, Berkeley and Los Angeles), pp. 303–26.
Adendorff, J. (1962) 'The role of the Bantu Investment Corporation in the economic development of the Bantu areas', *Finance and Trade Review*, V, 2, June.
Amin, Samir (1972) 'Underdevelopment and dependence in Black Africa – origins and contemporary forms', *The Journal of Modern African Studies*, X, 4, pp. 503–24.
Anonymous (1969) *South Africa: 'Resettlement' – the New Violence to Africans* (International Defence and Aid, London).
Anonymous (1976a) 'A chronology of resistance in South Africa', *Review of African Political Economy*, 7, pp. 119–24.
Anonymous (1976b) 'Transkei – economically viable?', *Bulletin of the Africa Institute of South Africa*, 14, 7 & 8, pp. 253–8.
Anonymous (1979) 'Venda becomes independent', *Informa*, XXVI, 12, December, pp. 1–8.
Anonymous (1980) 'Four years on: Transkei since "independence"', *Work in Progress*, no. 14, September (mimeo, Johannesburg).
Arrighi, Giovanni (1973) 'Labour Supply in Historical Perspective: A Study of the Proletarianisation of the African Peasantry in Rhodesia', in Giovanni Arrighi and John Saul, *Essays on the Political Economy of Africa* (Monthly Review Press, New York), pp. 180–234.
Ashford, Nicholas (1977) 'Africa's newest non-state runs into citizenship trouble', *The Times* (London), 7 July.

Baldwin, Alan (1975) 'Mass removals and separate development', *Journal of Southern African Studies*, 1, 2, April, pp. 215–27.
Bantu Investment Corporation (1975) *Homelands: The Role of the Corporations in the Republic of South Africa* (Johannesburg).
Baran, Paul (1957) *The Political Economy of Growth* (Monthly Review Press, New York and London).
Barber, James (1973) *South Africa's Foreign Policy 1945–1970* (Oxford University Press, London).
Barclays Bank (1977) *Economic Conditions in the Republic of Transkei* (*The Natal Witness*).
Bardill, John, Perrings, Charles and Southall, Roger (1977) 'The State and Labour Migration in the South African Political Economy, with Particular Respect to Gold Mining' (World Employment Programme Research, Working Paper, WEP 2-26/WP 19, International Labour Organization, Geneva).
Becker, W. (1970) 'Employment Opportunities for Graduates Offered by the Transkei', in W. Becker (ed.), *The Economic Development of the Transkei* (The Lovedale Press, Lovedale).
Beinart, William (1974a) 'Peasant Production, Underdevelopment and Stratification: Pondoland c. 1880–1930' (Paper presented to the University of Cape Town African Seminar, October 1974).
Beinart, William (1974b) 'Rural Production and Stratification in South Africa: Pondoland c 1894–1930' (mimeo).
Beinart, William (1975) 'The Policy of Industrial Decentralisation in South Africa', in *The Conditions of the Black Worker* (Study Project on External Investment in South Africa and Namibia, Uppsala), Paper no. 12, pp. 85–125.
Beinart, William and Bundy, Colin (1978) 'State Intervention and Rural Resistance: The Transkeian Territories, c 1900–1960' (Seminar paper presented to Centre for International and Area Studies, University of London, 13 October).
Bell, Trevor (1973) *Industrial Decentralisation in South Africa* (Oxford University Press, Cape Town).
Berkeley, Humphrey (1978/79) 'Why Transkei should be recognised', *Commonwealth*, December/January, pp. 42–3.
Blausten, Richard (1974) *Britain and the Bantustans* (Bow Group, London).
Blausten, Richard (1976) 'Foreign investment in the black homelands of South Africa', *African Affairs*, 75, 299, pp. 208–23.
Bonner, Philip (1980) 'Black Trade Unions in South Africa since World War II', in Robert M. Price and Carl G. Rosberg (eds), *The Apartheid Regime: Political Power and Racial Domination* (Institute of International Studies, University of California, Berkeley), pp. 174–93.
Bonner, Philip and Webster, Eddie (1979) 'Background' in 'Focus on Wiehahn', *South African Labour Bulletin*, 5, 2, August, pp. 1–12.

Botha, Roelf (1978) *South Africa: Plan for the Future – a Basis for Discussion* (Perskor, Johannesburg).
Bozzoli, Belinda (1978) 'Capital and the state in South Africa', *Review of African Political Economy*, 11, pp. 40–50.
Brown, Michael Barratt (1974) *The Economics of Imperialism* (Penguin, Middlesex).
Bundy, Colin (1972) 'The emergence and decline of a South African peasantry', *African Affairs*, 71, 285, pp. 369–88.
Bundy, Colin (1977) 'The Transkei Peasantry, c. 1890–1914: 'Passing Through a Period of Stress', in Robin Palmer and Neil Parsons (eds), *The Roots of Rural Poverty in Central and Southern Africa* (Heinemann Educational Books, London), pp. 201–20.
Bundy, Colin (1979) *The Rise and Fall of the South African Peasantry* (Heinemann Educational Books, London) and (University of California Press, Berkeley).
Bureau for Economic Research re Bantu Development (BENBO) (1975) *Transkei Economic Revue* (Pretoria).
Bureau for Economic Research re Bantu Development (BENBO) (1976) *Black Development in South Africa: The Economic Development of the Black Peoples in the Homelands of the Republic of South Africa* (Pretoria).
Butler, Jeffrey, Rotberg, Robert and Adams, John (1977) *The Black Homelands of South Africa: The Political and Economic Development of Bophuthatswana and Kwazulu* (University of California Press, Berkeley, Los Angeles and London).
Carter, Gwendolen, Karis, Thomas and Stultz, Newell (1967) *South Africa's Transkei: The Politics of Domestic Colonialism* (Heinemann Educational Books, London).
Charton, Nancy (1972) 'The Training of Officials in the Transkei, with a view to Manpower Mobilisation' (Paper presented to Annual Conference of the Teachers of African Government, South Africa).
Charton, Nancy (1976) 'Black élites in the Transkei', *Politikon*, 3, 2, October, pp. 61–74.
Cheadle, Halton (1979) 'A guide to the Industrial Conciliation Amendment Act', *South African Labour Bulletin*, 5, 2, August, pp. 12–26.
Cooper, Carole (1979) 'Wiehahn's hidden agenda', *Race Relations News*, 41, June, pp. 1–3.
Cooper, Carole and Ensor, Linda (1979) 'Summary of the Riekert Report', *South African Labour Bulletin*, 5, 4, November, pp. 7–37.
Davenport, T. R. H. (1977) *South Africa: A Modern History* (University of Toronto Press, Toronto and Buffalo).
Davies, Robert (1973) 'The white working class in South Africa', *New Left Review*, 82, November–December, pp. 40–59.
Davies, Robert, Kaplan, David, Morris, Mike and O'Meara, Dan (1976) 'Class struggle and the periodisation of the state in South Africa', *Review of African Political Economy*, 7, pp. 4–30.

De Kiewiet, C. W. (1941) *A History of South Africa: Social and Economic* (Oxford University Press, London).

De Villiers, Riaan (1980) 'Ciskei will market labour by computer', *RDM*, 30 May.

Desmond, Cosmas (1971) *The Discarded People* (Penguin, Middlesex).

Doxey, G. V. (1961) *The Industrial Colour Bar in South Africa* (Oxford University Press, London).

Duff, Tom (1979) 'Born to blush unseen', *The Star*, 11 June.

Dugard, John (1976a) 'Transkei and the United Nations' (Paper presented to the Conference of the South African Institute of International Affairs on 'The International Implications of Transkeian Independence').

Dugard, John (1976b) 'Transkei and international recognition', *Race Relations News*, 38, 10, October, pp. 1–2.

Duncan, Sheena (1979) 'The effects of the Riekert Report on the African population', *South African Labour Bulletin*, 5, 4, November, pp. 65–74.

Edgar, Robert (1976) 'Garveyism in Africa: Dr. Wellington and the American Movement in the Transkei', *Ufahamu*, VII, 3, pp. 31–57.

Feit, Edward (1971) *Urban Revolt in South Africa, 1960–1964: A Case Study* (Northwestern University Press, Evanston).

First, Ruth, Steele, Jonathan and Gurney, Christabel (1973) *The South African Connection: Western Investment in Apartheid* (Penguin, Middlesex).

Frank, Andre Gunder (1971) *Capitalism and Underdevelopment in Latin America* (Penguin, Middlesex).

Franklin, N. N. (1942) 'Cooperative credit in the Transkeian Territories', *South African Journal of Economics*, 10, 2, June, pp. 95–120.

Gerhart, Gail M. (1978) *Black Power in South Africa: The Evolution of an Ideology* (University of California Press, Berkeley, Los Angeles and London).

Giniewski, Paul (1961) *Bantustans: A Trek towards the Future* (Human and Rousseau, Cape Town).

Good, Kenneth (1976) 'Settler colonialism: economic development and class formation', *The Journal of Modern African Studies*, 14, 4, pp. 597–620.

Gordon, Dennis (1977) 'Lesotho's lesson in thin-ice skating', *RDM*, 24 January.

Grundy, Kenneth (1973) *Confrontation and Accommodation in Southern Africa: The Limits of Independence* (University of California Press, Berkeley and Los Angeles).

Hahn, Lorna (1976) 'What should the U.S. do?', *Africa Report*, May–June, pp. 6–10.

Haines, E. S. (1933) 'The Transkei trader', *South African Journal of Economics*, 1, 2, pp. 201–16.

Hammond-Tooke, W. D. (1965) 'Segmentation and fission in Cape Nguni political units', *Africa*, 35, 2, pp. 143–66.

Hammond-Tooke, W. D. (1968) 'The Transkeian council system 1895–1955: an appraisal', *The Journal of African History*, IX, 3. pp. 455–77.

Hammond-Tooke, W. D. (1975) *Command or Consensus: The Development of Transkeian Local Government* (David Philip, Cape Town).

Hart, Gillian (1972) *African Entrepreneurship* (Institute of Social and Economic Research, Rhodes University).

Harvey, W. B. and Dean, W. H. B. (1978) 'The independence of Transkei – a largely constitutional enquiry', *The Journal of Modern African Studies*, 16, 2, pp. 189–220.

Hepple, Alexander (1971) *South Africa: Workers Under Apartheid* (International Defence and Aid, London).

Hill, Christopher (1976) 'British Attitudes to Transkei Independence' (Paper presented to the Conference of the South African Institute of International Affairs on 'The International Implications of Transkeian Independence').

Hirschmann, David (1979) 'Changes in Lesotho's policy towards South Africa', *African Affairs*, 78, 311, pp. 177–96.

Horner, D. (1976) 'African labour representation', *South African Labour Bulletin*, 2, 9 and 10, pp. 23–7.

Horrell, Muriel (1959a) 'The Economic Development of the Reserves: The Extent to which the Tomlinson Commission's Recommendations are being Implemented' (SAIRR, Johannesburg, RR 93/59).

Horrell, Muriel (1959b) 'Second Interim Report on the Establishment of Bantu Authorities' (SAIRR, Johannesburg, RR 82/59).

Horrell, Muriel (1971) *Action, Re-action and Counter-action: A Brief Review of Non-white Political Movements in South Africa* (SAIRR, Johannesburg).

Horrell, Muriel (1973) *The African Homelands of South Africa* (SAIRR, Johannesburg).

Horrell, Muriel (1978) *Laws Affecting Race Relations in South Africa* (SAIRR, Johannesburg).

Horrell, Muriel et al. (1976) *A Survey of Race Relations in South Africa, 1976* (SAIRR, Johannesburg).

Houghton, Hobart (1976) *The South African Economy* (Oxford University Press, Cape Town, London and New York).

Hunter, Monica (1936) *Reaction to Conquest: Effects of Contacts with Europeans on the Pondo of South Africa* (Oxford University Press, London).

Innes, Duncan and O'Meara, Dan (1976) 'Class formation and ideology: the Transkei region', *Review of African Political Economy*, 7, September–December, pp. 69–86.

Innes, Duncan and Plaut, Martin (1978) 'Class struggle and the state', *Review of African Political Economy*, 11, pp. 51–61.

Ireland, Ralph (1972) 'Transkei: the significance of education for the development of the Republic of South Africa's first "Bantustan"', *Plural Societies*, 3, 1, pp. 39–58.

Johnson, R. W. (1977) *How Long will South Africa Survive?* (Macmillan, London and Basingstoke).

Johnstone, Frederick A. (1970) 'White prosperity and white supremacy in South Africa today', *African Affairs*, LXIX, 274, pp. 124–40.

Johnstone, Frederick A. (1976) *Class, Race and Gold: A Study of Class Relations and Racial Discrimination in South Africa* (Routledge & Kegan Paul, London and Boston).

Kahn, Ellison (1963) 'Some thoughts on the competency of the Transkeian Legislative Assembly and the sovereignty of the South African Parliament', *South African Law Journal*, 80, pp. 473–82.

Kane-Berman, John (1978) *Soweto: Black Revolt, White Reaction* (Ravan Press, Johannesburg).

Kirby, Alexander (1976) *South Africa's Bantustans: What Independence for the Transkei?* (World Council of Churches, Geneva).

Kotze, D. A. (1975) *African Politics in South Africa, 1964–1974* (C. Hurst and Company, London).

Kotze, H. J. (1973) 'Transkeian General Election', *Bulletin of the Africa Institute of South Africa*, 11, 9, pp. 349–52.

Kotze, H. J. (1976) 'The Transkei General Election', *Bulletin of the Africa Institute of South Africa*, 14, 9/10, pp. 339–42.

Krause, Otto (1976) 'The Implications of Independence for the Future Political Development of Blacks in South Africa' (Paper presented to the Conference of the South African Institute of International Affairs on 'The International Implications of Transkeian Independence').

Kuper, Leo (1965) *An African Bourgeoisie – Race, Class and Politics in South Africa* (Yale University Press, New Haven).

Laurence, Patrick (1976) *The Transkei: South Africa's Politics of Partition* (Ravan Press, Johannesburg).

Laurence, Patrick (1978) 'What they have, what they want', *RDM*, 12 April.

Laurence, Patrick (1981) 'Transkei poll will confirm Chief Kaiser's rule', *Guardian*, 8 September.

Le Cordeur, B. A. (1974) 'Natal and the Transkei to 1879', in C. C. Saunders and R. Derricourt (eds), *Beyond the Cape Frontier: Studies in the History of the Transkei and Ciskei* (Longman, London), pp. 163–84.

Leeuwenberg, Jeff (1976) *Transkei: A Study in Economic Regression* (Africa Bureau, London).

Legassick, Martin (1974a) 'Legislation, ideology and economy in post-1948 South Africa', *Journal of Southern African Studies*, 1, 1, pp. 5–35.

Legassick, Martin (1974b) 'South Africa: capital accumulation and violence', *Economy and Society*, III, 3. pp. 253–91.

Legassick, Martin (1975) 'South Africa: Forced Labour, Industrialization and Racial Differentiation', in Richard Harris (ed.), *The Political Economy of Africa* (Schenkman Publishing Company, Cambridge, Mass.), pp. 227–70.

Legassick, Martin and Wolpe, Harold (1976) 'The Bantustans and capital accumulation in South Africa', *Review of African Political Economy*, 7, pp. 87–107.
Legum, Colin (1977) 'Proof of Lesotho's UN hoax', *RDM*, 14 January.
Leistner, G. M. E. (1976) 'Economic Links with South Africa' (Paper presented to the Conference of the South African Institute of International Affairs on 'The International Implications of Transkeian Independence').
Leys, Colin (1975) *Underdevelopment in Kenya: The Political Economy of Neo-colonialism* (Heinemann Educational Books, London).
Leys, Roger (1975) 'South African gold mining in 1974: "the Gold of migrant labour"', *African Affairs*, 74, 295, pp. 196–208.
Lipton, Merle (1972a) 'Independent Bantustans?', *International Affairs*, 48, 1, pp. 1–19.
Lipton, Merle (1972b) 'The South African census and the Bantustan policy', *The World Today*, 28, 6, June, pp. 257–71.
Lodge, Tom (1977) 'Poqo and Rural Resistance in the Transkei, 1960–1965' (Paper delivered to the Societies of Southern Africa in the 19th and 20th Centuries Postgraduate Seminar, Institute of Commonwealth Studies, University of London, 12 January).
Macmillan, W. M. (1930) *Complex South Africa* (London).
Malan, T. and Hattingh, P. S. (1976) *Black Homelands in South Africa* (Africa Institute of South Africa, Pretoria).
Mare, Gerhard (1979) 'Relocation and Riekert: attempts at rural and urban stabilization', *South African Labour Bulletin*, 5, 4, November, pp. 37–48.
Mare, Gerhard (1980) *African Population Relocation in South Africa* (SAIRR, Johannesburg).
Maree, J. (1973) 'Bantustan economics', *Third World*, 2, 6, June.
Maree, J. and de Vos, P. J. (1975) *Underemployment, Poverty and Migrant Labour in the Transkei and Ciskei* (South African Institute of Race Relations, Johannesburg).
Marquard, Leo (1957) *South Africa's Colonial Policy* (SAIRR, Johannesburg).
Marx, Karl (1977) *Capital*, vol. 1 (Lawrence and Wishart, London).
Marx, Karl (1970) 'The Eighteenth Brumaire of Louis Bonaparte', in Karl Marx and Frederick Engels, *Selected Works* (Lawrence and Wishart, London, 1970), pp. 96–179.
Matanzima, Kaiser (1976) *Independence My Way* (Foreign Affairs Association, Pretoria).
Mayer, Philip (1961) *Townsmen or Tribesmen: Conservatism and the Process of Urbanisation in a South African City* (Oxford University Press, Cape Town).
Mayer, Philip (1966) 'The Tribal Elite and the Transkeian Elections of 1963', in P. C. Lloyd, *The New Elites of Tropical Africa* (Oxford University Press, London), pp. 236–308.

Mbanjwa, Thoko (1975) *Black Review 1974/75* (Black Community Programmes, Lovedale Press).
Mbeki, Govan (1964) *South Africa: The Peasants' Revolt* (Penguin, Middlesex).
Molnar, Thomas (1964) 'The Transkei: international decolonisation', *World View*, June, pp. 7-11.
Molteno, Robert (1971) 'South Africa's forward policy in Africa: milestones on the great north road', *The Round Table*, 243, pp. 329-45.
Moolman, J. H. (1977) 'Homelands only a partial solution', *RDM*, 16 December.
Moyer, Richard A. (1974) 'The Mfengu, Self-Defence and the Cape Frontier Wars', in C. C. Saunders and R. Derricourt (eds), *Beyond the Cape Frontier: Studies in the History of the Transkei and Ciskei* (Longman, London), pp. 101-26.
Munger, Edwin (1962) 'Transkei independence: fact or fantasy', *Africa Report*, 7, 5.
Nabudere, Dan (1977) *The Political Economy of Imperialism: Its Theoretical and Polemical Treatment from Mercantilist to Multilateral Imperialism* (Tanzania Publishing House, Dar es Salaam and Zed Press, London).
Nash, M. (1980) *Black Uprooting from 'White' South Africa – the Fourth and Final Stage of Apartheid* (South African Council of Churches, Braamfontein).
Ncokazi, Hector (1976) Untitled contribution in Black Viewpoint no. 4, *Transkei Independence* (Black Community Programmes, Durban).
Nieuwenhuysen, J. P. (1964) 'Economic Policy in the Reserves since the Tomlinson Report', *South African Journal of Economics*, 32, 1, pp. 3-24.
Nkrumah, Kwame (1965) *Neo-colonialism: The Last Stage of Imperialism* (Panaf Books, London).
Olivier, G. C. (undated) 'Plural Accommodation in South Africa: Problems, Perspectives and Solutions' (Political Science Department, University of Pretoria, mimeo).
O'Meara, Dan (1975) 'The African mine workers' strike and the political economy of South Africa', *Journal of Commonwealth and Comparative Studies*, 13, 2, pp. 146-73.
O'Sullivan, John (1976) 'How free is the Transkei?' *Daily Telegraph*, 26 October.
Palmer, R. and Parsons, N. (eds) (1977) *The Roots of Rural Poverty in Central and Southern Africa* (Heinemann Educational Books, London).
Pim, Howard (1934) *A Transkei Enquiry, 1933* (Lovedale Press, Lovedale).
Post, Ken (1972) ' "Peasantisation" and rural political movements in Western Africa', *Archives Européenes de Sociologie* (Paris), XIII, pp. 223-54.

Price, Robert M. (1980) 'Apartheid and White Supremacy: The Meaning of Government Led Reform in the South African Context', in Robert M. Price and Carl G. Rosberg (eds), *The Apartheid Regime: Political Power and Racial Domination* (Institute of International Studies, University of California, Berkeley), pp. 297–332.

Reader, D. H. (1961) *The Black Man's Portion: History, Demography and Living Conditions in the Native Locations of East London, Cape Province* (Oxford University Press, Cape Town).

Rhoodie, N. J. and Venter, H. J. (1960) *Apartheid: A Socio-historical Exposition of the Origin and Development of the Apartheid Idea* (Amsterdam).

Rogers, Barbara (1972) *South Africa: The Bantu Homelands* (International Defence and Aid, London).

Rogers, Barbara (1976) *Divide and Rule: South Africa's Bantustans* (International Defence and Aid Fund, London).

Rogers, H. (1933) *Native Administration in the Union of South Africa* (University of the Witwatersrand Press, Johannesburg).

Roux, Edward (1964) *Time Longer than Rope: A History of the Black Man's Struggle for Freedom in South Africa* (University of Wisconsin Press, Wisconsin).

Rutman, Gilbert (1971) 'Some economic costs of separate development in South Africa', *Co-Existence*, 8, 1, pp. 53–63.

Saul, John and Woods, Roger (1973) 'African Peasantries', in Giovanni Arrighi and John Saul (eds), *Essays on the Political Economy of Africa* (Monthly Review Press, New York), pp. 406–16.

Saunders, C. C. (1969) 'The second Transkeian General Election', *The South African Outlook*, January, p. 4.

Saunders, C. C. (1974) 'The Annexation of the Transkei' in C. C. Saunders and R. Derricourt (eds), *Beyond the Cape Frontier: Studies in the History of the Transkei and Ciskei* (Longman, London), pp. 185–98.

Savage, Michael (1975) 'Major Patterns of Group Interaction in South African Society', in Leonard Thompson and Jeffrey Butler (eds), *Change in Contemporary South Africa* (University of California Press, Berkeley and Los Angeles), pp. 280–302.

Seidman, Ann and Neva (1977) *U.S. Multinationals in Southern Africa* (Tanzania Publishing House, Dar es Salaam).

Seiler, John (1976) 'Perspectives, Process and Personnel in the Formulation of U.S. Policy towards South Africa: A Search for Clues to the Likely Evolution of U.S. Transkeian Policy' (Paper presented to the Conference of the South African Institute of International Affairs on 'The International Implications of Transkeian Independence').

Shivji, Issa G. (1973) *The Silent Class Struggle* (Tanzania Publishing House, Dar es Salaam).

Sklar, Richard (1967) 'Political science and national integration – a radical approach', *The Journal of Modern African Studies*, 5, 1, pp. 1–11.

Slovo, Joe (1976) 'South Africa – No Middle Road', in Basil Davidson, Joe Slovo and Anthony Wilkinson, *Southern Africa: The New Politics of Revolution* (Penguin, Middlesex), pp. 103–210.

South African Communist Party (1962) 'The Road to South African Freedom', reprinted in *African Communists Speak* (Moscow, Nauka Publishing House, 1970).

South African Institute of Race Relations (SAIRR) (1951–79), *A Survey of Race Relations in South Africa* (various authors) (Johannesburg).

South African Institute of Race Relations (SAIRR) (1960), *African Taxation: Its Relation to African Social Services* (Fact Paper no. 4, Johannesburg).

Southall, Roger J. (1976) 'Commentary: Transkei, Africa and Apartheid – the Implications of International Recognition' (Paper presented to Conference of the South African Institute of International Affairs on 'The International Implications of Transkeian Independence').

Southall, Roger, J. (1977) 'The beneficiaries of Transkeian "independence"', *The Journal of Modern African Studies*, 15, 1, pp. 1–23.

Southall, Roger J. (1978) Review of Butler, Jeffrey, Rotberg, Robert I. and Adams, John (1977), *The Black Homelands of South Africa: The Political and Economic Development of Bophuthatswana and Kwazulu* (University of California Press, Berkeley, Los Angeles and London), in *The Journal of Modern African Studies*, 16, 3, pp. 523–5.

Southall, Roger J. (1980a) 'Independence for the Transkei: Mystification and Diversion in the Model Bantustan', in John Seiler (ed.) *Southern Africa since the Portuguese Coup* (Westview Press, Boulder, Colorado), pp. 137–54.

Southall, Roger J. (1980b) 'African capitalism in contemporary South Africa', *Journal of Southern African Studies*, 7, 1, October, pp. 38–70.

Southall, Roger J. (1980c) 'New perspectives on South Africa', *The Journal of Modern African Studies*, 18, 4, December, pp. 713–25.

Southall, Roger J. (1981) 'Buthelezi, Inkatha and the politics of compromise', *African Affairs*, 80, 321, October, pp. 453–81.

Spence, Jack (1964) 'British policy towards the High Commission Territories', *The Journal of Modern African Studies*, 2, 2, pp. 221–46.

Stultz, Newell (1964) '"Creative self-withdrawal" in the Transkei', *Africa Report*, 9, 4, pp. 18–23.

Stultz, Newell (1973) 'South Africa's "apartheid" election of 1948 reconsidered', *Plural Societies*, III, 4 (Winter), pp. 25–38.

Stultz, Newell (1976) 'Transkei: a party for the patrons', *The Star*, 1 November.

Stultz, Newell (1977) 'Transkei Independence in Separatist Perspective', *Journal of African Studies*, 4, 4, pp. 414–32.

Stultz, Newell (1979) 'Why is Transkei still portrayed as a stooge?', *The Star*, 27 July.

Stultz, Newell (1980) *Transkei's Half Loaf: Race Separatism in South Africa* (Yale University Press, New Haven and London; and David Philip, Cape Town).
Tatz, Colin M. (1962) *Shadow and Substance in South Africa: A Study in Land and Franchise Policies Affecting Africans, 1910–1960* (University of Natal Press, Pietermaritzburg).
Taylor, Geoffrey (1976) 'Are the doubts about the Transkei self-fulfilling?', *Guardian* (London), 21 October.
Theal, G. M. (1908–10) *History of South Africa, 1795–1872* (5 vols) (George Allen and Unwin, London).
Thompson, Leonard (1971) 'The Subjection of the African Chiefdoms, 1870–1898', in Monica Wilson and Leonard Thompson (eds), *The Oxford History of South Africa*, vol. II, *South Africa 1870–1966* (Clarendon, Oxford), pp. 245–84.
Trapido, Stanley (1971) 'South Africa as a comparative study of industrialisation', *Journal of Development Studies*, 7, 3, pp. 309–20.
Turok, Ben (1961) *The Pondo Revolt* (Congress of Democrats, South Africa).
Vigne, Randolph (1966?) *The Transkei – a South African Tragedy* (Africa Bureau, London).
Wilson, Francis (1971) 'Farming, 1866–1966', in Monica Wilson and Leonard Thompson (eds), *The Oxford History of South Africa*, vol. II, *South Africa 1870–1966* (Clarendon, Oxford), pp. 104–17.
Wilson, Francis (1972a) *Labour in the South African Gold Mines 1911–1969* (Cambridge University Press, Cambridge).
Wilson, Francis (1972b) *Migrant Labour in South Africa: Report to the South African Council of Churches* (South African Council of Churches and Spro-Cas, Johannesburg).
Wilson, Monica (1959) 'The early history of the Transkei and Ciskei', *African Studies*, 18, 4, pp. 167–78.
Wilson, Monica (1969) 'Cooperation and Conflict: The Eastern Cape Frontier', in Monica Wilson and Leonard Thompson (eds), *The Oxford History of South Africa*, vol. I, *South Africa to 1870* (Clarendon, Oxford), pp. 233–71.
Wilson, Monica (1971) 'The Growth of Peasant Communities', in Monica Wilson and Leonard Thompson (eds), *The Oxford History of South Africa*, vol. II, *South Africa 1870–1966* (Clarendon, Oxford), pp. 49–103.
Woddis, Jack (1967) *Introduction to Neo-colonialism: The New Imperialism in Asia, Africa and Latin America* (International Publishers, New York).
Wolf, Eric (1966) *Peasants* (Prentice-Hall, Englewood Cliffs, New Jersey).
Wolpe, Harold (1972) 'Capitalism and cheap labour-power in South Africa: from segregation to apartheid', *Economy and Society*, 1, pp. 426–56.

Wolpe, Harold (1975) 'The Theory of Internal Colonialism: The South African Case', in I. Oxaal, T. Barnett and D. Booth (eds), *Beyond the Sociology of Development: Economy and Society in Latin America and Africa* (Routledge & Kegan Paul, London and Boston), pp. 229–52.

Wolpe, Harold (1976) '"The white working class" in South Africa', *Economy and Society*, 5, 2, pp. 197–240.

Wolpe, Harold (1978) 'The Changing Class Structure of South Africa: The African Petit-Bourgeoisie', in Paul Zarembka (ed.), *Research in Political Economy* (JAI Press, Greenwich, Connecticut), pp. 143–74.

Note

1. The material in this section previously held by the author has now been deposited with the African Collection of Yale University Library, New Haven, Connecticut 0652, USA.

Index*

Abolition of Passes and Co-ordination of Documents Act (1952) 43
Abraham, Hans, Commissioner-General of the Xhosa 156, 165, 170n.31
Act No. 46 of 1968 (The Promotion of Economic Development of Homelands) 166
Act of Union (1910) 10, 21, 95, 249, 268
Adam, Heribert 120, 282, 300
Adams, John 296; Butler *et al.* 297, 299, 302
Administration
See: Bantu Administration; Transkei, Administration; Transkei, Administrative Structures
African National Congress (ANC)
activities
Defiance Campaign 45; Pondo Revolt 109, 110, 113, 127; Protests 93, 108; TNIP opposition 259, 260, 263, 264, 310
banning 40, 48, 114, 256, 262; demands 92; formation 31; middle class, and 172; Slovo argument, and 11; Youth League 31
African states, relationship with South Africa dialogue 54–5; Front Line States 290; 'independence' and 249–50; Organization of African Unity 3, 55, 131; regional relations 49, 289–290

Africanization
of bureaucracy 181; strategy 148–9, 158; of teachers 182–3; of trade 116, 158, 163–4; of urban petty commerce 164
Afrikaner Party 32, 33
Agriculture
African middle class and, 195–6; capitalist agriculture, inhibition of 76–7; commercial 23, 299; decline of African 37, 74–5; general 219; government schemes 107, 224–30; grain trade 83, 84; irrigation projects 227–9; Nguni pastoral 64; peasantization 68–73; productivity 220–3; settler 22–24; subsistence 15, 26, 80–1

See also: Land, Land tenure, Livestock, Production, Farmers
Aliens and Travellers Control Act (1977) 256
Anglo-Boer War (1899–1902) 21, 28
Angola 25, 55, 193, 215
civil war 56
Anti-Bantu Authorities Committee 112
Apartheid
agriculture and, 15, 24; capitalism and, 21; commerce, African, and, 187; deracialization of 254–5; education 34, 182; general 6, 10, 20–56, 281–3; goals 39; ideology 20–1, 33; implementation 33–44; labour policy 23, 29–33, 41, 43; neo-colonial strategy 115; opposition to; international 47, 48, Transkei 127; resettlement 267–8, 293–4, 311; residence rights 25, 43, 288; segregation 17n.6, 34, 253–4, 286–7

See also: Separate development, Pass Laws
Arenstein, Roley 110

Back, D. 85
Banda, Hastings, President of Malawi 181, 214
Bantu Administration, Department of
elections, and 134; Minister of Bantu Administration and Development 50, 107, 155, 157 resettlement, and 43–4
Bantu Authorities
established 104, 108; opposition 127, 151; TNIP, and 137
Bantu Authorities Act (1951) 35, 45, 50, 105
Bantu Authorities system
creation of 153; general 15, 37, 45, 47, 89, 97–8; Pondoland, collapse of, 111; revolt against 48, 108–13
Bantu Education Act (1953) 34, 154
Bantu Homelands Amendment Bill (1977) 285
Bantu Homelands Citizenship Act (no. 26 of 1970) 50, 292
Bantu Homelands Constitution Act (no. 21 of 1971) 50
Bantu Homelands Development Corporations Act (1965) 37

*Compiled by Shirley Ross.

330 INDEX

Bantu Investment Corporation (BIC) 37–8, 158
established 153
Bantu Labour (Settlement of Disputes) Act (1953) 40
Bantu Laws Amendment Acts
(no. 23 of 1972) 50; (of 1973) 50; (Nov. 1974) 232; (no. 12 of 1978) 293
Bantu (Urban Areas) Consolidation Act 193
Bantustans
constitutional development 48–55; neo-colonial concept and, 9–10; opposition to policy 154; programme 'divide and rule' 34, 35, 173
Bantustan strategy
consolidation / constellation / confederation 288–294, 307n.35; critique 301–304; general 36, 37, 281–3; homeland leaders and, 284–5; perspectives on 295–304; policy options 286–290

See also: Separate development policy
Basotho
people 35; homeland characteristics 51, 141
Beaumont Commission (1916) 73
Bell, Trevor 38
BENBO 219, 267
Ben-Dak, J. D., adviser to Matanzima 181, 182, 199n.27
Berkeley, Humphrey, adviser to Matanzima 273–4
Bikitsha, Charles, Secretary, Department of Health, Transkei 180–1
Black consciousness
suppression of 262; teachers and, 184–5
Black Peoples' Convention (BPC) 3, 40, 129, 262
Black United Front 3, 285
Bolshevik Revolution of 1917 29
Bophuthatswana homeland
characteristics of 5, 35, 50, 51; destruction of legislative building 3; independence 4, 266, 284
Border areas
economy 38–9; Transkei 52, 53
Botha, M. C., Minister of Bantu Administration and Development 1, 52
Botha, P. Roelf, member, Prime Minister's Planning Advisory Council 287
Botha, P. W., Prime Minister 287, 288, 311
Botha, R. F., South African Minister of Foreign Affairs 268, 271
Botswana (formerly Bechuanaland) 10, 46, 47, 215, 249
Boycotts
Democratic Party and, 131; Pondo Revolt 112, 113; trading stores 96; visit of Prince of Wales 93
Brownlee, W. T., Chief Magistrate 150
Bundy, Colin, 68, 69, 72, 83
Bunga/Council 33, 87
abolition/replacement 97–98; established at Butterworth, Idutywa, Nqamakwe, Tsomo, Thembuland, Griqualand, Xalanga and Pondoland 91; powers 91–2, 176; structure 90, 93–5
Bunting, S. P., Communist Party candidate Thembuland 73, 88
action against 93
Buthelezi, Chief Gatsha, Chief of Kwazulu, SABA leader 285
Inkatha movement and 262, 301–2
Buthelezi, Wellington 97
Butler, Jeffrey 296, 297, 299, 302
Butterworth 76, 159
importance of, 165–6

Caledon Code (1809) 23
Carter, Gwendolen 11, 117, 134, 295, 296, 299
Carter, J., US President 56
Cattle-Killing, The 66, 69
Cecil Rhodes Act 76

Chieftaincy
abuse of power 106–7; chiefdoms 105; constitutional powers 115; electoral influence 123–6; Mfengu 98n.5; power of 86, 87, 98, 106, 113, 121–2, 225–226; revival of 35, 45, 104–105; salaries 174; Transkei bourgeoisie and, 173–6; Transkei Legislative Assembly and, 116, 118, 121; TNIP and, 121, 123–6, 135, 137; undermining 88, 89, 176, 225
Ciskei homeland
characteristics of 35, 51; general 50, 53, 65, 69, 71, 72, 73; 'independence' 290–292, 311
Ciskei National Independence Party (CNIP) 290, 291
Citizenship
Bantu 47, 50, 58n.49, 115, 132, 290, 293, 298; Ciskei 292; traders 194; Transkei coloureds 191; Transkei whites 168; urban blacks 265–6
Clarke, W. J., founder of Transkeian Territories European Civic Association 149
Class and Class Structure
Bunga and, 94–5; economic formation 8, 9; labour and race 27–33; race relations and, 12, 13, 15; stratification in 'Native Reserve' 18n.14, 84, 85, 88, 130, 287
Class structure, Bantustan
bureaucrats 178; chiefs and politicians 173–6; class coherence 195–8; Development Corporations and, 190; general 116, 130, 147, 172–6, 247–8, 275, 301; origin 173; significance to separate development policy 194–8; teachers 183, 197; traders and businessmen 185–94; TNIP and, 135; Urban capital and, 164–8

INDEX 331

See also: Chieftaincy, Traders
Colonial rule 45
hut tax 67, 71, 75; Transkei 60–7
Colonialism
theory of internal 10–17
Coloured Labour Party 285
Commission of Inquiry, into position of Europeans in Transkei (1962)
formation 156, 157; general 161
Congress Alliance 172
Congress of Democrats 172
Constitution, development of 48–51, 115, 283, 291
See also: Transkei Constitution Act
Co-operatives
agricultural 97, 226–7, 229
Corruption
bureaucratic 179–80; elections 122–3, 128, 304n.4; political 196–7
Criminal Law Amendment Act (1953) 40
Cuban, military in Africa 56
Customs Union 205
Cwele, Brigadier 259, 260, 310

Dalindyebo, Sabata
ANC and, 260, 310; Paramount 105, 108, 114, 123, 126, 128, 129, 130, 131; DPP leader 258; arrest 259–260
Davies, Robert 302
Dean, W. H. B., Professor of Law, Cape Town University 5–6
Decolonization
African 47; South African 103, 146, 158, 281–2
Defiance Campaign (1951–52) 108
De Kiewiet, C. W. 24
Democratic Party (DP)
amalgamation 258; elections and, 118–19, 123; formation 118; leadership 128–9; multiracialism 251; policy 128–31, 136, 141; teachers' support of, 184–5, 198

Democratic Progressive party (DPP)
formation 258; as opposition 261, 309; repression of 259
Deracialization
concept 254–5; repression and, 264; within the white core 287
Desmond, Cosmas 225
Development Corporations
activities 190, 229, 230–31, 233, 238; establishment of, 187; job creation 211
See also: Xhosa Development Corporation, Transkei Development Corporation, Bantu Investment Corporation
de Wet Nel, M. D. C., Minister of Native Affairs 97
Diamonds 70
Diedrichs, Nico, South African State President 1
Diko, Cromwell 180
as TPFP leader 257
'Divide and rule' programme 34, 35, 173
Dugard, John, Professor of Law, University of Witwatersrand 5
Durban 38, 41
D'Urban, Sir Benjamin, Governor 63, 65
Dutch East India Company 64

East Coast Fever
anti-dipping movement 96–7; of (1910–11) 75; of (1897 and 1912–13) 95–6
East London 38
Eastern Pondoland Peoples' Party 127
Economy, Homelands
border 38–9; general 202–203, 208–9, 283–4
See also: Transkei, economy
Economy, South African
Apartheid, and 33, 39; general 11–12, 44, 68; history 21–2, 27–8; production, capitalist 14–17, 25–7, 68

Education
Bantu 34, 154, 182–5, 199n.30; call for abolition of Bantu 113; for Transkei whites 168; student politics 185
Electoral Law Amendment Act (1979) 261
Electoral process
candidate selection 123, 124; chiefs' influence 121–126; patronage 126; urban influence 132–5, 145n.77; voting procedure 122, 133; general 120–21, 125
See also: Transkei, elections
Elite, Homeland
See: Class Structure, Bantustan
Ethiopia 49
European investment in Transkei 237–9
Extension of University Education Act (1958) 34

Faku, Paramount Chief of the Pondo 271
Farmers
African elite 195–6; white, in Transkei 147
Farmers and Traders Association/Civic Association
founded 150
Fingoland 60, 61
hut tax 67; land tenure 226; proletarianization 72
FOSKOR 27
Fox, F. W. 85
Franchise and Ballot Act (1882) 90
Frank, André Gunder 7, 8
Fyfe-King, Lt.-Col. R., Chief Magistrate 150

Ganyile, Anderson, ANC Youth Leaguer 110
Garvey, Marcus 97
Gazankulu, homeland 35, 50
characteristics 51
Gcaleka 60, 61, 62, 66
Gcalekaland 61, 67
Glenelg, Lord 65
Glen Grey Bill (Act no. 25, 1894) 76, 90, 91, 92, 93

Glen Grey system 76, 91
Gold 21, 22, 42, 70, 75, 77, 78, 213–16
Good, Kenneth 302
Government Notice R764 (May 1976) trade licenses 193
Government Service Amendment Act (1974) 185
Grain
 native trade 83, 84
Grey, Sir George, Governor 65
Griqualand East 60
 Chief Magistracy 67; division (Willowvale, Kentani) 67; Griqualand West, diamonds 70; hut tax 67; proletarianization 72; territory disputes 268–70
Group Areas Act 43
Guzana, Knowledge, DP leader 127–32, 184, 251

Hammond-Tooke, W. D. 95
Hartzenburg, Ferdie Deputy Minister of Bantu Administration 293
Harvey, W. B., Professor of Law, Boston 5–6
Havenga, N. C., leader of Afrikaner Party 32, 33
Headmen
 appointment and power 88–9, 98; general 173; salaries 174; subordinated to chiefs 104, 106
Heckroodt, W. H., head of Commission of Inquiry 157, 161
Hendricks, Rev. Abel, President, Methodist Conference 256
Hertzog, General, Prime Minister 31, 32, 92
Hertzogites 31
Hintsa, Chief of the Gcaleka, 1830s 63
Homelands, in generai
 border economy 38, 39; characteristics 35, 51, 283; citizenship 47, 50, 115, 132, 290, 293; constitutional development 283, 291; economy 202–3, 208–9, 283–4; elections 120; employment 38, 39, 217; South Africa government relations 284–295
Houphouet-Boigny, F., Ivory Coast leader 54
Hughes, T. Gray, UP Member of Parliament 154, 156, 164
Hunter, Monica 107

Idutywa 60, 76, 165
 hut tax 67
Immorality Act (no. 23 of 1957) 253, 254, 285
Independence'
 constitution 115; declaration of juridical 1; move to 52–5, 140–2; opposition to 2–4, international 3, local 2–3, 131, 141–2, 284–5; potential gains 265; politics of 274–5; theory 103, 114, 202–3, 247–8, 286
Indian Reform Party 285
Industrial and Commercial Workers union (ICU) 28, 29
Industrial Conciliation Act (1956) 40, 41
Industrial Conciliation Amendment Act (no. 74 of 1979) 287
Industrial Development Corporation 27
Industry
 decentralization 38; general 240; foreign capital 237–9; policy 230; white capital 230–1, 234–7
Inkatha movement, Chief Buthelezi's banning 262; of Kwazulu 285; strategy 301–302
Innes, Duncan 16, 175
Intelligence Service and State Security Act (1977) 256
Internal colonialism, theory 10–17
Internal Security Act (1976) 40, 255
International Court of Justice 49
Iron and Steel Corporation (ISCOR) 27

Jojo, Chief S. G. 124
Jokl, E. 85
Jonathan, Leabua (Prime Minister of Lesotho) 54

Kadalie, Clements 28
Kaffraria, British 65
Kane-Berman, John 135
KaNgwane, homeland 35, 50, 51, 285
Karis, Thomas 11, 295
Kenya 10, 47
 Kenya analogy 154–5; Transkei recognition, and 250
Kenyatta, Jomo 155, 181
Keswa, Brigadier, Commissioner of the Defence Force 310
Kornhoof, Piet, SA Minister of Co-operation and Development 289
Kotze, D. A. 122, 133
Koyana, Digby, Transkeian Foreign Minister 250, 251
Kuper, Leo 183
Kwazulu, homeland 35, 38, 50, 51

Labour, migration
 development of 72; general 26, 30, 75; migrant labour 42–3, 132, 209–18; mining and, 72, 77, 78, 216–17; sectors 78, 212; statistics 58n.48, 77, 132, 209–10, 215
Labour, policy
 'Civilized Labour Policy' 29–30; controls 42–3; forced labour 107; general 23, 25, 29–33; stabilization 40; unions 28, 40–2, 232–3
Labour, recruiting 78–80, 82, 214–15
 traders and 147–8
Labour Party 29
Labour Relations Regulation Amendment Act (1973) 41
Land
 African loss of 73; allocation of 57n.33, 86, 107, 288; landlessness 86–7; quality of Transkei land 220, 222–223

INDEX 333

See also: Natives Land Act, Natives Trust and Land Act
Land claims
 by bantustan leaders 52–3, 265, 268–70, 291
Land tenure
 franchise and 90
 general 14, 23–4, 76, 196; government schemes 224–227; 'one-man-one-lot' 76–77, 85; Xhosa 62
Laurence, Patrick 131, 247
League of Nations 49
Lebowa, homeland 35, 38, 50, 51
Legal aspects
 apartheid in South West Africa 49; state recognition 5–6, 18–19n.32; trader rights 150–1, 158, 163, 186
Legassick, Martin 22
Leistner, G. M. E. 211
Lesotho/Basutoland 10, 25, 46, 47, 61, 215, 249, 310
 contrast with Transkei 5, 278n.74; Transkei recognition, and 250, 276n.9
Letlaka, Tsepo, Minister of Justice 263
Leys, Colin 9, 179, 181
Liaison Committee
 formation 156, 160; TTCA, and 161, 163; urban cause, and 161, 163, 166
Liberia 49
Liberal Party 128, 130
 and teachers 184
Liberation movements
 activities 263, 310; Matanzima support 270; possible support 261, 301; prospects 303–4

See also: African National Congress, Poqo, Pan-Africanist Congress
Lipton, Merle 229
Livestock
 cattle 86; general 97; projects 229; sheep 87; tax 207; Transkei ownership 85–7, 221
Louw, SA Foreign Minister 47
Ludidi, Pascoe, Secretary-General TNIP 137, 277n.37

Mabude, Saul, local District Authority Chairman, Pondoland 109, 110
Macmillan, Harold, British Premier 47
Macmillan, W. M. 75
Magistrates/Native Commissioners administrative powers 88, 147; white settlers, and 149
Maize 21, 220
Maize Quota Act (1931) 84
Mabuza, Enos, Chief Minister of KaNgwane 285
Makhuluspani movement 109
Makiwane, Tennyson, assassination 260, 264
Malan, D. F. 32
Malawi
 labour supply 214–15
Maluti-Herschel South Sotho Central Committee 141
Mamba, E., leader, Transkei Vigilance Association 94
Mandela, Nelson 130, 259
Mangope, Lucas 3, 284
 as Chief of Bophuthatswana 3; as President 284
Maninja, Lingham 116
Maritz, Franco, 181
Maritz, J. P. 181
Marx, Karl 9, 275
Maseru 250
Masters and Servants Law (1856) 23
Masters and Servants Laws 24
Masters and Servants Ordinances 25
Matanzima, George 131, 133, 196
 Minister of Justice 252; as Prime Minister 260, 262, 310, 311; rise to power 258
Matanzima, Kaiser
 apartheid, and 252–3; assassination attempts 48, 118, 262, 263; bureaucrats, and 181, 182; business interests 192, 196–7, 229; Chief Minister campaign 117–18; daughter's rustication 263; elections, and 122, 123, 124, 125, 126; extrusion, of whites and 155, 158, 162, 164, 165, 168; 'independence', and 1, 3, 52–3, 140–42, 247; philosophy of middle class 198; relations with South Africa 268–74, 311; retirement 309; rise to power 105, 108, 121; salary as Prime Minister 174; as State President 258; as TNIP leader 116, 118, 120, 129–131, 133, 140, 298; as TTA chairman 114, 115

See also: Transkei National Independence Party
Matanzima regime
See: Transkei National Independence Party
Mayaba, A. M., President of TRACOC 197
Mayer, Philip 117
Mbeki 130
Mbeki, Govan 234
Mda, Caledon, leader of TNPP 258
Methodist Church of South Africa banning in Transkei 256
metropole-periphery concept 7–8
Mfengu 60, 61, 62, 66
 chieftaincy 98n.5; history, economy 62; land tenure 76; peasantization 69; settlement 65
Military 266, 272
 Transkei 181, 266, 272; Security forces 39, 139, 140, 263, 310
Millenarian movements 66, 97
Mine Natives' Wages Commission (1944) 75, 77, 81
Mines, Chamber of, President 79, 80
Mines and Works Amendment Act (1926) 29
Mining
 early development 70; labour 72, 77, 78, 216–17; labour recruiting 79–80, 82

Missions 65
Methodists 69; missionaries 146, 154; peasantization and, 69, 71
Mlanda, Dr J. 257
Mlanjeni, prophet, colonial resistance 65
Mopeli, Kenneth, Chief Minister, Sotho homeland 141
of QwaQwa 285
Moshesh, Chief Jeremiah 259, 277n.44, 285
Motlana, Ntatho 301
Mozambique 25, 55, 193
labour supply 78, 214–15
Mpephu, Chief Patrick, of Venda 284, 285
Mpondo 61, 67, 70, 71
Mpondomise 61, 62
Mrwetyana, Vuyani, editor, fled from Transkei 262
Mugabe, regime 250
Mulder, Dr Connie, SA Minister of Plural Relations 285, 290
Munger, Edwin 130, 184
Muzorewa, Bishop Abel 251, 303

Namibia/South West Africa 12, 25, 49
National African Federated Chambers of Commerce (NAFCOC) 193, 194
National Party 29, 31, 45
homelands creation, and 2, 4, 103; post-1948 racial policies 33, 148–9; (Purified) National Party 32; strategies, Bantustan 286–290, 292–4
Native Affairs Act (1920) 45, 92
Native Economic Commission (1930–2) 77, 81, 82, 186
Native Labour Regulation Act (1911) 25
Native Laws Amendment Act (1952) 42
Native Laws and Customs Commission (1883) 90
Native Locations Act (1879) 76
Native Recruiting Corporation (NRC)
formation 79; traders, and 147–8
Native Reserves/African Reserves 14, 20, 23
Native (Urban Areas) Consolidation Act (1945) 43, 187
Natives Land Act (1913) 14, 24, 26, 82, 92; effects 74, 79; purpose 85; statistics 73; white settlement, and 147
Natives Land Act (1913) Amendment Bill (1926) 92
Natives' Representative Council 33, 92, 94
Natives Taxation and Development Act (1925) 75
Natives Taxation and Development Act (1958) 36
Natives Trust and Land Act (1936) 20, 24, 52, 147, 195, 287, 288
opposition to 52, 53
Natives (Urban Areas) Act (1923) 25, 186
Ncokazi, Hector 129, 130–1, 184, 194, 257
Ndamse, Curnick 123–4, 257
Ndamse, Tutor, Paramount Chief of Western Pondoland 128, 309
Ndebele 20
homeland 35, 50, 51; people 35
Ndzumo, Paul, Transkei Minister of Agriculture 223
Ndzumo, S. K., Transkei Minister of the Interior 260
Neo-colonialism
concept 7–10, 18n.31; related to bantustans 9–10; strategy 45, 103–4, 114–15

See also: Underdevelopment
New Democratic Party (NDP)
amalgamation 258; elections, and 132; election results 119; formation 129
Ngangelizwe, Thembu Paramount 61, 66
Ngceba, Martin, Chief of Transkeian Security Police 262; Brigadier 263; attack against 310
Ngqika 60, 61, 65, 66
Ngquza Hill massacre 112
Nguni
See: Transkei
Nigeria and Transkei 273
Ninth Frontier War (1877–1878) 60, 67
Njisane, Professor M., Ambassador to Pretoria 268
Nkrumah, Kwame, President of Ghana 7
Nongquase, Xhosa visionary 66
Nota, G. 125
Ntsanwisi, Hudson, of Gazankulu 285
Ntshongwana, Liston, Transkei Ministry of Foreign Affairs 273, 274
Nyamakazi, Simon, President of TRACOC 192, 197
Nyasaland 25, 47

O'Meara, Dan 16, 175
Organization of African Unity (OAU) 3, 55, 131
and Transkei recognition 249–50

Pact government (1924–9) 28, 29
Pan-Africanist Congress (PAC) 297, 308n.77; anti-TNIP activity 263; banning 40, 48, 114, 256, 262; campaign 48
Parliamentary Registration Act (1887) 90
Pass Laws 25, 26, 32, 43, 72, 132; protest 48, 113, 172
Paton, Alan, leader of Liberal Party 128
Patronage
chiefs 106–7; political 126, 128; traders 84; TNIP network 120, 188
Peasantization
dependence 71, 72, 73; economic boom 70, 71; emergence 68; missions, and 69; stratification 84, 85; undermined 74–7, 81
Pedi, people 35

INDEX 335

Permanent Committee for the Location of Industry and the Development of Border Areas 38
Phatudi, Dr Cedric 284, 285
Pikashe, B. C., former DP national organizer 258
Pityana, Barney, SASO general secretary 131
Pondo Revolt 48, 108–14, 122, 154, 225
  Commission of inquiry 112; Government attack 112, 113; Hill Committee 109–11, 112, 113; Kenya analogy, and 154, 155; Ikongo formation 109; reprisal 113; significance of 114, 148, 173
Pondoland 60, 62
  exports 70, 71, 72, 78; TNIP, and 257, 258, 261, 263, 271, 309
Population
  bantustan 35, 293; density 37; Transkei 74, 211
Population Registration Act (1950) 43
Poqo
  activity 143n.26, 154; general 162; PAC, and 48; repression of 127; TNIP opposition 118
Portuguese East Africa 23
Poto, Victor
  Chief Minister campaign 116, 117; leader Democratic Party 117, 127; Paramount Chief, Western Pondoland 106, 114; Poto faction 121, 133; teacher support of 184
Poverty
  conditions 81, 220; general 209; income 219, 220, 221
Proclamations
  no. 352 (1894) 91; no. 11 (1922) 82; no. 191 (1932) 91; no. 164 (1934) 82; no. 244 (1934) 82, 186, 188; no. 180 (1956) 104; no. 110 (1957) 106; no. 400 122, 127, 128, 131, 198, 255; R150 (1979) 286
Production, capitalist mode of

general concept 14, 18n.27; labour migration, and 26–27; in South Africa 14–17, 68
Production, pre-capitalist modes of 13
  non-capitalist modes 26, 42
Progressive Party 296
Progressive-Reform Party 2
Prohibition of Mixed Marriages Act (no. 55 of 1949) 253, 254, 285
Proletarianization 30, 31, 32, 34, 40
  agriculture, and 230; differentiated 87–8; land laws, and 76, 79, 85; mining 72, 75
Promotion of Bantu Self-Government Bill (1959) 15, 46, 153
Promotion of the Economic Development of the Homelands Act (1968) 39
Public Security Act (1977)/Transkeian Public Security Act 255, 262, 263
Publications Act (1977) 256

Qamata project 227–8
Quail, Professor George and Ciskei Commission 290
QwaQwa, homeland 35, 51, 305n.6

Rand Revolt (1922) 29
Reid-Daly, Ronald, Major-General, head of Defence Force 310
Relocation
  See: Resettlement
Representation of Natives in Parliament Bill (1926) 92
Repression
  against DP 131, 257; against the press 261–2, 309; banning of organizations 262; general 127; policies of TNIP 255–9; Pondo Revolt 113; Protest against 259; South African policies 40
Resettlement 37, 44, 267–8, 293–4, 311
Residence rights 25, 43, 288

Revolt
  against Bantu Authorities 3, 48, 108–13; of 1960–1, 127; Thembuland disturbance 143n.26
  See also: Pondo Revolt
Rhodes, Cecil, Prime Minister of the Cape 90, 91, 92
Rhodesia/Zimbabwe 10, 25, 47, 55, 289, 290, 310
  labour recruiting 214–15
Riotous Assemblies Act (1956) 40, 255
Rotberg, Robert 296; Butler et al. 297, 299, 302
Rubusana, Rev. Walter 150

Salukapatwa, Mlizo 118
Sandile, Chief of Ngqika, deposition 65
Sarili, Xhosa paramount 66
SASOL 27
Savage, Michael 300
Sebe, Chief Lennox, Ciskei leader 290, 291, 292, 311
Security forces
  bantustan 39; TNIP, and 139, 140, 263, 310
Segregation 17n.6, 34, 253–254, 286–7
'Separate Development' policy
  African petty-bourgeoisie, and 194–8; constructive possibilities 297–300; critique 21, 300–4; opposition to, by teachers 184, 185; policy options 148, 286–290, 294; support for, by bureaucrats 180; support for, by Matanzima 117, 136; theory 1, 20–1, 247–248, 251–2
  See also: Bantustan strategy
Settlers, Extrusion of white
  Commission of Inquiry 156, 157, 161; compensation 157–9, 164–7, 170n.29; consequences 155, 157, 160; division of interest groups 160–1; general 146, 148–9; Government policy 151–3, 156–9, White Paper 157–8; Liaison Committee 156, 160, 161, 163,

Settlers – *cont.*
166; Transkeian Territories European Civic Association (TTCA) 149–51, 154–156, 161–4; urban capital 164–8; white resistance 152, 153, 154, 160; zoning 158–159, 165

Settlement, white
exodus of traders 164; government 147, 149, 157; history of early 146–8; remaining in homelands 168; settler society 302; urban 148

See also: Transkeian Territories European Civic Association (TTCA)

Shangaan, people 20, 35
Sharpeville 54, 114
massacre 48
Shivji, Issa G. 18n.31
Shone, Rev. P. 257
Sicgau, Botha
death of 258, 309; Paramount Chief of Eastern Pondoland 105, 108–9, 112, 143n.31; State President 258

Sicgau, Chief Mpondombini, son of Botha Sicgau 259; 277n.40

Sicgau, Chief Ntzihayesizwe, son of Botha Sicgau 259

Sicgau, Stella, daughter of Botha Sicgau
arrest 259; Cabinet reappointment 261, 271; Minister of the Interior 254; Pondo elite and, 309; resignation 257

Sicgau, Chief Vukaibambe 110, 113
Slovo, Joe 11, 12, 13
Smith, Ian, regime in Rhodesia 55
Smuts, General 29, 32, 92
Snelling, Sir Arthur 232
Sotho
chiefdoms 61; North & South 20; TNIP, and 257, 271

South Africa, economy
apartheid, and 33, 39; general 11–12, 44, 68; history 21–2, 27–8; production, capitalist 14–17, 25–7, 68

South African Black Alliance (SABA) 285

South African Communist Party 11, 12, 13
banning 262

South African Congress of Trade Unions
banning 262

South African Council of Churches
banning 262

South African Defence Force (SADF) 266, 272
South African Party 29, 31
South African Students' Organization (SASO) 3, 40, 129, 131, 185, 262
South West Africa/Namibia 25
apartheid 49; relationship to South Africa 12
South West Africa Peoples Organization (SWAPO)
banning 262
Soweto
Transkei relations, and 135, 142; upheaval 34, 40, 43, 44, 56, 119, 193
Sparg, companies 167, 190
Spilkin, companies 167, 190
Stallard Commission (1921) 25
Stanford, A. H., Chief Magistrate 150
Stanford, Walter 149
Status of Trankei Act (1976) 1, 253, 266
Steyn, F. S., Nationalist MP 49
Strijdom, Prime Minister 45
Strikes
Durban 41, 44, 53; industrial 223–33; legislation against 40; of 1920, 28; of mineworkers in 1946 31, 93
Student unrest 185, 263
Stulz, Newell 5, 6, 11, 295, 297–9, 304
Sugar industry in Natal 78, 210
Suppression of Communism Act (1950) 40, 124, 127, 255
arrests made 262
Swazi people 20, 35, 61
Swaziland 10, 46, 47, 215, 249

Tambo, Oliver 130
Tanganyika/Tanzania 25, 47
labour supply 214
Taxation
East Coast fever, and 96; fixing of rates 90, 106, 207; for administration 75, 91; hut taxes 67, 71, 75; livestock 207
Teachers
See: Class Structure – Bantustan Education
Terrorism Act (1967) 40
Thembu 61, 62, 66, 67
proletarianization 72; Qamata project 227–8; Thembuland 61, 108; TNIP and 258, 271, 309
Thembu Paramount 93
Tomlinson Commission 36–38, 46, 107, 153, 187
agriculture policy 223–5, 229; industry policy 230
Tourism 237
Trade unions
black trade unions 28, 40, 41, 42; opposition to 29, 232; Wage Board, and 233
Traders, African
concessions 193–4; development corporations, and 187–8; licences 188–94; organizations 191–4; restraints on growth 186–7, 193; Xhosa Development Corporation monopoly, and 189
Traders, white
characteristics 153–4; fight for rights 150–51, 153–4, 160–4; history of, 147–8, 150; monopoly 82–4, 148, 153; patron role 84; Pondo revolt 111–12; replacement by blacks 116, 158, 163–4, 189; TNIP, and 137; under homeland government 157, 163; United Party, and 156
Trading Amendment Act (no. 5 of 1964) 158, 188, 197
Trading Rights, Native
extension of in 1934, 150
Transkei, Administration
division of functions 106; financing of 204–8, 272–3

INDEX 337

Transkei, Administrative Structure
Bantu Authorities 104; Bunga 90–98; Direct rule 88; District and District Authorities 105–6; early development 60–7; franchise 90, 92; general 45–7; headman and chiefs 88–9; Location Boards 90; Magistrates 88; Regions and Regional Authorities 105–106, 188; representation in Republic Parliament 92–3; Tribal Authorities 105–7, 123, 133

See also: Bantu Authorities system, Transkei Territorial Authority, Transkei, legislature, Transkei, bureaucracy
Transkei, border areas 52, 53
Transkei, bureaucracy
corruption 179–80; growth 176–7; ideology 180–1; salary 178; whites 181
Transkei, citizenship
statistics 132

See also: Citizenship
Transkei, economy
agriculture 222–30; dislocation of agriculture 73–77; early mercantile 63–4; general 222, 240; government financing 204–8; income levels 219–21; industry 230–40; labour export 209–18; peasantization 68–73

See also: Agriculture, Industry, Traders
Transkei, elections
of Chief Minister 116–18; corruption 122–3, 128; general elections 118–19, 309; of municipal councils 254; urban vote 133, 135; voter participation 141
Transkei, general characteristics 5, 25, 51
Transkei, history
early colonial 60–7; frontier trade 63–4; frontier wars 64–6; territory formation 52, 53, 67, 249
Transkei, independence 1, 53–6
beginnings of, 98

See also 'Independence'
Transkei, legislature
Chieftaincy and 116, 118, 121; division on party lines 118; formation 115; leadership campaign 116–17; occupational background of members 175; opposition role 127–32, 257–8, 261; salaries 174
Transkei, military 181, 266, 272
Transkei, as model
critique 301–4; general 2, 282; 'neo-colonial' system 104; official doctrine 4–5; perspectives on, 295–304
Transkei, neo-colonialism and 6–7
Transkei, recognition 56
financing, and 206–7, 264; general 248–51; Transkei–South Africa relations, and 266, 267; withheld, 6
Transkei, relations with South Africa
finances 272–4; general 274–5; military alignment 266, 272; land and citizenship strains 265, 268–70; resettlement policy 267–8; state of diplomatic relations 268–71, 274
Transkei, society
class formation 85, 88; education 182–5; income 174, 219–21; land tenure, Xhosa, 62; language 61; people 60–1; political units/chiefdoms 62; politics and class 130; population 74, 211; trade with settlers 63–4; women's role 77, 221

See also: Chieftaincy, Traders, Transkei, Economy
Transkei, White capital 39, 166
Transkei Constitution Act (1963) 115, 116, 157, 161, 162, 176; Republic of Transkei Constitution Act (1976) 253, 265, 266
Transkei Development Corporation 180, 192
and industrial investment 234, 235, 236, 237, 239, 240
Transkei Education Act (1966) 183
Transkei Legislative Assembly (TLA)
See: Transkei, legislature
Transkei National Independence Party (TNIP)
chiefs, and 121, 123–6, 135, 137; dependent status 204; development strategy 222; election results 118–19, 309; explanation for success of 120, 126; formation 118; general characteristics 116, 135; independence, and, 52–3; labour export and, 218; labour policy 232; 'nationalists' 249–51 nomination procedures 124–5; opposition by teachers 184–5; popular resistance 262–3; principles 136; racial policy 168, 251–5; relations with South Africa 265–74, 310–11; repression of opposition 127–32, 255–64; separate development and, 117, 136, 251–2; structure 136–40; urban electorate, and 132–5, 137–8

See also: Matanzima, George; Matanzima, Kaiser
Transkei National Progressive Party (TNPP)
amalgamation 258; formation 258
Transkei People's Freedom Party (TPFP)
as opposition 257
Transkei Self-Government Act (1963) 46
Transkei Territorial Authority (TTA)
dissolution 106; formation 97–8, 105; self-government creation and, 114, 115, 176–7

Transkei Territorial Civic Association 111
Transkei Chamber of Commerce (TRACOC) 189, 191–3
Transkei General Council (TGC)/Transkeian Territories General Council (TTGC)
general 94; opposition 94; structure 91; United TTGC 91, 94
Transkeian Public Security Act (1977) 255, 262, 263
Transkeian Territories European Civic Association (TTCA)
division 155–6; formation 149; leadership 150; policies 150–1, 154; traders cause and, 161–4; Umtata Council 156; White Citizens Association 164
Transkeian Townships Board 165
Transkeians, urban 132–5, 265–6
Tribal Authorities
functions 106, 107, 123, 133; structure 105
Tribal society
Bantu peoples 20; Transkei peoples 60, 61; 'tribalism' 125–6
Trust and Lands Act (1936)
See: Natives Trust and Lands Act
Tsomo 76
Tsonga, people 35
Tswana, people 35
Tutu, Bishop Desmond 301

Umkonto we Sizwe/Spear of the Nation
formed by ANC militants 48
Umtata, capital of Transkei 3, 76, 152, 159
importance of 165–7; Umtata government 50, 88
Underdevelopment
creation of 72–88; theory 73
Undesirable Organizations Act (1978) 256
Unemployment 39, 218
Union of Soviet Socialist Republics (USSR)
influence in Africa 56
United Kingdom
and Transkei recognition 250
United Nations 3, 47, 48, 131, 206
Pondo cause 113; Transkei recognition, and 249–50
United Party 2, 31, 46, 49
fusion 92; TTCA, and 162; white support 149
United States of America (USA)
investment in Transkei 239; policy 55, 56, 59n.75; recognition of Transkei 250; UN votes 47, 48
United Transkei Territories 67
Unlawful Organizations Act (1962) 40, 48, 255
Urban
Transkeians 132–5, 265–6; Urban Areas Acts 25, 43, 186, 187, 193; vote 133, 135

van der Merwe, Professor B. 263
Van der Walt, Hennie, National Party MP, Chairman of Central Consolidation Committee 288, 289
Van Rooyen, Renier, Chairman of Pep 236
Venda, homeland
government characteristics 50, 51; independence 4; people 20, 35
Verwoerd, Hendrik 46, 114
independent commonwealth concept 56, 104, 289, 294; Verwoerdian purpose 49; white extrusion and, 151, 152, 153, 156–8, 160, 168
Verwoerdian concept
See: Verwoerd, Hendrik
Viedge Brothers, wholesale firm 190
Vorster, B. J., as Prime Minister 3, 17n.6, 52, 53, 56, 253, 268, 287, 288

Wage Act (1957) 40
Wage Act (1977) 233
Wage Board
formed 29; purpose 233
Wage labour
development of 67–73, 221; sectors 78
Wage rates
bureaucrats 174, 178; Deferred Pay system 83; general 151; in industry 232, 246n.157; in mining 80, 81, 99n.39, 217; teachers 183
War of the Axe (1846) 65
White Citizens' Association (WCA)
formation 164
Wickstead, Richard, journalist 262
Wiehahn Report 41
Wilson, Francis 210
Witwatersrand Native Labour Association (WNLA)
established 1896, 79
Wolpe, Harold 10–11, 13–14, 15, 16
Women
agriculture, and 77; boycotts by 96; industry, and 240, 246n.157; role in reserve society 221;
World War I 28

Xhosa
Cattle-killing 66, 69; society stratification 84; wars 65–6
Xhosa, peoples 1, 20, 35, 60–1
nationalism 247, 311
Xhosa Development Corporation (XDC) 138
established 38; loans to black businessmen 158, 159, 167; reserve trade, and 163–4, 165, 189–92
Yutar, Dr Percy 259

Zambia
labour supply 214
Zimbabwe/Rhodesia 10, 25, 47, 55, 289, 290, 310
labour recruiting 214–15
Zoning Committee
established 1964, 158
Zoning Proclamation (December 1965) 158, 165
Zulu 20, 35, 61, 62